T0374818

APULEIUS

APOLOGIA
FLORIDA
DE DEO SOCRATIS

LCL 534

APULEIUS

APOLOGIA
FLORIDA
DE DEO SOCRATIS

EDITED AND TRANSLATED BY

CHRISTOPHER P. JONES

HARVARD UNIVERSITY PRESS
CAMBRIDGE, MASSACHUSETTS
LONDON, ENGLAND
2017

Library of Congress Control Number 2016957657
CIP data available from the Library of Congress

ISBN 978-0-674-99711-0

*Composed in ZephGreek and ZephText by
Technologies 'N Typography, Merrimac, Massachusetts.
Printed on acid-free paper and bound by
Maple Press, York, Pennsylvania*

CONTENTS

GENERAL INTRODUCTION

1. APULEIUS' LIFE AND CAREER

Almost all the evidence for Apuleius' life is contained in the *Apologia* and the *Florida*. His birthdate fell about 125, perhaps before that date rather than after.[1] He does not name his father, and he mentions his mother not at all, but only a brother (*Apol.* 23.1); there is no authority for the *praenomen* Lucius that he is given in older texts. He was born in Madauros in the province of Africa (modern Mdaourouch in western Algeria), which was founded by one of the Flavian emperors as a military colony, *colonia Flavia Augusta veteranorum,* and was situated, in Apuleius' words, "on the very border of Numidia and Gaetulia" (*Apol.* 24.1).[2] The colony had a constitution on the Roman model, with a fixed scale of magistracies, and Apuleius describes his father as having held them all, ending with the exceptional honor of being the sole *duumvir* when the titular holder was the emperor (as the title implies, there were normally two). This suggests that Apu-

---

[1] Birthdate: Appendix A. I use the conventional title *Apologia*, though it has no ancient authority: Hijmans, "Apuleius Orator," 1712, and see further below, Introduction to the *Apologia*.

[2] G. Souville, *PECS* 51–542; *Barrington Atlas* 32 A 4.

leius' family belonged to the original stock of settlers, the civic aristocracy (*Apol.* 24.8, with Appendix C). From their father Apuleius and his brother inherited an estate worth two million sesterces (*Apol.* 23.1), a considerable fortune, though far below the hundreds of millions of some wealthy senators and imperial freedmen.[3] According to Augustine, he performed the duties of provincial *sacerdos,* the annual high priest of the imperial cult, which implies a considerable degree of wealth and status.[4]

Apuleius received an expensive education, for which he was sent to Carthage, the capital of the province, where he spent his adolescent years. For his advanced studies he went to Athens, and it was perhaps here that he came under the influence of a Platonic teacher (some have guessed Sextus, the nephew or grand-nephew of Plutarch) and became known as a *philosophus Platonicus,* as he is called on an inscription from Madauros.[5] The first through the third centuries were the apogee of public speakers of the type known as "sophists" (*sophistai*), many of whom, such as Aristides and Herodes Atticus, had a deep knowledge of philosophical literature. Apuleius himself has sometimes been classified as a sophist, though he talks

[3] R. P. Duncan-Jones, *The Economy of the Roman Empire,* 2nd ed. (Cambridge, 1982), 343–44.

[4] *Apuleius . . . sacerdos provinciae pro magno fuit ut munera ederet venatoresque vestiret, Ep.* 138.19 (*Corpus Scriptorum Ecclesisticorum Latinorum* 44.146).

[5] S. Gsell, ed., *Inscriptions Latines de l'Algérie* (Paris, 1922), 1:2115: *[——ph]ilosopho [Pl]atonico [Ma]daurenses cives ornament[o] suo. D(ecreto) d(ecurionum) p(ublica) [p(ecunia)].*

of himself only as a philosopher in the "school" of Plato, and all his extant works to different degrees reflect his allegiance to Platonism.[6]

By the time he delivered the *Apologia,* probably spoken in 158/9 though revised and published later, Apuleius claims to have used up a large part of his inheritance in "distant travels, long studies, and frequent acts of generosity" (*Apol.* 23.1). In this and other works, he claims to have visited several cities of the eastern empire, the farthest east being Hierapolis in Phrygia, famous as containing one of the entrances to the Underworld, which he visited personally (*De mundo* 17, 327, if that work is genuine). At some date in the later 150s, he married a wealthy widow of Oea in Tripolitania (now Tripoli in western Libya); his wife, Pudentilla, was older than he was, and was the mother of two sons, the elder being a certain Sicinius Pontianus, whom Apuleius had come to know in Athens (*Apol.* 72.3). After Pontianus' death, Pontianus' younger brother, Pudens, together with his backers accused Apuleius of having used magic to make Pudentilla fall in love with him; the *Apologia* represents his speech in his own defense, though how closely it approximates to the original cannot be known. His publication of a written version strongly suggests that he won his case.

Some other dates emerge from the *Florida,* an unconnected series of extracts from longer works now lost. One of the longest (*Flor.* 9) is from a speech given at Carthage in honor of the proconsul Severianus Honorinus, perhaps

---

[6] For Apuleius as a sophist, Harrison, *Apuleius: A Latin Sophist;* on his "impersonation" of Plato, Fletcher, *Apuleius' Platonism.*

in 162/3. One or two years later the proconsul was Salvidienus Orfitus, whose term is firmly dated to 163/4 (*Flor.* 17). Perhaps the last in date, and Apuleius' last datable work, is a speech for his fellow African, his "friend and fellow pupil" (*amicus et condiscipulus*), Strabo Aemilianus, ex-consul (*consularis*) and, the author hopes, shortly (*brevi*) to be proconsul (*Flor.* 16, esp. 16.40). Strabo was consul suffect in 156, and since seventeen or eighteen years normally passed between consulate and proconsulate, that might imply a date in the early 170s, though *brevi* cannot be pressed.[7]

Already by the time of the *Apologia,* Apuleius claims to have written several works in verse and prose and on various subjects. Of the surviving and undisputed works, the most famous is the *Metamorphoses,* or *Golden Ass.*[8] The date of composition is unclear, though a late date, perhaps in the 170s, seems more likely than an early one. Since he tells the story in the first-person singular, there is a temptation to read the work as autobiographical, and many readers, such as Augustine, have yielded to it. The

---

[7] Severianus Honorinus: *PIR* C 1230, *PIR* S p. 242. Salvidienus Orfitus: *PIR* C 1447; R. Syme, *REA* 61 (1959) 318–19 = *Roman Papers* (Oxford, 1979), 3:468–69. Strabo Aemilianus: *PIR* S 923. Cf. Apuleius' hope that Severianus' son Honorinus (*PIR* C 1218) will "rapidly" (*cito, Flor.* 9.40) return to Carthage as proconsul, though that time could hardly be less than twenty years off. For the proconsular dates of Honorinus and Orfitus, B. E. Thomasson, *Laterculi Praesidum* (Göteborg, 1984), 1:382.

[8] For an account of all the known works, preserved and lost, disputed and undisputed, Harrison, *Apuleius: A Latin Sophist,* 10–36.

last book in particular, in which the protagonist represents himself as a *Madaurensis* (*Met.* 11.27.9), might indicate that Apuleius spent the last years of his life as a successful advocate in Rome and a devotee of the goddess Isis, and it would not be surprising if his success as speaker and author had finally brought him to settle in the capital. There is perhaps a hint in the disputed *De mundo*, where he speaks of "our Vesuvius" as an active volcano:[9] "our" might suggest that he had settled in Italy, or at least in Naples, which two centuries before Virgil had made his home. The *De mundo* is addressed by the author to a son, Faustinus, who is also the addressee of the second book of the *De Platone.* That work is also of disputed authenticity, but if "Faustinus" is a real person, he may be Apuleius' son by a later marriage.[10]

2. STYLE AND VOCABULARY

Apuleius' style is one of his most prominent features.[11] In general, he uses clauses and sentences aligned on the same syntactical plane, with only a few subordinate clauses (*parataxis*), rather than sentences built up into long "periods" (*hypotaxis*), and reaching completion only at the close. Even his longer sentences are syntactically complete even before they are complete in meaning. *Apology*

---

[9] *De mundo* 17 (326): *ut Liparae, ut Aetna, ut Vesuvius etiam noster solet.*

[10] *De Platone* 2.1 (219); *De mundo, praef.* (285). On the *De Platone* see now Stover, *A New Work by Apuleius.*

[11] For an excellent survey, Kenney, *Apuleius,* 28–38.

2.8–12 is an example in which a sentence of over ninety words has several such "pauses":

> Igitur et priusquam causa ageretur, facile intellectu cuivis fuit qualisnam accusatio futura esset, | cuius qui fuerat professor et machinator idem fieri auctor timeret, | ac praesertim Sicinius Aemilianus, qui si quippiam veri in me explorasset, nunquam profecto tam cunctanter hominem extraneum tot tantorumque criminum postulasset, | qui avunculi sui testamentum quod verum sciebat pro falso infamarit, | tanta quidem pertinacia, ut, cum Lollius Vrbicus v. c. verum videri et ratum esse debere de consilio consularium virorum pronuntiasset, contra clarissimam vocem iuraverit vecordissimus iste, tamen illud testamentum fictum esse, | adeo ut aegre Lollius Vrbicus ab eius pernicie temperarit.

By contrast, a feature that Apuleius shares with periodic writers such as Cicero, but not with paratactic ones such as Sallust and Tacitus, is his frequent use of connectives (connecting relatives, particles, adverbs) to indicate the links of thought between sentences. In chapter 1 of the *Apology,* the examples are *quippe* (2), *quo* (3), *quamquam* (4), *nam* (5), *quae, ibi vero* (6). A stylistic tic serving a similar function is his use of *potius,* often followed by *quam,* which occurs some forty-five times in the *Apology,* as opposed to about seventeen in the whole of the *Metamorphoses.*

Apuleius makes equally frequent use of figures of sound and sense. To take examples only from the opening chapters of the *Apology:*

Alliteration: *oPtigit Purgandae aPud imPeritos Philoso-phiae et Probandi mei* (1.3)

Antistrophe: *innocens potest . . . nocens non potest* (1.2)

Antithesis and homoeoteleuton: *prius apud te coeptam quam apud se cogitatam* (1.1), *non tam crimina iu-dicio quam obiectamenta iurgio prolata* (1.6)

Metaphor: *ut comminus ageret . . . calumniis velitatur* (2.6)

Pleonasm: *certus . . . eram proque vero obtinebam* (1.1), *copia et facultas* (1.3)

Simile: *pudor veluti vestis quanto obsoletior est, tanto incuriosius habetur* (3.3)

While comparatively straightforward in his syntax, Apuleius is very adventurous in his vocabulary. In particular, like other prose writers of the second century, he uses compounds that either appear in his works for the first time or are otherwise found only or mainly in early poetry or prose. For example, the nouns terminating in *-mentum* include the following (I ignore examples in writers later than Apuleius: all examples from the *Apologia*):[12]

agnomentum (56.7: only here)
concrementum (49.4: only here)
deliramentum (29.1: also Elder Pliny, M. Aurelius)
dissimulamentum (87.6: only here and in *Flor.* 3.7)
eiectamentum (35.4: otherwise, only in Tacitus, *Germania*)
illectamentum (98.1, 102.7: only here)

---

[12] Cf. the lists of "new words" in Butler-Owen, *Apulei Apologia,* lix–lxii.

inhonestamentum (3.8: otherwise, only in C. Gracchus)
obiectamentum (1.6: only here)
terriculamentum (64.2: only here and in *De Deo* 15.7)[13]

Apuleius' prose rhythms, and especially his use of a limited number of rhythmical schemes with which to round out a clause, sentence, or paragraph (*clausulae*), correspond to classical usage. In the first three chapters of the *Apology,* the only exception, *subito tacens* (2.1), may well be corrupt. The reason is perhaps that all three of the works included in this volume originated as speeches, or at least take the form of written speeches, and orators such as Cicero and Apuleius used rhythm as a form of punctuation to allow the ear to recognize breaks in sense.

Apart from these technicalities, Apuleius uses syntax for pictorial effects, as when the description of the hovering eagle in *Flor.* 2.8–11 beautifully conveys the idea of the majestic bird hovering high in the sky before it swoops down on its prey; the series of short phrases at the end, *unde unguibus inuncet vel agnum incuriosum vel leporem meticulosum vel quodcumque esui animatum vel laniatui fors obtulit,* suggests the suddenness of the bird's attack, and the sibilants and labials of *vel agnum incuriosum vel leporem meticulosum,* contrasting with the alliteration of *animaTum vel laniaTui fors obTulit,* convey the contrast between the unsuspecting animals and the brutality of their impending slaughter. Similarly, the simple syntax that he employs in certain narratives, for example the

[13] This word, in combination with *occursaculum* and *formidamen* (both unique to Apuleius) in the same clause, is clearly meant to reinforce the idea of terrifying strangeness.

death of Philemon (*Flor.* 16.6–18), reminiscent of the mode in which he begins and ends the tale of *Cupid and Psyche* (*Met.* 4.28, 6.24), illustrates his artful deployment of literary registers.

3.1. RECEPTION

To 1469

The afterlife, or "reception," of the three works included in this present volume is best discussed together; I take first the *Apologia* and the *De Deo Socratis,* since the fate of the *Florida* is somewhat divergent. Though Apuleius must have had readers in the decades following his death, there is no certain trace until the polymath Neoplatonist, Porphyry, in the late third century.[14] If a quotation by Jerome can be trusted, Porphyry in his *Against the Christians* cited both Apollonius of Tyana and Apuleius as performing miracles "in order to secure the wealth of rich females" (*ut divitias acciperent a divitibus mulierculis*).[15]

Writing not long after Porphyry, Lactantius pairs the same two philosophers, but only with a reference to their "wonders" (*mira*), which suggests the *Golden Ass* rather than the *Apologia.* A ceiling painting from a building in Trier, constructed between 315 and 326, contained a por-

[14] The supposed letter of Septimius Severus in the *Historia Augusta, Albinus* 12.12, is evidence only for late fourth-century knowledge of Apuleius.

[15] Hier. *Hom. in Psalm. LXXXI* (Migne, *PL* 26.1130); Gaisser, *The Fortunes of Apuleius,* 23, 24 with n. 91; this of course does not apply to Apollonius.

trait of Apuleius, though he is not named, and he also had
a statue in the Baths of Zeuxippos in Constantinople, re-
built by Constantine about 330.[16] Thereafter, there is no
certain reference to him until later in the same century,
when there comes a cluster of them: a reference in the
Historia Augusta, his image on a token issued at Rome (a
so-called contorniate), and (decisive for his survival) the
work of an otherwise unknown Sallustius. In Rome in 395
and again in Constantinople in 397, this student of rhetoric corrected (*emendavi*) a copy of the *Apologia,* the *Metamorphoses,* and perhaps also the *Florida,* and this copy is
the ancestor of all copies of all three works. Sallustius is
presumably responsible for the division of the *Apologia*
into two books, with the second beginning at chapter 66;
if he also corrected the *Florida,* he is presumably responsible for the division into four books at chapters 1.1, 9.15,
16.1, and 18.1.[17]

The crucial reason for the survival of Apuleius was the
interest of his fellow African, Augustine, bishop of Hippo.
He had read the *Metamorphoses,* but refers to it not by
the manuscript title but by the title that was to become
canonical, *Asinus Aureus.* He also makes passing reference to the *Apologia,* saying that Apuleius wrote it to defend himself against the "charge of magical arts" (*crimen*

[16] Gaisser, *The Fortunes of Apuleius,* 25–28. On Apuleius'
statue in the baths of Zeuxippos, R. Stupperich, "Das Statuenpro-
gramm in den Zeuxippos-Thermen. Überlegungen zur Besch-
reibung des Christodoros von Koptos," *Istanbuler Mitteilungen*
32 (1982): 229–30.

[17] For the process of correction implied by Sallustius' *emendavi,* J. E. G. Zetzel, "The Subscriptions in the Manuscripts of
Livy and Fronto and the Meaning of *Emendatio*," *CP* 75 (1980):
38–59.

artium magicarum, Civ. Dei 8.19). By contrast, the *De Deo Socratis* he knew intimately, and rebuts it at length in Books 8 and 9 of the *City of God,* and his extensive quotations allow the manuscript readings to be improved in several places. Between Augustine in early fifth-century Africa and Priscian in Justinian's Constantinople, several writers show knowledge both of the *Metamorphoses* and of the *Apologia.*[18]

The *Florida* is a collection of excerpts from speeches of Apuleius, probably all of them spoken in Africa; it is uncertain whether the *Florida* were included in Sallustius' copy or were added later. There seem to be no references in Late Antiquity, but a medieval Spanish glossary, the so-called *Abolita,* shows knowledge of the *Florida* and of all the works of Apuleius that survived until the later Middle Ages. At some stage, several chapters of the *Florida* became detached from the original collection and came down by a different channel of transmission as the opening chapters of the *De Deo Socratis.*[19]

A copy of the three works came by an unknown route from Constantinople to southern Italy, and from that a copy (F) was made at the Benedictine monastery of Monte Cassino, probably under the abbot Desiderius in the late eleventh century. From this ultimately descend all the other extant manuscripts, the most important being a later one made at Monte Cassino about 1200 (ϕ).[20] One manuscript from Monte Cassino had reached northern Italy by the early fourteenth century, and some early humanists

[18] Gaisser, *The Fortunes of Apuleius,* 53–60.
[19] On the separate tradition of this work, see below.
[20] For more on the manuscripts, see below, "The Manuscript Tradition."

show knowledge of Apuleius, including works not contained in F and ϕ. Thereafter, he began to acquire literary admirers, above all Boccaccio and Petrarch, and knowledge of him began to spread and further manuscripts to be made. Both F and ϕ were brought to Florence in the 1350s and eventually found their way to the Laurentian Library, where they remain. After the first printed edition of the complete works in 1469, "Apuleius was let loose upon the world."[21]

1469 to the Present

The first edition (Rome, 1469) was edited by Giovanni Andrea Bussi (Joannes Andreas de Buxis), bishop of Aleria in Corsica, who produced other first editions, including those of Virgil and Ovid. The next major step was Filippo Beroaldo's edition of the *Metamorphoses* (Rome, 1501). The two Giuntine editions (Florence, 1512 and 1522), edited respectively by Mariano Tucci (Marianus Tuccius) and Bernardo Pisano (Bernardus Philomathes Pisanus), were the first to use the manuscripts of the Laurentian Library. Fulvio Orsini (Fulvius), though greatly interested in Apuleius, did not produce his own edition, but made many important conjectures.[22]

After this largely Italian phase of Apuleian studies, near the end of the sixteenth century a new phase began

---

[21] Gaisser, *The Fortunes of Apuleius,* 172. See also pp. 66–75 (early humanists), 77–82 (Petrarch), 93–121 (Boccaccio), 157–72 (the *editio princeps*).

[22] "Fulvius" is therefore more than a "vir doctus laudatus apud Oudendorpium" (Zimmerman, *Apulei Metamorphoseon,* xlviii).

north of the Alps, particularly in the Netherlands. A series of editions appeared in quick succession, from Gustaf Stewechius (Lyon, 1587), Petrus Colvius (Leyden, 1588),[23] Bonaventura Vulcanius (Leyden, 1594), Johannes Wowerius (Basel, 1606), Geverhart Elmenhorstius (Frankfurt, 1621), Petrus Scriverius (Amsterdam, 1624), and later in the century Julianus Floridus (Paris, 1688). The posthumous edition of Franz Oudendorp (1786–1823, Leyden, reprinted London, 1825), and the edition of G. F. Hildebrand (Leipzig, 1842), teacher at the famous Royal Orphanage of Halle (Saxony), represent the last of this mainly Dutch tradition.

The first separate study of the *Apologia* was the edition of Isaac Casaubon (Heidelberg, 1594), soon followed by the commentary of the jurist Scipione Gentili (Scipio Gentilis: Hanover, 1607),[24] and the edition (Paris, 1635) of the roving Englishman John Price (Johannes Pricaeus).[25]

The first half of the nineteenth century inaugurated a new, mainly German, phase of Apuleian scholarship, concomitant with the rise of "scientific" philology, and in textual criticism with the method associated with the name of Lachmann.[26] Only a few years after Hildebrand's edi-

---

[23] This brilliant scholar died in his mid-20s: Hildebrand, *Apulei Opera Omnia,* 1.lxxxiii.

[24] A. De Benedictis, *Dizionario Biografico degli Italiani* (Rome, 1999), 53: 268–72.

[25] On this interesting figure, M. H. Crawford, *Oxford Dictionary of National Biography* (Cambridge, 2004), 45:295–96.

[26] As is now well-known, Lachmann's method had many antecedents: S. Timpanaro, *The Genesis of Lachmann's Method* (Chicago, 2005). On Keil's discovery and its subsequent modification, Zimmerman, *Apulei Metamorphoseon,* xiv–xviii.

tion appeared the Habilitationsschrift of Heinrich Keil, later known for his editions of the Younger Pliny and the Latin grammarians.[27] Almost by the way, Keil used his paleographical acumen and his acquaintance with the libraries of Italy to prove that F was the ancestor of all manuscripts of Apuleius containing the *Florida, Metamorphoses,* and *Apologia,* and that ϕ was a copy of F. Keil advised that editors of those works should regard all other witnesses as *deteriores,* and this principle informed the editions of Apuleius' chief editor in the twentieth century, Rudolf Helm.[28] The theory that the so-called vulgate manuscripts could contain readings obliterated in F, and hence could be witnesses in their own right, was first adumbrated by Johannes van der Vliet, and carried further by D. S. Robertson in a fundamental article of 1924.[29]

The manuscript tradition of the *philosophica,* together with the "orphan" chapters of the *Florida,* was not unraveled until the late nineteenth century, with the edition of Aloysius Goldbacher (Vienna, 1876). Goldbacher overlooked the earliest witness, the Bruxellensis, though Vulcanius had already used some of its readings in his edition of 1594. Among Erwin Rohde's many contributions to the study of Apuleius was his rediscovery of this manuscript

[27] Keil, *Observationes criticae,* 77–81. On Keil, P. Wirth, *Neue Deutsche Biographie* (Berlin, 1977), 11:404.

[28] Cf. J. A. Hanson, ed., *Apuleius:* Metamorphoses, 2nd. ed. (Cambridge, MA, 2014), 1.xiii: "Modern editors . . . have rightly seen their task as reproducing a legible text of F, making use of other manuscripts and conjectures only where F is unreadable or patently in error."

[29] Robertson, "Manuscripts of the *Metamorphoses.*"

(1882).[30] Van der Vliet produced the first Teubner edition
(1900), though his boldness in conjecture appears to have
dissatisfied the publishers, who quickly replaced his edition with that of Paul Thomas (1908).

After 1900 Apuleian scholarship developed in several
countries of Europe and (later) the United States. Paul
Vallette's published thesis on the *Apologia* (1908) led to
his Budé edition of 1924, and he and D. S. Robertson
(1940–1945) collaborated to produce the still-standard
edition of the *Metamorphoses*. After translating the *Apologia and Florida* (1909), H. E. Butler collaborated with
A. S. Owen to produce a still valuable commentary on the
Apologia (1914). The first Loeb (1915) of the *Metamorphoses* was edited by Stephen Gaselee, who combined
W. Adlington's translation (1566) with Helm's second edition (1907) for the text, in which he made some changes
but gave no apparatus. In the United States, a group of
scholars connected with the University of Indiana, notably
W. A. Oldfather and B. E. Perry, produced the still invaluable *Index Apuleianus* (1934). J. Arthur Hanson's Loeb
edition of the *Metamorphoses* appeared posthumously in
1989 (corrected reprint, 1996). This present volume is the
first Loeb of the *Apologia, Florida,* and *De Deo Socratis.*

3.2. THE MANUSCRIPT TRADITION

The textual history of the three works translated in this
volume is best treated as a unit, since the *Apologia* and the
larger part of the *Florida* have a common history, and a

[30] Rohde, "Zur handschriftliche Überlieferung."

lesser part of the *Florida* comes down with the *De Deo Socratis.*[31]

As already mentioned, the archetype of all extant manuscripts of the *Apologia, Metamorphoses,* and most of the *Florida,* transmitted in that order, is Laurentianus 68.2, copied at Monte Cassino in the later eleventh century (F). But other witnesses are indispensable, since F has been degraded in various ways, and in particular by a tear in folio 160 containing part of Book 8 of the *Metamorphoses.* The next most important witness is Laurentianus 29.2, also Cassinese and dated about 1200 (ϕ), which was copied after the tear. In 1924 D. S. Robertson showed that some fourteenth-century manuscripts of his Class I descended from a hyparchetype that had been copied from F before the tear and was therefore earlier than ϕ. Since 1942 another important witness has become known, Assisi 706 (C) with some pages of the *Apologia.* Some have supposed that C and the Class I manuscripts represent a line of transmission independent of F, but this view has not found favor.

The larger part of the *Florida,* conventionally divided into twenty-three chapters, is transmitted in F and ϕ, and in both manuscripts the *Florida* follow the *Apologia* and the *Metamorphoses.* The *Florida* is an assemblage of passages varying in length from a few lines to several pages, divided by the manuscripts into four "books." All are extracts from lost speeches of Apuleius, though none represents a complete speech, with the possible exception of

[31] For the following, Olsen, *L'Étude des Auteurs classiques latins,* 11; Zimmermann, *Apulei Metamorphoseon,* xii–xxiii; on

the longest, number 16. It is generally agreed that the extracts were not made by Apuleius himself, but are a later compilation. The title *Florida* is of disputed meaning. It refers either to the "florid" nature of the extracts or to their resemblance to an anthology, though whoever chose the title might have had both meanings in mind.[32]

What I have printed after chapter 23 as chapters 1* to 5* of the *Florida,* which I have called the "orphan chapters" rather than the more usual "false preface," has a different textual history and appears in the principal manuscripts of the *De Deo Socratis* as the opening of that work, though some manuscripts mark the last extract (here 5*) as a preface to the *De Deo Socratis,* which may be correct. These manuscripts all descend from a single, lost archetype, and fall into two classes, α and δ. To α belongs the oldest witness, B of the late ninth century, and two other early manuscripts, V and M, of the tenth/eleventh and the eleventh/twelfth centuries, respectively. The oldest manuscript of δ is the eleventh-century N, which also contains Pliny's *Letters* in the ten-book version.[33] There are also several lesser witnesses of the eleventh through the fourteenth centuries. Important readings in the *De Deo Socratis* are also preserved in manuscripts of St. Augustine, who cites the work several times.

Assisi 706, Piccioni, "*De magia* di Apuleio," and "Sull'Assisiate 706."   [32] Discussion in Lee, *Apuleius' Florida,* 1–3.

[33] For these dates, Olsen, *L'Étude des Auteurs classiques latins,* 19 (V), 16 (M and N); R. Klibansky and F. Regen, *Die Handschriften der philosophischen Werke des Apuleius* (Göttingen, 1993), 119, date V to the tenth century. I am grateful to G. Magnaldi for advice on these dates.

3.3. THE PRESENT EDITION

For the readings of the manuscripts, I have relied on the reports of earlier editors. I have also usually relied on my predecessors in identifying the first authors of such conjectures as I cite, though in accordance with the policy of the Loeb Classical Library, I have silently incorporated uncontroversial conjectures.[34] I have used the apparatus to indicate (1) manuscript readings rejected by modern editors that I have accepted, in which case I have put my preferred reading before the colon and the source of my text after it; (2) conjectural additions or excisions made by editors from the Renaissance on, marked by *add(idit)* and *del(evit)*. I have incorporated a very few conjectures of my own, indicating them as in (1). For the works contained in F and its descendants, I have used the siglum ω to indicate readings that appear in both F and φ, in F when its reading differs from φ, and in φ when F is illegible; I have used *u(ulgata)* to designate manuscripts later than F and φ, which often contain excellent readings that may be either true variants or conjectures. For the "orphan chapters" of the *Florida* and the *De Deo Socratis*, I have used ω to indicate the presumed reading of the archetype, occasionally referring to readings of individual manuscripts.

For the *Apologia* and the *Florida*, I have used the traditional chapter divisions and the subdivisions introduced

[34] Some conjectures attributed to Renaissance or later editors may have been anticipated by copyists: for the importance of the *recentiores* in the *Apologia* and the *Florida,* Reynolds, *Texts and Transmission,* 15–16.

by Vallette.[35] The "orphan chapters" of the *Florida* and the *De deo Socratis* have traditionally been divided into chapters, but otherwise only by Oudendorp's pagination; I have subdivided the chapters into smaller units numbered within each chapter. In matters of orthography I have followed the *Oxford Latin Dictionary*, though aware that some "unclassical" spellings in the manuscripts may go back to Apuleius himself, and I have also resolved abbreviations such as *v(iro) c(larissimo)*. I have not listed all the editors and authors of conjectures that I have cited; full lists are given by Hildebrand for all the works in this volume, for the *Apologia* and *Florida* by Helm, Martos, and Vallette, for the *De Deo Socratis* by Thomas, Beaujeu, and Moreschini. The *British Museum Catalogue of Printed Books* 6 (1954), 242–60, is also a rich source of bibliographic information.[36]

I owe thanks to several friends for reading parts or all of my manuscript, for sending me their published or unpublished work, for saving me from many errors, and for suggesting many improvements: Glen Bowersock, Stephen Harrison, Giuseppina Magnaldi, Francesca Piccioni, and Antonio Stramaglia (Magnaldi, Piccioni, and Stramaglia

[35] Helm begins chapter 65 at *en ultro,* Vallette, whom I have followed, at *de nomine* in the next sentence.

[36] I have usually retained Latinate names, e.g., Pricaeus, I(ohannes), not Price, J(ohn). The "Contarenus" frequently cited by Helm is Vincenzo Contarini (1577–1616), author of *Variarum Lectionum Liber* (Venice, 1606); information kindly supplied by Giuseppe Pezzini.

are preparing an Oxford text of the three works included here). Juan Martos kindly sent me his invaluable edition of the *Apologia* and the *Florida* (Madrid, 2015). Anne Power compiled the index with efficiency and vigilance. To all of these I owe my sincerest gratitude.

BIBLIOGRAPHIES AND ABBREVIATIONS

For very full bibliographies of the *Apologia* and *Florida,* see J. Martos, *Apología o Discurso sobre la Magia en Defensa propria: Floridas* (Madrid, 2015), lvi–cii.

GENERAL

Abt, A. *Die Apologie des Apuleius von Madaura und die antike Zauberei: Beiträge zur Erläuterung der Schrift De magia.* Giessen, 1908.

Bradley, K. R. *Apuleius and Antonine Rome: Historical Essays.* Toronto, 2012.

———. "Apuleius' *Apologia:* Text and Context." In *Apuleius and Africa*, edited by B. T. Lee et al., 23–24. New York, 2014.

Calder, W. M. III, et al. *The Unknown Socrates.* Wauconda, IL, 2002.

Flamand, J.-M. "Apulée de Madaure." In *Dictionnaire des Philosophes antiques,* edited by R. Goulet, 1:298–317. Paris, 1994.

Fletcher, R. *Apuleius' Platonism: The Impersonation of Philosophy.* Cambridge, 2014.

Gaisser, J. H. *The Fortunes of Apuleius and the* Golden Ass. Princeton, 2008.

Harrison, S. J. *Apuleius: A Latin Sophist.* Oxford, 2000.

Hijmans, B. L. "Apuleius Philosophus Platonicus." *ANRW* II 36.1 (1987): 395–475.

———. "Apuleius Orator: 'Pro se de Magia' and 'Florida.'" *ANRW* II 34.2 (1994): 1708–84.

Keil, H. *Observationes criticae in Catonis et Varronis de re rustica libros.* Halle, 1849.

Marshall, P. K., and L. D. Reynolds. "Apuleius." In Reynolds, *Texts and Transmission*, 15–18.

Lévi, N. "La Chronologie de la vie et de l'œuvre d'Apulée: Essai de synthèse et nouvelles hypothèses." *Latomus* 73 (2014): 693–720.

Nock, A. D. *Essays on Religion and the Ancient World.* Edited by Z. Stewart. Oxford, 1972.

Oldfather, W. A., H. V. Canter, and B. E. Perry. *Index Apuleianus. American Philological Association Monographs* 3. Middletown, CT, 1934.

Reynolds, L. D., ed. *Texts and Transmission: A Survey of the Latin Classics.* Oxford, 1983.

Rohde, E. "Zu Apuleius." *RhMus* 40 (1885): 66–113. = Rohde, *Kleine Schriften,* 2:43–74.

———. *Kleine Schriften.* 2 vols. Tübingen, 1901.

Schwabe, L. Art. "Apuleius (9)." *RE* 2 (1895): 246–58.

Stover, J. A. *A New Work by Apuleius: The Lost Third Book of the* De Platone. Oxford, 2016.

Taylor, T. "Magic and Property: The Legal Context of Apuleius' *Apologia.*" *Antichthon* 45 (2011): 149–66.

BIBLIOGRAPHIES AND ABBREVIATIONS

MANUSCRIPTS AND TEXT HISTORY

Lowe, E. A. "The Unique Manuscript of Apuleius' *Metamorphoses* (Laurentian. 68.2) and Its Oldest Transcript (Laurentian. 29.2)." *CQ* 14 (1920): 150–55. = Lowe, *Paleographical Papers 1907–1965,* 92–98.

———. *Paleographical Papers 1907–1965.* Oxford, 1972.

Magnaldi, G. "*L'editio princeps* del *De Deo Socratis* di Apuleio." In *Sulle orme degli antichi,* edited by M. Capasso, 379–401. Lecce, 2016.

Marshall, P. K., and L. D. Reynolds. "Apuleius." in Reynolds, *Texts and Transmission,* 15–18.

Olsen, B. M. *L'Étude des Auteurs classiques latins aux XIe et XIIe Siècles* 1. Paris, 1982.

Pecere, O. "Qualche riflessione sulla tradizione di Apuleio a Montecassino." In *Studi Apuleiani,* edited by O. Pecere and A. Stramaglia, 37–60. Cassino, 2003.

Piccioni, F. "Il *De magia* di Apuleio: Un Testimone trascurato, I: Il codice Assisiate 706." In *Linguaggi del Potere, Potere del Linguaggio,* edited by E. Bona and M. Curnis, 365–75. Alessandria, 2010.

———. "Sull'Assisiate 706 del *De magia* di Apuleio." *Segno e Testo* 11 (2013): 165–210.

Piccioni, F. "On Some *loci vexati* in Apuleius' *Florida*." *Mnemosyne* (forthcoming).

Reynolds, L. D., ed. *Texts and Transmission: A Survey of the Latin Classics.* Oxford, 1983.

Robertson, D. S. "The Manuscripts of the *Metamorphoses* of Apuleius." *CQ* 18 (1924): 27–42, 85–99.

———. "The Assisi Fragments of the *Apologia* of Apuleius." *CQ* 6 (1956): 68–80.

Rohde, E. "Zur handschriftliche Überlieferung der philosophischen Schriften des Apuleius." *Rheinisches Museum* 37 (1882): 146–51.

Watt, W. S. "Ten Notes on Apuleius, *Apologia.*" *Mnemosyne* 47 (1994): 517–20.

TEXTS, COMMENTARIES, TRANSLATIONS

Beaujeu, J. *Apulée: Opuscules philosophiques (Du Dieu de Socrate; Platon et sa Doctrine; Du monde) et Fragments* (Budé). Paris, 1973.

Butler, H. E. trans. *The Apologia and Florida of Apuleius of Madaura.* Oxford, 1909.

Butler, H. E., and A. S. Owen, eds. *Apulei Apologia sive Pro se de Magia Liber.* Oxford, 1914.

Hammerstaedt, J. *Apuleius:* De Magia. Darmstadt, 2002.

Hanson, J. A. *Apuleius,* Metamorphoses (The Golden Ass). 2 vols. Cambridge, MA, 1989.

Harrison, S. J., J. L. Hilton, and V. J. C. Hunink. *Apuleius: Rhetorical Works.* Oxford, 2001.

Helm, R., ed. *Apuleius II, 1: Apologia (De Magia).* 4th ed. (Teubner). Stuttgart, 1963.

Hildebrand, G. F., ed. *L. Apuleii Opera Omnia.* 2 vols. Leipzig, 1842.

Hunink, V. *Apuleius of Madauros: Pro se De Magia (Apologia). I: Text.* Amsterdam, 1997.

———. *Apuleius of Madauros: Pro se De Magia (Apologia). II: Commentary.* Amsterdam, 1997.

Kenney, E. J. Apuleius: *Cupid & Psyche.* Cambridge, 1990.

Lee, B. T. *Apuleius'* Florida: *A Commentary. Texte und Kommentare* 25. Berlin, 2005.

BIBLIOGRAPHIES AND ABBREVIATIONS

Marchesi, C. *Apuleio di Madaura: Della Magia.* Bologna, 1955.

Martos, J. *Apología o Discurso sobre la Magia en Defensa propria: Floridas.* Madrid, 2015.

Moreschini, C. *Apulei De Philosophia Libri* (Teubner). Leipzig, 1991.

Novák, R. *Quaestiones Apuleianae.* Prague, 1904.

Thomas, P., ed. *Apulei Platonici Madaurensis De Philosophia Libri* (Teubner). Leipzig, 1908.

Trzaskoma, S. M. "Apuleius: *De Deo Socratis.*" In *The Unknown Socrates,* edited by W. M. Calder III et al., 245–304. Wauconda, IL, 2002.

Vallette, P. *Apulée: Apologie, Florides.* 2nd ed. (Budé). Paris, 1960.

Vliet, J. van der, ed. *Lucii Apulei Platonici Madaurensis Apologia sive De Magia Liber et Florida* (Teubner). Leipzig, 1900.

Zimmerman, M. *Apulei Metamorphoseon Libri XI* (OCT). Oxford, 2012.

ABBREVIATIONS

ANRW   H. Temporini et al., eds., *Aufstieg und Nie-dergang der römischen Welt* (Berlin, 1972–)

Aristotle   fragments cited from O. Gigon, ed., *Aristotelis Opera III: Librorum Deperditorum Fragmenta* (Berlin, 1987)

Barrington Atlas   R. J. A. Talbert, ed., *Barrington Atlas of the Greek and Roman World* (Princeton, 2000)

FLP	E. Courtney, ed., *The Fragmentary Latin Poets* (Oxford, 2003)
FPL	J. Blänsdorf, ed., *Fragmenta Poetarum Latinorum epicorum et lyricorum* (Teubner), 4th ed. (Berlin, 2011)
MRR	T. R. S. Broughton, *The Magistrates of the Roman Republic* (New York, 1951–1986)
OCD	S. Hornblower and A. Spawforth, eds., *The Oxford Classical Dictionary,* 4th ed. (Oxford, 2012)
OLD	R. W. Glare, ed., *The Oxford Latin Dictionary,* 2nd ed. (Oxford, 2012)
PECS	R. Stillwell, ed., *The Princeton Encyclopedia of Classical Sites* (Princeton, 1976)
PIR	E. Groag, A. Stein et al., eds., *Prosopographia Imperii Romani,* 2nd ed. (Berlin, 1933–2015)
RE	G. Wissowa et al., eds., *Paulys Real-Encyclopädie der classischen Altertumswissenchaft* (Stuttgart, 1893–1980)
ROL	E. H. Warmington, ed., *Remains of Old Latin* (Loeb), 4 vols. (London, 1935–1940)

APOLOGIA

INTRODUCTION

1. THE CHARGE AGAINST APULEIUS

The *Apologia* takes the form of a speech in his own defense that Apuleius delivered at Sabrata, a coastal town in
northwestern Tripolitania (now Sabratah in Libya); the
actual building in which the trial probably took place has
been uncovered by excavation.[1] The trial took the form of
a judicial hearing (*cognitio*), presided over by the proconsul, Claudius Maximus, who had arrived at Sabrata on
his annual judicial tour (*conventus*). How far the written
version of the speech represents what Apuleius spoke on
the occasion is uncertain, but whatever its relation to the
original, it constitutes the only forensic speech to survive
from the imperial period.[2]

The accusation that Apuleius was a magician, though it
gives the work its conventional title, formed only part of
the general charge, which was that he had used magical

---

[1] Sabratha was a prosperous port city of eastern Tripolitania:
Barrington Atlas 35 E 2: Bradley, *Apuleius and Antonine Rome*,
4. On the general background of the trial: Bradley, "Apuleius'
Apologia."   [2] The thesis that the text represents an imaginary speech spoken on an imaginary occasion cannot be proved
or disproved, but I agree with the verdict of Bradley, *Apuleius
and Antonine Rome*, 20, "inherently implausible."

and other means to marry a rich widow of Oea, Pudentilla, or as his opponents alleged, had "broken into Pudentilla's house in my greed for profit" (*lucri cupiditate invasisse Pudentillae domum,* 66.1), thus defrauding her potential heirs and legatees.[3] Apuleius' stepson, Sicinius Pudens, was the principal injured party, but being below age could not represent himself[4] and was instead represented by his uncle, Sicinius Aemilianus, whose lawyer (*patronus*) was Tannonius Pudens; another interested party was Herennius Rufinus, the father-in-law of Sicinius Pontianus, the recently deceased elder brother of Sicinius Pudens.[5] A few days before the trial, Apuleius had been arguing a different case on behalf of his wife when Aemilianus first accused him of having murdered Pudens' brother Pontianus, and then dropped the charge. Aemilianus now handed in a formal denunciation (*delatio*), of which Apuleius gives the opening (102.9–3.10), "My lord Maximus, I formally accuse this man before you . . . of most numerous and flagrant crimes." Technically, one or more of the charges were "capital," which could have meant death or a lesser penalty, such as exile, though under the *cognitio* procedure the proconsul would have been guided as much

[3] Nock, *Essays on Religion,* 316–17, with n. 47, "I take it that the gravamen of the charge against Apuleius lay in the fact that the disposition of Pudentilla's property was affected." On the legal background to the speech, Abt, *Die Apologie des Apuleius,* 8–14; Taylor, "Magic and Property"; Bradley, *Apuleius and Antonine Rome,* 4–7. See further below, section 2.

[4] Boys below the age of seventeen could not represent themselves: Ulpian in *Dig.* 3.1.1.3.

[5] For a list of the persons involved, see below, section 4.

4

by precedent as by the law, and in particular by applicable decisions (*constitutiones*) of the emperors.

Apuleius does not mention any statute law under which he is being accused. At one point he says that magic, "so I am told," is something "entrusted to the laws," and he proceeds to mention the well-known provision of the Twelve Tables against charming away crops from a neighbor's field (47.3). The most directly applicable law was Sulla's *lex Cornelia de sicariis et veneficis,* which continued in force well into Late Antiquity and forms a whole section of Justinian's *Digest.* Later jurists explicitly ruled that love-magic was not criminal, so long as it did not cause bodily harm or death, but magic used for fraudulent purposes would have fallen under the law.[6] Other than this reference, the only occurrences of the word *lex* in the entire work are jocular allusions to the Augustan marriage laws (88.3, 103.3).

What Apuleius calls the most serious charge (57.1), though he mainly deals with it by ridicule, was contained in a deposition by a third party, Junius Crassus. According to this, he had conducted magical ceremonies at night in company with a friend, Appius Quintianus. Here the accusers might have appealed to Augustus' *Lex Iulia de maiestate,* since nocturnal gatherings, already suspect in the period of the republic, were especially so under the emperors, who were always alert to possible conspiracy. But on this charge too, Apuleius' adversaries did not need to invoke statute law. Many emperors since Augustus had

---

[6] *Lex Cornelia: Digest* 48.8; Abt, *Die Apologie des Apuleius,* 8–14; Taylor, "Magic and Property," 152–53. Later jurists: *Digest* 48.3.2 (Marcianus).

issued decisions in cases of alleged conspiracy; Pliny's instructions (*mandata*) from Trajan in his province of Pontus and Bithynia included a ban on associations (*hetaeriae*), which Christians understood as forbidding their predawn services (*Epp.* 10.96.7).

In reaching his verdict, the magistrate had broad powers of discretion, and in particular would take into account the social standing of the accused; penalties for those of the "better sort" (*honestiores*) were typically more lenient than for the "humbler sort" (*humiliores*).[7] Hence Apuleius is at pains to convey that he is a Roman citizen, native of a Roman colony in which his father had been the emperor's representative as mayor; he had received a testimonial from a previous proconsul, Lollianus Avitus; he was born rich, though he had spent much of his fortune in the pursuit of knowledge; he was a celebrated orator, fluent in both Latin and Greek, a world-traveler, and above all a philosopher of the Platonic school. Throughout, he represents himself as of the same educated class as the proconsul and his advisors, and totally different from the unlettered local gentry bringing the case. Though the outcome of the trial is unknown, it can hardly be doubted that Apuleius won, since he would not have published the speech in case of an adverse verdict.

2. MAGIC IN THE *APOLOGIA*

Already by the time of Porphyry and Lactantius, Apuleius was credited with magical powers. The belief that the *Metamorphoses* was autobiographical, and showed the

---

[7] Taylor, "Magic and Property," 153–55.

author's own pursuit of occult knowledge (*non quidem curiosum sed qui velim scire vel cuncta vel certe plurima, Met.* 1.2.6), could well have arisen before Augustine: it may explain how Sallustius or an unknown forerunner joined the *Metamorphoses* and the *Apologia* in a single manuscript. The title of *De magia* that Sallustius or an earlier copyist gave to the speech is misleading, in that the work is by no means a treatise "on magic." Apuleius' main concern is to show that he had married his wife reluctantly and had not used her fortune to his own advantage, and the rebuttal of the charges of magical practice is only a part of his argument, which he treats as an issue to be disposed of before coming to the charge of fraud. Rather than *De magia,* Apuleius might have given the speech a title such as *Pro se contra Sicinium Aemilianum.*

Yet magic was a stark reality in ancient life, and the charge would not have seemed implausible on its face.[8] Given his rhetorical stance, Apuleius would not want to display a detailed knowledge of magic, and the work cannot be treated as a treasure chest of magical lore.[9] He takes pains to cite literary justifications for the practices with which he is charged: thus on fish he cites Homer, Nicander, and Ennius among poets, Aristotle and Theophrastus among philosophers (39–41); on predictions, Varro and the Younger Cato (42); on epilepsy he

[8] Bradley, *Apuleius and Antonine Rome,* 7–12.

[9] This does not apply to Abt's admirable dissertation; he rebuts earlier scholars who overinterpreted the work in this sense, for instance, by taking Apuleius' discussion of mirrors as evidence for their use in ancient magic (Abt, *Die Apologie des Apuleius,* 24–27).

adapts a passage of Plato's *Timaeus* (49–50). By so doing he diverts the charge of magic onto a knowledge of literature and uses it to reinforce his self-presentation as a cultured philosopher, no different in this respect from his judge, Claudius Maximus.

3. STRUCTURE OF THE *APOLOGIA*

4. THE PEOPLE INVOLVED

Letters and numbers in parentheses indicate entries in *PIR*, where they exist.

Aemilia Pudentilla (A 425): married first to Sicinius Amicus and then to Apuleius; mother of Sicinius Pontianus and Sicinius Pudens.

Appii: friends of Apuleius at Oea, including Appius Quintianus (A 951), accused of joining with him to perform magical rites.

Apuleius (A 958): defendant, second husband of Aemilia Pudentilla.

---

[10] In the accusation, this topic came before the discussion of their marriage in the country.

Calpurnianus: a friend of Apuleius who produced allegedly incriminating evidence against him.

Capitolina: owner of some wood that Cornelius Saturninus made into a statuette.

Cassius Longinus: tutor (representative at law) of Pudentilla.

Claudius Maximus (C 933, 934): proconsul of Africa 158/9, presiding at Apuleius' trial.

Cornelius Saturninus: woodworker.

Corvinius Celer: public treasurer (quaestor publicus) of Oea.

Gavii: adversaries in a suit against Apuleius' wife Pudentilla.

(L. Hedius Rufus) Lollianus Avitus (H 40): proconsul of Africa (probably) 157/8.

Herennia (?): daughter of Herennius Rufinus; the widow of Sicinius Pontianus, and intended by her father as wife of his younger brother Pudens.

Herennius Rufinus (H 123): allegedly son of a bankrupt father, father of (Herennia).

Iunius Crassus (I 746): owner of the house in which Apuleius and Appius Quintianus allegedly practiced magic.

(Q.) Lollius Urbicus (L 327): Prefect of the City who heard a case involving Sicinius Aemilianus.

Saturninus: craftsman in wood.

(Sicinius—): father of the following three Sicinii.

Sicinius Aemilianus (S 696): principal accuser, uncle of Sicinius Pontianus and Sicinius Pudens.

Sicinius Amicus (S 697): first husband of Aemilia Pudentilla.

APOLOGIA

Sicinius Clarus (S 698): intended by his father, Sicinius—, to be Pudentilla's second husband, after the death of Amicus.

Sicinius Pontianus (S 701): Roman knight, elder son of Sicinius Amicus and Aemilia Pudentilla, now dead.

Sicinius Pudens (S 702): younger brother of Pontianus, collaborating with Herennius Rufinus and Sicinius Aemilianus in their case against Apuleius.

Tannonius Pudens (T 13): *advocatus* (representative in court) of Sicinius Aemilianus and Sicinius Pudens.

Thallus: slave of Apuleius, allegedly used by him in performing magic.

[APOLOGIA]¹

1. Certus equidem eram proque vero obtinebam, Maxime
Claudi quique in consilio estis, Sicinium Aemilianum, se-
nem notissimae temeritatis, accusationem mei prius apud
te coeptam quam apud se cogitatam penuria criminum
2 solis conviciis impleturum; quippe insimulari quivis inno-
3 cens potest, revinci nisi nocens non potest. Quo ego uno
praecipue confisus gratulor medius fidius, quod mihi copia
et facultas te iudice optigit purgandae apud imperitos phi-
4 losophiae et probandi mei. Quamquam istae calumniae ut
prima specie graves, ita ad difficultatem defensionis re-
5 pentinae fuere. Nam, ut meministi, dies abhinc quintus an
sextus est, cum me causam pro uxore mea Pudentilla adversus Granios agere aggressum de composito necopi-
nantem patroni eius incessere maledictis, et insimulare
magicorum maleficiorum ac denique necis Pontiani pri-
6 vigni mei coepere. Quae ego cum intellegerem non tam

¹ MADAVRENSIS APVLEI PLATONICI APOLOGIA DE MAGIA
LIBER PRIMVS φ

¹ On the titles given in φ here and after ch. 65, see General
Introduction.   ² Roman magistrates and governors sitting
in judgment had a panel (*consilium*) of handpicked advisers (*as-
sessores*) to assist them in forming a verdict.

‹SPEECH IN SELF-DEFENSE›[1]

1. *I* was convinced and considered it a certainty, Claudius Maximus and you who are present as his advisers,[2] that Sicinius Aemilianus, an old man notoriously foolhardy, had launched his suit against me in your court before duly thinking it over with himself, and that for lack of any real charges he would fill his prosecution with insults and nothing more. For one can defame an innocent man, but only 2 convict a guilty one. That thought in itself gives me confidence, 3 and I must say I am delighted to have been granted an opportunity and an occasion to clear the name of Philosophy, and to justify myself in the eyes of ignorant people, with you as my judge; though these slanders were 4 grave at first sight, and at the same time were so unexpected as to make a defense difficult. For as you will remember, 5 it was only five or six days ago that, after I had begun to argue a case on behalf of my wife Pudentilla against the Granius family, Aemilianus' lawyers colluded in attacking me by surprise with their insults, and finally began to accuse me of practicing black magic and even of murdering my stepson Pontianus. Realizing that these 6 were not so much charges made to stand up in court as

crimina iudicio quam obiectamenta iurgio prolata, ultro eos ad accusandum crebris flagitationibus provocavi. Ibi vero Aemilianus cum te quoque acrius motum et ex verbis rem factam videret, quaerere occepit ex diffidentia latibulum aliquod temeritati.

2. Igitur Pontianum fratris sui filium, quem paulo prius occisum a me clamitarat, postquam ad subscribendum

2 compellitur, ilico oblitus est, de morte cognati adulescentis subito tacens.[2] Tanti criminis descriptione tamen ‹ne›[3] omnino desistere videretur, calumniam magiae, quae facilius infamatur quam probatur, eam solum sibi delegit ad

3 accusandum. Ac ne id quidem de professo audet, verum postera die dat libellum nomine privigni mei Sicini Pu-

4 dentis admodum pueri et adscribit se ei assistere, novo more per alium lacessendi, scilicet ut obtentu eius aetatu-

5 lae ipse insimulationis falsae non plecteretur. Quod tu cum sollertissime animadvertisses et idcirco eum denuo iussisses proprio nomine accusationem delatam sustinere,

6 pollicitus ita facturum ne sic quidem quitus est ut comminus ageret percelli, sed iam et adversum te contumaciter

7 eminus calumniis velitatur. Ita totiens ab accusandi periculo profugus in assistendi venia perseveravit.

8 Igitur et priusquam causa ageretur, facile intellectu cuivis fuit qualisnam accusatio futura esset, cuius qui fue-

9 rat professor et machinator idem fieri auctor timeret, ac praesertim Sicinius Aemilianus, qui si quippiam veri in me

---

[2] tacens *u*: tacerem *ω*: tacere *Petschenig: an* tacere cepit (*i.e.*, coepit), *cf. Mart. 12.83.6?*

[3] ne *add. u*

14

slurs designed to provoke a quarrel, I in return challenged those men, demanding repeatedly that they bring an accusation. At that point, however, Aemilianus saw that you too were annoyed, and that facts had been made out of words, and so he lost confidence and began to look for a way to cover up his recklessness.

2. Consequently, after loudly claiming a little while ago that I had killed his own brother's son Pontianus, as soon as he was forced to put his name to the charge, he immediately forgot him, and suddenly fell silent about his young 2 relative's death. And yet, not to seem altogether to abandon a charge for such a crime, and because the allegation of magical practice is more easily insinuated than proved, he made his whole charge consist of that. Even 3 that, though, he does not dare to do openly; no, on the next day he laid a charge in the name of my stepson Sicinius Pudens, a very young boy, and also stated that he is supporting him (an original way of harassing someone by 4 proxy), no doubt so that, hiding behind Pudens' early youth, he himself would not be punished for his false insinuations. But with your great acuteness you had ob- 5 served that, and so had ordered him to undertake the suit in his own name. Though he promised to do so, he still 6 could not be driven to engage face to face, but now, in defiance even of yourself, he fires off his slanders from a distance. So many times, then, has he shirked the risk of 7 bringing a charge and has clung to his excuse of "assisting."

Thus even before the case came on, anyone could eas- 8 ily see what kind of charge this was going to be, when the very person who was its prompter and inventor was afraid to be its sponsor, especially when that person was Sicinius 9 Aemilianus. If he had discovered anything true about me,

explorasset, nunquam profecto tam cunctanter hominem
10 extraneum tot tantorumque criminum postulasset, qui
avunculi sui testamentum quod verum sciebat pro falso
11 infamarit, tanta quidem pertinacia, ut, cum Lollius Vrbicus v(irum) c(larissimum) verum videri et ratum esse
debere de consilio consularium virorum pronuntiasset,
contra clarissimam vocem iuraverit vecordissimus iste, ta-
12 men illud testamentum fictum esse, adeo ut aegre Lollius
Vrbicus ab eius pernicie temperarit.

3. Quam quidem vocem et tua aequitate et mea innocentia fretus spero in hoc quoque iudicio erupturam,
quippe qui sciens innocentem criminatur eo sane facilius,
quod iam, ut dixi, mentiens apud praefectum urbi in am-
2 plissima causa convictus est. Namque peccatum semel ut
bonus quisque postea sollicitius cavet, ita qui ingenio malo
est confidentius integrat ac iam de cetero quo saepius, eo
3 apertius delinquit; pudor enim veluti vestis quanto obso-
4 letior est, tanto incuriosius habetur. Et ideo necessarium
arbitror pro integritate pudoris mei, priusquam ad rem
5 aggrediar, maledicta omnia refutare. Sustineo enim non
modo meam, verum etiam philosophiae defensionem,
cuia magnitudo vel minimam reprehensionem pro maximo
6 crimine aspernatur, propter quod paulo prius patroni
Aemiliani multa in me proprie conficta et alia communiter
in philosophos sueta ab imperitis mercennaria loquacitate

---

3 Lollius Urbicus (*PIR* L 327) crowned a distinguished career
by a long tenure as prefect of the city of Rome, in which capacity
he judged the case that Apuleius mentions here. As a Roman
senator he had the title of *vir clarissimus,* here translated "right
honorable": by an untranslatable wordplay, Apuleius applies the
same adjective to his decision, "very clear."

he would certainly never hesitated as he did to charge an
outsider to the family with crimes so numerous and so
grave, considering that he defamed his very own uncle's   10
will as false, though knowing it to be genuine, and was so   11
persistent in doing so that when the right honorable Lollius Urbicus, acting on the advice of men of consular rank,
had declared that it appeared genuine and must be considered valid, despite this clearest of decisions this utter
madman swore nonetheless that the will was false, and   12
Lollius Urbicus could scarcely restrain himself from sending him to perdition.[3]

3. Relying alike on your sense of justice and on my innocence, I hope that the same verdict will ring out in this
trial also, since in full knowledge of the truth he is accusing an innocent man, something all the easier for him in
that, as I said, he has already been convicted of lying in a
most important case before the Prefect of the City. Just as   2
any honest man, after doing wrong, is more careful not to
do so thereafter, equally a man of evil character does so
again more confidently, and thereafter transgresses both
more frequently and more openly (for honor is like cloth-   3
ing—the shabbier it gets, the more carelessly it is treated).
Hence I think it necessary for the preservation of my own   4
honor to rebut all his slanders before I come to the actual charge. It is not only my defense that I am undertak-   5
ing but Philosophy's too, whose exalted status refuses to
accept even the slightest aspersion as if it were the gravest of charges. I do so because Aemilianus' lawyers, with   6
their paid loquacity, a little while ago spouted many things,
some of them made up against me personally, and others
that ignorant people tend to aim at philosophers collec-

7   effutierunt. Quae etsi possunt ab his futiliter[4] blaterata ob
mercedem et auctoramento impudentiae depensa haberi,
iam concesso quodam more rabulis id genus, quo ferinae[5]
8   solent linguae suae virus alieno dolori locare, tamen vel
mea causa paucis refellenda sunt, ne is, qui sedulo laboro
ut ne quid maculae aut inhonestamenti in me admittam,
videar cuipiam, si quid ex frivolis praeteriero, id agnovisse
9   potius quam contempsisse. Est enim pudentis animi et
verecundi, ut mea opinio fert, vel falsas vituperationes
gravari, cum etiam hi, qui sibi delicti alicuius conscii sunt,
tamen, cum male audiunt, impendio commoveantur et
10 obirascantur, quamquam, exinde ut male facere coeperunt, consueverint male audire, quod, si a ceteris silentium est, tamen ipsi sibimet conscii sunt posse se merito
11 increpari. Enimvero bonus et innoxius quisque rudis et
imperitas auris ad male audiendum habens, et laudis assuetudine contumeliae insolens, multo tanta ex animo
laborat ea sibi immerito dici, quae ipse possit aliis vere
12 obiectare. Quod si forte inepta videbor et oppido frivola
velle defendere, illis debet ea res vitio verti, quibus turpe
est etiam haec obiectasse, non mihi culpae dari, cui honestum erit etiam haec diluisse.

    4. Audisti igitur paulo prius in principio accusationis ita
dici: "accusamus apud te philosophum formosum et tam
2   Graece quam Latine" (pro nefas!) "disertissimum." Nisi
fallor enim, his ipsis verbis accusationem mei ingressus est

---

[4] futiliter *Colvius*: utiliter ω
[5] ferine (*i.e.,* ferinae) *u*: ferme ω

tively. One might consider everything of that sort the fool-   7
ish prattle of hirelings, payments that they make after
contracting to act shamelessly, since it is the accepted way
of ranters of the kind to hire out their savage tongues'
venom to inflict pain on others. And yet I must briefly   8
rebut them, even if only on my own account, since I am
extremely careful not to be touched by any stain or disgrace, and I do not want anyone to think, if I ignored one
of these trivial charges, that I do so because I acknowledge
it when in fact I despise it. For it is the mark of an honor-   9
able and self-respecting mind, in my opinion, to object
even to false censure. Even those who have some misdeed
on their conscience nonetheless become very irritated and
angry when they hear evil report of themselves, despite   10
having got used to evil report from the moment they began to do evil. Even if they hear nothing said by others,
still they know within themselves that they are rightly liable to reproach. By contrast, every upright and inno-   11
cent person has ears that are sensitive and unused to hearing evil. Though familiar with praise they are strangers to
abuse, and are pained to the very marrow when something
is undeservedly said against themselves that they could
truthfully charge against others. If then I seem to be de-   12
fending myself against charges that are silly and perfectly
trivial, the blame should fall on those people, who are
disgraced by making these as well as other allegations. The
fault is not with me, but I will earn credit for refuting even
things of this kind.

4. You heard them say this not long ago at the start of
the prosecution: "We accuse a handsome philosopher in
your court and" (shocking to say!) "one very eloquent both
in Greek and in Latin." For if I am not mistaken, those   2

Tannonius Pudens, homo vere ille quidem non disertissi-
3 mus. Quod utinam tam gravia formae et facundiae crimina
vere mihi opprobrasset! Non difficile ei respondissem
quod Homericus Alexander Hectori:

4   οὔ τοι ἀπόβλητ᾽ ἐστὶ θεῶν ἐπικυδέα δῶρα
     ὅσσα κεν αὐτοὶ δῶσιν, ἑκὼν δ᾽οὐκ ἄν τις ἕλοιτο.

5 munera deum gloriosissima nequaquam aspernanda; quae
tamen ab ipsis tribui sueta multis volentibus non obtin-
6 gunt. Haec ego de forma respondissem; praeterea, licere
7 etiam philosophis esse voltu liberali; Pythagoram, qui primus sese[6] philosophum nuncuparit, eum sui saeculi excel-
8 lentissima forma fuisse; item Zenonem illum antiquum
Velia oriundum, qui primus omnium sollertissimo artificio
⟨argumenta⟩[7] ambifariam dissolverit, eum quoque Zeno-
9 nem longe decorissimum fuisse, ut Plato autumat; itemque
multos philosophos ab ore honestissimos memoriae prodi,
qui gratiam corporis morum honestamentis ornaverint.
10   Sed haec defensio, ut dixi, aliquam multum a me remota est, cui praeter formae mediocritatem continuatio
etiam litterati laboris omnem gratiam corpore deterget,
habitudinem tenuat, sucum exsorbet, colorem obliterat,
11 vigorem debilitat. Capillus ipse, quem isti aperto menda-

---

[6] sese *Lipsius*: se esse ω   [7] argumenta *add. Helm*

---

[4] Apuleius actually uses Paris' more usual name in Homer,
"Alexander."   [5] *Il.* 3.65–66.
[6] This Latin paraphrase may be a late interpolation for the
benefit of Greekless readers.
[7] Apuleius is usually thought to refer to Zeno's version of the
argument by *reductio ad absurdum*.

were the words with which Tannonius Pudens, certainly
someone of no great eloquence, began his accusation. If   3
only he had been telling the truth when he brought such
grave charges of handsomeness and eloquence against me!
It would have been easy to answer him in the words of
Homer's Paris[4] to Hector:

> Not to be spurned are the wonderful gifts of the   4
>   gods;
> They give them as they please, but no man could get
>   them by wishing.[5]

The most glorious gifts of the gods are by no means to be 5
rejected, but they are usually given by the gods themselves, and many people want them without receiving
them.[6] That is what I would have answered about my
looks. Furthermore, I could have said that even philoso-   6
phers may be decent-looking; that Pythagoras himself, the 7
first man to call himself a philosopher, was the most outstandingly handsome man of his time; similarly, that the   8
famous Zeno of antiquity, who came from Velia, the very
first person to refute hypotheses by the most ingenious de-
vice of self-inconsistency,[7]—this Zeno too was extremely
handsome, according to Plato; and many philosophers are   9
likewise recorded as being very good-looking, and to have
added to their physical grace by the further adornment of
character.

But as I said, such a defense is far from relevant to me, 10
since apart from my unprepossessing looks, my continuous occupation with literary study obliterates all my physical charm, and makes my body thin, my vitality feeble,
my complexion pale, and my energy weak. Even my hair,   11
though by a patent lie they said that I let it grow in order

21

cio ad lenocinium decoris promissum dixere, vides quam
12 sit amoenus ac delicatus—horrore implexus atque impeditus, stuppeo tomento adsimilis et inaequaliter hirtus et
globosus et congestus, prorsum inenodabilis diutina incuria non modo comendi, sed saltem expediendi et discrimi-
13 nandi. Satis, ut puto, crinium crimen, quod illi quasi capitale intenderunt, refutatur.

5. De eloquentia vero, si qua mihi fuisset, neque mirum neque invidiosum deberet videri si, ab ineunte aevo
unis studiis litterarum ex summis viribus deditus, omnibus
aliis spretis voluptatibus ad hoc aevi, haud sciam anne
super omnis homines impenso labore diuque noctuque
cum despectu et dispendio bonae valetudinis eam quae-
2 sissem. Sed nihil ab eloquentia metuant, quam ego, si quid
3 omnino promovi, potius spero quam praesto. Sane quidem, si verum est quod Statium Caecilium in suis poema-
tibus scripsisse dicunt, innocentiam eloquentiam esse, ego
vero profiteor ista ratione ac praefero me nemini omnium
4 de eloquentia concessurum. Quis enim me hoc quidem
pacto eloquentior vivat, quippe qui nihil unquam cogitavi
5 quod eloqui non auderem? Eundem me aio facundissimum esse, nam omne peccatum semper nefas habui; eundem disertissimum, quod nullum meum factum vel dic-
6 tum extet, de quo disserere publice non possim, ita ut iam
de versibus dissertabo quos a me factos quasi pudendos

---

8 Apuleius plays with the assonance of *crinium* and *crimen,*
and with the connection of *capitale* with *caput* (head).

9 Caecilius Statius was a writer of Latin adaptations of Greek
New Comedy (*fabula palliata*), whose death Jerome places in 168
BC: this fragment is *ROL* 1.552, Caecilius fr. 255.

to make my looks seductive, you see how charming and
coiffed it is; it sticks up in tangles and knots, it resembles   12
mattress stuffing, it is unevenly matted, coiled, and tufted,
and has become totally inextricable through my neglecting
even to untangle and straighten it, let alone to comb it.
That, I think, sufficiently answers the affair of my hair,   13
with which they charged me as if it were a capital crime.[8]

5. As for my eloquence, however, if ever I possessed
any, no one should think it cause for surprise or envy if,
having dedicated myself with all my strength to nothing
but the study of literature from my earliest years, and having rejected all other pleasures throughout my life, I may
perhaps have surpassed all human beings in the tireless
effort with which I have pursued eloquence night and day,
to the neglect and the detriment of my health. But let my   2
opponents have no fear of my eloquence, for whatever
advances I have made are more a matter of aspiration than
achievement. Certainly, if what Caecilius Statius is said to   3
have written in his poems is true, that innocence is eloquence,[9] on that ground, yes, I assert and I declare that I
will yield to nobody on the score of eloquence. For by that   4
logic what person alive is more eloquent than I, who have
never had a thought I did not dare to say aloud? I also   5
claim to be more copious in speech than anyone, because
I have always held that every misdeed is impious, and most
ready of speech, because there is no deed or word of mine
on which I cannot readily speak in public. Indeed, I will   6
now expound verses of my own composition that those

protulerunt, cum quidem me animadvertisti cum risu illis
suscensentem, quod eos absone et indocte pronuntiarent.

6. Primo igitur legerunt e ludicris meis epistolium de
dentifricio versibus scriptum ad quendam Calpurnianum,
qui cum adversum me eas litteras promeret, non vidit profecto cupiditate laedendi, si quid mihi ex illis fieret crimi-
2 nosum, id mihi secum esse commune. Nam petisse eum a
me aliquid tersui dentibus versus testantur:

3   Calpurniane, salue properis versibus.
        Misi, ut petisti, mundicinas[8] dentium,
        nitelas oris ex Arabicis frugibus,
        tenuem, candificum, nobilem pulvisculum,
        complanatorem tumidulae gingivulae,
        converritorem pridianae reliquiae,
        ne qua visatur tetra labes sordium,
        restrictis forte si labellis riseris.

4 Quaeso, quid habent isti versus re aut verbo pudendum,
5 quid omnino quod philosophus suum nolit videri? Nisi
forte in eo reprehendendus sum, quod Calpurniano pul-
visculum ex Arabicis frugibus miserim, quem multo ae-
quius erat spurcissimo ritu Hiberorum, ut ait Catullus, sua
sibi urina

        dentem atque russam pumicare gingivam.

---

[8] mundicinas *Lipsius*: munditias ω

---

[10] Apuleius plays on the similarity of the words *fas/facundia*
and *disertus/dissero,* both of which pairs may have the same root
(*figura etymologica*); *disserto* in the next sentence is formed from
the supine of *dissero.*
[11] *FLP* and *FPL*[2], Apuleius fr. 2; the meter is iambic senarius.

people brought up as if they were shameful, while you,
Maximus, noticed that I was both amused and annoyed at
the harsh and ignorant way they spoke them.[10]

6. First, then, they read out one of my trifles—a little
missive in verse on the subject of dentifrice addressed to
one Calpurnianus. When he produced that letter against
me, his eagerness to do me harm utterly blinded him to
the fact that if anything in it proved criminal, that was his
business as much as mine, for the lines show that he had   2
asked me for something to clean his teeth with.[11]

> I say hello, Calpurnianus, with these hasty lines.   3
> I've sent you something to clean your teeth,
> To brighten your smile with Arabian spices.
> It's a fine, whitening, excellent powder,
> Guaranteed to shrink swollen gums,
> To brush away yesterday's leftovers,
> So that no ugly stain of dirt appears
> If you chance to laugh with opened lips.

I ask you, what is shameful about these lines, either in   4
subject or language? Is there anything about them that a
philosopher would not wish to be thought his? Unless per-   5
haps I am to be faulted for sending Calpurnianus a powder
made from "Arabian spices," when it would have been
more fitting for him to observe that disgusting custom of
the Spaniards. They, in Catullus' words, use their own
urine

> To scrape their teeth and reddish gums.[12]

---

[12] Catullus 39.19, with *pumicare* in place of *defricare*: perhaps
a deliberate substitution rather than an error of memory, since
pumice was used as a depilatory, not as a dentifrice.

7. Vidi ego dudum vix risum quosdam tenentis, cum
munditias oris videlicet orator ille aspere accusaret et den-
tifricium tanta indignatione pronuntiaret, quanta nemo
2 quisquam venenum. Quidni? Crimen haud contemnen-
dum philosopho, nihil in se sordidum sinere, nihil uspiam
3 corporis apertum immundum[9] pati ac foetulentum, praesertim os, cuius in propatulo et conspicuo usus homini
creberrimus, sive ille cuipiam osculum ferat, seu cum
quiquam sermocinetur, sive in auditorio dissertet, sive in
4 templo preces alleget. Omnem quippe hominis actum
sermo praeit, qui, ut ait poeta praecipuus, dentium muro
5 proficiscitur. Dares nunc aliquem similiter grandiloquum:
diceret suo more cum primis cui ulla fandi cura sit impensius cetero corpore os colendum, quod esset animi vesti-
6 bulum et orationis ianua et cogitationum comitium. Ego
certe pro meo captu dixerim nihil minus quam oris illu-
7 viem libero et liberali viro competere, est enim ea pars
hominis loco celsa, visu prompta, usu facunda. Nam quidem feris et pecudibus os humile est et deorsum ad pedes
deiectum, uestigio et pabulo proximum; nunquam ferme
nisi mortuis aut ad morsum exasperatis conspicitur: hominis vero nihil prius tacentis, nihil saepius loquentis con-
templere.

8. Velim igitur censor meus Aemilianus respondeat,

[9] apertum immundum *u*: apertum mundum *ω*

---

[13] Another play on words, this one between *orator* (speaker)
and *oris* (mouth).   [14] As the logic shows, Apuleius means
that the charge would be grave if it were false, not if it were true,
because all these habits are essential for a philosopher.

[15] *Il.* 4.350 and elsewhere.

7. Just now I saw some people here scarcely able to restrain their mirth, no doubt because the speaker there was sharply attacking oral hygiene and uttering the word "dentifrice" with more indignation than any one has ever uttered "poison."[13] And why not? For a philosopher it is no trifling charge[14] that he allows no dirt to settle on him, and leaves no exposed part of his body dirty or smelly, least of all his mouth, a visible and conspicuous feature that humans use very frequently, whether to offer someone a kiss, converse with another, address an audience, or offer prayers in a temple. Speech precedes every human action, and, as the chief of poets says, it starts from "the barrier of the teeth."[15] Now imagine someone similarly lofty of speech: he would say in his own way that someone with any interest in oratory is particularly obliged to devote more attentive care to his mouth than to the rest of his body, since it is the vestibule of the mind, the portal of speech, the forum where thoughts meet. I at any rate cannot put it better than to say that nothing is less appropriate to a freeborn, well-educated man than a dirty mouth. In a human being the mouth is a feature set high up, readily noticed, and an instrument of eloquence, while in wild and domesticated animals the mouth is set low down and turned toward the feet, is close to where they walk and feed, and is almost never seen except when they are dead or goaded into biting: in a man, by contrast, there is nothing you notice sooner when he is silent or oftener when he talks.

8. I would therefore like my critic Aemilianus to tell me

unquamne ipse soleat pedes lavare; vel, si id non negat,
contendat maiorem curam munditiarum pedibus quam
2 dentibus impertiendam. Plane quidem, si quis ita ut tu,
Aemiliane, nunquam ferme os suum nisi maledictis et calumniis aperiat, censeo ne ulla cura os percolat neque ille
exotico pulvere dentis emaculet, quos iustius carbone de
rogo obteruerit, neque saltem communi aqua perluat;
3 quin ei nocens lingua mendaciorum et amaritudinum
praeministra semper in foetutinis et olenticetis suis iaceat.
4 Nam quae, malum, ratio est linguam mundam et laetam,
vocem contra spurcam et taetram possidere, viperae ritu
5 niveo denticulo atrum venenum inspirare? Ceterum qui
sese sciat orationem prompturum neque inutilem neque
iniucundam, eius merito os, ut bono potui poculum, prae-
6 lavitur. Et quid ego de homine nato diutius? Belua imma-
nis, crocodillus ille qui in Nilo gignitur, ea quoque, ut
comperior, purgandos sibi dentis innoxio hiatu praebet.
7 Nam quod est ore amplo, sed elingui et plerumque in aqua
recluso, multae hirudines dentibus implectuntur; eas illi,
cum egressus in praeripia fluminis hiavit, una ex [avibus][10]
fluvialibus amica avis iniecto rostro sine noxae periculo
exsculpit.

9. Mitto haec: venio ad ceteros versus ut illi vocant
amatorios, quos tamen tam dure et rustice legere ut odium
2 moverent. Sed quid ad magica maleficia, quod ego pueros
3 Scriboni Laeti, amici mei, carmine laudavi? An ideo magus, quia poeta? Quis unquam fando audivit tam ‹veri›[11]

[10] avibus *del. Brantius*   [11] veri *add. Krüger*

---

[16] This famous habit of crocodiles is first mentioned by
Herodotus, 2.68.

in reply whether he himself ever makes a practice of washing his feet, or, if he does not deny doing so, whether he holds that one should devote more care to keeping the feet clean than the teeth. Of course, if someone is like you, 2 Aemilianus, and almost never opens his lips except to utter insults and slanders, I would not advise him to spend any care on his mouth, or clean his teeth with imported powder; it would be more appropriate to scrub them with ash from a funeral pyre, or at least not wash them in ordinary water. No, his malicious tongue, which serves up his lies 3 and acrimony, should remain permanently in its cesspools and dung heaps. For what sense is there, confound it, in 4 possessing a clean, pleasing mouth and at the same time a filthy, foul voice—in injecting black venom with a white fang like a viper? If however someone knows that the 5 speech he is about to make is not unhelpful or unpleasant, he rightly begins by washing his mouth, as one washes a cup for a healthy drink. But why should I say more about 6 human beings? That colossal monster, the crocodile born in the Nile—he too, I find, offers his teeth to be cleaned by harmlessly opening his jaws. Since his mouth is huge 7 but tongueless, and is usually open under water, many leeches get caught in his teeth; so that when he emerges and opens his mouth on the riverbank, a friendly waterbird pokes its beak in and cleans it with no risk of harm to itself.[16]

9. I leave all this aside, and come to other poems of mine, "love poems" according to them, though they read them out so stiffly and coarsely as to inspire revulsion. But 2 how is criminal magic involved if a poem I wrote was in praise of my friend Scribonius Laetus' boy slaves? Does 3 being a poet make me a magician? Whoever heard so

APULEIUS

similem suspicionem, tam aptam coniecturam, tam proxi-
4 mum argumentum? "Fecit versus Apuleius." Si malos, crimen est, nec id tamen philosophi, sed poetae; sin bonos,
5 quid accusas? "At enim ludicros et amatorios fecit." Num
ergo haec sunt crimina mea, et nomine erratis, qui me
6 magiae detulistis? Fecere tamen et alii talia, etsi vos igno-
ratis: apud Graecos Teius quidam et Lacedaemonius et
7 Cius[12] cum aliis innumeris, etiam mulier Lesbia, lascive
illa quidem tantaque gratia, ut nobis insolentiam linguae
8 suae dulcedine carminum commendet; apud nos vero Aedituus et Porcius et Catulus, isti quoque cum aliis innu-
9 meris. At philosophi non fuere. Num igitur etiam Solonem
fuisse serium virum et philosophum negabis, cuius ille
lascivissimus versus est:

μηρῶν ἱμείρων καὶ γλυκεροῦ στόματος.

10 Et quid tam petulans habent omnes versus mei, si cum isto
11 uno contendantur? Vt taceam scripta Diogenis Cynici et
Zenonis Stoicae sectae conditoris, id genus plurima. Recitem denuo, ut sciant me eorum non pigere:

12   Et Critias mea delicia est et salva, Charine,
            pars in amore meo, vita, tibi remanet.
        Ne metuas, nam me ignis et ignis torreat ut vult;
            hasce duas flammas, dum potiar, patiar.

[12] Cius *Bosscha*: civis ω

---

[17] The male poets are Anacreon of Teos, Alcman of Sparta,
and Simonides of Ceos (on whose erotic poetry see West, *Iambi
et Elegi Graeci*[2], Simonides frr. 21, 22); the female is of course
Sappho.   [18] West, *Iambi et Elegi Graeci*[2], Solon fr. 25.2.

30

plausible a suspicion expressed, so compelling an inference, so conclusive an argument? "Apuleius has written 4
poems." If they were bad, that is an accusation, but still
one against a poet, not a philosopher; and if they were
good, what is your charge? "Well, he wrote frivolous, 5
erotic poems." Are these then your charges against me,
and you picked the wrong word when indicting me for
magic? Others too have written such things, not that you 6
would know—among the Greeks, certain men from Teos,
from Sparta, from Ceos, and countless others, and a lady 7
from Lesbos too, with such sauciness and such charm indeed that the sweetness of her poems makes up for her
improper language.[17] In our literature, however, there are 8
Aedituus, Porcius, Catulus, these and countless others.
True, they were not philosophers. Well, would you then 9
deny that Solon was a respectable citizen and a philosopher, even though he wrote that very risqué line:

"Of lovely thighs and honeyed mouth"?[18]

Do all the lines I have written include anything so naughty 10
as that one by itself? Not to mention the writings of Diog- 11
enes the Cynic and Zeno, the founder of the Stoic school,
many of which are like that. I will read mine out again so
that those people know that I am not ashamed of them.[19]

Critias is my beloved, yet for you, 12
Dearest Charinus, half my love's reserved.
Fear not: this double fire may burn me as it will,
I will endure these two flames just to win you.

[19] Courtney, *FLP* 392, Apuleius 3; Blänsdorf, *FPL*[2] 362, Apuleius 3.

Hoc modo sim vobis, unus sibi quisque quod ipse est;
    hoc mihi vos eritis, quod duo sunt oculi.

13 Recitem nunc et alios, quos illi quasi intemperantissimos
postremum legere:

Florea serta, meum mel, et haec tibi carmina dono.
    Carmina dono tibi, serta tuo genio,
carmina uti, Critia, lux haec optata canatur
    quae bis septeno vere tibi remeat,
serta autem ut laeto tibi tempore tempora vernent,
    aetatis florem floribus ut decores.
Tu mihi des[13] contra pro verno flore tuum uer,
    ut nostra exuperes munera muneribus.
Pro implexis sertis complexum corpore redde,
    proque rosis oris savia purpurei.
Quod si animum inspires donaci, iam carmina nostra
    cedent victa tuo dulciloquo calamo.

10. Habes crimen meum, Maxime, quasi improbi co-
2 misatoris de sertis et canticis compositum. Hic illud etiam
reprehendi animadvertisti, quod, cum aliis nominibus pueri vocentur, ego eos Charinum et Critian appellitarim.
3 Eadem igitur opera accusent C. Catullum, quod Lesbiam
pro Clodia nominarit, et Ticidam similiter, quod quae
Metella erat Perillam scripserit, et Propertium, qui Cyn-

---

[13] des *Krüger*: das ω: da *u*

---

[20] Courtney, *FLP* 392, Apuleius 4; Blänsdorf, *FPL*[2] 362–63,
Apuleius 4.

Only let me be to both as each is to himself;
You both will be to me as dear as my two eyes.

Let me also read other ones too, which they saved for the   13
end as the last word in immorality:[20]

These flowery wreaths and songs, my sweet, I give
    you.
Flowers for you, and wreaths for your guardian spirit:
Songs, my Critias, to celebrate this longed-for day,
Which comes around with your fourteenth spring,
And wreaths to adorn your brows in this happy
    season,
So that you may adorn with flowers your youthful
    flower.
But in return repay my spring flowers with your
    spring
And outdo my gifts with gifts of yours.
For intertwining wreaths entwine your limbs with
    mine
And for roses give kisses from your ruby lips.
But if you breathe your soul into the reed, ah, then
My poems will yield the victory to your sweet flute.

10. That is what I am charged with, Maximus; you
would think it the work of a shameless reveler on the subject of garlands and serenades. On this point, you noticed   2
that they faulted me for calling the boys not by their real
names but "Charinus" and "Critias." Well, on the same   3
grounds they should accuse Gaius Catullus because he
used the name "Lesbia" instead of "Clodia," and Ticidas
similarly because he used "Perilla" for the actual Metella,
and Propertius who writes "Cynthia" as a cover for Hostia,

33

thiam dicat, Hostiam dissimulet, et Tibullum, quod ei sit
4 Plania in animo, Delia in versu. Et quidem C. Lucilium,
quamquam sit iambicus, tamen improbarim, quod Gentium et Macedonem pueros directis nominibus carmine
5 suo prostituerit. Quanto modestius tandem Mantuanus
poeta, qui itidem ut ego puerum amici sui Pollionis bu-
colico ludicro laudans et abstinens nominum sese quidem
6 Corydonem, puerum vero Alexin vocat. Sed Aemilianus,
vir ultra Vergilianos opiliones et busequas rusticanus,
agrestis quidem semper et barbarus, verum longe auste-
rior, ut putat, Serranis et Curiis et Fabriciis, negat id genus
7 versus Platonico philosopho competere. Etiamne, Aemiliane, si Platonis ipsius exemplo doceo factos? Cuius nulla
carmina extant nisi amoris elegia; nam cetera omnia, credo
8 quod tam lepida non erant, igni deussit. Disce igitur versus Platonis philosophi in puerum Astera, si tamen tantus
natu potes litteras discere:

---

21 This passage is a *locus classicus* for such pseudonyms in
classical Latin poetry and is the only testimony for the women's
actual names, except for Ovid, *Tr.* 2.433–38 on Perilla. On Ticidas,
or Ticida, a contemporary of Catullus, Courtney, *FLP* 228.

22 Most of Lucilius' poetry, including his poem or poems on
Gentius and Macedo (fr. 273–74 Marx; *ROL* 3.95, fr. 308–9), was
hexametric; *iambicus* here means "satiric" (*OLD* sv).

23 Verg. *Ecl.* 2, on which see W. Clausen, *A Commentary on
Virgil:* Eclogues (Oxford, 1994), 61–85, especially 64. The first
mention of this tradition is in Martial (references in Clausen).
Pollio, better known as a statesman, a patron of Virgil and a historian, also wrote love poetry (Plin. *Ep.* 5.3.5; Courtney, *FLP*
254–56).

24 An Atilius Serranus (cf. 88.7) is mentioned by Cicero and
other authors as being called from the plow to serve in the First

and Tibullus, because he has Plania in his thoughts but
Delia in his poetry.[21] For that matter I would fault Gaius 4
Lucilius, even though it is satire that he writes, for prosti-
tuting the boys Gentius and Macedo by their actual names
in his poem.[22] How much more seemly was the Mantuan 5
poet who does just as I do, and uses pseudonyms in a playful eclogue to praise his friend Asinius Pollio's boy slave,
calling himself Corydon and the boy Alexis.[23] But Aemil- 6
ianus, who is more of a bumpkin than Virgil's shepherds
and cowherds, incurably rustic and uncouth, though in his
own estimation far sterner than a Serranus, a Curius or a
Fabricius, says that poems like that are unseemly for a
Platonic philosopher.[24] Really, Aemilianus, even if I prove 7
I wrote them with Plato himself as my exemplar? His only
extant poems are love elegies, since all the others he committed to the flames, no doubt because they were less elegant. So listen to the philosopher Plato's lines on the boy 8
Aster, in case even at your age you can take a lesson in
literature:[25]

Punic War (cf. Kaster on Cic. *Sest.* 72). M'. Curius Dentatus and
C. Fabricius Luscinus were consuls and generals of the third
century BC famed for their frugality and simplicity of life. Apuleius is called a Platonist in a fragmentary inscription from his
hometown of Madauros (*Inscriptions Latines de l'Algérie,* 2115)
and by several Late Antique writers (Harrison, *Apuleius,* 5n19).

    [25] *Anth. Pal.* 7.670 (Page, *Further Greek Epigrams,* "Plato,"
no. 2). This and the next epigram are commonly ascribed to Plato
in antiquity, but they are in fact Hellenistic. The play on the name
Aster (star) is impossible to reproduce in English: there is a well-
known translation of this poem by Shelley, "To Stella, From the
Greek of Plato": "Thou wert the morning star among the living, / Ere thy fair light had fled;— / Now having died, thou art as
Hesperus giving / New light unto the dead."

ἀστὴρ πρὶν μὲν ἔλαμπες ἐνὶ ζωοῖσιν Ἑῷος·
νῦν δὲ θανὼν λάμπεις Ἕσπερος ἐν φθιμένοις.

9 Item eiusdem Platonis in Alexin Phaedrumque pueros
coniuncto carmine:

νῦν ὅτε μηδὲν Ἄλεξις ὅσον μόνον εἶφ' ὅτι καλός,
ὦπται καὶ πάντῃ πᾶσι περιβλέπεται.
θυμέ, τί μηνύεις κυσὶν ὀστέον, εἶτ' ἀνιήσει
ὕστερον; οὐχ οὕτω Φαῖδρον ἀπωλέσαμεν;

10 Ne pluris commemorem, novissimum versum eius de
Dione Syracusano si dixero, finem faciam:

ὦ ἐμὸν ἐκμήνας θυμὸν ἔρωτι Δίων.

11. Sed sumne ego ineptus, qui haec etiam in iudicio?
An vos potius calumniosi, qui etiam haec in accusatione,
2 quasi ullum specimen morum sit versibus ludere? Catullum ita respondentem malivolis non legistis?

Nam castum esse decet pium poetam
ipsum, versiculos nihil necesse est

3 Diuus Adrianus cum Voconi amici sui poetae tumulum
versibus muneraretur, ita scripsit:

Lasciuus versu, mente pudicus eras,

quod nunquam ita dixisset, si forent lepidiora carmina
4 argumentum impudicitiae habenda. Ipsius etiam divi

---

26 *Anth. Pal.* 7.100 (Page, *Further Greek Epigrams,* "Plato,"
no. 6).   27 Catull. 16.5–6.
28 Courtney, *FLP* 382, Hadrianus 2. Voconius is probably
Pliny's friend Voconius Romanus of Saguntum (*PIR* L 210), or less
probably Martial's friend Voconius Victor (*PIR* V 613).

You once shone among the living as the eastern Star;
Now dead, you shine as the Evening Star among the
shades.

And again the lines of Plato uniting the boys Alexis and   9
Phaedrus in one poem:[26]

Alexis I only said was fair,
And now he's looked at everywhere,
For everyone to see.
My heart, you'll rue it if you show
Bones to dogs. Was it not so
Phaedrus was lost to me?

Not to recall more lines, I will quote one last one by him   10
about Dion of Syracuse before I finish:

Ah, Dion, who maddened my heart with love.

11. But am I not a fool to mention even these things in
court? Or rather are you not a slanderer to include even
these things in your charge, as if trifling in verse was any
index of character! Have you never read how Catullus   2
made this reply to malicious critics,[27]

"A virtuous poet should be chaste
Himself: his poems needn't be"?

When the deified Hadrian adorned his friend Voconius'   3
tomb with a poem, here is what he wrote:

Playful in verse, but pure in heart were you[28]

Yet he never would have said so if witty poetry had to
be thought proof of immorality. I remember having read   4

Adriani multa id genus legere me memini. Audes igitur,[14]
Aemiliane, dicere male id fieri, quod imperator et censor
5 divus Adrianus fecit et factum memoriae reliquit? Ceterum Maximum quicquam putas culpaturum, quod sciat
Platonis exemplo a me factum? Cuius versus quos nunc
percensui tanto sanctiores sunt, quanto apertiores, tanto
6 pudicius compositi, quanto simplicius professi; namque
haec et id genus omnia dissimulare et occultare peccantis,
profiteri et promulgare ludentis est; quippe natura vox
innocentiae, silentium maleficio distributa.

12. Mitto enim dicere alta illa et divina Platonica, raris-
simo cuique piorum gnara,[15] ceterum omnibus profanis
incognita: geminam esse Venerem deam, proprio quam-
2 que amore et diversis amatoribus pollentis; earum alteram
vulgariam, quae sit percita populari amore, non modo
humanis animis, verum etiam pecuinis et ferinis ad libidinem imperitare ui immodica trucique, perculsorum ani-
3 malium serva corpora complexu vincientem; alteram vero
caelitem Venerem, praedita quae sit optimati amore, solis
hominibus et eorum paucis curare, nullis ad turpitudinem
4 stimulis vel illecebris sectatores suos percellentem; quippe
Amorem eius non amoenum et lascivum, sed contra in-
comptum et serium pulchritudine honestatis virtutes amatoribus suis conciliare, et si quando decora corpora com-
5 mendet, a contumelia eorum procul absterrere; neque
enim quicquam aliud in corporum forma diligendum

---

[14] audes igitur *u*: aude sis *ω*   [15] gnara *u*: ignara *ω*

---

[29] In fact, no emperor after Domitian held the office of censor.
[30] Apuleius seems to be thinking of Venus' son Cupid (*OLD
amor* 4), rather than of the disembodied feeling of love.

many such poems by the deified Hadrian himself. I challenge you, Aemilianus, to say that it is wrong to do something that Hadrian, an emperor and a censor,[29] both did and told posterity that he had done? Moreover, do you 5 think Maximus will fault anything that he knows I did with Plato as a precedent? Those lines of his that I repeated just now are all the more innocent for their frankness, all the more chastely written for their open declaration. For 6 to disguise and conceal these things and everything like them shows wrongdoing, to admit and broadcast them shows playfulness, since by nature's dispensation speech and innocence, silence and guilt belong together.

12. For I pass over those lofty, godlike doctrines of Plato, known to only a very few pious souls, but unknown to all the uninitiated, which say that there are twin Venuses, each presiding over her own kind of love and over opposite kinds of lovers. One of these Venuses is plebeian, 2 provoked by ordinary passion, who forces not only human souls but those of tame and wild animals into deeds of lust by her unbridled and savage power, locking in embrace the enslaved bodies of the creatures that she strikes; the 3 other by contrast is the heavenly Venus, the mistress of exalted love, who cares only for humans and for few of them, and does not drive her devotees to commit shameful acts by means of goads or allurements. Her Love[30] is not 4 sweet and mischievous, but on the contrary unkempt and stern, and by means of moral beauty unites his lovers with the virtues. If ever he makes handsome bodies desirable, he keeps them at a safe distance from abuse, for there is 5 nothing lovable about physical grace except what reminds

quam quod admoneant divinos animos eius pulchritudi-
6 nis, quam prius veram et sinceram inter deos videre. Quapropter, etsi pereleganter[16] Afranius hoc scriptum relin-
quat, "amabit sapiens, cupient ceteri," tamen si verum
velis, Aemiliane, vel si haec intellegere unquam potes, non
tam amat sapiens quam recordatur.

13. Da igitur veniam Platoni philosopho versuum eius
de amore, ne ego necesse habeam contra sententiam
2 Neoptolemi Enniani pluribus philosophari. Vel si tu id non
facis, ego me facile patiar in huiuscemodi versibus culpari
3 cum Platone. Tibi autem, Maxime, habeo gratiam propen-
sam, cum has quoque appendices defensionis meae idcirco necessarias, quia accusationi rependuntur, tam at-
4 tente audis. Et ideo hoc etiam peto, quod mihi ante ipsa
crimina superest audias, ut adhuc fecisti, libenter et diligenter.
5 Sequitur enim de speculo longa illa et censoria oratio,
de quo pro rei atrocitate paene diruptus est Pudens cla-
mitans: "Habet speculum philosophus! Possidet speculum
6 philosophus!" Ut igitur habere concedam (ne aliquid ob-
iecisse te credas, si negaro), non tamen ex eo accipi me
7 necesse est exornari quoque ad speculum solere. Quid
enim? Si choragium thymelicum possiderem, num ex eo
argumentarere etiam uti me consuesse tragoedi syrmate,
histrionis crocota, [orgia][17] mimi centunculo? Non opinor.

---

[16] etsi pereleganter *Krüger*: et (ut *u*) semper eleganter ω
[17] orgia *del. Krüger*

---

[31] Afranius was a much-admired comic writer of the later second century: for this line, A. Daviault, ed., *Comoedia Togata*
(Budé), Afranius 225.

40

blessed souls of the true, unblemished beauty they once
beheld among the gods. For these reasons, though Afra- 6
nius has left this well-turned line, "Love is for the wise
man, desire is for the rest,"[31] still, if you want the truth,
Aemilianus, or if you are ever able to understand such
things, the wise man does not so much love as he recol-
lects.

13. So give Plato allowance for his love poems, or else
I shall be forced to talk philosophy at length, against the
advice of Ennius' Neoptolemus;[32] but if you do not, I will 2
be quite content to join Plato in being blamed for such
poetry. To you, however, Maximus, I have the greatest 3
gratitude for listening so attentively to these subsidiary
parts of my defense, which I have to make in order to
answer the charge. And so I make this further request, that 4
you hear what I still have to say before coming to the actual
charges in the way you have hitherto: with goodwill and
attention.

For next comes that long, censorious speech about a 5
mirror, a subject so shocking that Pudens virtually burst
himself with shouting, "A philosopher has a mirror! A philosopher owns a mirror!" Even were I to admit to having 6
one (in case you think you have scored a point if I deny it),
still it does not necessarily follow that I habitually dress
myself before a mirror. Why, suppose I owned a theatrical 7
wardrobe, surely you would not argue that I habitually
wore the tragic actor's robe, the dancer's saffron dress, the
buffoon's motley, as well? No, I don't think you would. On

[32] Ennius, *Andromacha* fr. 28 Jocelyn, *philosophandum est paucis.*

Nam et contra plurimis rebus possessu careo, usu fruor.
8 Quod si neque habere utendi argumentum est neque non
utendi non habere, et speculi non tam possessio culpatur
quam inspectio, illud etiam doceas[18] necesse est, quando
et quibus praesentibus in speculum inspexerim, quoniam
ut res est, magis piaculum decernis speculum philosopho
quam Cereris mundum profano videre.

14. Cedo nunc, si et inspexisse me fateor, quod tandem
crimen est imaginem suam nosse eamque non uno loco
conditam, sed quoquo uelis parvo speculo promptam ges-
2 tare? An tu ignoras nihil esse aspectabilius homini nato
quam formam suam? Equidem scio et filiorum cariores
esse qui similes videntur et publicitus simulacrum suum
3 cuique, quod videat, pro meritis praemio tribui. Aut quid
sibi statuae et imagines variis artibus effigiatae volunt?
Nisi forte quod artificio elaboratum laudabile habetur, hoc
natura oblatum culpabile iudicandum est, cum sit in ea vel
4 magis miranda et facilitas et similitudo. Quippe in omnibus manu faciundis imaginibus opera diutina[19] sumitur,
neque tamen similitudo aeque ut in speculis comparet;
5 deest enim et luto vigor et saxo color et picturae rigor et
motus omnibus, qui praecipua fide similitudinem repraesentat, cum in eo visitur imago mire relata, ut similis, ita
6 mobilis et ad omnem nutum hominis sui morigera. Eadem
semper contemplantibus aequaeva est ab ineunte pueritia
ad obeuntem senectam, tot aetatis vices induit, tam varias

---

[18] doceas *u, cf. 20.3:* docear ω   [19] diutina *u:* diutino ω

---

[33] At the mysteries of Demeter (Ceres) at Eleusis, certain
"symbols" were revealed to initiates.

the contrary, there are many things of which I lack the possession but enjoy the use. So, if possession is no proof 8 of use, and nonuse is no proof of nonpossession, and if blame attaches not so much to owning a mirror but to looking at it, you need to show when and in whose presence I looked in the mirror; since as it is, you consider it a greater sin for a philosopher to see a mirror than for someone uninitiated to see Ceres' symbols.[33]

14. Tell me now, if I do grant that I have looked in a mirror—what crime, I ask you, is it to know one's own appearance, and carry it not stored up in a single place, but to any place you wish, available in a little mirror? As 2 you surely know, there is no more enjoyable sight for any human being than that of his own appearance. I certainly know both that sons are dearer if they resemble their fathers, and that in public life everyone is rewarded for his merits by having his own statue to look at. Otherwise, what 3 is the point of statues and pictures reproduced by this or that art? Unless perhaps something is considered laudable if it is the laborious product of skill, and culpable if the free gift of Nature; and yet Nature has even more amazing quickness and accuracy than skill. For all representations 4 that have to be handmade require lengthy effort, and even so the resemblance does not appear as it does as in a mirror. For clay lacks liveliness, stone color, painting relief, 5 all lack motion, and motion reproduces likeness with especial fidelity, since it is through motion that we see an image wonderfully rendered, as mobile as it is precise, and obedient to the mover's every gesture. The same image is 6 always contemporary with the beholder from earliest boyhood to extreme old age, so many are the changes of life that it assumes, so many the states of the body that it

43

habitudines corporis participat, tot vultus eiusdem laetan-
7 tis vel dolentis imitatur. Enimvero quod luto fictum vel
aere infusum vel lapide incusum[20] vel cera inustum vel
pigmento illitum vel alio quopiam humano artificio adsi-
mulatum est, non multa intercapedine temporis dissimile
redditur et ritu cadaveris unum vultum et immobilem pos-
8 sidet, tantum praestat imaginis artibus ad similitudinem
referendam levitas illa speculi fabra et splendor opifex.

15. Aut igitur unius Agesilai Lacedaemonii sententia
nobis sequenda est, qui se neque pingi neque fingi un-
2 quam diffidens formae suae passus est, aut si mos omnium
ceterorum hominum retinendus videtur in statuis et imaginibus non repudiandis, cur existimes imaginem suam
cuique visendam potius in lapide quam in argento, magis
3 in tabula quam in speculo? An turpe arbitraris formam
4 suam spectaculo assiduo explorare? An non Socrates philosophus ultro etiam suasisse fertur discipulis suis, crebro
5 ut semet in speculo contemplarentur, ut qui eorum foret
pulchritudine sibi complacitus, impendio procuraret ne
6 dignitatem corporis malis moribus dedecoraret, qui vero
minus se commendabilem forma putaret, sedulo operam
7 daret ut virtutis laude turpitudinem tegeret? Adeo vir
omnium sapientissimus speculo etiam ad disciplinam mo-
8 rum utebatur. Demosthenen vero, primarium dicendi artificem, quis est qui non sciat semper ante speculum quasi

---

[20] incusum *ed. Iuntina*: incussum ω

---

[34] Agesilaus II, king of Sparta from 400 to 359.
[35] Cf. Diog. Laert. 2.33, "He recommended to the young the
constant use of the mirror, to the end that handsome men might

APOLOGIA

shares, so many the expressions of the same person's face,
whether happy or sad, that it imitates. By contrast, what is   7
molded in clay, poured in bronze, hammered in stone,
burned in wax, applied in paint or reproduced by any other
human art, after no great interval of time becomes unlike
and possesses a single, fixed expression like a corpse, so far   8
does the artful smoothness, the creative brilliance of a
mirror surpass the arts of portraiture in reproducing a
likeness.

15. Either therefore we must adopt the opinion of one
man, Agesilaus of Sparta, who being diffident about his
appearance never allowed either statues or portraits of
himself,[34] or else, if we think we should preserve the gen-   2
eral custom of not refusing statues and pictures, why
should you think that everyone should see his image in
stone rather than in silver, in a picture rather than in a
mirror? Or do you perhaps think it disgraceful to check   3
one's appearance by careful scrutiny? Do they not say that   4
the philosopher Socrates went so far as to advise his pupils
to observe themselves in a mirror often?[35] In that way, if   5
any of them was complacent about his beauty, he should
be very careful not to sully the dignity of his body by evil
habits: if on the other hand any of them thought himself to   6
have less than attractive looks, he should make every effort
to cloak his homeliness by earning praise for virtue. So   7
much did even that wisest of all men use a mirror for moral
instruction. As for Demosthenes, that supreme master of   8
oratory, does anyone not know that he always practiced his

acquire a corresponding behavior, and ugly men conceal their
defects by education" (trans. R. D. Hicks. Loeb Classical Library).

9   ante magistrum causas meditatum? Ita ille summus orator cum a Platone philosopho facundiam hausisset, ab Eubulide dialectico argumentationes edidicisset, novissimam
10   pronuntiandi congruentiam ab speculo petivit. Vtrum igitur putas maiorem curam decoris in adseveranda oratione suscipiendam rhetori iurganti an philosopho obiurganti, apud iudices sorte ductos paulisper disceptanti an apud omnis homines semper disserenti, de finibus agrorum litiganti an de finibus bonorum et malorum docenti?

11   Quid quod nec ob haec debet tantummodo philoso-
12   phus speculum invisere? Nam saepe oportet non modo similitudinem suam, verum etiam ipsius similitudinis rationem considerare: num, ut ait Epicurus, profectae a nobis imagines velut quaedam exuviae iugi fluore a corporibus manantes, cum leve aliquid et solidum offenderunt, illisae reflectantur et retro expressae contraversim respondeant;
13   an, ut alii philosophi disputant, radii nostri seu mediis oculis proliquati et lumini extrario mixti atque ita uniti, ut
14   Plato arbitratur, seu tantum oculis profecti sine ullo foris adminiculo, ut Archytas putat, seu intentu aëris acti,[21] ut
15   Stoici rentur, cum alicui corpori inciderunt spisso et splendido et levi, paribus angulis quibus inciderant resultent ad faciem suam reduces atque ita, quod extra tangant ac visant, id intra speculum imaginentur.

     16. Videnturne vobis debere philosophi haec omnia

[21] acti *Helm*: facti ω

[36] Milesian philosopher of the mid-fourth century, supposed to have invented several famous puzzles in logic.
[37] Philosopher of Tarentum (ca. 400–350 BC), famous for his mathematical discoveries.

speeches before a mirror as if before a teacher? Conse-   9
quently, once he had learned eloquence from the philosopher Plato and argumentation from the logician Eu-
bulides,[36] he finally resorted to a mirror for the proper
way to speak. Who then do you think should be more   10
careful about his grooming to give weight to his words—a
lawyer who disputes or a philosopher who rebukes, someone briefly arguing before an empanelled jury or one for
ever discoursing before all mankind, one litigating about
the limits of an estate or rather one expounding the limits
of good and evil?

What is more, even these are not the only reasons for   11
a philosopher to look in a mirror. For often he should   12
contemplate not only his likeness but the cause of likeness
itself. Are images projected from us, as Epicurus says, flying in a continuous stream from our bodies like a kind of
skin, so that, on meeting something smooth and solid, they
then rebound on impact and bounce back so as to appear
reversed? Or as other philosophers maintain, do rays from   13
us—whether because they emanate from the center of the
eye, mingle and so unite with the light outside, as Plato
believes, or because they merely start from the eyes with-   14
out any external assistance, as Archytas thinks,[37] or because they are driven by air pressure, as the Stoics hold—,
when they strike an object that is compact, shiny and   15
smooth, do they bounce back at the angle of collision and
return to the face from which they started, so that the
object that they touch and contact outside the mirror becomes an image within it?

16. Do you people think that Philosophy should in-

vestigare et inquirere, et cuncta specula vel uda vel suda

2 soli ‹non›[22] videre? Quibus praeter ista quae dixi etiam
illa ratiocinatio necessaria est, cur in planis quidem speculis ferme pares optutus et imagines videantur, in tumidis
vero et globosis omnia defectiora, at contra in cavis auc-

3 tiora; ubi et cur laeva cum dexteris permutentur; quando
se imago eodem speculo tum recondat penitus, tum foras

4 exerat; cur cava specula, si exadversum soli retineantur,

5 appositum fomitem accendant; qui fiat ut arcus in nubibus
varie, duo soles aemula similitudine visantur, alia prae-

6 terea eiusdem modi plurima, quae tractat volumine ingenti Archimedes Syracusanus, vir in omni quidem geo-
metria multum ante alios admirabilis subtilitate, sed haud
sciam an propter hoc vel maxime memorandus, quod ins-

7 pexerat speculum saepe ac diligenter. Quem tu librum,
Aemiliane, si nosses ac non modo campo et glebis, verum
etiam abaco et pulvisculo te dedisses, mihi istud crede,
quamquam taeterrimum os tuum minimum a Thyesta tra-
gico demutet, tamen profecto discendi cupidine speculum
inviseres et aliquando relicto aratro mirarere tot in facie
tua sulcos rugarum.

8 At ego non mirer, si boni consulis me de isto distortis-
simo vultu tuo dicere, de moribus tuis multo truculentio-

9 ribus reticere. Ea res est: praeter quod non sum iurgiosus,

---

[22] non *add. van der Vliet*

---

[38] If the text is correct, this is perhaps a "polar" expression,
meaning "any at all."   [39] Apuleius refers to the phenome-
non of double suns (*parhelion,* or "sun dog").

[40] Archimedes (ca. 287–212) wrote a now lost work on mirrors
(*Katoptrika*).

vestigate and examine all these matters, and yet that she
alone should not see any mirrors, either wet ones or dry?[38]
Beside the questions I have mentioned, she must also   2
understand the reason why in plane mirrors objects and
their reflections seem almost identical, while in convex,
rounded ones everything seems diminished, and in concave ones magnified; when and why left and right are re-   3
versed; under what circumstances the image in one and
the same mirror sometimes recedes inward, at other times
protrudes outward; why concave mirrors, if they are held   4
to face the sun, set fire to fuel placed next to them; how it   5
is that a rainbow looks multicolored, while two suns look
closely similar;[39] and many questions of the same sort that   6
Archimedes of Syracuse discusses in a large volume, a man
who in all branches of geometry was admirable above all
others for his ingenuity, but I rather think deserves particular mention for having frequently and minutely studied the mirror.[40] If you had known that book, Aemilianus,   7
and had devoted yourself not merely to the field and the
soil, but also to the board and powder,[41] though your hideous face differs very little from Thyestes in tragedy, still
curiosity would certainly have made you look in a mirror;
you would occasionally have abandoned the plow and marveled at all the furrows seaming your face.

I, though, should not wonder if you preferred me to   8
speak about that deformed face of yours, and to say nothing about your much more violent character. The fact is   9

[41] Boards covered with sand or fine dust were used for making
erasable calculations or for drawing figures and diagrams, like the
modern white- or blackboard.

etiam libenter te nuper usque albus an ater esses ignoravi,
10 et adhuc hercle non satis novi. Id adeo factum, quod et tu
11 rusticando obscurus es et ego discendo occupatus; ita et
tibi umbra ignobilitatis a probatore obstitit, et ego numquam studui male facta cuiusquam cognoscere, sed semper potius duxi mea peccata tegere quam aliena indagare.
12 Igitur hoc mihi adversum te usu venit, quod qui forte
constitit in loco lumine conlustrato atque eum alter e tene-
13 bris prospectat; nam ad eundem modum tu quidem, quid
ego in propatulo et celebri agam, facile e tenebris tuis
arbitraris, cum ipse humilitate abdita et lucifuga non sis
mihi mutuo conspicuus.

17. Ego adeo servosne tu habeas ad agrum colendum
an ipse mutuarias operas cum vicinis tuis cambies, neque
2 scio neque labor: at tu me scis eadem die tris Oeae manu
misisse, idque mihi patronus tuus inter cetera a te sibi
edita obiecit, quamquam modico prius dixerat me uno
3 servo comite Oeam venisse. Quod quidem velim mihi re-
spondeas, qui potuerim ex uno tris manu mittere, nisi si et
4 hoc magicum est. Tantamne esse mentiendi caecitatem
dicam an consuetudinem? "Venit Apuleius Oeam cum uno
servo"; dein pauculis verbis intergarritis, "Apuleius Oeae
5 una die tris manu misit." Ne illud quidem credibile fuisset,
cum tribus venisse, omnes liberasse. Quod tamen si ita
fecissem, cur potius tris servos inopiae signum putares
6 quam tris libertos opulentiae? Nescis profecto, nescis,

---

[42] For this proverbial saying, Catull. 93.2; Cic. *Phil.* 2.41.

this: apart from the fact that I am not quarrelsome, until
very recently I was also happy not to know whether you
were black or white,[42] and even now in fact I do not really
know you. The reason is that you were an obscure rustic   10
and I was a busy scholar, and hence your inferiority was a   11
shadow protecting you from investigation, while I at the
same time have never been interested in hearing of anybody's wrongdoing, but have always thought it better to
cover my own lapses than to pry into other people's. So   12
when I am placed opposite you, I have the same experience as when someone chances to stand in a brightly illuminated place while another watches him from the dark:
in the same way you observe what I do openly and in   13
public, while you yourself, obscure, concealed and skulk-
ing, are not equally visible to me.

17. Moreover, I neither know nor care to know whether
you own slaves to cultivate your land, or whether you yourself exchange hired workmen with your neighbors; while   2
you know that I freed three slaves in a single day at Oea,
and your lawyer included that in his charge among other
things you told him, even though shortly before he said I
had only a single slave with me when I arrived in Oea. As   3
to that, I would like you to answer me how I could free
three after starting with one, unless this was another con-
juring trick. I am unsure whether to call such mendacity   4
blind or habitual. "Apuleius arrived in Oea with single
slave," then after a few words of blather, "Apuleius liber-
ated three slaves at Oea in a single day." That too would   5
have been incredible, to have arrived with three and liber-
ated them all; but even had I done so, why should you
think three slaves a sign of poverty rather than three freedmen a sign of wealth? You do not realize, Aemilianus,   6

51

Aemiliane, philosophum accusare, qui famulitii paucitatem obprobraris, quam ego gloriae causa ementiri debuissem, quippe qui scirem non modo philosophos, quorum me sectatorem fero, verum etiam imperatores populi Romani paucitate servorum gloriatos. Itane tandem ne haec
7   quidem legere patroni tui: M. Antonium consularem solos octo servos domi habuisse, Carbonem vero illum, qui rebus potitus est, uno minus, at enim M. Curio tot adoreis longe incluto, quippe qui ter triumphum una porta egerit,
8   ei igitur M. Curio duos solos in castris calones fuisse? Ita ille vir de Sabinis deque Samnitibus deque Pyrro trium-
9   phator paucioris servos habuit quam triumphos. M. autem Cato nihil oppertus, ut alii de se praedicarent, ipse in oratione sua scriptum reliquit, cum in Hispaniam consul pro-
10 ficisceretur, tris servos solos ex urbe duxisse; quoniam ad villam publicam venerat, parum visum qui uteretur, iussisse duos pueros in foro de mensa emi, eos quinque in
11 Hispaniam duxisse. Haec Pudens si legisset, ut mea opinio est, aut omnino huic maledicto supersedisset aut in tribus servis multitudinem comitum philosophi quam paucitatem reprehendere maluisset.

    18. Idem mihi etiam paupertatem obprobravit, accep-
2   tum philosopho crimen et ultro profitendum. Enim paupertas olim philosophiae vernacula est, frugi, sobria, parvo

---

43 M. Antonius was a famous orator, consul in 99 and grandfather of Mark Antony; Cn. Papirius Carbo was an associate of Cinna and Marius and was consul in 85 and 84. On M'. Curius, above, n. 24; he triumphed twice in 290 and once in 275.

44 M. Porcius Cato "the Elder," consul in 195 (Malcovati, ed., *Oratorum Romanorum Fragmenta*[3] 24 fr. 51). The Villa Publica

no, that you are accusing a philosopher when you reproach me for having few slaves. That is something that I ought to have made up as a boast, since I know that not only philosophers, whose disciple I claim to be, but also generals of the Roman people have boasted of having few slaves. Can it really be that your lawyers have not even read this— 7 that the consular Marcus Antonius had just eight slaves at home; the well known Carbo for his part, who made himself master of the state, had one less; and Manius Curius, far-famed for all his distinctions, since he thrice conducted a triumph through a single gate—Manius Curius, I say, had just two batmen in his camp? Hence that great 8 man, who triumphed over the Sabines, over the Samnites, and over Pyrrhus, had fewer slaves than triumphs.[43] As for 9 Marcus Cato, he did not wait for others to praise him, but put on record in a speech of his own that when starting for Spain as consul, he brought just three slaves from the city; but after he had been to the Villa Publica, they seemed too 10 few for his needs, and so he ordered two slaves to be bought off the stand in the Forum, and took those five to Spain.[44] If Pudens had read that, in my opinion, he would 11 either have omitted this slander altogether, or he would have chosen to criticize a retinue of three slaves as too large for a philosopher, not too small.

18. At the same time, he also reproached me for my poverty, a charge that a philosopher welcomes and claims willingly. For Poverty has long been the maidservant of 2 Philosophy; she is virtuous, steady, content with little, ea-

was situated in the Campus Martius and outside the *pomoerium*, so that when visiting it to recruit troops, Cato was technically outside the city.

potens, aemula laudis, adversum divitias possessa, habitu

3 secura, cultu simplex, consilio benesuada. Neminem umquam superbia inflavit, neminem impotentia depravavit,
neminem tyrannide efferavit, delicias ventris et inguinum

4 neque vult ullas neque potest; quippe haec et alia flagitia
divitiarum alumni solent. Maxima quaeque scelera si ex
omni memoria hominum percenseas, nullum in illis pau-

5 perem reperies, ut contra haud temere inter illustris viros
divites comparent, sed quemcunque in aliqua laude mira-

6 mur, eum paupertas ab incunabulis nutricata est. Paupertas, inquam, prisca apud saecula omnium civitatium condi-
trix, omnium artium repertrix, omnium peccatorum inops,
omnis gloriae munifica, cunctis laudibus apud omnis na-

7 tiones perfuncta. Eadem est enim paupertas apud Graecos in Aristide iusta, in Phocione benigna, in Epaminonda

8 strenua, in Socrate sapiens, in Homero diserta. Eadem
paupertas etiam populo Romano imperium a primordio
fundavit, proque eo in hodiernum diis immortalibus sim-

9 pulo et catino fictili sacrificat. Quod si modo iudices de
causa ista sederent C. Fabricius, Cn. Scipio, Manius Curius, quorum filiae ob paupertatem de publico dotibus
donatae ad maritos ierunt portantes gloriam domesticam,

10 pecuniam publicam, si Publicola regum exactor et Agrippa
populi reconciliator, quorum funus ob tenuis opes a po-

---

45 Literally, "owned in opposition to wealth," apparently, "that
saves the possessor from the dangers of wealth."

46 Aristides "the Just" was an Athenian general of the early
fifth century; Phocion "the Good" was an Athenian statesman and
general of the late fourth century; Epaminondas of Thebes broke
the power of Sparta in the 360s by his brilliant generalship.

ger for praise, a defense against wealth for her owner,[45] a
secure possession, simple in dress, wise in counsel. Never   3
has she puffed someone up with conceit, corrupted him
with lawlessness, maddened him with tyranny, neither
desirous nor capable of the pleasures of gluttony or sex.
For these and other transgressions are the way of those   4
brought up in wealth. If you recall the greatest crimes in
human history, you will find no poor man involved in them,
while by contrast scarcely any of the rich can be found   5
among men of distinction: everyone we admire for some
achievement has been raised by Poverty from the cradle.
Poverty, I repeat, was the founder of every state in olden   6
times, the inventor of every skill, with no faults to impart
and every excellence to bestow, enjoying every kind of
praise among all the nations of the earth. For this same   7
Poverty is justice in Aristides, humaneness in Phocion,
vigor in Epaminondas,[46] wisdom in Socrates, eloquence in
Homer. This same Poverty from earliest times secured the   8
empire of the Roman people, which consequently to this
day uses a ladle and an earthenware bowl to sacrifice to
the immortal gods. Now, just suppose the judges presiding   9
in this case were Gaius Fabricius, Gnaeus Scipio, Manius
Curius, whose daughters were so poor that they received
dowries from the public funds, and went to their husbands
bringing only their household's renown and the people's
money;[47] suppose the judges were Publicola, who ex-   10
pelled the kings, and Agrippa who reconciled the people,

[47] For Fabricius and Curius, n. 24; Cn. Cornelius Scipio Calvus was consul in 222 and uncle of the better-known Scipio Africanus the Elder.

11 pulo Romano collatis sextantibus adornatum est, si Atilius
Regulus, cuius agellus ob similem penuriam publica pecu-
12 nia cultus est, si denique omnes illae veteres prosapiae
consulares et censoriae et triumphales brevi usura lucis ad
iudicium istud remissae audirent, auderesne paupertatem
philosopho exprobrare apud tot consules pauperes?

19. An tibi Claudius Maximus idoneus auditor videtur
ad irridendam paupertatem, quod ipse uberem et pro-
2 lixam rem familiarem sortitus est? Erras, Aemiliane, et
longe huius animi frustra es, si eum ex fortunae indulgentia, non ex philosophiae censura metiris, si virum tam
austerae sectae tamque diutinae militiae non putas ami-
ciorem esse coercitae mediocritati quam delicatae opulentiae, fortunam velut tunicam magis concinnam quam
3 longam probare; quippe etiam ea, si non gestetur sed[23]
trahatur, nihilo minus quam lacinia praependens impedit
et praecipitat.

4 Etenim omnibus ad vitae munia utendis quicquid aptam moderationem supergreditur, oneri potius quam usui
5 exuberat. Igitur et immodicae divitiae velut ingentia et
enormia gubernacula facilius mergunt quam regunt, quod
6 habent irritam copiam, noxiam nimietatem. Quin ex ipsis
opulentioribus eos potissimum video laudari, qui nullo

---

[23] sed (*i.e.*, set) *Elmenhorstius*: et ω

---

[48] P. Valerius Publicola was several times consul after the ex-
pulsion of the kings and was credited with several popular measures. Menenius Agrippa, consul in 503, convinced the Roman
plebs to end their secession in 494/3. M. Atilius Regulus is the
celebrated general, consul in 267 and 256, who died in captivity
at Carthage.

men who because of their meager resources had funerals furnished with the people's pennies, or Atilius Regulus, 11 whose little farm was cultivated at public expense because he too was poor,[48] suppose in short all those men of an- 12 cient stock, past consuls, censors, triumph holders, were given a brief spell of daylight to preside at this trial and to listen—would you dare to upbraid a philosopher for poverty before so many consular paupers?

19. Or is that you think Claudius Maximus the right person to hear poverty mocked, just because he himself is blessed with a rich and plentiful fortune? You are wrong, 2 Aemilianus, you are entirely mistaken about his views if you judge him by the blessings of fortune and not by the standards of philosophy, and if you do not suppose that a man of such strict beliefs and such long military service is more inclined to disciplined moderation than to pampered opulence, and that he esteems wealth as he does a tunic, for its propriety not for its excess. Wealth too, if it 3 is trailed rather than worn, impedes and trips one up no less than a garment hanging down in front.[49]

Indeed with all things that we use for the tasks of life, 4 anything that exceeds proper limits is an excrescence more burdensome than useful. Hence vast wealth too, like a 5 huge, bulky rudder, sinks you rather than steering you, because its abundance is useless, its excess harmful. Yes, 6 those whom I see most praised among wealthy people are

[49] In full dress, the male Roman citizen wore a long undergarment (*tunica*) beneath the toga; the young Julius Caesar and others wore very long tunics, or ones with elaborate fringes.

strepitu, modico cultu, dissimulatis facultatibus agunt et
divitias magnas administrant sine ostentatione, sine super-
7 bia, specie mediocritatis pauperum similes. Quod si etiam
ditibus ad argumentum modestiae quaeritur imago quaepiam et color paupertatis, cur eius pudeat tenuioris, qui
eam non simulate, sed vere fungimur?

20. Possum equidem tibi et ipsius nominis controver-
siam facere, neminem nostrum pauperem esse qui super-
vacanea nolit, possideat[24] necessaria, quae natura oppido
2 pauca sunt. Namque is plurimum habebit, qui minimum
desiderabit; habebit enim quantum volet qui volet mini-
3 mum. Et idcirco divitiae non melius in fundis et in fenore
quam in ipso hominis animo aestimantur, qui si est avaritia
egenus et ad omne lucrum inexplebilis, nec montibus auri
satiabitur, sed semper aliquid, ante parta ut augeat, men-
4 dicabit. Quae quidem vera confessio est paupertatis: omnis enim cupido acquirendi ex opinione inopiae venit, nec
5 refert quam magnum sit quod tibi minus est. Non habuit
tantam rem familiarem Philus quantam Laelius, nec Laelius quantam Scipio, nec Scipio quantam Crassus Dives,
6 at enim nec Crassus Dives quantam volebat; ita cum omnis
superaret, a suamet avaritia superatus est omnibusque
7 potius dives visus est quam sibi. At contra hi philosophi
quos commemoravi non ultra volentes quam poterant, sed
congruentibus desideriis et facultatibus iure meritoque
8 dites et beati fuerunt. Pauper enim fis[25] appetendi eges-

---

[24] possideat *Elmenhorstius*: poscit ω
[25] fis *u*: sis ω

---

[50] All these are persons of the later second century BC: both
L. Furius Philus and C. Laelius were senators and friends of P.

those who act without bustle, who have modest tastes and unostentatious means, and manage their large fortunes without show or pride, in their everyday appearance looking like paupers. But if even the rich aim for a kind of 7 image or semblance of poverty to show their modesty, why should poverty embarrass those less fortunate, for whom it is not feigned but real?

20. I might also have a dispute with you about the very meaning of the word, saying that none of us is poor if he does not want the superfluities and owns the necessities, which by their nature are very few. For one who has the 2 least desires will have the most resources, since by wanting the least he will have all he wants. That is why riches 3 are better measured not by lands and revenues than by a man's inner self. If avarice makes him needy and unsatisfied whatever his profit, he will not be content even with mountains of gold, but will be forever scrounging to increase his previous gains. And that indeed is truly to con- 4 fess poverty: for all desire for gain comes from a sense of want, and it makes no difference how great something is if it seems to you too little. Philus did not have so large 5 an estate as Laelius, nor Laelius as Scipio, nor Scipio as Crassus the Rich, but not even Crassus the Rich had as much as he wanted, so that though he surpassed everyone 6 his own avarice surpassed him, and everyone thought him rich except himself.[50] But by contrast those philosophers 7 I mentioned, who did not want more than they could command, and whose desires and resources were in balance, were justly and properly deemed rich and fortunate. For 8

Cornelius Scipio the Younger; P. Licinius Crassus Dives ("Rich") was a wealthy orator and an opponent of the Younger Scipio.

tate, dives non egendi satietate, quippe qui inopia deside-
9 rio, opulentia fastidio cernuntur. Igitur, Aemiliane, si pauperem me haberi vis, prius avarum esse doceas necesse
est. Quod si nihil in animo deest, de rebus extrariis quantum desit non laboro, quarum neque laus in copia neque
culpa in penuria consistit.

21. Sed finge haec aliter esse ac me ideo pauperem,
quia mihi fortuna divitias invidit easque, ut ferme evenit,
aut tutor imminuit aut inimicus eripuit aut pater non reliquit: hocine homini opprobrari, pauperiem, quod nulli ex
animalibus vitio datur, non aquilae, non tauro, non leoni?
2 Equus si virtutibus suis polleat, ut sit aequabilis vector et
cursor pernix, nemo ei penuriam pabuli exprobrat: tu mihi
vitio dabis non facti vel dicti alicuius pravitatem, sed quod
vivo gracili lare, quod paucioris habeo, parcius pasco, le-
3 vius vestio, minus obsono? Atqui ego contra, quantulacum-
que tibi haec videntur, multa etiam et nimia arbitror et
cupio ad pauciora me coercere, tanto beatior futurus
4 quanto collectior. Namque animi ita ut corporis sanitas
expedita, imbecillitas laciniosa est, certumque signum est
5 infirmitatis pluribus indigere. Prorsus ad vivendum velut
ad natandum is melior, qui onere liberior; sunt enim similiter etiam in ista vitae humanae tempestate levia susten-
6 tui, gravia demersui. Equidem didici ea re praecedere
maxime deos hominibus, quod nulla re ad usum sui indi-
geant, igitur ex nobis cui quam minimis opus sit, eum esse
deo similiorem.

you become poor from the urge to acquire, you become rich from the satiety of needing nothing, since desire is a mark of poverty, satiety of wealth. If therefore, Aemilianus, you want people to think me poor, you are bound first to prove me greedy; if however I lack nothing in my own judgment, I do not care how much I lack in externals, which if abundant are no ground for praise, if scanty no ground for censure. 9

21. But suppose it is otherwise, and that I am poor because fate begrudged me a fortune and, as often happens, it was either mismanaged by a guardian, seized by an enemy, or left to someone else by my father: is that something to blame a human being for—poverty, which no one counts against an animal, whether an eagle, or a bull, or a lion? If a horse is valued for his own qualities, 2 for example that he is a quiet mount and a fast runner, no one blames him for shortness of fodder; so do you fault me not because I am somehow vicious in word or deed, but because I live in a small house and have few slaves, whom I feed thriftily and dress lightly, and I shop cheaply? However slight these things seem to you, I for my part think 3 them much, yes, too much, and I try to restrict myself to fewer of them, so as to increase my happiness and my self-restraint both at once. For a healthy mind resembles 4 a healthy body in being unencumbered, while illness is heavily swaddled, and to have many needs is a sure sign of weakness. Indeed, in life as in swimming you are all the 5 better for being free of burdens, for just as in this storm of human life what is light buoys you up, what is heavy drags you down. I certainly have found that what particu- 6 larly makes gods superior to humans is that they need nothing for their own use, so that whichever of us needs the least more closely resembles a god.

22. Proinde gratum habui,[26] cum ad contumeliam dice-
2 retis rem familiarem mihi peram et baculum fuisse. Quod
utinam tantus animi forem, ut praeter eam supellectilem
nihil quicquam requirerem, sed eundem ornatum digne
gestarem, quem Crates ultro divitiis abiectis appetivit.
3 Crates, inquam, si quid credis, Aemiliane, vir domi inter
Thebanos proceres dives et nobilis amore huius habitus,
quem mihi obiectas, rem familiarem largam et uberem
populo donavit, multis servis a sese remotis solitatem delegit, arbores plurimas et frugiferas prae uno baculo spre-
4 vit, villas ornatissimas una perula mutavit, quam postea
comperta utilitate etiam carmine laudavit flexis ad hoc
Homericis versibus, quibus ille Cretam insulam nobilitat.
5 Principium dicam, ne me haec ad defensionem putes con-
finxisse:

πήρη τις πόλις ἐστὶ μέσῳ ἐνὶ οἴνοπι τύφῳ,

etiam cetera tam mirifica, quae si tu legisses, magis mihi
peram quam nuptias Pudentillae invidisses.
6 Peram et baculam tu philosophis exprobrares: igitur et
equitibus faleras et peditibus clipeos et signiferis vexilla et
denique triumphantibus quadrigas albas et togam palma-
7 tam? Non sunt quidem ista Platonicae sectae gestamina,
sed Cynicae familiae insignia, verum tamen hoc Diogeni
et Antistheni pera et baculum, quod regibus diadema,

26 habui cum *Casaubon*: habitum ω

51 Crates of Thebes was a pupil of Diogenes of Sinope, on
whom see below; for his poem, L. Paquet, *Les Cyniques grecs*
(Ottawa, 1975), 110, Crates fr. 1; the present line is a parody of
Od. 19.172.

22. So I was grateful when you said by way of an insult that my possessions consisted of a sack and a stick. Why, I 2 wish I was so strong-minded as to need absolutely nothing but those items, and was worthy to carry the equipment that Crates actually desired when he had thrown away his fortune. Crates, I repeat, if you can believe it, Aemilianus, 3 a man rich and famous among the nobles of his native Thebes, so loved this appearance that you fault me for that he presented the people with his large and prosperous estate, renounced his many slaves, chose solitude, threw over his many fruitful orchards for a single stick, and exchanged his well-furnished country houses for a single sack. After discovering how useful the sack was, he even 4 praised it in a poem, adapting for the purpose the lines in which Homer exalts Crete. I will recite the opening, in 5 case you think I made up this in my own defense:

> There is a town called Sack, in the midst of the wine-
> dark Folly.

And there are other gems, which if you had read them you would have envied me my sack more than my marriage with Pudentilla.[51]

You would fault philosophers for their sack and stick: 6 would you then you fault horsemen for their medallions, infantrymen their shields, standard-bearers their standards, finally triumph holders their chariot drawn by four white horses and their palm-embroidered toga? True, sack 7 and stick are not what followers of Plato carry, but are emblems of the Cynic sect, but even so these items were for Diogenes and Antisthenes the equivalent of a king's

quod imperatoribus paludamentum, quod pontificibus ga-
8 lerum, quod lituus auguribus. Diogenes quidem Cynicus
cum Alexandro magno de veritate regni certabundus ba-
9 culo vice sceptri gloriabatur. Ipse denique Hercules invic-
tus (quoniam haec tibi ut quaedam mendicabula nimis
10 sordent), ipse, inquam, Hercules lustrator orbis, purgator
ferarum, gentium domitor, is tamen deus, cum terras per-
agraret, paulo prius quam in caelum ob virtutes ascitus est,
neque una pelli vestitior fuit neque uno baculo comitatior.

23. Quod si haec exempla nihili putas ac me non ad
causam agendam, verum ad censum disserendum vocasti,
ne quid tu rerum mearum nescias, si tamen nescis, profiteor mihi ac fratri meo relictum a patre HS XX paulo se-
2 cus, idque a me longa peregrinatione et diutinis studiis et
3 crebris liberalitatibus ⟨non⟩[27] modice imminutum. Nam
et amicorum plerisque opem tuli et magistris plurimis
4 gratiam rettuli, quorundam etiam filias dote auxi. Neque
enim dubitassem equidem vel universum patrimonium im-
pendere, ut acquirerem mihi quod maius est: contemp-
5 tum[28] patrimonii. Tu vero, Aemiliane, et id genus homines
uti tu es, inculti et agrestes, tanti re vera estis quantum
habetis, ut arbor infecunda et infelix, quae nullum fructum ex sese gignit, tanti est in pretio, quanti lignum eius
6 in trunco. At tamen parce postea, Aemiliane, paupertatem

[27] non *add. Casaubon*
[28] contemptum *u*: contemptu *ω*

[52] Antisthenes, an associate of Socrates, was regarded as the
founder of Cynicism; Diogenes of Sinope was the most notorious
Cynic of the fourth century, and his encounter with Alexander III
of Macedon at Corinth gave rise to many anecdotes. The *lituus*

diadem, a general's cloak, a priest's cap, an augur's ritual staff.[52] Diogenes the Cynic indeed, when disputing   8
with Alexander the Great on the subject of true kingship,
boasted of his staff as if it were a scepter. The invinci-   9
ble Hercules himself—since you find the former things
disgusting, beggar's baggage as it were—Hercules him-   10
self, I repeat, who cleansed the world, expelled wild animals, defeated savage tribes, nonetheless while roaming
the earth shortly before he was summoned to the skies
because of his virtues—that god was dressed only in a
single pelt and accompanied only by a single staff.

  23. But perhaps you think these precedents worthless,
and you brought me into court not to plead my case but
to state my wealth. To let you know every detail of my
affairs, then, if you do not already, I declare that our father left my brother and me roughly two million sesterces,
which I have considerably lessened by my distant travels,   2
long education, and frequent liberalities. For I assisted   3
several of my friends and also showed my thanks to my
many teachers, even giving a dowry to the daughters of
some of them. Nor indeed would I have hesitated to spend   4
my entire inheritance to procure something more important for myself—a contempt for inheritances. You, how-   5
ever, Aemilianus and people like you, ignorant bumpkins,
you really are worth no more than what you possess, like
a barren, sterile tree that yields no crop of its own, but is
valued only for its trunk as timber. Even so, Aemilianus,   6
please refrain from rebuking anyone for poverty in fu-

was a crooked staff used by augurs to delimit their field of vision
when watching for omens.

cuipiam obiectare, qui nuper usque agellum Zarathensem, quem tibi unicum pater tuus reliquerat, solus uno
7 asello ad tempestivum imbrem triduo exarabas. Neque
enim diu est cum te crebrae mortes propinquorum imme-
ritis hereditatibus fulserunt, unde tibi potius quam ob istam taeterrimam faciem Charon nomen est.

24. De patria mea vero, quod eam sitam Numidiae et
Gaetuliae in ipso confinio meis scriptis ostendistis,[29] quibus memet professus sum cum Lolliano Avito c(larissimo)
v(iro) praesente publice dissererem, "Seminumidam" et
2 "Semigaetulum," non video quid mihi sit in ea re pudendum, haud magis[30] quam Cyro maiori, quod genere mixto
3 fuit Semimedus ac Semipersa. Non enim ubi prognatus,
sed ut moratus quisque sit spectandum, nec qua regione,
sed qua ratione vitam vivere inierit, considerandum est.
4 Holitori et cauponi merito est concessum holus et vinum
ex nobilitate soli commendare, vinum Thasium, holus
Phliasium; quippe illa terrae alumna multum ad meliorem
saporem iuverit et regio fecunda et caelum pluvium et
5 ventus clemens et sol apricus et solum sucidum. Enimvero
animo hominis extrinsecus in hospitium corporis immi-
granti quid ex istis addi vel minui ad virtutem vel malitiam

---

[29] ostendistis *Rohde,* Kleine Schriften, *2.67n1*: ostendi scis ω
[30] magis *van der Vliet*: minus ω

---

[53] On the site of Zaratha, see Appendix B. The taunt about the
donkey implies that the soil was too hard to plow without oxen,
whereas Aemilianus had only a single donkey and had to wait for
rain to soften the soil (Butler and Owen, *Apulei Apologia*).
[54] Charon was the ferryman of the River Styx: the implication
is that Aemilianus murdered his relatives for their money.

ture, seeing that until very recently you used to plow a small farm at Zaratha, the only one your father left you, all by yourself with one donkey in three days' time after a chance rainfall.[53] For it is only a little while since the deaths of your relatives in quick succession made you rich from undeserved legacies, which is how you got the name of "Charon," even more than from your hideous face.[54]

7

24. Now as for my native city: it lies on the very border of Numidia and Gaetulia, as you showed from a work of mine, a speech delivered in public before the right honorable Lollianus Avitus, in which I called myself half Numidian and half Gaetulian.[55] Well, I do not see what I have to regret about that, any more than the elder Cyrus had to regret that he was of mixed birth, half Median and half Persian.[56] What we must consider in a person is not his birthplace but his character, not in which land but on what principle he began the course of life. We rightly allow the greengrocer and the innkeeper to recommend their produce or their wine by the excellence of the soil, wine from Thasos or vegetables from Phlious, let us say; such articles, the products of the earth, get a superior taste with the help of a fertile region, a rainy climate, a gentle wind, warm sun, and moist soil. By contrast, a man's soul comes from without and lodges in the body as a guest, and how can such factors cause him to be more or less good or

2

3

4

5

---

55 That is, Madauros: see Introduction. L. Hedius Rufus Lollianus Avitus (*PIR* H 40) was consul in 144 and proconsul of Africa (probably) in 157/8, the year before Claudius Maximus.

56 Cyrus the Great, founder of the Achaemenid Empire in the sixth century, was the son of the Persian king Cambyses and of Mandane, daughter of the Median king Astyages.

6   potest? Quando non in omnibus gentibus varia ingenia provenere, quamquam videantur quaedam stultitia vel sollertia insigniores? Apud socordissimos Scythas Anacharsis sapiens natus est, apud Athenienses catos Meletides

7   fatuus. Nec hoc eo dixi, quo me patriae meae paeniteret,

8   etsi adhuc Syphacis oppidum essemus. Quo tamen victo ad Masinissam regem munere populi Romani concessimus ac deinceps veteranorum militum novo conditu splendidissima colonia sumus, in qua colonia patrem habui loco

9   principis duoviralem cunctis honoribus perfunctum, cuius ego locum in illa re publica, exinde ut participare curiam coepi, nequaquam degener pari, spero, honore et existi-

10 matione tueor. Cur ergo illa protuli? Ut mihi tu, Aemiliane, minus posthac suscenseas, potiusque ut veniam impertias, si per neglegentiam forte non elegi illud tuum Atticum Zarath ut in eo nascerer.

     25. Nonne vos puditum est haec crimina tali viro audiente tam adseverate obiectare, frivola et inter se repug-

2   nantia simul promere et utraque tamen reprehendere? At non contraria accusastis? Peram et baculum ob austerita-tem,[31] carmina et speculum ob hilaritatem, unum servum ut deparci,[32] tris libertos ut profusi, praeterea eloquen-

3   tiam Graecam, patriam barbaram? Quin igitur tandem

---

[31] austeritatem *Fuluius*: auctoritatem *ω*
[32] deparci *ω*, *vide Robertson, "The Assisi Fragments," 74*

---

[57] Anacharsis was a legendary Scythian prince of the sixth century; Meletides was a proverbial fool, first mentioned in the fifth century.   [58] Syphax was a Numidian chieftain whom the Elder Scipio defeated in battle in 203, after which Rome recognized Massinissa as king of all Numidia. Madauros became

bad? Has it not always been true that every nation has   6
produced different degrees of intelligence, though some
nations seem to be more striking for stupidity or astute-
ness? The philosopher Anacharsis was born among the
doltish Scythians, the buffoon Meletides among the clever
Athenians.[57] I do not say this because I am ashamed of my   7
native place, even were it still the home town of Syphax.
Still, after his defeat we passed by gift of the Roman peo-   8
ple to king Massinissa, and thereafter, newly refounded
with veteran soldiers, we became a most distinguished colony, in which colony my father had the position of mayor
in the emperor's place, when he had held every office.[58] I   9
have maintained his position in that city from when I first
began to be a member of the city council, not at all un-
worthily of him and, I hope, with equal honor and repute.
Why then have I brought all this up? So that you will be   10
less angry with me in future, Aemilianus, or rather that
you will pardon me for my mistake in not choosing your
Attic Zarath to be born in.

25. Were you not ashamed to hurl these charges so
insistently in the hearing of such a man, to make two frivolous and mutually incompatible charges simultaneously
and yet to find fault on both grounds? For were your ac-   2
cusations not contradictory? A bag and a stick to portray
me as a puritan, poems and a mirror as a dandy, one slave
as a miser, three freedmen as a spendthrift, and after that
eloquence in speaking Greek and a barbarous origin?
Won't you come to your senses at last, and remember that   3

a veteran colony under the Flavian emperors (AD 70–96). Apuleius' father had taken the emperor's place as *praefectus* (deputy),
with powers of a *duovir* (chief magistrate): see Appendix C.

expergiscimini ac vos cogitatis apud Claudium Maximum
dicere, apud virum severum et totius provinciae negotiis
4 occupatum? Quin, inquam, vana haec convicia aufertis?
Quin ostenditis quod insimulavistis: scelera immania et
inconcessa maleficia et artis nefandas? Cur vestra oratio
rebus flaccet, strepitu viget?

5   Aggredior enim iam ad ipsum crimen magiae, quod
ingenti tumultu ad invidiam mei accensum frustrata ex-
pectatione omnium per nescio quas anilis fabulas defra-
6 glavit. Ecquandone vidisti, Maxime, flammam stipula exortam claro crepitu, largo fulgore, cito incremento, sed
7 enim materia levi, caduco incendio, nullis reliquiis? Em
tibi illa accusatio iurgiis inita, verbis aucta, argumentis
defecta, nullis post sententiam tuam reliquiis calumniae
permansura.

8   Quae quidem omnis Aemiliano fuit in isto uno desti-
nata, me magum esse, et ideo mihi libet quaerere ab eru-
9 ditissimis eius advocatis, quid sit magus. Nam si, quod ego
apud plurimos lego, Persarum lingua magus est qui nostra
sacerdos, quod tandem crimen est, sacerdotem esse et rite
nosse atque scire atque callere leges caerimoniarum, fas
10 sacrorum, ius religionum, si quidem magia id est quod
Plato interpretatur, cum commemorat, quibusnam disciplinis puerum regno adulescentem Persae imbuant?
Verba ipsa divini viri memini, quae tu mecum, Maxime,
recognosce:

---

59 For the agricultural practice of burning stubble (not hay, as
sometimes translated), see Verg. *G.* 1.84–93, 3.99–100, with the
commentaries of Thomas and Mynors; the practice has lasted into
modern times.

you are speaking before Claudius Maximus, an upright man busy with the affairs of the entire province? I repeat, 4 won't you drop this empty abuse? Won't you prove your allegations—monstrous crimes, forbidden magic, the black arts? Why is your speech so weak on facts and so strong on noise?

(*Turning to address Maximus.*) Well, I now come to 5 the actual charge of magic, which he set ablaze with a tremendous roar to make me disliked, and then, disappointing everyone's expectation, doused it with a few old wives' tales. Have you ever, Maximus, seen a fire starting 6 from stubble? It crackles loudly, shines brightly, spreads quickly, but lacking fuel its flames die down and leave no trace.[59] Well, that is like this prosecution: begun with in- 7 sults, heaped up with verbiage, short of proofs, but after your verdict fated to leave no trace of its slanders.

Since Aemilianus rested it entirely on this one point, 8 that I was a magician, I would like to inquire of his most learned advocates what a magician is. For if a magician in 9 the Persian language is what a priest is in ours, as I have read in many authors, what kind of crime is it to be a priest and to have the right information, knowledge and mastery of the ceremonial rules, ritual requirements, and sacred laws? Provided of course that Plato understands what 10 magic is when he recalls the lessons that the Persians use to initiate a youth in kingship. I remember the very words of that inspired man, and you, Maximus, may recall them together with me:[60]

[60] Pl. *Alc.* 1.121E–22A. As a Stoic, Maximus would know his Plato.

11 δὶς ἑπτὰ δὲ γένομενον ἐτῶν τὸν παῖδα παραλαμ-
βάνουσιν οὓς ἐκεῖνοι βασιλείους παιδαγωγοὺς
ὀνομάζουσιν· εἰσὶ δὲ ἐξειλεγμένοι Περσῶν οἱ ἄρι-
στοι δόξαντες ἐν ἡλικίᾳ τέτταρες, ὅ τε σοφώτατος
καὶ ὁ δικαιότατος καὶ ὁ σωφρονέστατος καὶ ὁ
ἀνδρειότατος. ὧν ὁ μὲν μαγείαν τε διδάσκει τὴν
Ζωροάστρου τοῦ Ὠρομάζου—ἔστι δὲ τοῦτο θεῶν
θεραπεία—διδάσκει δὲ καὶ τὰ βασιλικά.

26. Auditisne magiam, qui eam temere accusatis, ar-
tem esse dis immortalibus acceptam, colendi eos ac vene-
2 randi pergnaram, piam scilicet et divini scientem, iam
inde a Zoroastre et Oromaze auctoribus suis nobilem,
3 caelitum antistitam, quippe qui inter prima regalia docetur nec ulli temere inter Persas concessum est magum
4 esse, haud magis quam regnare? Idem Plato in alia sermo-
cinatione de Zalmoxi quodam Thraci generis, sed eiusdem
artis viro ita scriptum reliquit: τὰς δὲ ἐπῳδὰς εἶναι τοὺς
5 λόγους τοὺς καλούς. Quod si ita est, cur mihi nosse non
6 liceat vel Zalmoxi bona verba vel Zoroastri sacerdotia? Sin
vero more vulgari eum isti proprie magum existimant, qui
communione loquendi cum deis immortalibus ad omnia
quae velit incredibili quadam ui cantaminum polleat, oppido miror, cur accusare non timuerint quem posse tan-
7 tum fatentur. Neque enim tam occulta et divina potentia
8 caveri potest itidem ut cetera. Sicarium qui in iudicium
vocat, comitatus venit; qui venenarium accusat, scrupulo-

---

61 Zoraster, or Zarathustra, was an Iranian religious reformer
of the early first millennium BC; Oromazes (Ahura Mazda) was
the supreme god in his system and was later believed to be his
father.

And when the boy is twice seven years, those whom   11
they call the royal tutors take him into their charge:
these are four men chosen as the best Persians of
mature years, namely, the most wise, just, temper-
ate, and brave. Of these one teaches him the magic
lore of Zoroaster, son of Oromazes, which is the
worship of the gods; he also teaches him kingship.[61]

26. You hear that magic, which you thoughtlessly charge
me with, is an art pleasing to the immortal gods, thoroughly expert in worshiping and honoring them, unques-
tionably pious and skilled in divine lore, famous from   2
the time of he originators, Zoroaster and Oromazes, and
priestess of the gods in heaven; and hence magic is among   3
the first lessons of kingship, and no Persian is readily per-
mitted to be a magician any more than be a king. Plato   4
again in another dialogue has written about a certain Zalmoxis, who though Thracian by origin was distinguished
in this same art, that "his charms are words of beauty."[62]
If that is so, why may not *I* know Zalmoxis' "words of   5
beauty" or Zoroaster's priestly lore? But if those people   6
have the commonplace idea that "magician" strictly means
someone able to fulfill his every wish by spells that have
some kind of extraordinary power, I am very puzzled why
they are not afraid to accuse someone who they say is so
powerful. For one cannot guard against a power so mys-   7
terious and supernatural as that in the way one can against
other things. A man who brings a murderer to court comes   8
with a bodyguard; one who accuses a poisoner is more

---

[62] Pl. *Chrm.* 157A. Zalmoxis is a legendary Thracian figure
whom Plato represents as a healer and deified king.

9 sius cibatur; qui furem arguit, sua custodit. Enimvero qui
magum qualem isti dicunt in discrimen capitis deducit,
quibus comitibus, quibus scrupulis, quibus custodibus
perniciem caecam et inevitabilem prohibeat? Nullis scilicet, et ideo id genus crimen non est eius accusare, qui
credit.

27. Verum haec ferme communi quodam errore imperitorum philosophis obiectantur, ut partim eorum qui
corporum causas meras et simplicis rimantur irreligiosos
putent eoque aiant deos abnuere, ut Anaxagoram et Leu-
cippum et Democritum et Epicurum ceterosque rerum
2 naturae patronos, partim autem, qui providentiam mundi
curiosius vestigant et impensius deos celebrant, eos vero
vulgo magos nominent, quasi facere etiam sciant quae
sciant fieri, ut olim fuere Epimenides et Orpheus et Pytha-
3 goras et Ostanes, ac dein similiter suspectata Empedocli
4 catharmoe, Socrati daemonion, Platonis τὸ ἀγαθόν. Gratulor igitur mihi, cum et ego tot ac tantis viris adnumeror.

5 Ceterum ea quae ab illis ad ostendendum crimen
obiecta sunt, vana et inepta ⟨et⟩[33] simplicia, vereor ne
6 ideo tantum crimina putes, quod obiecta sunt. "Cur," inquit, "piscium quaedam genera quaesisti?" Quasi id cog-

[33] ⟨et⟩ *add. u*

---

[63] Anaxagoras was a cosmological philosopher of the fifth century; Leucippus later in the same century was the teacher of
Democritus and the father of the atomic theory.
[64] Epimenides of Crete was a holy man of the seventh or sixth
century; Ostanes, or Hostanes, was a Persian *magus* and the reputed author of works on magic and related topics.

74

scrupulous about his food; one who charges a burglar protects his property. By contrast, if someone brings a capital 9
case against a magician of the sort they describe, what bodyguards, what scruple, what protection can save him from invisible and inevitable perdition? None, of course, and hence to bring such a charge shows that one does not believe it.

27. But thanks to an almost universal error of the ignorant, philosophers are often faced with this kind of reproach. They think those who investigate the basic, unitary causes of matter to be irreligious, and hence they accuse them of denying the gods' existence, as they did Anaxagoras, Leucippus, Democritus, Epicurus and other champions of the natural order.[63] As for that branch, how- 2
ever, which devotes particular study to universal providence and greatly honors the gods, people commonly label them "magicians," as if convinced that they can cause things to occur which they know do occur; ancient examples are Epimenides, Orpheus, Pythagoras and Ostanes;[64] and thereafter Empedocles' *Purifications*,[65] Soc- 3
rates' Guiding Spirit, Plato's The Good came under similar suspicion. I congratulate myself, then, on being included 4
in such a large and distinguished company.

On the other hand, the allegations that those people 5
have made in order to prove a crime is empty, foolish and naïve, but I fear (*addressing Maximus*) that you may think they are criminal for the simple reason that they have been alleged. "Why," they say, "did you go looking for certain 6

---

[65] Empedocles, the Sicilian philosopher of the mid-fifth century, set out his philosophical views in a poem or poems entitled *Purifications*, of which several papyrus fragments survive.

nitionis gratia philosopho facere non liceat, quod luxurioso
7 gulae causa liceret. "Cur mulier libera tibi nupsit post
annos XIII viduitatis?" Quasi non magis mirandum sit
8 quod tot annis non nupserit. "Cur prius, quam tibi nuberet, scripsit nescio quid in epistula quod sibi videbatur?"
Quasi quisquam debeat causas alienae sententiae reddere.
9 At enim maior natu non est iuvenem aspernata. Igitur hoc
ipsum argumentum est nihil opus magia fuisse, ut nubere
10 vellet mulier viro, vidua caelibi, maior iuniori. Iam et illa
similia: "Habet quiddam Apuleius domi quod sancte colit." Quasi non id potius crimen sit, quod colas non habere.
11 "Cecidit praesente Apuleio puer." Quid enim si iuvenis,
quid si etiam senex assistente me corruisset vel morbo
12 corporis impeditus vel lubrico soli prolapsus? Hiscine argumentis magian probatis, casu puerili et matrimonio
mulieris et obsonio piscium?

28. Possem equidem bono periculo vel his dictis contentus perorare; quoniam mihi pro accusationis longitu-
dine largiter aquae superest, cedo, si videtur, singula con-
2 sideremus. Atque ego omnia obiecta, seu vera seu falsa
sunt, non negabo, sed perinde atque si facta sint fatebor,
3 ut omnis ista multitudo, quae plurima undique ad audiendum convenit, aperte intellegat nihil in philosophos non
modo vere dici, sed ne falso quidem posse confingi, quod
non ex innocentiae fiducia, quamvis liceat negare, tamen
potius habeant defendere.
4   Primum igitur argumenta eorum convincam ac refu-

---

66 More literally, "there remains an abundant amount of water," forensic and other speeches being commonly measured by a
water clock; the opposing parties were allowed equal time.

kinds of fish?" As if a philosopher may not do for the sake
of science what an epicure might do to please his appetite.
"Why did a freeborn woman marry you after being thir- 7
teen years a widow?" As if it were not the greater surprise
that she had gone so many years unmarried. "Why before 8
her marriage to you did she write a certain something or
other to please herself?" As if anyone should give reasons
for another's decision. "Ah, but though well on in years, 9
she did not reject a young man." Well, this fact is enough
to prove that no magic was needed for a woman to want
to marry a man, a widow a bachelor, an older person a
younger. The next charges too are similar: "Apuleius has 10
something at home that he worships devoutly." As if it was
not more of a charge to have nothing to worship. "A boy 11
collapsed in Apuleius' presence." Well, suppose an adult
or an old man had collapsed in my presence, weakened by
bodily illness or slipping on a polished floor? Are these the 12
arguments you prove magic with—a boy's fall, a woman's
marriage, the purchase of fish?

28. I might indeed without serious risk be content to
say no more than this, and end my speech here, but given
the length of the prosecution I have ample time still left
on the clock,[66] so let us consider each point separately, if
you please. And indeed I will not deny but rather will 2
admit every one of the charges, whether true or false, just
as if they were facts. In that way, all this crowd, which 3
has come streaming from all sides to listen, may clearly
see that nothing can be truthfully alleged against philosophers, or indeed falsely fabricated, that their trust in
their own innocence would not allow them to defend, even
though they might deny them.

First therefore I will disprove their testimony, and 4

77

tabo nihil ea ad magian pertinere. Dein etsi maxime magus forem, tamen ostendam neque causam ullam neque
occasionem fuisse, ut me in aliquo maleficio experirentur.
5 Ibi etiam de falsa invidia deque epistulis mulieris perperam lectis et nequius interpretatis deque matrimonio meo
ac Pudentillae disputabo, idque a me susceptum officii
6 gratia quam lucri causa docebo; quod quidem matrimonium nostrum Aemiliano huic immane quanto angori
quantaeque dividiae fuit. Inde omnis huiusce accusationis
7 obeundae ira et rabies et denique insania exorta est. Quae
si omnia palam et dilucide ostendero, tunc denique te,
Claudi Maxime, et omnis qui adsunt contestabor puerum
illum Sicinium Pudentem privignum meum, cuius obtentu et voluntate a patruo eius accusor, nuperrime curae
8 meae eruptum, postquam frater eius Pontianus et natu
9 maior et moribus melior diem suum obiit, atque ita in me
ac matrem suam nefarie efferatum, non mea culpa, desertis liberalibus studiis ac repudiata omni disciplina, scelestis accusationis huius rudimentis patruo Aemiliano potius
quam fratri Pontiano similem futurum.

29. Nunc, ut institui, proficiscar ad omnia Aemiliani
huiusce deliramenta orsus ab eo, quod ad suspicionem
magiae quasi validissimum in principio dici animadvertisti, nonnulla me piscium genera per quosdam piscatores
2 pretio quaesisse. Utrum igitur horum ad suspectandam
3 magian valet? Quodne piscatores mihi piscem quaesierunt? Scilicet ergo phrygionibus aut fabris negotium istud
dandum fuisse atque ita opera cuiusque artis permutanda,

show that it has nothing to do with magic. Next I will show
that, even if I were a thoroughgoing magician, they had no
reason or opportunity to catch me in some act of magic.
In that connection I will also refute them by discussing   5
their ungrounded jealousy, the lady's letter that they have
incorrectly quoted and maliciously interpreted, and my
marriage with Pudentilla, which I will show that I contracted in order to do my duty by another, not to profit
myself. That marriage of ours certainly caused Aemilianus 6
immense anguish and vexation; that gave rise to the anger,
the fury, in a word the madness that made him undertake
this whole prosecution. If I prove all of this openly and   7
convincingly, then, Claudius Maximus, I will finally assert
before you and before all those present that the boy there,
Sicinius Pudens my stepson, under whose cover and with
whose assent his uncle is prosecuting me, very recently
broke away from my tutelage when his brother Pontianus,   8
who was both his senior in years and his superior in character, had passed away; and it was this, not any fault of   9
mine, that threw him into a wicked rage against me and
his very own mother, so that he gave up humane studies,
shook off all control, and has taken his first villainous lessons by this prosecution, sure as he is to resemble his
uncle Aemilianus rather than his brother Pontianus.

29. Well, as promised, I will now go on to all the ravings
of Aemilianus here, starting with what he mentioned right
away as the strongest reason to suspect magic, as you observed: that I paid certain fishermen to get different sorts
of fish for me. So which of these things is a valid reason to   2
suspect sorcery? Was it that fishermen tried to get me fish?   3
No doubt, then, I should have entrusted the task to tapestry or carpentry workers, thus reversing the task of each

si vellem calumniis vestris vitare, ut faber mihi piscem
4 everreret, ut piscator mutuo lignum dedolaret. An ex eo
intellexistis maleficio quaeri pisciculos, quod pretio quae-
rebantur? Credo, si convivio vellem, gratis quaesissem.
5 Quin igitur etiam ex aliis plerisque me arguitis? Nam
saepe numero et vinum et holus et pomum et panem pre-
6 tio mutavi. Eo pacto cuppedinariis omnibus famem decernis: quis enim ab illis obsonare audebit, si quidem statuitur
omnia edulia quae depenso parantur non cenae, sed magiae desiderari?

7   Quod si nihil remanet suspicionis, neque in piscatoribus mercede invitatis ad quod solent, ad piscem capi-
endum (quos tamen nullos ad testimonium produxere,
8 quippe qui nulli fuerunt), neque in ipso pretio rei venalis
(cuius tamen quantitatem nullam taxavere, ne, si mediocre pretium dixissent, contemneretur, si plurimum,
9 non crederetur)—si in his, ut dico, nulla suspicio est, respondeat mihi Aemilianus, quo proximo signo ad accusationem magiae sit inductus.

    30. "Pisces," inquit, "quaeris." Nolo negare. Sed, oro
te, qui pisces quaerit, magus est? Equidem non magis
arbitror quam si lepores quaererem vel apros vel altilia.
2 An soli pisces habent aliquit occultum aliis, sed magis cognitum? Hoc si scis quid sit, magus es profecto; sin nescis,
3 confitearis necesse est id te accusare quod nescis. Tam
rudis vos esse omnium litterarum, omnium denique vulgi
fabularum, ut ne fingere quidem possitis ista verisimiliter?
4 Quid enim competit ad amoris ardorem accendendum
piscis brutus et frigidus aut omnino res pelago quaesita?

profession, if I wanted to escape your slanders, so that a carpenter should net me a fish, and in turn a fisherman should carve wood. Or was it because I offered to pay for 4 fish that you inferred that I wanted them for black magic? Had I wanted them for a feast, no doubt I would have offered nothing. Why then don't you use many other items 5 to convict me? I have often paid money for wine, vegetables, fruit, and bread. In that way you condemn the whole 6 tribe of grocers to starvation, for who will dare to shop from them, once it is the rule that all foods that one gets by purchase are wanted for magic, not for dinner?

But if there is no further ground for suspicion, neither 7 in my hiring fishermen to do their usual work and catch fish (none of them, however, have they produced as witnesses, since they never existed), nor in the actual price of 8 the purchase (the amount of which they did not specify, in case any price they named would be laughable if moderate and incredible if excessive): if, I repeat, there is no ground 9 for suspicion in all this, let Aemilianus tell me what evidence in particular led him to charge me with magic.

30. "You go looking for fish," says he. I don't wish to deny it. But, I ask you, is someone who looks for fish a magician? No more so, in my opinion, that if I looked for hare, boar, or poultry. Or do only fish have some special 2 property known to magicians but hidden from others? If you know what this is, you must be a magician; if not, you are obliged to confess that you do not know the meaning of your own charge. Are you people so ignorant of all polite 3 literature, and even of all popular fable, that you cannot even make those stories of yours plausible? For how is a 4 cold, stupid fish, or anything at all drawn from the sea, suitable for lighting the flames of love? Unless perhaps you

Nisi forte hoc vos ad mendacium induxit, quod Venus dici-
5 tur pelago exorta. Audi sis, Tannoni Pudens, quam multa
nescieris, qui de piscibus argumentum magiae recepisti.
6 At si Virgilium legisses, profecto scisses alia quaeri ad hanc
7 rem solere; ille enim, quantum scio, enumerat vittas mollis et verbenas pinguis et tura mascula et licia discolora,
praeterea laurum fragilem, limum durabilem, ceram li-
quabilem, nec minus quae iam in opere serio scripsit:

8   Falcibus et messae ad lunam quaeruntur aenis
      pubentes herbae nigri cum lacte veneni.
      Quaeritur et nascentis equi de fronte revulsus
      et matri praereptus amor.

9 At tu piscium insimulator longe diversa instrumenta magis
attribuis, non frontibus teneris detergenda sed dorsis
squalentibus excidenda, nec fundo revellenda sed profundo extrahenda, nec falcibus metenda sed hamis inun-
10 canda. Postremo in maleficio ille venenum nominat, tu
pulmentum, ille herbas et surculos, tu squamas et ossa, ille
pratum decerpit, tu fluctum scrutaris.
11   Memorassem tibi etiam Theocriti paria et alia Homeri
et Orphei plurima, et ex comoediis et tragoediis Graecis
et ex historiis multa repetissem, ni te dudum animadver-
tissem Graecam Pudentillae epistulam legere nequivisse.

---

67 Referring to *Ecl.* 8.64–65, 73–75, 80–82.

68 *Aen.* 4.513–16: "this time," because the previous quotation
was from the *Eclogues.*

69 The so-called *hippomanes* (horse madness), supposed to be
a growth on the head of a newborn foal that worked as a love
charm.

70 For this charge, chapters 80 to 84.

were led to invent this lie because they say Venus rose
from the sea. Let me tell you, Tannonius Pudens, how 5
little you knew when you took fish to be a proof of magic,
whereas if you had read Virgil, you would certainly have 6
known that the things usually required for this purpose are
different. For as far as I know he lists soft wreaths of wool, 7
leafy boughs, balls of incense, threads of different colors,
and moreover laurel leaves that crackle, mud that hardens,
wax that softens,[67] all of which he included, this time in a
serious poem:[68]

> And, reaped with brazen sickles beneath the moon, 8
> Herbs are sought, rich with juice of black poison;
> And, torn from the forehead of a foal at birth,
> The love charm snatched from the dam.[69]

But you with your allegations against fish suppose that ma- 9
gicians use very different means, not one trimmed from
soft foreheads but skimmed from scaly backs, not torn
from the earth but drawn from the deep, not harvested
with sickles but impaled on hooks. Finally, Virgil talks of 10
using poison to cast a spell while you talk of savories, he
talks of herbs and twigs while you talk of scales and bones,
he culls a meadow while you scour the deep.

I would also have quoted you similar lines of Theoc- 11
ritus and many others of Homer and Orpheus, I would
have cited many passages from Greek tragedy and comedy
and from histories, except that I noticed long ago that
you could not read Pudentilla's letter written in Greek.[70]

12 Igitur unum etiam poetam Latinum attingam; versus ipsos
[quos]³⁴ agnoscent qui Laevium legere:

13 Philtra omnia undique eruunt:
  antipathes illud quaeritur,
  trochiscili, ungues, taeniae,
  radiculae, herbae, surculi,
  saurae inlices bicodulae,
  hinnientium dulcedines.

31. Haec et alia quaesisse me potius quam pisces longe
verisimilius confinxisses (his etenim fortasse per famam
pervulgatam fides fuisset), si tibi ulla eruditio adfuisset.
Enimvero piscis ad quam rem facit captus nisi ad epulas
coctus? Ceterum ad magian nihil quicquam videtur mihi
2 adiutare. Dicam unde id coniectem. Pythagoram plerique
Zoroastri sectatorem similiterque magiae peritum arbitrati tamen memoriae prodiderunt, cum animadvertisset
proxime Metapontum in litore Italiae suae, quam subsici-
vam Graeciam fecerat, a quibusdam piscatoribus everri-
3 culum trahi, fortunam iactus eius emisse et pretio dato
iussisse ilico piscis eos, qui capti tenebantur, solvi retibus
4 et reddi profundo; quos scilicet eum de manibus amissu-
rum non fuisse, si quid in his utile ad magian comperisset.
5 Sed enim vir egregie doctus et veterum aemulator memi-
nerat Homerum, poetam multiscium vel potius cuncta-

³⁴ quos *del. Salmasius*

⁷¹ Courtney, *FLP* 140, Laevius 27; Blänsdorf, *FPL*², 148, Laevius 27. Laevius was a poet of the early first century BC, notable
for his word coinages and varied meters.
⁷² The so-called *hippomanes,* on which see above, n. 69.

So I will mention just one other Latin poet; those who   12
have read Laevius will recognize the actual lines:[71]

> They search out love charms everywhere,   13
> They seek the famous elixir,
> Wheels, nail clippings, ribbons,
> Roots, herbs, twigs,
> Lures from fork-tailed lizards,
> Charms from neighing horses.[72]

31. It would have been more plausible of you to allege
that I had gone looking for these and other things, rather
than fish, if you had had the slightest education, since you
would have got some credence from the common belief
about them: but what use is a fish once caught except when
cooked for dinner? But for magic I think it is of no use at
all. I will give my reason for supposing so. Most people   2
think that Pythagoras was a disciple of Zoroaster and no
less skilled in magic, and yet they have recorded that he
was on the shore very near Metapontum in his adoptive
Italy, which he had made into a second Greece, when he
noticed certain fishermen hauling in a dragnet. He bought   3
whatever their catch happened to be, but after paying the
price immediately told them to free the fish caught in their
nets and return them to the deep. Surely he would not   4
have let them slip from his grasp if had he discovered them
to be of any use in magic? But no, as an exceptionally   5
learned man and a follower of the ancients, he remem-
bered that Homer, a poet and polymath, or rather a su-

rum rerum adprime peritum, vim omnem medicaminum non mari, sed terrae ascripsisse, cum de quadam saga ad hunc modum memoravit:

ἣ τόσα φάρμακα ᾔδη, ὅσα τρέφει εὐρεῖα χθών,

6 itemque alibi carminum similiter:

τῇ πλεῖστα φέρει ζείδουρος ἄρουρα
φάρμακα, πολλὰ μὲν ἐσθλὰ μεμιγμένα, πολλὰ δὲ
λυγρά,

7 cum tamen numquam apud eum marino aliquo et piscolento medicavit nec Proteus faciem nec Vlixes scrobem nec Aeolus follem nec Helena creterram nec Circe pocu-
8 lum nec Venus cingulum. At vos soli reperti estis ex omni memoria, qui vim herbarum et radicum et surculorum et lapillorum quasi quadam colluvione naturae de summis montibus in mare transferatis et penitus piscium ventribus
9 insuatis. Igitur ut solebat ad magorum cerimonias advocari Mercurius carminum vector et illex animi Venus et Luna noctium conscia et manium potens Trivia, vobis auctoribus posthac Neptunus cum Salacia et Portuno et omni choro Nerei ab aestibus fretorum ad aestus amorum transferentur.

32. Dixi cur non arbitrer quicquam negotii esse magis
2 et piscibus. Nunc, si videtur, credamus Aemiliano solere pisces etiam ad magicas potestates adiutare. Num ergo propterea quicumque quaerit et ipse magus est? Eo qui-

---

[73] *Il.* 11.741; *Od.* 4.229–30.   [74] Respectively, *Od.* 4.456–58 (Proteus), 11.25 (Odysseus), 10.19–22 (Aeolus), 10.234–38 (Circe), *Il.* 14.214–17 (Aphrodite/Venus).

[75] The text is uncertain.

preme expert on every topic, ascribed all the efficacy of
potions not to the sea but to the earth, when he wrote this
about a certain sorceress:

> Who knew all the herbs bred by the broad earth,

and similarly in another passage of his poetry,   6

> There the grain-giving earth brings forth the most
> herbs,
> many good when mixed, and many harmful,[73]

while by contrast, nowhere in Homer did Proteus use   7
something maritime and fishy to charm his appearance,
Ulysses his ditch, Aeolus his bag, Helen her wine bowl,
Circe her cup, or Venus her girdle.[74] You are the first   8
people in human memory found to transfer the power of
herbs, roots, twigs, and gems in a kind of natural confu-
sion from mountaintops to the sea, and to sew them deep
in the bellies of fish. Hence, just as magicians used to   9
summon to their rites Mercury the bringer of spells,[75]
Venus the temptress of the heart, Moon the partner of the
Night, and Trivia the ruler of the shades, Neptune with
Salacia,[76] Portunus, and Nereus' entire troop will henceforth be transferred on your authority from the surges of
the sea to the surges of love.

32. I have said why I do not think magicians have
any business with fish, but now, if I may, let us accept   2
Aemilianus' assertion that even fish increase the powers of
magic. But surely that does not prove that whoever goes
looking for fish is also a magician himself? At that rate,

---

[76] The Roman goddess of the sea, whose name recalled the
adjective *salax* (highly sexed).

dem pacto et qui myoparonem quaesierit pirata erit, et qui
3 vectem perfossor, et qui gladium sicarius. Nihil in rebus
omnibus tam innoxium dices, quin id possit aliquid aliqua
obesse, nec tam laetum, quin possit ad tristitudinem in-
4 tellegi. Nec tamen omnia idcirco ad nequiorem suspicionem trahuntur, ut si tus et casiam et myrram ceterosque id genus odores funeri tantum emptos arbitreris, cum
5 et medicamento parentur et sacrificio. Ceterum eodem
piscium argumento etiam Menelai socios putabis magos
fuisse, quos ait poeta praecipuus flexis hamulis apud Pha-
6 rum insulam famem propulsasse. Etiam mergos et delphi-
nos et Scyllam tu eodem referes; etiam gulones omnes, qui
impendio a piscatoribus merguntur; etiam ipsos piscato-
7 res, qui omnium generum piscis arte adquirunt. "Cur ergo
tu quaeris?" Nolo equidem nec necessarium habeo tibi
8 dicere, sed per te, si potes, ad hoc quaesisse me argue. Ut
si elleborum vel cicutam vel sucum papaveris emissem,
item alia eiusdem modi quorum moderatus usus salutaris,
sed commixtio vel quantitas noxia est, quis aequo animo
pateretur, si me per haec veneficii arcesseres, quod ex illis
potest homo occidi?

33. Videamus tamen, quae fuerint piscium genera tam
necessaria ad habendum tamque rara ad repperiendum,
2 ut merito statuto praemio quaererentur. Tria omnino no-
3 minaverunt, unum falsi, duo mentiti; falsi, quod leporem
marinum fuisse dixerunt qui alius omnino piscis fuit,

---

77 *Od.* 4.368–69.

78 Probably the mythical monster rather than the seabird *ciris,*
believed to be Scylla the daughter of Nisus, turned into a bird
after betraying her father and perpetually hunted by him in the
form of a sea eagle: Hunink, *Apuleius of Madauros,* 106–7.

looking for a galley makes one a pirate, for a crowbar a burglar, for a sword a murderer. In all of nature you 3 can name nothing so harmless that it cannot somehow do harm, nor so cheerful that it can escape a sinister construction. And yet a sinister suspicion cannot be forced on everything, as if you were to think that people buy frankincense, cassia, myrrh and other such perfumes only for a funeral, when they obtain them both as medicines and as offerings. Moreover, by the same argument from fish you 5 will suppose that Menelaus' companions were magicians too because, so the supreme poet says, they used fishhooks to stave off hunger on the island of Pharos.[77] You will put 6 seagulls, dolphins and Scylla[78] in the same class, as well as the whole tribe of gluttons, who drown in debt to fishermen, and indeed even fishermen, who collect fish of every kind by profession. "Why then do *you* go looking for fish?" 7 I myself do not wish or think myself obliged to tell you, but if you can, prove by your own wits that that was what I wanted them for. Suppose for example I had bought hel- 8 lebore, hemlock, or poppy juice and other such items as well, medicinal when used moderately but harmful when mixed or excessive, who would put up with listening to you if you charged me with poisoning because of them, just because they can be used to kill someone?

33. Let us however see what kinds of fish these were, so essential to own and so difficult to find that it was worth agreeing on a price to get them. They named three in all, 2 one erroneously and two mendaciously. Erroneously, be- 3 cause they said "sea hare" when it was altogether a differ-

quem mihi Themison servus noster medicinae non igna-
rus, ut ex ipso audisti, ultro attulit ad inspiciendum; nam

4 quidem leporem nondum etiam invenit. Sed profiteor me
quaerere et cetera, non piscatoribus modo, verum etiam
amicis meis negotio dato, quicumque minus cogniti generis piscis inciderit, ut eius mihi aut formam commemorent
aut ipsum vivum, si id nequierint vel mortuum ostendant.

5 Quam ob rem id faciam, mox docebo. Mentiti autem sunt
callidissimi accusatores mei, ut sibi videntur, cum me ad
fidem[35] calumniae confinxerunt duas res marinas impudi-

6 cis vocabulis quaesisse. Quas Tannonius ille cum utrius-
que sexus genitalia intellegi vellet, sed eloqui propter
infantiam causidicus summus nequiret, multum ac diu
haesitato tandem virile "marinum" nescio qua circumlo-

7 cutione male ac sordide nominavit; sed enim feminal nullo
pacto repperiens munditer dicere ad mea scripta confugit
et quodam libro meo legit: "interfeminium tegat et femo-
ris obiectu et palmae velamento."

34. Hic etiam pro sua gravitate vitio mihi vertebat,

2 quod me nec sordidiora dicere honeste pigeret. At ego illi
contra iustius exprobrarim, quod qui eloquentiae patroci-
nium vulgo profiteatur etiam honesta dictu sordide blate-
ret ac saepe in rebus nequaquam difficilibus fringultiat vel

3 omnino obmutescat. Cedo enim, si ego de Veneris statua
nihil dixissem neque interfeminium nominassem, quibus

[35] fidem *Fulvius*: finem ω

---

[79] Allegedly, Aemilianus used *marinum* (marine), similar
sounding to *mas, maris* (male), to avoid naming the fish called
veretilla (next n.); similarly, for *feminal* (female pudenda), he
borrowed a term from Apuleius.

ent fish that my slave Themison (who has no small knowledge of medicine, as you heard him say himself) without
prompting brought for me to look at; a sea hare he has
not yet even found. But I admit I am looking for other   4
kinds too, and have given a commission not only to fishermen but also to my friends; for any unusual kind of fish
they come across, they are either to inform me of its appearance, or to show me either the actual thing alive, or if
they cannot, then dead. I will tell you later my reason for
doing this. But my very crafty accusers, as they suppose   5
themselves to be, were lying when to make their slander
plausible they alleged that I tried to get two "obscenely
named" sea creatures. Tannonius there intended this to be   6
taken to mean the genital organs of either sex but, being
too tongue-tied, this consummate lawyer could not say the
words, so after hesitating for a very long time and using a
strange circumlocution, he finally called the male organ
by an ugly, vulgar word "the marine"; but not finding any   7
way to mention the female one with propriety,[79] he took
refuge in my writings and read in a certain book of mine,
"Let her hide her interloin both with the screen of her
thigh and the cover of her palm."

34. Moreover, as the stern judge he is, he faulted me
because I did not shrink from mentioning even more sor-
did items outright. But *I* would be more justified for re-   2
proaching him with the fact that he publicly proclaims
himself a champion of eloquence, and then vulgarly blath-
ers even things it is decent to say, and often stammers or
turns completely dumb over things not awkward at all. For   3
tell me, if I had said nothing about a statue of Venus and
had not used the word "interloin," what words, may I ask,

tandem verbis accusasses crimen illud tam stultitiae quam
4 linguae tuae congruens? An quicquam stultius quam ex
nominum propinquitate vim similem rerum coniectam?

5   Et fortasse an peracute repperisse vobis videbamini, ut
quaesisse me fingeretis ad illecebras magicas duo haec
marina, veretillam et virginal (disce enim nomina rerum
Latina, quae propterea varie nominavi, ut denuo instruc-
6 tus accuses). Memento tamen tam ridiculum argumentum
fore desiderata ad res venerias marina obscena, quam si
dicas marinum pectinem comendo capillo quaesitum vel
aucupandis volantibus piscem accipitrem aut venandis
apris piscem apriculam aut eliciendis mortuis marina cal-
7 varia. Respondeo igitur ad hunc vestrum locum, non minus insulse quam absurde commentum, me hasce nugas
marinas et quiscilias litoralis neque pretio neque gratis
quaesisse.

35. Illud etiam praeterea respondeo, nescisse vos quid
2 a me quaesitum fingeretis. Haec enim frivola quae nominastis pleraque in litoribus omnibus congestim et acerva-
tim iacent et sine ullius opera quamlibet leviter motis fluc-
3 ticulis ultro foras evolvuntur. Quin ergo dicitis me eadem
opera pretio impenso per plurimos piscatores quaesisse de
litore conchulam striatam, testam hebetem, calculum te-
retem; praeterea cancrorum furcas, echinum caliculos,
4 lolliginum ligulas; postremo assulas, festucas, resticulas et

---

80 Neither of these fish is identified: *veretilla,* which I have
translated "cockle," got its name from its resemblance to a penis
(*veretrum*), and *virginal* is similarly derived from *virgo* (virgin).
Cunner is a species of wrasse (Webster).

81 *Pecten* (comb) means "scallop," while *accipiter, apricula*
and *calvaria* are unidentified; three of these appear in the quota-

would you have used to make that charge of yours, which so well suits both your stupidity and your vocabulary? Is 4 there anything more stupid than to take words that sound alike to denote similar objects?

And yet maybe you thought you had found a very clever 5 ruse—alleging that I had tried to get these two sea creatures, a cockle and a cunner, for their magical powers of attraction[80] (for let me tell you the creatures' Latin names, which I have mentioned separately, so that you have learned something before you accuse me again). But remember, it would be just as absurd to argue that 6 obscenely-named sea creatures are desired for sexual purposes as to say that one wanted a comb fish to comb one's hair, a hawk fish to catch birds, a boar fish to hunt boar, sea skulls to raise the dead.[81] My reply to this passage of 7 your speech, a fabrication as tasteless as it is absurd, is that I did not try to get this sea trash or shore refuse either for a price or for nothing.

35. I will also make this reply: you had no idea what you alleged I was looking for. These scraps that you mentioned 2 usually lie in heaps and piles on every shore, and furthermore are tossed up automatically when wavelets are ever so slightly rolled landwards. You might just as well say, 3 then, that I spent money on numerous fishermen to search the shore for a striped cockle shell, a worn-down mussel shell, a smooth pebble, and in addition crabs' claws, sea urchins' suckers, squids' tentacles, and finally splinters, straws, bits of string, spotted oyster shells, and finally sea 4 moss, seaweed, other flotsam such as you find on every

tion from Ennius below (ch. 39). A modern equivalent would be to want swordfish for fencing, catfish for catching mice, etc.

ostrea [Pergami][36] vermiculata; denique muscum et al-
gam, cetera maris eiectamenta, quae ubique litorum ventis expelluntur, salo expuuntur, tempestate reciprocantur,
5 tranquillo deseruntur? Neque enim minus istis quae commemoravi accommodari possunt similiter ex vocabulo
6 suspiciones. Posse dicitis ad res venerias sumpta de mari
spuria et fascina propter nominum similitudinem; qui
minus possit ex eodem litore calculus ad vesicam, testa ad
7 testamentum, cancer ad ulcera, alga ad querqueram?[37] Ne
tu, Claudi Maxime, nimis patiens vir es et oppido plurima[38] humanitate, qui hasce eorum argumentationes diu
hercle perpessus sis. Equidem, cum haec ab illis quasi
gravia et vincibilia dicerentur, illorum stultitiam ridebam,
tuam patientiam mirabar.

    36. Ceterum quam ob rem plurimos iam piscis cogno-
verim, quorundam adhuc nescius esse nolim, discat Aemi-
2 lianus, quoniam usque adeo rebus meis curat. Quamquam
est iam praecipiti aevo et occidua senectute, tamen, si vi-
3 detur, accipiat doctrinam seram plane et postumam; legat
veterum philosophorum monumenta, tandem ut intellegat non me primum haec requisisse, sed iam pridem
maiores meos, Aristotelem dico et Theophrastum et Eu-

---

36 Pergami *del. Lennep*
37 querqueram (querc-) *Colvius*: querquerum ω
38 plurima *Colvius*: proxima ω

---

82 Some or all of these words were close in sound or identical
to ones with a sexual sense, such as *testa* (shard) to *testis* (testicle),
furca (claw or fork) to the female *pudenda;* for others the double
entendre can only be guessed.

shore, driven there by the wind, spewed from the brine, tossed around by a storm, stranded in calm. For those 5 items I just mentioned can similarly be made suspicious by means of their names.[82] You could say holias and prick- 6 lebacks[83] taken from the sea can help with sex because of the similarity of their names; couldn't a pebble from the same shore help just as much with a bladder, a shell with a will, a crab with a sore, seaweed with a chill?[84] Really, 7 Claudius Maximus, you are a very patient man, and ex- tremely kind, to put up so very long with these people's arguments. Speaking for myself, I smiled at their stupidity and marveled at your patience when they mentioned such items as if they were grave and overwhelming.

36. But let me tell Aemilianus why I have already learned about many fish, and would wish to acquire knowl- edge of certain others even now, since he is so very inter- ested in my affairs. Though he is now in his declining years 2 and at the sunset of old age, still, if I may, I want him to get some education, even if very late and in the next life. Let him read the treatises of the ancient philosophers, and 3 learn at last that I was not the first to investigate these subjects: it was my predecessors long ago, I mean Aris-

[83] The word *spurium* designated both a species of fish and the female *pudenda;* the various meanings of *fascinum* included "pe- nis" and a kind of seashell. According to Webster, "prickleback" is another name for "stickleback," and "holia" is a kind of salmon.

[84] These wordplays are impossible to render in English: *cal- culus* (small stone) suggests gallstone in the bladder (*vesica*), *testa* suggests *testamentum* (will), *cancer* (crab) also means "tumor," *alga* (seaweed) suggests *algor* (chill).

4 demum et Lyconem ceterosque Platonis minores, qui plurimos libros de genitu animalium deque victu deque particulis deque omni differentia reliquerunt.

5   Bene quod apud te, Maxime, causa agitur, qui pro tua eruditione legisti profecto Aristotelis περὶ ζῴων γενέσεως, περὶ ζῴων ἀνατομῆς, περὶ ζῴων ἱστορίας multiiuga volumina, praeterea problemata innumera eiusdem, tum ex eadem secta ceterorum, in quibus id genus varia

6 tractantur. Quae tanta cura conquisita si honestum et gloriosum illis fuit scribere, cur turpe sit nobis experiri, praesertim cum ordinatius et cohibilius eadem Graece et Latine adnitar conscribere et in omnibus aut omissa ad-

7 quirere aut defecta supplere? Permittite, si opera est, quaedam legi de magicis meis, ut sciat me Aemilianus

8 plura quam putat quaerere et sedulo explorare. Prome tu librum e Graecis meis, quos forte hic amici habuere, sed utique[39] naturalium quaestionum atque eum maxime, in quo plura de piscium genere tractata sunt; interea, dum hic quaerit, ego exemplum rei competens dixero.

    37. Sophocles poeta Euripidi aemulus et superstes— vixit enim ad extremam senectam—, cum igitur accusaretur a filio suomet dementiae, quasi iam per aetatem desiperet, protulisse dicitur Coloneum suam, peregregiam tragoediarum, quam forte tum in eo tempore conscribe-

2 bat, eam iudicibus legisse nec quicquam amplius pro

[39] sed utique *Lipsius*: sedulique ω

[85] Arist. fr. 295 Gigon. Theophrastus was a pupil of Aristotle, who chose him over Eudemus to be his successor as head of the Peripatetic school; Lyco was Theophrastus' successor at one remove and led the school for much of the third century.

totle, Theophrastus, Eudemus, Lyco,[85] and others later than Plato. These have left us very many books on the generation of animals, their diet, their anatomy, and all their characteristic features. 4

How lucky, Claudius Maximus, that you are the judge in the case. Learned as you are, you have certainly read Aristotle's many different volumes *On the generation of animals, On the anatomy of animals, Natural History,* and the same author's countless *Problems* too, as well as works by others of the same school that treat various subjects of the kind. If it was honorable and praiseworthy for them to write on such subjects that they had so laboriously discovered, what is disgraceful in my investigating them, especially since I struggle to expound these same topics more systematically and concisely in Greek and in Latin, either remedying omissions in them all or correcting errors? (*To Maximus and his advisors:*) If it is not inconvenient, permit certain of my works on magic to be read out, so that Aemilianus can learn that I study and go deeply into more topics than he thinks. (*To a servant of the court:*) You there, produce one of my works in Greek that my friends may have with them, and above all one of my *Natural Questions,* particularly the one where I have discussed types of fish several times. (*To the court:*) In the meantime, while this man is looking, I will cite a precedent suited to the case. 5 6 7 8

37. Sophocles, a poet who rivaled and outlived Euripides, for he reached extreme old age—well, when his own son accused him of dementia, alleging that his age was now making him foolish, they say he brought out his *Oedipus at Colonus,* that tragic masterpiece, which he was just then writing. He read this out to the jurors, and said 2

defensione sua addidisse, nisi ut audacter dementiae con-
3 demnarent, si carmina senis displicerent. Ibi ego comperior omnis iudices tanto poetae adsurrexisse, miris laudibus eum tulisse ob argumenti sollertiam et coturnum
facundiae, nec ita multum omnis afuisse quin accusatorem
potius dementiae condemnarent.

4   Invenisti tu librum? Beasti. Cedo enim experiamur an
et mihi possint in iudicio litterae meae prodesse. Lege
pauca de principio, dein quaedam de piscibus. At tu interea, dum legit, aquam sustine.

    38. Audisti, Maxime, quorum pleraque scilicet legeras
2 apud antiquos philosophorum. Et memento de solis piscibus haec volumina a me conscripta, qui eorum coitu pro-
gignantur, qui ex limo coalescant, quotiens et quid anni
cuiusque eorum generis feminae subent, mares suriant,
3 quibus membris et causis discrerit natura viviparos eorum
et oviparos (ita enim Latine appello quae Graeci ζῳοτόκα
4 et ᾠοτόκα) et, ne per omnes animalium genitus[40] pergam,
deinde de differentia et victu et membris et aetatibus ceterisque plurimis scitu quidem necessariis, sed in iudicio
alienis.

5   Pauca etiam de Latinis scriptis meis ad eandem peri-
tiam pertinentibus legi iubebo, in quibus animadvertes
cum res[41] cognitu raras, tum nomina etiam Romanis inu-
sitata et in hodiernum quod sciam infecta, ea tamen nomina labore meo et studio ita de Graecis provenire, ut

---

[40] per omnes animalium genitus *Casaubon*: perose animalium
genita ω
[41] res *Bosscha*: me ω

nothing further in his defense except that they should go
ahead and unhesitatingly find him guilty of dementia if
they disliked this poem of his old age. At that point, so I   3
find, all the judges rose to applaud the great poet, and
showered extraordinary praise on him for the artistry of
the plot and the elevation of the language, while they were
all very near to condemning his accusers for dementia
instead.

Have you found the book? Many thanks. Well, let us   4
see whether I too can be aided by my works in a trial. (*To
a servant of the court:*) Read a little from the preface, and
then some passages about fish. (*To another servant of the
court:*) You there, stop the clock for a minute while he
reads. (*The first servant reads.*)

38. Most of what you have heard, Maximus, you have
read in the ancient philosophers. Remember too that   2
these works of mine only concerned fish: which of them
are engendered by coitus, which congeal from mud, how
often and at what time of year the female of each species
is excited and the male is aroused, by what features and   3
for what reasons nature marks the viviparous off from the
oviparous (since those are my Latin terms for what the
Greeks call *zoötoka* and *oötoka*). Not to go through all   4
the creatures' ways of generation, next I discussed their
differences, diets, body parts, lifespans, and many other
items essential for science but out of place in a courtroom.

I will also order a few passages to be read out from my   5
Latin writings relevant to the same branch of the sciences.
In them you will notice scarcely known facts and also
words unfamiliar to Romans, ones never coined before to
my knowledge; however, thanks to my effort and research,
those words, though of Greek origin, nonetheless have the

6 tamen Latina moneta percussa sint. Vel dicant nobis, Aemiliane, patroni tui, ubi legerint Latine haec pronuntiata
vocabula. De solis aquatilibus dicam, nec cetera animalia
7 nisi in communibus differentîs attingam. Ausculta igitur
quae dicam. Iam me clamabis magica nomina Aegyptio
8 vel Babylonico ritu percensere: σελάχεια, μαλάκεια,
μαλακόστρακα, χονδράκανθα, ὀστρακόδερμα, καρχα-
ρόδοντα, ἀμφίβια, λεπιδωτά, φολιδωτά, δερμόπτερα,
9 στεγανόποδα, μονήρη, συναγελαστικά—possum etiam
pergere; sed non est operae in istis diem terere, ut sit mihi
tempus aggredi ad cetera. Haec interim quae dixi pauca
recita Latine a me enuntiata.

39. Utrum igitur putas philosopho non secundum Cy-
nicam temeritatem rudi et indocto, sed qui se Platonicae
scholae meminerit, utrum ei putas turpe scire ista an nescire, neglegere an curare, nosse quanta sit etiam in istis
providentiae ratio an de diis immortalibus matri et patri
2 credere? Q. Ennius hedyphagetica versibus scripsit. Innu-
merabilia genera piscium enumerat, quae scilicet curiose
cognorat. Paucos versus memini, eos dicam:

3   Omnibus ut Clipea praestat mustela marina!
     Mures sunt Aeni, aspra ostrea plurima Abydi,
     Mytilenae est pecten Charadrumque apud Ambraciai
     [finis],[42]

[42] finis del. *Salmasius*

[86] Egypt and Babylonia were regions notorious for the practice of magic.   [87] Trans. Warmington, *ROL* 1.409, altered to
conform with Courtney, *FLP*, Ennius fr. 28. Text and translation
of this passage are very uncertain.

stamp of Latin. If not, your lawyers should tell us, Aemil- 6
ianus, where they read these terms expressed in Latin. I
will talk only of aquatic creatures, not touching on other
ones except when they share distinguishing features. Lis- 7
ten therefore to what I have to say. You will immediately
clamor that I am listing words of magic in Egyptian or
Babylonian style:[86] sharks, mollusks, creatures with soft 8
shells, with hard shells, with cartilaginous skeletons, with
sharp teeth, amphibious, with scales, with plates, with
membranous wings, with webbed feet, creatures solitary
and gregarious. I could go on, but it is not worth it to spend 9
the day on these matters, so that I have time to get to other
ones. (*To a servant of the court:*) In the meantime read out
these few terms I mention as translated into Latin. (*The
servant reads out the Latin translations.*)

39. Well then, do you think a philosopher, not one unlettered and ignorant like a shameless Cynic, but one who
remembers that he follows Plato—do you think it a disgrace for him to know these things or not, to neglect them
or to study them, to know how much of the design of
Providence is visible even in these things, or instead to
believe what his father and mother tell him about the immortal gods? Quintus Ennius wrote a poem called *Delica-* 2
cies, in which he lists innumerable kinds of fish, which he
had no doubt studied carefully. I remember a few lines,
and will quote them:[87]

How the turbot from Clupea beats them all! 3
There are mussels at Aenus, prickly oysters aplenty at
    Abydus.
There's the scallop at Mytilene and at Charadrus in
    Ambracia.

Brundisii sargus bonus est; hunc, magnus si erit,
   sume.
Apriculum piscem scito primum esse Tarenti.
Surrenti elopem fac emas glaucumque aput Cumas.
Quid scarum praeterii cerebrum Iovis paene supremi
(Nestoris ad patriam hic capitur magnusque bonus-
   que),
melanurum, turdum, merulamque umbramque
   marinam?
Polypus Corcyrae, calvaria pinguia acharnae.

4   Alios etiam multos[43] versibus decoravit, et ubi gentium
quisque eorum, qualiter assus aut iurulentus optime sa-
piat, nec tamen ab eruditis reprehenditur; ne ego repre-
hendar, qui res paucissimis cognitas Graece et Latine pro-
priis et elegantibus vocabulis conscribo.

40. Cum hoc satis dixi, tum aliud accipe. Quid enim
tandem, si medicinae neque instudiosus neque imperitus
2   quaepiam remedia ex piscibus quaero? Ut sane sunt plurima cum in aliis omnibus rebus eodem naturae munere
interspersa atque interseminata, tum etiam nonnulla in
3   piscibus. An remedia nosse et ea conquirere magi potius
esse quam medici, quam denique philosophi putas, qui
4   illis non ad quaestum, sed ad suppetias usurus est? Veteres
quidem medici etiam carmina remedia vulnerum norant,
ut omnis vetustatis certissimus auctor Homerus docet, qui
facit Ulixi de vulnere sanguinem profluentem sisti canta-
mine. Nihil enim quod salutis ferendae gratia fit, crimino-
sum est.

[43] multos *Pricaeus*: multis ω

At Brindisi the sar is good, and buy it if it's big.
The little boar fish, I tell you, is excellent at
    Tarentum.
At Surrentum be sure to buy halibut, and bluefish at
    Cumae.
Why, I forgot parrot fish, almost Lord Jupiter's brains
(in Nestor's homeland you get it big and tasty),
and small wrasse, plain wrasse, dark wrasse, maigre,
cuttlefish at Corcyra, fat brains of bass,
purple fish, pilot fish, mussels, and sweet sea urchins
    too.

Many others too he honors with his poetry, saying where 4
in the world each is, and how to bake or stew them for the
best flavor, and yet scholars do not fault him; so I am not
to be faulted either when I use correct, stylish language,
both Greek and Latin, to record facts that very few know.

40. That is enough on that subject, so let me tell you
this too. What does it matter, I ask you, if as someone not
uninterested or unskilled in medicine I go looking for certain cures from fish? In fact there many such cures in ev- 2
erything, scattered and implanted like seeds by Nature's
impartial bounty, and some of them in fish. Do you think 3
that to know and to collect cures marks someone as a
magician rather than a doctor, or indeed a philosopher, if
he is going to use them not for gain but to help others?
Why, the doctors of old knew that even spells could cure 4
wounds, as Homer, the most reliable authority of all antiquity, tells us when he makes a spell stanch the blood
from Ulysses' wound.[88] Nothing done to effect a cure is
criminal.

[88] *Od.* 19.456–58.

5   "At enim," inquit, "piscem cui rei nisi malae proscidisti,
quem tibi Themison servus attulit?" Quasi vero non paulo
prius dixerim me de particulis omnium animalium, de situ
earum deque numero deque causa conscribere ac libros
6 ἀνατομῶν Aristoteli et explorare studio et augere. Atque
adeo summe miror quod unum a me pisciculum inspec-
tum sciatis, cum iam plurimos, ubicumque locorum oblati
7 sunt, aeque inspexerim, praesertim quod nihil ego clanculo sed omnia in propatulo ago, ut quivis vel extrarius
arbiter adsistat, more hoc et instituto magistrorum meorum, qui aiunt hominem liberum et magnificum debere,
8 si quo eat, in primori fronte animum gestare. Hunc adeo
pisciculum, quem vos leporem marinum nominatis, pluri-
9 mis qui aderant ostendi. Necdum etiam decerno quid
vocem,[44] nisi quaeram sane accuratius, quod nec apud
veteres philosophos proprietatem eius piscis reperio,
quamquam sit omnium rarissima et hercule memoranda;
10 quippe solus ille, quantum sciam, cum sit cetera exossis,
duodecim numero ossa ad similitudinem talorum suillo-
11 rum in uentre eius conexa et catenata sunt. Quod Aristoteles numquam profecto omisisset scripto prodere, qui
aselli piscis solius omnium in medio alvo corculum situm
pro maximo memoravit.

    41. "Piscem," inquit, "proscidisti." Hoc quis ferat—
philosopho crimen esse, quod lanio vel coquo non fuisset?
2 "Piscem proscidisti." Quod crudum, id accusas? Si cocto

---

[44] vocem *Colvius*: vocent ω

[89] Aristotle wrote an eight-volume work *On Anatomy,* frr.
293–304 Gigon.

"Ah," he says, "but for what purpose did you dissect the   5
fish that your slave Themison brought you, if not for an
evil one?" As if indeed I did not say a while ago that my
works concern the parts of every animal, about their location, numbers, and purpose, and that I study the books of
Aristotle *On Anatomy* closely and add to them.[89] And yet   6
it really surprises me that you know I examined one little
fish, seeing that I have examined many before this just
as much, wherever they came my way. This is mainly be-   7
cause I do nothing in secret, but everything in the open,
so that any bystander, even a stranger, can be present; that
was the custom and the practice of my teachers, who say
that a man of free and lofty disposition should have his
thoughts imprinted on his forehead wherever he goes. In   8
fact, I showed this little fish that you call a "sea hare" to
many bystanders. Even to this day indeed, I cannot make   9
out what to call it, at least without more research, since I
find that not even the ancient philosophers described the
properties of this particular fish, though it is especially
rare and certainly very remarkable. For this is the only   10
fish, so far as I know, which though otherwise boneless has
twelve bones in its stomach, conjoined and interlinked so
as to resemble the knucklebones of a pig. Aristotle would   11
certainly never have failed to make a record of the fact,
considering that he records as a very notable fact that the
hake is the only fish with its heart in the middle of its
stomach.

41. "You dissected a fish," says he. Who can tolerate
that—a charge brought against a philosopher that would
never have been brought against a butcher or a cook? "You   2
dissected a fish." "It was raw," is that your accusation?

ventrem rusparer, hepatia suffoderem, ita ut apud te puerulus ille Sicinius Pudens suomet obsonio discit, eam rem
non putares accusandam; atqui maius crimen est philoso-
3 pho comesse piscis quam inspicere. An hariolis licet ioci-
nera rimari, philosopho contemplari non licebit, qui se
sciat omnium animalium haruspicem, omnium deum sa-
4 cerdotem? Hoc in me accusas, quod ego et Maximus in
Aristotele miramur? Cuius nisi libros bibliothecis exege-
ris et studiosorum manibus extorseris, accusare me non
potes. Sed de hoc paene plura quam debui.
5 Nunc praeterea vide, quam ipsi sese revincant; aiunt
mulierem magicis artibus, marinis illecebris a me petitam
eo in tempore, quo me non negabunt in Gaetuliae medi-
terraneis montibus fuisse, ubi pisces per Deucalionis dilu-
6 via repperientur. Quod ego gratulor nescire istos legisse
me Theophrasti quoque περὶ δακέτων καὶ βλητικῶν et
Nicandri θηριακά, ceterum me etiam veneficii reum pos-
7 tularent; at quidem hoc negotium ex lectione et aemula-
tione Aristoteli nactus sum, nonnihil et Platone meo ad-
hortante, qui ait eum, qui ista vestiget, ἀμεταμέλητον
παιδιὰν ἐν βίῳ παίζειν.
42. Nunc quoniam pisces horum satis patuerunt, accipe aliud pari quidem stultitia, sed multo tanta vanius et
2 nequius excogitatum. Scierunt et ipsi argumentum pisca-
rium futile et nihil futurum, praeterea novitatem eius ri-

---

90 That is, skeletons left over from the flooding of the earth in
the time of Deucalion, the Greek equivalent of Noah.
91 A loose quotation of Pl. *Ti.* 59D.

Suppose I had scraped out the stomach from a cooked fish and dug into the liver, as that boy Sicinius Pudens is learning to do when he banquets with you: you would not think of making a charge of that, and yet for a philosopher it is a worse crime to eat fish than to examine them. Or are soothsayers free to scrutinize livers, but a philosopher not free to study them, though knowing himself to be the mystic reader of every creature, the priest of every god? Do you accuse me of an activity for which Maximus and I admire Aristotle? You cannot accuse *me* without removing *his* books from the libraries and wrenching them from the hands of scholars. But I have almost said more on the topic than I should.

Furthermore, just see how *they* contradict themselves. According to them, I used magical arts and marine charms to seduce a woman, though just then, as they will fully admit, I was among the mountains of inner Gaetulia, where you find fish from Deucalion's flood.[90] Well, it's lucky for me they do not know that my reading also includes Theophrastus' *On animals that bite and stun* and Nicander's *On Remedies for poisonous bites:* otherwise they would accuse me of being a poisoner too. But in fact I began this pursuit from my reading of Aristotle and my desire to surpass him; my master Plato gave me no slight encouragement too, when he says that one who examines such matters "spends his life in a game he will not regret."[91]

42. Now that these people's fish have been sufficiently laid bare, here is something else, an invention of equal stupidity but very much more flimsy and malicious. Even they knew that their fishy argument would be useless and worthless, and moreover that its oddity was absurd (for

diculam (quis enim fando audivit ad magica maleficia disquamari et exdorsari piscis solere?), potius aliquid de
3 rebus pervulgatioribus et iam creditis fingendum esse. Igitur ad praescriptum opinionis et famae confinxere puerum quempiam carmine cantatum remotis arbitris, sccrcto loco, arula et lucerna et paucis consciis testibus, ubi incan-
4 tatus sit, corruisse, postea nescientem sui excitatum, nec ultra isti quidem progredi mendacio ausi; enim fabula ut impleretur, addendum etiam illud fuit, puerum eundem
5 multa praesagio praedixisse. Quippe hoc emolumentum canticis accipimus, praesagium et divinationem, nec modo vulgi opinione, verum etiam doctorum virorum auctori-
6 tate hoc miraculum de pueris confirmatur. Memini me apud Varronem philosophum, virum accuratissime doctum atque eruditum, cum alia eiusdem modi, tum hoc etiam legere: Trallibus de eventu Mithridatici belli magica percontatione consultantibus puerum in aqua simulacrum Mercuri contemplantem quae futura erant CLX versibus
7 cecinisse. Itemque Fabium, cum quingentos denarium perdidisset, ad Nigidium consultum venisse; ab eo pueros carmine instinctos indicavisse, ubi locorum defossa esset crumina cum parte eorum, ceteri ut forent distributi;
8 unum etiam denarium ex eo numero habere M. Catonem philosophum, quem se a pedisequo in stipe Apollinis accepisse Cato confessus est.

---

92 M. Terentius Varro is the polymath and prolific author of the first century BC. Tralles in Caria (Asia Minor) resisted Mithradates VI of Pergamum in the First Mithridatic War (89–85 BC).

93 P. Nigidius Figulus, reputed to be second only to Varro for

whoever heard that scaling and filleting a fish was customary in malevolent magic?), and that they needed to fabri-
cate something else out of things more commonly said and
already believed. So to conform with belief and rumor,   3
they alleged that I had used a spell to bewitch some boy,
once I had gotten observers out of the way, in a secret
place, with a small altar, a lantern and a few accomplices
looking on; on being bewitched he collapsed, and when he
came round later he did not know where he was. But *they*   4
indeed did not dare to carry their lie further; to complete the drama they should have added that the same boy
prophesied and made many predictions. For we are told   5
that foresight and divination are the reward of spells, and
not only popular belief but the authority of notable scholars too attest to this miraculous power in young boys. I   6
recall having read various things of the same kind in the
philosopher Varro, a man of the most exact scholarship
and erudition; one of them was that when the people of
Tralles used magic to inquire about the outcome of the
Mithridatic war, a boy gazing at a reflection of Mercury
in water gave a prophecy of the future in a hundred and
sixty lines of poetry.[92] Similarly, after losing five hundred   7
denarii Fabius came to consult Nigidius, who bewitched
some boys by means of a spell, and they revealed just
where there was a buried purse with some of the money,
and how the rest had been divided up; moreover, the phi-   8
losopher Marcus Cato had one denarius out of the total,
which he admitted that an attendant had given him during
a collection for Apollo.[93]

his learning, was said to engage in magic; Fabius is unknown; M.
Cato is the Younger Cato, Stoic and opponent of Julius Caesar.

109

43. Haec et alia apud plerosque de magis et pueris lego equidem, sed dubius sententiae sum, dicamne fieri posse
2 an negem, quamquam Platoni credam inter deos atque homines natura et loco medias quasdam divorum potestates intersitas, easque divinationes cunctas et magorum
3 miracula gubernare. Quin et illud mecum reputo: posse animum humanum, praesertim puerilem et simplicem, seu carminum avocamento sive odorum delenimento soporari et ad oblivionem praesentium exsternari et paulisper remota corporis memoria redigi ac redire ad naturam suam, quae est immortalis scilicet et divina, atque ita velut quodam sopore futura rerum praesagare.

4 Verum enimvero, utut[45] ista sese habent, si qua fides hisce rebus impertienda est, debet ille nescio qui puer providus, quantum ego audio, et corpore decorus atque
5 integer deligi et animo sollers et ore facundus, ut in eo aut divina potestas quasi bonis aedibus digne diversetur, si tamen ea pueri corpore includitur, an ipse animus expergitus cito ad divinationem suam redigatur, quae ei prompte insita et nulla oblivione saucia et hebes facile resumatur.
6 Non enim ex omni ligno, ut Pythagoras dicebat, debet Mercurius exsculpi.

7 Quod si ita est, nominate, quis ille fuerit puer sanus, incolumis, ingeniosus, decorus, quem ego carmine dignatus sim initiare. Ceterum Thallus, quem nominastis, me-
9 dico potius quam mago indiget; est enim miser morbo

---

45 utut *Colvius*: ut ω

94 Pl. *Symp.* 202E–3A; Apuleius himself discusses this theory in *De Deo Socratis* 6.

43. Though I certainly read this and other things like it in many authors, I hesitate whether to call them possible or not; though I do believe Plato's doctrine that certain 2 heavenly powers are situated by their nature and position halfway between gods and humans, and that they control all forms of divination and wonders of magic.[94] I also re- 3 flect on the fact that the human soul, especially when young and innocent, can be lulled to sleep either by seductive spells or by soothing odors, and can thus be distracted into forgetting the present; then, in a brief suspension of its physical memory, it reverts and returns to its true nature, which of course is immortal and divine, and thus foretells future events in a kind of trance.

Yet at the same time, whether this is true or not, if these 4 stories deserve any credence this supposed boy must, so I hear, be chosen for his beautiful and unblemished body, acute intelligence and eloquent speech, so that either the 5 divine power can have a sort of suitable home in which to lodge decently, if indeed it is enclosed within the boy's body, or so that the soul itself once aroused can quickly be restored to its predictive power, which must enter readily and be easily recovered, not diminished or dulled by forgetfulness. For as Pythagoras said, not every kind of wood 6 is right for carving a Mercury.[95]

If all this is true, kindly give us the name of this boy, 7 healthy, whole, intelligent, handsome, whom I thought saw fit to enchant with a spell. But you named Thallus, 8 who needs a doctor rather than a magician, for the poor 9 boy is so racked by epilepsy that he often needs no spells

[95] Iambl. *VP* 245 attributes a similar saying to the Pythagoreans in general.

comitiali ita confectus, ut ter an quater die saepe numero
sine ullis cantaminibus corruat omniaque membra conflic-
tationibus debilitet, facie ulcerosus, fronte et occipitio
conquassatus, oculis hebes, naribus hiulcus, pedibus ca-
10   ducus. Maximus omnium magus est, quo praesente Thallus diu steterit: ita plerumque morbo ceu somno vergens
inclinatur.

44. Eum tamen vos carminibus meis subversum dixis-
2   tis, quod forte me coram semel decidit. Conservi eius plerique adsunt, quos exhiberi denuntiastis. Possunt dicere
omnes quid in Thallo despuant, cur nemo audeat cum eo
3   ex eodem catino cenare, eodem poculo bibere. Et quid
ego de servis? Vos ipsi videtis. Negate Thallum multo
prius quam ego Oeam venirem corruere eo morbo soli-
4   tum, medicis saepe numero ostensum, negent hoc conservi
eius, qui sunt in ministerio vestro; omnium rerum con-
victum me fatebor, ⟨nisi⟩[46] rus adeo iam[47] diu ablegatus
est in longinquos agros, ne familiam contaminaret, quod
5   ita factum nec ab illis negari potest; eo nec potuit hodie a
nobis exhiberi. Nam ut omnis ista accusatio temeraria et
repentina fuit, nudius tertius nobis Aemilianus denuntia-
vit, ut servos numero quindecim apud te exhiberemus.
6   Adsunt XIIII, qui in oppido erant. Thallus solus, ut dixi,
quod ferme ad centesimum lapidem longe ex oculis[48] est,
is Thallus solus abest, sed misimus qui eum curriculo ad-
7   vehat. Interroga, Maxime, XIIII servos quos exhibemus,
Thallus puer ubi sit et quam salve agat, interroga servos
accusatorum meorum. Non negabunt turpissimum puerum, corpore putri et morbido, caducum, barbarum, rus-

[46] nisi *add. u*   [47] rus adeo iam *ignotus in* φ: rusa de
omnium ω   [48] ex oculis *u*: exoleis ω

to collapse three or four times a day, exhausts his whole
frame with his spasms, has sores on his face, bruises on his
head in front and behind, shortsighted eyes, flaring nostrils and unsteady feet. A man is a magician without equal 10
if Thallus can stand for long in his presence, so often does
his disease make him sway like one half asleep.

44. He is the one, however, whom according to you I
prostrated with my spells, just because he once happened
to fall over in my presence. Most of his fellow slaves are 2
here, since you demanded that I produce them. All of
them can say what it is about Thallus they detest, why
none of them dares to eat with him from the same dish or
drink from the same cup. But why mention slaves? You 3
can see for yourselves. Deny that Thallus habitually collapsed from that same disease long before I came to Oea,
and was many times shown to doctors, let his fellow slaves 4
who are in your service deny it, and I will admit to being
refuted on all counts, except that I sent him quite recently to an estate far away to save the servants from infec-
tion, as even my accusers cannot deny to be true; hence I 5
could not produce him even today. For just as the whole
prosecution has been hasty and improvised, so it was also
only the day before yesterday when Aemilianus requested
that I should produce no less than fifteen slaves in your
court. Fourteen who were in town are present; only Thal- 6
lus, as I said, having indeed been packed off almost a
hundred miles away in the country, only Thallus is not
here, though I have sent someone to bring him by carriage. Ask the fourteen slaves I have produced, Maximus, 7
where the boy Thallus is and how well he is doing, ask my
accusers' slaves, and they will not deny that the boy is very
ugly, wasted and diseased in body, an epileptic, inartic-

8 ticanum. Bellum vero puerum elegistis, quem quis sacrificio adhibeat, cuius caput contingat, quem puro pallio
9 amiciat, a quo responsum speret. Vellem hercle adesset:
tibi eum, Aemiliane, permisissem, ut teneres ipse, ut[49]
interrogares. Iam in media quaestione hic ibidem pro tribunali oculos trucis in te invertisset, faciem tuam spuma-
bundus conspuisset, manus contraxisset, caput succussis-
set, postremo in sinu tuo corruisset.

45. XIIII servos quos postulasti exhibeo. Cur illis ad
quaestionem nihil uteris? Unum puerum atque eum caducum requiris, quem olim abesse pariter mecum scis. Quae
alia est evidentior calumnia? XIIII servi petitu tuo adsunt,
2 eos dissimulas; unus puerulus abest, eum insimulas. Postremo quid vis? Puta Thallum adesse: vis probare eum
praesente me concidisse? Ultro confiteor. Carmine id factum dicis? Hoc puer nescit, ego non factum revinco, nam
3 caducum esse puerum nec tu audebis negare. Cur ergo
carmini potius quam morbo attribuatur eius ruina? An
evenire non potuit ut forte praesente me idem pateretur,
4 quod saepe alias multis praesentibus? Quod si magnum
putarem caducum deicere, quid opus carmine fuit, cum
incensus gagates lapis, ut apud physicos lego, pulchre et
facile hunc morbum exploret, cuius odore etiam in vena-
liciis vulgo sanitatem aut morbum venalium experiantur?
5 Etiam orbis a figulo circumactus non difficile eiusdem
valetudinis hominem vertigine sui corripit, ita spectacu-

---

[49] ut teneres ipse, ut *u*: et tenerem si ω

ulate yokel. A fine boy indeed you have chosen for some- 8
one to use for sacrifice, to touch on the head, to dress in a
white cloak, to expect an oracle from. I really wish he were 9
here; I would have given him over to you, Aemilianus, to
hold and to interrogate for yourself. In the very middle of
the examination, here before the very judgment seat, he
would have turned wild eyes on you, spattered your face
with froth, clenched his fists, shaken his head, and finally
collapsed in your arms.

45. I have produced the fourteen slaves you asked for.
Why don't you use *them* at all for questioning? You demand a single slave, an epileptic too, when you know as
well as I do about his long absence. How can a malicious
charge be more obvious? Fourteen slaves are here as you
requested, and you ignore them: one mere boy is not here,
and you implicate him. What is it you want at last? Sup- 2
pose Thallus was here, do you want to prove that he collapsed in my presence? I freely admit it. Do you say it
happened because of a spell? The boy doesn't know that,
and I assert it did not happen, for even you will not dare
to deny that the boy was epileptic. Why then is his collapse 3
to be ascribed to a spell rather than to disease? Could it
not happen by coincidence that I was there when he had
the same fit as often elsewhere with many people present?
But if I thought it important to prostrate an epileptic, why 4
did I need a spell? For when jet-stone is heated, according
to scientists I have read, it detects this disease excellently
and easily. In the slave markets too they use its smell to
test whether a slave on sale is healthy or diseased. Even a 5
wheel turned by a potter can easily hypnotize someone
with that disease just by turning, so much does the sight

lum rotationis eius animum saucium debilitat. Ac multo
plus ad caducos consternendos figulus valet quam magus.

6   Tu frustra postulasti, ut servos exhiberem; ego non de
nihilo postulo ut nomines, quinam testes huic piaculari
sacro adfuerint, cum ego ruentem Thallum impellerem.

7   Unum omnino nominas puerulum illum Sicinium Pudentem, cuius me nomine accusas; is enim adfuisse se dicit.
Cuius pueritia etsi nihil ad religionem refragaretur, tamen

8   accusatio fidem deroget. Facilius fuit, Aemiliane, ac multo
gravius, tete ut ipsum diceres interfuisse et ex eo sacro
coepisse dementire potius quam totum negotium quasi
ludicrum pueris donares. Puer cecidit, puer vidit; num
etiam puer aliqui incantavit?

    46. Hic satis veteratorie Tannonius Pudens, cum hoc
quoque mendacium frigere ac prope iam omnium vultu et
murmure explosum videret, ut vel suspiciones quorundam
spe moraretur, ait pueros alios producturum qui sint aeque a me incantati, atque ita ad aliam speciem argumenti

2   transgressus est. Quod quamquam dissimulare potui, tamen ut omnia, ita hoc quoque ultro provoco; cupio enim
produci eos pueros, quos spe libertatis audio confirmatos
ad mentiendum. Sed nihil amplius dico: ut producantur.

3   Postulo igitur et flagito, Tannoni Pudens, ut expleas quod
es pollicitus. Cedo pueros istos, quibus confiditis: produc,
nomina qui sint: mea aqua licet ad hoc utare. Dic, inquam,

4   Tannoni. Quid taces, quid cunctaris, quid respectas? Quod

---

96 Literally, "did not militate against his religious scruple."

of its rotation overpower his weakened senses. Yes, a potter is much better than a magician at making epileptics collapse.

You had no good reason to ask me to produce my slaves; 6
but I have every reason to expect you to name the witnesses present at this rite of expiation, when I pushed Thallus as he was falling. You name none at all except that 7
boy Sicinius Pudens, in whose name you are accusing me, since he claims to have been there. Even if his youth did not diminish the sanctity of his oath,[96] still his being an accuser weakens his credit. It would have been easier, Ae- 8
milianus, and much more damning if you claimed to have been there yourself and had begun to lose your mind after that ceremony, rather than entrusting the whole business to young boys like a toy. A boy collapsed, a boy looked on: was it some boy who cast the spell too?

46. At this point, Tannonius Pudens was very cunning. He saw from the expressions and murmurs of almost everyone that this lie too had failed and fallen flat. So, perhaps to feed some people's suspicions with false hopes, he said he would produce other slaves whom I had similarly entranced, and in this way he crossed into another line of argument. Though I might have paid it no attention, I ac- 2
tually challenge it as I do all these charges. For I want those slaves exhibited, though I hear that they have been encouraged to lie by the prospect of getting their freedom. But I say no more: let them exhibit them. I insist and 3
I demand, therefore, Tannonius Pudens, that you keep your promise. Let us have those slaves you are relying on: let us hear who they are by name. You can use my time for the purpose. I say again, speak up, Tannonius. Why do 4
you not speak, why hesitate, why look around? Well, if *he*

117

si hic nescit quid didicerit aut nomina oblitus est, at tu,
Aemiliane, cede huc, dic quid advocato tuo mandaveris,
5 exhibe pueros. Quid expalluisti? Quid taces? Hocine accusare est, hocine tandem[50] crimen deferre, an Claudium
Maximum, tantum virum, ludibrio habere, me calumnia
6 insectari? Quod si forte patronus tuus verbo prolapsus est
et nullos pueros habes quos producas, saltem XIIII servis
quos exhibui ad aliquid utere.

47. Aut cur sisti postulabas tantam familiam? Magiae
accusans de XV servis denuntiasti: quid, si de vi accusares,
2 quot tandem servos postulares? Sciunt ergo aliquid XV
servi et occultum est? An occultum non est et magicum
est? Alterum horum fatearis necesse est: aut inlicitum non
fuisse in quo tot conscios non timuerim, aut si inlicitum
3 fuit, scire tot conscios non debuisse. Magia ista, quantum
ego audio, res est legibus delegata, iam inde antiquitus XII
tabulis propter incredundas frugum inlecebras interdicta,
igitur et occulta non minus quam taetra et horribilis, plerumque noctibus vigilata et tenebris abstrusa et arbitris
4 solitaria et carminibus murmurata, cui non modo servo-
5 rum, verum etiam liberorum pauci adhibentur. Et tu XV
servos vis interfuisse? Nuptiaene illae fuerunt an aliud
celebratum officium an convivium tempestivum? XV servi
sacrum magicum participant quasi XV viri sacris faciundis

[50] tandem *Owen*: tantum *ω*

97 The Twelve Tables were a set of statutes compiled in 451
and 450 in response to popular pressure. This measure against
luring crops by magic into another's fields is mentioned in several
sources (*ROL* 3.478–81).

does not know his instructions or has forgotten the names, then you, Aemilianus, come forward, say what orders you gave to your lawyer, produce the slaves. Why have you 5 blenched? Why fall silent? Is this what it means to prosecute? Is this after all what it means to bring a charge? Or does it mean making a fool of a man like Claudius Maximus and heaping false accusations on me? But if your 6 lawyer perhaps made a verbal slip and you have no slaves to produce, at least make some use of the fourteen slaves I have produced.

47. Otherwise, why did you demand that I produce so large a group of slaves? For a charge of magic you had fifteen slaves summoned: why, supposing you were charging me with violence, however many slaves would you be requesting? So is there something fifteen slaves know, and 2 yet it is a secret? Or it is not a secret, and yet involves magic? One of these two alternatives you will have to admit: either it was nothing illegal, since I was not afraid to have so many accessories to it, or it was illegal, in which case so many accessories should not have known about it. Your magic, so I am told, is something that we leave to the 3 law. Even in antiquity, the Twelve Tables forbade it because of the incredible practice of charming away crops.[97] Hence it is not only something secret but something sinister and horrible, usually practiced at night, buried in darkness, screened from witnesses, muttered in spells, and few free men are involved in it, let alone slaves. 4 And yet you say that fifteen slaves were there? Was that a 5 wedding or some other crowded function, or an elaborate banquet? Do fifteen slaves participate in a magical ceremony as if they were the Board of Fifteen for the Perfor-

6 creati? Cui tamen rei tot numero adhibuissem, si conscientiae nimis multi sunt? XV liberi homines populus est,
7 totidem servi familia, totidem vincti ergastulum. An adiu-
torio multitudo eorum necessaria fuit, qui diutine hostias
lustralis tenerent? At nullas hostias nisi gallinas nominastis. An ut grana turis numerarent, an ut Thallum proster-
nerent?

48. Mulierem etiam liberam perductam ad me domum
dixistis eiusdem ⟨ac⟩[51] Thalli valetudinis, quam ego pollicitus sim curaturum, eam quoque a me incantatam cor-
2 ruisse. Ut video, vos palaestritam, non magum accusatum
3 venistis: ita omnis qui me accessere dicitis cecidisse. Negavit tamen quaerente te, Maxime, Themison medicus, a
quo mulier ad inspiciendum perducta est, quicquam ultra
passam nisi quaesisse me, ecquid illi aures obtinnirent et
4 utra earum magis; ubi responderit dexteram sibi aurem
nimis inquietam, confestim discessisse.

5 Hic ego, Maxime, quamquam sedulo impraesentiarum
a laudibus tuis tempero, necubi tibi ob causam istam videar blanditus, tamen sollertiam tuam in percontando ne-
6 queo quin laudem. Dudum enim, cum haec agitarentur et
illi incantatam mulierem dicerent, medicus qui adfuerat
abnueret, quaesisti tu nimis quam prudenter, quod mihi
7 emolumentum fuerit incantandi. Responderunt: "Ut mulier rueret." "Quid deinde? Mortua est?" inquis. Negarunt.
"Quid ergo dicitis? Quod Apulei commodum, si ruisset?"

[51] ac *add. Butler*

---

[98] The Fifteen Men for the Performance of Rites was one of
the four major colleges of the Roman priesthood.

[99] Hens were particularly used for sacrifices to the dead.

120

mance of Sacrifice?[98] But for what purpose would I have   6
involved so many people, if they are too many to be accessories? Fifteen free men are a crowd, fifteen slaves a
household, fifteen convicts a chain gang. Or did I need a   7
swarm of them as helpers, to restrain the sacrificial victims
for a long time? But the only victims you mentioned were
hens.[99] Were they meant to count the grains of incense, or
to knock Thallus down?

48. Moreover, you said that a woman of free birth was
brought to my home having the same illness as Thallus, I
promised to cure her, and I bewitched her so that she too
collapsed. I see: it's a wrestler, not a magician, you have   2
come to accuse, since you say everyone who came to me
fell over. And yet, Maximus, when you questioned Themi-   3
son the doctor, who brought the woman for me to examine, he said that nothing happened to her except that I
asked whether if she had ringing in her ears and in which
ear more: after replying that her right ear was very trou-   4
blesome, she immediately left.

On this point, Maximus, though for the moment I   5
am taking great care to restrain my praises of you, since
I do not wish to give the impression of having flattered
you because of this trial, yet I cannot help praising your
skill as an interrogator. Some while ago, when these mat-   6
ters were under discussion and those people said that
I had bewitched the woman, while the doctor in at-
tendance denied it, you asked with extraordinary shrewdness what I had to gain from bewitching her. They replied: 7
"To make the woman fall down." "So what?" you said;
"Is she dead?" "No," they said. "What are you saying then?
What would Apuleius have gained if she had fallen?"

121

8 Ita enim pulchre ac perseveranter tertio quaesisti, ut qui
scires omnium factorum rationes diligentius examinandas
ac saepius causas quaeri, facta concedi, eoque etiam patronos litigatorum causidicos nominari, quod cur quaeque
9 facta sint expediant. Ceterum negare factum facilis res est
et nullo patrono indiget; recte factum vel perperam do-
cere, id vero multo arduum et difficile est. Frustra igitur
an factum sit anquiritur, quod nullam malam causam ha-
10 buit ut fieret. Ita facti reus apud bonum iudicem scrupulo
quaestionis liberatur, si nulla fuit ei ratio peccandi.

11 Nunc quoniam neque incantatam neque prostratam
mulierem probaverunt et ego non nego petitu medici a me
inspectam, dicam tibi, Maxime, cur illud de aurium tinnitu
12 quaesierim, non tam purgandi mei gratia in ea re, quam
tu iam praeiudicasti neque culpae neque crimini confi-
nem, quam ut ne quid dignum auribus tuis et doctrinae
13 tuae congruens reticuerim. Dicam igitur quam brevissime
potuero; etenim admonendus es mihi, non docendus.

49. Plato philosophus in illo praeclarissimo Timaeo
caelesti quadam facundia universum mundum molitur.[52]
2 Igitur postquam de nostri quoque animi trinis potestatibus sollertissime disseruit, et cur quaeque membra nobis
divina providentia fabricata sint aptissime docuit, causam
3 morborum omnium trifariam percenset. Primam causam

---

[52] molitur *Rossbach, Berl. Philol. Wochenschr. 1897*: moli-
tus ω

---

[100] The first part of the compound *causidicus* (advocate) in
fact derives from *causa*, not in the sense of "cause" but of "legal
case."   [101] The following is a condensation of *Ti.* 81E–86A.

For in this way, elegantly and persistently, you asked them 8
three questions, knowing as you do that the motives of
every action require careful scrutiny, that very often examination of motives leads to admission of facts, and
moreover that lawyers on behalf of litigants are called "advocates" because they explain why any particular thing was
done.[100] Yet to deny that something was done is an easy 9
step, requiring no advocate: proving that what was done
was right or wrong—that is what is really onerous and difficult. It is therefore pointless to inquire if something was
done if there was no sinister reason for doing it. Hence 10
someone accused of an act before an upright judge is free
from concern about being cross-examined if he had no
motive to commit wrong.

Well then, since they have not proved that I either 11
bewitched the woman or caused her to fall over, and I do
not deny having examined her at her doctor's request, I
will tell you, Maximus, why I asked that question about the
ringing in her ears. It is not that I want to clear myself, 12
since you have already judged the matter not to border on
blame or crime: no, I do not want to pass over anything
that is worth your hearing and consistent with your erudition. So I will speak as briefly as I can, my task being to 13
remind you, not to teach you.

49. In that sublime *Timaeus* of his, the philosopher
Plato uses a sort of divine eloquence to construct the entire universe.[101] Well, after also discoursing in great detail 2
about the three faculties of our souls, and persuasively
showing how each part of us is constructed by divine providence, he reviews the causes of all disease under three
headings. The first cause he attributes to the basic com- 3

primordiis corporis adtribuit, si ipsae elementorum quali-
tates, uvida et frigida, et his duae adversae non congruent;
id adeo evenit, cum quaepiam earum modo excessit aut
4 loco demigravit. Sequens causa morborum inest in eorum
vitio, quae iam concreta ex simplicibus elementis una tamen specie coaluerunt, ut est sanguinis species et visceris
et ossi et medullae, porro illa quae ex hisce singularibus
5 mixta sunt. Tertio in corpore concrementa varii fellis et
turbidi spiritus et pinguis humoris novissima aegritudi-
num incitamenta sunt.

50. Quorum e numero praecipuast materia morbi comitialis, de quo dicere exorsus sum, cum caro in humorem
crassum et spumidum inimico igni conliquescit et, spiritu
indidem parto, ex candore compressi aeris albida et tu-
2 mida tabes fluit. Ea namque tabes si foras corporis prospi-
ravit, maiore dedecore quam noxa diffunditur; corporis[53]
enim primorem cutim vitiligine insignit et omnimodis
3 maculationibus convariat. Sed cui hoc usu venerit, numquam postea comitiali morbo adtemptatur; ita aegritudinem animi gravissimam levi turpitudine corporis compen-
4 sat. Enimvero si perniciosa illa dulcedo intus cohibita et
bili atrae sociata venis omnibus furens pervasit, dein ad
summum caput viam molita dirum fluxum cerebro immiscuit, ilico regalem partem animi debilitat, quae ratione
pollens verticem hominis velut arcem et regiam insedit.
5 Eius quippe divinas vias et sapientis meatus obruit et ob-
turbat; quod facit minore pernicie per soporem, cum potu
et cibo plenos comitialis morbi praenuntia strangulatione

---

[53] corporis *Casaubon*: pectoris ω

ponents of the body, when the actual quality of these elements, wet and cold, and their two opposites, are out of balance; now this happens when any one of them exceeds its due amount or leaves its proper place. The next cause 4 of illness lies in a defect of those substances that, when once they are combined out of their primary elements, coalesce into a single substance, that of blood, flesh, bone, or marrow for example, and furthermore into those substances that combine these separate ones. Thirdly, the 5 combination of various kinds of gall, turbulent gas and viscous humor constitute the last precipitators of illness.

50. Of all these the chief source of epilepsy, with which I began, is when flesh is dissolved by a malignant heat into a thick, frothy moisture; this produces a gas, and this vapor, condensed into a white substance, produces a pale and foamy discharge. Now if that discharge finds its way 2 to the surface of the body, it disperses, inflicting shame rather than harm on the patient, since it marks his outer skin with blisters and covers it with a variety of blotches. But once this has happened to someone, he is never again 3 attacked by epilepsy, and so gets a slight disfigurement of the body in exchange for a very grave disease of the mind. However, if once that infectious secretion, trapped inside 4 and combined with black bile, travels feverishly through all the veins and then forces its way to the head and infuses the brain with its pestilent virus, it immediately weakens the royal part of the soul, which because it rules by reason occupies the topmost part of a man, as it would a citadel or a palace. The virus blocks and disrupts the soul's divine 5 paths and ways of wisdom. It does so with less damage during sleep, for then people who are full of food and drink feel a slight pain from tightness of breath, a symp-

6 modice angit. Sed si usque adeo aucta est, ut etiam vigilantium capiti offundatur, tum vero repentino mentis nubilo obtorpescunt et moribundo corpore, cessante animo

7 cadunt. Eum nostri non modo maiorem et comitialem, verum etiam divinum morbum, ita ut Graeci ἱερὰν νόσον, vere nuncuparunt, videlicet quod animi partem rationalem, quae longe sanctissimast, eam violet.

51. Agnoscis, Maxime, rationem Platonis quantum

2 potui pro tempore perspicue explicatam; cui ego fidem arbitratus causam divini morbi esse, cum illa pestis in caput redundavit, haudquaquam videor de nihilo percontatus, an esset mulieri illi caput grave, cervix torpens, tem-

3 pora pulsata, aures sonorae. [et][54] Ceterum, quod dexterae auris crebriores tinnitus fatebatur, signum erat morbi penitus adacti. Nam dextera corporis validiora sunt eoque minus spei ad sanitatem relinquunt, cum et ipsa aegritu-

4 dini succumbunt. Aristoteles adeo in Problematis scriptum reliquit, quibuscumque[55] caducis a dextero morbus

5 occipiat, eorum esse difficiliorem medelam. Longum est, si velim Theophrasti quoque sententiam de eodem morbo recensere, est enim etiam eius egregius liber de caducis.

6 Quibus tamen in alio libro, quem de invidentibus animalibus conscripsit, remedio esse ait exuvias stelionum, quas velut senium more ceterorum serpentium temporibus

---

54 et *del. Salmasius*
55 quibuscumque *Scipio Gentilis*: quibus aeque ω

---

102 Epilepsy was called *morbus comitialis* because an epileptic fit occurring at public assembly (*comitium*) was considered ominous and required the assembly to be terminated.

tom of epilepsy. But if it has increased so much as to flood 6
someone's brain even when awake, then his mind is suddenly dulled and he grows faint from a sudden darkening
of the intellect, his body becomes lifeless, his conscious-
ness fails, and he collapses. This our ancestors rightly 7
called not only the "greater illness" and "epilepsy," but also
the "divine illness,"[102] just as the Greeks say the "sacred
illness," evidently because the rational part of the soul, by
far the most sacred part of us, is what it attacks.

51. You recognize Plato's theory, Maximus, expounded
as clearly as I could for the occasion. Accepting on his 2
authority that the sacred illness occurs when that distem-
per has risen to the head, I do not think it was at all ir-
relevant to ask that woman if her head was heavy, her neck
slack, her temples throbbing, her ears ringing. However, 3
when she alleged that the ringing was more persistent in
her right ear, that showed that the disease was far advanced, since the right-hand parts of the body are the
stronger, and therefore hold out less hope of recovery
when they too succumb to illness. Aristotle indeed has 4
written in his *Problems* that cure is more difficult for any
epileptic in whom the illness begins on the right side.[103] It 5
would take too long if I tried to review Theophrastus'
opinion too about the same illness; he also has an excellent
study of epileptics. In a different work, though, one he 6
wrote about malevolent animals, he says that the castoff
skin of newts, which like other reptiles they slough off at
fixed times as if it were their old age, can serve as a cure;

[103] Fr. 767 (*Aristotelis Opera* 3.774); this is not in the extant
Problems, which are of disputed authenticity.

7 statutis exuant; sed nisi confestim eripias, malignone praesagio an naturali adpetentia ilico convertuntur et devo-
8 rant. Haec idcirco commemoravi nobilium philosophorum disputata, simul et libros sedulo nominavi nec ullum
ex medicis aut poetis volui attingere, ut isti desinant mirari, si philosophi suapte doctrina causas morborum et
remedia noverunt.

9 Igitur cum ad inspiciendum mulier aegra curationis
gratia ad me perducta sit atque hoc et medici confessione
qui adduxit ac mea ratiocinatione recte factum esse con-
10 veniat, aut constituant magi et malefici hominis esse mor-
bis mederi, aut, si hoc dicere non audent, fateantur se in
puero et muliere caducis vanas et prorsus caducas calumnias intendisse.

52. Immo enim, si verum velis, Aemiliane, tu potius
caducus qui iam tot calumniis cecidisti. Neque enim gravius est corpore quam corde collabi, pede potius quam
mente corruere, in cubiculo despui quam in isto splendi-
2 dissimo coetu detestari. At tu fortasse te putas sanum,
quod non domi contineris, sed insaniam tuam, quoquo te
duxerit, sequeris. Atqui contende, si vis, furorem tuum
cum Thalli furore: invenies non permultum interesse, nisi
3 quod Thallus sibi, tu etiam aliis furis. Ceterum Thallus
oculos torquet, tu veritatem; Thallus manus contrahit, tu
patronos; Thallus pavimentis illiditur, tu tribunalibus.
Postremo ille quidquid agit in aegritudine facit, ignorans

---

104 Theophr. fr. 362B (Fortenbaugh et al., eds., *Theophrastus of Eresus: Sources*, 2.156)   105 Here and in the next sentence Apuleius plays on the meanings of *cado* and *caducus* in a way that defies precise translation.   106 Another untranslatable pun, *contraho* meaning to "clasp together" and "assemble, collect."

but unless you snatch the skin promptly away, malicious 7
presentiment or natural appetite makes them promptly
turn and devour it.[104] I have mentioned these matters as 8
discussed by famous philosophers and have named their
works too, choosing not to cite any doctor or poet, so that
these people may no longer be surprised by the fact that
philosophers use their own research to learn the causes
and cures of disease.

Well then, when a sick woman had been brought to me 9
to examine in hope of a cure, and since it is established
both by the testimony of the doctor who brought her and
my own arguments that this was the proper procedure,
these people must show either that curing illnesses marks 10
a sorcerer and a dealer in evil magic, or, if they dare not
say that, they must admit that the slanderous charges they
brought concerning an epileptic boy and woman were
baseless and indeed fated to fall.[105]

52. But if you want the truth, Aemilianus, *you* are really
the one about to fall, since your many calumnies have already fallen flat. For it is no more grave to slip bodily than
mentally, for the foot to trip than the mind, to rouse abhorrence in the bedroom than disgust in this most august
assembly. Perhaps you think yourself sane because you are 2
not confined at home, but you follow wherever your insanity leads you. And yet just compare your madness, if you
will, with the madness of Thallus: you will find no great
difference between the two, except that his madness affects only himself, yours affects others too. And yet Thal- 3
lus twists his eyes, you twist the facts; Thallus clutches his
fists, you clutch at lawyers;[106] Thallus crashes onto floors,
you crash into courtrooms; finally, whatever he does he
does from illness, and his errors are due to ignorance,

4 peccat; at tu, miser, prudens et sciens delinquis, tanta vis morbi te instigat. Falsum pro vero insimulas; infectum pro facto criminaris; quem innocentem liquido scis, tamen accusas ut nocentem.

53. Quin etiam (quod praeterii) sunt quae fatearis
2 nescire, et eadem rursus, quasi scias, criminaris. Ais enim me habuisse quaedam sudariolo involuta apud lares Pontiani; ea involuta quae et cuius modi fuerint, nescisse te confiteris, neque praeterea quemquam esse qui viderit;
3 tamen illa contendis instrumenta magiae fuisse. Nemo tibi blandiatur, Aemiliane: non est in accusando versutia ac ne impudentia quidem, ne tu arbitreris. Quid igitur? Furor infelix acerbi animi et misera insania crudae senectutis.
4 His enim paene verbis cum tam gravi et perspicaci iudice egisti: "Habuit Apuleius quaepiam linteolo involuta apud lares Pontiani. Haec quoniam ignoro quae fuerint, idcirco magica fuisse contendo. Crede igitur mihi quod dico, quia
5 id dico quod nescio." O pulchra argumenta et aperte crimen revincentia! "Hoc fuit, quoniam quid fuerit ignoro." Solus repertus es, Aemiliane, qui scias etiam illa quae
6 nescis, tantum super omnis stultitia evectus es; quippe qui sollertissimi et acerrimi philosophorum ne is quidem confidendum esse aiunt quae videmus, at tu de illis quoque adfirmas, quae neque conspexisti umquam neque audisti.
7 Pontianus si viveret atque eum interrogares, quae fue-
8 rint in illo involucro, nescire se responderet. Libertus eccille, qui clavis eius loci in hodiernum habet et a vobis stat,

while your crimes, you wretch, are conscious and deliber-   4
ate, so powerful is the malady that urges you on. You allege
falsehood as if truth; you allege falsity as if fact; a man you
fully know to be innocent you accuse as if he were guilty.

53. Furthermore, as I omitted to mention, some things
by your own confession you did not know, and yet you
denounce the same things as if you did. You say I kept   2
certain objects in Pontianus' house shrine wrapped up in
a cloth; you admit that you did not know what things were
wrapped up or what their nature was, and moreover that
nobody was known to have seen them, but nonetheless
you assert they were equipment for magic. Don't let any-   3
one flatter you, Aemilianus: your accusation shows no cunning or even impudence, as you perhaps imagine. What
then does it show? The sterile ravings of a bitter heart,
the pathetic madness of a harsh old man. For these are   4
more or less the words you used when addressing so grave
and perspicacious a judge: "Apuleius kept certain things
wrapped in a cloth in Pontianus' house shrine; what they
were I do not know, and hence I insist that they were
magical. Believe what I say, therefore, since I am saying
what I do not know." Splendid arguments, such manifest   5
proofs of the charge! "It was this, though what it was I
don't know." You are the first person in history, Aemilianus, to know even what he doesn't know, so far do you
surpass everyone in your stupidity; for the most intelligent   6
and penetrating of philosophers say that we cannot trust
even what we see, but you make assertions even about
things that you have never observed and never heard.

If Pontianus were alive and you were to ask him what   7
was in that cloth, he would reply that he did not know. The   8
freedman there, who keeps the keys of that place to this

131

numquam se ait inspexisse, quamquam ipse aperiret utpote promus librorum qui illic erant conditi, paene cotidie
et clauderet, saepe nobiscum, multo saepius solus intraret,
linteum in mensa positum cerneret sine ullo sigillo, sine

9   vinculo. Quidni enim? Magicae res in eo occultabantur: eo
neglegentius adservabam, sed enim libere scrutandum et
inspiciendum si liberet, etiam auferendum temere expo-
nebam, alienae custodiae commendabam, alieno arbitrio

10 permittebam. Quid igitur impraesentiarum vis tibi credi?
Quodne Pontianus nescierit, qui individuo contubernio
mecum vixit, id te scire, quem numquam viderim nisi pro

11 tribunali? An quod libertus adsiduus, cui omnis facultas
inspiciendi fuit, quod is libertus non viderit, te qui num-

12 quam eo accesseris vidisse? Denique ut quod non vidisti,
id tale fuerit quale dicis. Atqui, stulte, si hodie illud suda-
riolum tu intercepisses, quicquid ex eo promeres, ego
magicum negarem.

     54. Tibi adeo permitto, finge quidvis, eminiscere, exco-
gita, quod possit magicum videri: tamen de eo tecum de-

2   certarem. Aut ego subiectum dicerem aut remedio acceptum aut sacro traditum aut somnio imperatum. Mille alia
sunt quibus possem more communi et vulgatissima obser-

3   vationum consuetudine vere refutare. Nunc id postulas,
ut, quod deprehensum[56] et detectum[57] tamen nihil me
apud bonum iudicem laederet, id inani suspicione incertum et incognitum condemnet.

4   Haud sciam an rursus, ut soles, dicas: "Quid ergo illud

---

56 deprehensum *u*: reprehensum ω
57 detectum *Fulvius*: detentum ω

day and is in court on your behalf, says he never looked into it, though as the custodian of the books stored there he personally opened and locked it almost daily; he often entered it with me, but more often alone, and saw the napkin placed on a table with no seal and no cord. For of 9 course—there were magical objects hidden inside it, and hence I preserved it so carelessly, so that anyone could examine, inspect or even remove it at his pleasure, I entrusted it to another to guard, I left it for another to control. So what do you want us to believe this time? That you 10 know something unknown to Pontianus, who lived inseparably with me under the same roof, while you I have never seen except in court? Or that you saw something that a 11 conscientious freedman did not see, though he had every opportunity to inspect it, while you never set foot in the place? Lastly, that something you did not see was such as 12 you say it was? You fool, even if you had filched that cloth only today, I would deny that anything you produced from it was magical.

54. Indeed, I give you leave to imagine, invent, suppose anything that might seem to be magical, and even so I would dispute what you said about it. I would say either 2 that it was a replacement, or that I had been given it as a medicine, or received it in a rite, or commanded in a dream. There are countless other charges that common practice and the most ordinary of everyday customs would allow me to refute with truth. As it is, this is something 3 that would not harm me before an upright judge, even were it detected and proved, and yet you expect it to incriminate me when it is an empty suspicion, vague and unverified.

I suppose you will say as usual, "What then was that 4

fuit, quod linteo tectum apud lares potissimum depo-
suisti?" Itane est, Aemiliane? Sic accusas, ut omnia a reo
5 percontere, nihil ipse adferas cognitum? "Quam ob rem
piscis quaeris?" "Cur aegram mulierem inspexisti?" "Quid
in sudario habuisti?" Utrum tu accusatum an interrogatum
venisti? Si accusatum, tute argue quae dicis; si interrogatum, noli praeiudicare quid fuerit, quod ideo te necesse
6 est interrogare, quia nescis. Ceterum hoc quidem pacto
omnes homines rei constituentur, si ei, qui nomen cuiuspiam detulerit, nulla necessitas sit probandi, omnis contra
facultas percontandi. Quippe omnibus sic, ut forte negotium magiae facessitur, quicquid omnino egerint obicie-
7 tur. Votum in alicuius statuae femore signasti: igitur magus
es. Aut cur signasti? Tacitas preces in templo deis allegasti:
igitur magus es. Aut quid optasti? Contra, nihil in templo
precatus es: igitur magus es. Aut cur deos non rogasti?
Similiter, si posueris donum aliquod, si sacrificaveris, si
8 verbenam sumpseris. Dies me deficiet, si omnia velim per-
sequi, quorum rationem similiter calumniator flagitabit.
Praesertim quod conditum cumque, quod obsignatum,
quod inclusum domi adservatur, id omne eodem argumento magicum dicetur aut e cella promptaria in forum
atque in iudicium proferetur.

55. Haec quanta sint et cuius modi,[58] Maxime, quantus-
que campus calumniis hoc Aemiliani tramite aperiatur,

---

[58] cuius modi *Colvius*: cuiusce modi ω

---

[107] Written requests to the gods (*vota*) were often plastered
on their statues; praying under one's breath suggested that the
prayer was for something shameful or underhand, cf. Pers. *Sat.*
2.3–16.

object wrapped in a napkin that you stored in a household shrine of all places?" Really, Aemilianus? Is that how you accuse, merely by plying the accused with questions and not producing any known fact yourself? "Why do you look 5 for fish?" "Why did you examine a sick woman?" "What did you have in the napkin?" Did you come here to accuse or to interrogate? If to accuse, prove what you say: if to interrogate, don't presume to know what your ignorance obliges you to ask. Moreover, on that principle anyone 6 at all can be set up as a defendant, if someone who has named another in a case has no compulsion to provide proof, and yet every opportunity to ask questions. For then everyone who happens to be accused of magic will have his whole past brought up against him. You have 7 put a prayer on the thigh of some statue, so you're a sorcerer, for why else did you put it there? You offered silent prayers to the gods in a temple: so you're a sorcerer, or what were you praying for?[107] On the contrary, you made no prayer in a temple, so you're a sorcerer, or why didn't you ask something of the gods? And similarly if you offered some gift, made some sacrifice, took up a sacred branch. The entire day will not be enough for me if I try to list 8 everything for which a slanderer will demand a motive in this way. In particular, anything kept at home in a storeroom, or under seal, or locked up—by the same line of argument any such thing will be called magical, or will be brought out of the storeroom into the forum and into the court.

55. The number and the nature of these charges, Maximus, the wide scope for slander Aemilianus is opening

quantique sudores innocentibus hoc uno sudariolo adfe-
2 rantur, possum equidem pluribus disputare, sed faciam
quod institui: etiam quod non necesse est confitebor et
3 interrogatus ab Aemiliano respondebo. Interrogas, Aemiliane, quid in sudario habuerim. At ego, quamquam omnino positum ullum sudarium meum in bibliotheca Pon-
4 tiani possim negare ac, ‹si›[59] maxime fuisse concedam,
5 tamen habeam dicere nihil in eo involutum fuisse (quae si
dicam, neque testimonio aliquo neque argumento revin-
car; nemo est enim qui attigerit, unus libertus, ut ais, qui
6 viderit); tamen, inquam, per me licet fuerit refertissimum.
Sic enim, si vis, arbitrare, ut olim Vlixi socii thesaurum
repperisse arbitrati sunt, cum utrem ventosissimum man-
7 ticularentur. Vin dicam, cuius modi illas res in sudario
obvolutas laribus Pontiani commendarim? Mos tibi geretur.
8   Sacrorum pleraque initia in Graecia participavi, eorum
quaedam signa et monumenta tradita mihi a sacerdotibus
sedulo conservo. Nihil insolitum, nihil incognitum dico.
Vel unius Liberi patris mystae qui adestis, scitis quid domi
conditum celetis et absque omnibus profanis tacite vene-
9 remini. At ego, ut dixi, multiiuga sacra et plurimos ritus et
varias caerimonias studio veri et officio erga deos didici.
10 Nec hoc ad tempus compono, sed abhinc ferme triennium
est, cum primis diebus quibus Oeam veneram publice disserens de Aesculapii maiestate eadem ista prae me tuli et

---

[59] si *add. H. A. Koch, Rh. Mus.* 30 *(1875), 640, item Goldbacher*

---

[108] *Od.* 10.19–55.
[109] Liber was a Roman god of vegetation identified with Dio-

by this path, the great trouble he is bringing on innocent people with this one little napkin—I could indeed say
more to discuss all this, but I will proceed as I have begun,   2
concede even what I need not, and answer Aemilianus'
questions. You ask what I kept in the napkin, Aemilianus.   3
I could indeed deny that I had put any napkin in Pontianus' book chest, and even if I were fully to concede that I   4
had, I would could well say that I had nothing wrapped in
it (and if I did say so, no testimony or argument could   5
refute me, since no one touched it and, so you claim, just
one freedman saw it); even so, I repeat, for all I care it was   6
chock full. Yes, imagine *that,* if you want, as once Ulysses'
companions imagined they had found a treasure when in
fact they were rifling through a bag full of wind.[108] Do you   7
want me to tell you what sort of things wrapped in a napkin
I entrusted to Pontianus' house shrine? I will oblige you.

I have been initiated into many mysteries in Greece,   8
and the priests entrusted me with certain symbols and
tokens of them, which I store carefully. What I say is nothing strange or secret. For instance, merely to take such
initiates of Liber Pater as are here,[109] you know what you
keep hidden at home and venerate silently, apart from all
those who are not initiated. But I, as I said, have learned   9
all kinds of observances, many rituals, and various ceremonies in my pursuit of truth and my reverence for the
gods. I am not making this up on the spot, since about   10
three years ago, within a few days of my arrival in Oea,
when speaking in public on the majesty of Asclepius, I

nysus; as Liber Pater he was one of the principal deities of Sabratha, where the trial was being held; cf. J. B. Ward-Perkins,
PECS 779–80.

11 quot sacra nossem percensui. Ea disputatio celebratissima
est, vulgo legitur, in omnibus manibus versatur, non tam
facundia mea quam mentione Aesculapii religiosis Oeen-
12 sibus commendata. Dicite aliquis, si qui forte meminit,
huius loci principium. (—) Audisne, Maxime, multos sug-
gerentis? Immo, ecce etiam liber offertur. Recitari ipsa
haec iubebo, quoniam ostendis humanissimo vultu audi-
tionem te istam non gravari. (—)

56. Etiamne cuiquam mirum videri potest, cui sit ulla
memoria religionis, hominem tot mysteriis deum con-
scium quaedam sacrorum crepundia domi adservare atque ea lineo texto involvere, quod purissimum est rebus
2 divinis velamentum? Quippe lana, segnissimi corporis ex-
crementum, pecori detracta, iam inde Orphei et Pythagorae scitis profanus vestitus est; sed enim mundissima
lini seges inter optimas fruges terra exorta non modo indutui et amictui sanctissimis Aegyptiorum sacerdotibus, sed
opertui quoque rebus sacris usurpatur.

3 Atque ego scio nonnullos et cum primis Aemilianum
4 istum facetiae sibi habere res divinas deridere. Nam, ut
audio partim Oeensium qui istum novere, nulli deo ad hoc
aevi supplicavit, nullum templum frequentavit, si fanum
aliquod praetereat, nefas habet adorandi gratia manum
5 labris admovere. Iste vero nec dis rurationis, qui eum pas-
cunt ac vestiunt, segetis ullas aut vitis aut gregis primitias
impertit; nullum in villa eius delubrum situm, nullus locus

---

110 *Flor.* 18 is the preface of a speech in honor of Asclepius,
spoken by Apuleius at Carthage.

111 Touching the hand to the lips when passing a shrine or an
altar was a customary way of showing respect to the god in question.

openly mentioned these same facts, and listed all the rites
familiar to me. That discourse of mine is very well known,   11
is widely read, is frequently in every hand, and pleases the
pious people of Oea not so much because of my eloquence
but of my mention of Asclepius.[110] Will someone who hap-   12
pens to remember it give the beginning of that passage?
(*Several people present speak up.*) Do you hear, Maximus,
the many people supplying the words? Why, look, someone has actually produced the book. I will order the actual
words to be read out, since the kindly expression on your
face shows that you have no objection to hearing them. (*A
servant of the court reads the passage.*)

56. Moreover, can it seem surprising to someone who
has any notion of religion that a man privy to so many
mysteries of the gods keeps certain ritual emblems at
home and wraps them in a cloth of linen, the purest material for veiling sacred objects? For wool, produced from   2
the most slothful of creatures, shorn from a dumb animal,
was already the dress of the profane by the laws of Orpheus and Pythagoras: while linen, that purest of plants,
one of the finest crops to spring from the earth, serves not
only to dress and clothe the most holy priests of Egypt, but
also to cover sacred objects.

And yet I know some people, especially Aemilianus   3
here, find amusement in mocking the practices of religion.
As some who know him at Oea have told me, to this day   4
he has never prayed to a god or attended a temple; if ever
he passes a shrine, he thinks it sacrilege to touch his hand
to his lips in adoration.[111] In fact this man does not even   5
share any of his crops or vines, or the firstborn of his flocks,
with the agricultural gods who feed and clothe him; he has
no shrine set up in his country house, no sacred place or

6   aut lucus consecratus. Et quid ego de luco et delubro lo-
quor? Negant vidisse se qui fuere unum saltem in finibus
7   eius aut lapidem unctum aut ramum coronatum. Igitur
agnomenta ei duo indita: "Charon," ut iam dixi, ob oris et
animi diritatem, sed alterum, quod libentius audit ob deo-
8   rum contemptum, "Mezentius." Quapropter facile intellego hasce ei tot initiorum enumerationes nugas videri, et
fors anne ob hanc divini contumaciam non inducat animum verum esse quod dixi, me sanctissime tot sacrorum
9   signa et memoracula custodire. Sed ego, quid de me
Mezentius sentiat, manum non verterim, ceteris autem
clarissima voce profiteor: si qui forte adest eorundem sol-
lemnium mihi particeps, signum dato, et audiat[60] licet
10   quae ego adservem. Nam equidem nullo umquam periculo compellar, quae reticenda accepi, haec ad profanos
enuntiare.

    57. Ut puto, Maxime, satis videor cuivis vel iniquissimo
animum explesse et, quod ad sudarium pertineat, omnem
criminis maculam detersisse, ac bono iam periculo ad testimonium illud Crassi, quod post ista quasi gravissimum
legerunt, a suspicionibus Aemiliani transcensurus.

2   Testimonium ex libello legi audisti gumiae cuiusdam et
desperati lurconis Iuni Crassi, me in eius domo nocturna
sacra cum Appio Quintiano amico meo factitasse, qui ibi
mercede deversabatur. Idque se ait Crassus, quamquam
in eo tempore vel Alexandreae fuerit, tamen taedae fumo

---

[60] audiat *u*: audias ω

---

[112] For Charon, see above, ch. 23.2; Mezentius is the paradig-
matic "despiser of the gods" of the *Aeneid* (*contemptor divum,
Aen.* 7.648).

140

grove. But why talk of grove or shrine? Those who have   6
been there say they have never seen even a single stone
smeared with oil, or single branch adorned with a garland
on his estate. Hence people have given him two nick-   7
names, "Charon," as I said earlier, because of his horrible
face and character, while the other one, which he prefers
to be called as a despiser of the gods, is "Mezentius."[112] So   8
I readily understand why my mentioning all these mysteries seems to him like nonsense, and it is perhaps this defiance of religion that makes him incapable of seeing the
truth of what I said: that I most reverently guard the symbols and tokens of so many rites. As for me, I could not   9
care less what Mezentius thinks of me, but to everyone
else I proclaim as loudly as I can: if anyone happens to be
present who has taken part in the same rites as I, let him
so indicate, and he may hear what I keep stored away. As   10
for *me,* no danger to myself could ever induce me to describe to the profane what I received as a secret.

57. In my opinion, Maximus, I think I have quite satisfied even the most unfriendly listener and, as far as the
napkin is concerned, to have wiped away every smear left
by the charge, and will now in full confidence turn from
Aemilianus' insinuations to Crassus' evidence, which they
read out last as if it were the most damning.

You heard how they read the written testimony of some   2
glutton and hopeless drunkard, Junius Crassus, to the effect that while in his house I performed nocturnal rites
together with my friend Appius Quintianus, who was stay-
ing there as a lodger. Though Crassus was actually in Alexandria at the time, nonetheless he says found this out

141

3 et avium plumis comperisse. Scilicet eum, cum Alexandreae symposia obiret—est enim Crassus iste, qui non
invitus de die in ganeas conrepat—, in illo cauponio ni-
dore pinnas de penatibus suis advectas aucupatum, fumum domus suae agnovisse patrio culmine longe exor-
4 tum. Quem si oculis vidit, ultra Vlixi uota et desideria hic
quidem est oculatus; Vlixes fumum terra sua emergentem
compluribus annis e litore prospectans frustra captavit,
Crassus in paucis quibus afuit mensibus eundem fumum
5 sine labore in taberna vinaria sedens conspexit. Sin vero
naribus nidorem domesticum praesensit, vincit idem saga-
citate odorandi canes et vulturios; cui enim cani, cui vul-
turio Alexandrini caeli quicquam abusque Oeensium fini-
6 bus oboleat? Est quidem Crassus iste summus helluo et
omnis fumi non imperitus, sed profecto pro studio bi-
bendi, quo solo censetur, facilius ad eum Alexandriam vini
aura quam fumi perveniret.

58. Intellexit hoc et ipse incredibile futurum; nam dicitur ante horam diei secundam ieiunus adhuc et abstemius
2 testimonium istud vendidisse. Igitur scripsit haec se ad
hunc modum comperisse: postquam Alexandria revenerit,
domum suam recta contendisse, qua iam Quintianus mi-
grarat; ibi in vestibulo multas avium pinnas offendisse,
praeterea parietes fuligine deformatos; quaesisse causas
ex servo suo, quem Oeae reliquerit, eumque sibi de meis
3 et Quintiani nocturnis sacris indicasse. Quam vero subtiliter compositum et verisimiliter commentum me, si quid
eius facere vellem, non domi meae potius facturum fuisse,
4 Quintianum istum, qui mihi assistit, quem ego pro amici-

---

[113] Odysseus when detained by Calypso longed to see "even
the smoke rising from his land," *Od.* 1.57–59; cf. 5.156–58.

from torch smoke and bird feathers. No doubt as he went 3
around parties in Alexandria (since this Crassus is the sort
who quite happily slips into taverns in the daytime), in that
stuffy inn he detected feathers blown from his hearth and
recognized the smoke of his house rising high over his
ancestral roof. If he saw this with his own eyes, the man 4
must have better vision than Ulysses ever prayed or longed
for;[113] Ulysses watched from the shore year after year
looking in vain for smoke rising from his homeland, yet
Crassus in the few months of his absence had no trouble
seeing the same smoke as he sat in a wine bar. But if his 5
nostrils really picked up odors from home, the man surpasses dogs and vultures in keenness of smell; for what
dog, what vulture under the Alexandrian sky could sniff
anything from somewhere so distant as the territory of
Oea? True, Crassus is an out-and-out debauchee, familiar 6
with smoke of every kind, but given his love of drink, his
only claim to notice, surely a whiff of wine rather than of
smoke would more easily have reached him in Alexandria.

58. Even *he* realized that this would be incredible, for
they say he sold that deposition before eight in the morning, while still fasting and sober. So this is how he wrote 2
that he had found all this out: on returning from Alexandria, he hurried straight home, Quintianus having already
moved out; there in the hallway he found many bird feathers, and in addition the walls besmirched with black soot;
he inquired from his own slave, whom he had left at Oea,
what the reason was, and *he* informed him about the nocturnal rites conducted by me and Quintianus. What an 3
artful concoction, what a plausible story, to suppose that
if I had wanted to do anything of the sort, I would not have
preferred to do it at home; to suppose that Quintianus 4

143

tia quae mihi cum eo artissima est proque eius egregia
eruditione et perfectissima eloquentia honoris et laudis
5 gratia nomino, hunc igitur Quintianum, si quas avis in
cena habuisset aut, quod aiunt, magiae causa interemisset,
puerum nullum habuisse, qui pinnas converreret et foras
6 abiceret, praeterea fumi tantam vim fuisse, ut parietes
atros redderet, eamque deformitatem, quoad habitavit,
7 passum in cubiculo suo Quintianum! Nihil dicis, Aemiliane, non est veri simile, nisi forte Crassus non in cubiculum reversus perrexit, sed suo more recta ad focum.

8 Unde autem servus Crassi suspicatus est noctu potissimum parietes fumigatos? An ex fumi colore? Videlicet
fumus nocturnus nigrior est eoque diurno fumo differt.
9 Cur autem ‹tam›[61] suspicax servus ac tam diligens passus
est Quintianum migrare prius quam mundam domum
redderet? Cur illae plumae quasi plumbeae tam diu ad-
10 ventum Crassi manserunt? Non insimulet Crassus servum
suum: ipse haec potius de fuligine et pinnis mentitus est,
dum non potest nec in testimonio dando discedere longius
a culina.

59. Cur autem testimonium ex libello legistis? Crassus
ipse ubi gentium est? An Alexandriam taedio domus re-
meavit? An parietes suos detergit? An, quod verius est, ex
2 crapula helluo attemptatur? Nam equidem hic Sabratae
eum hesterna die animadverti satis notabiliter in medio
foro tibi, Aemiliane, obructantem. Quaere a nomenclato-

[61] tam *addidi*

here, who is supporting me, whom I mention with honor and praise because of the close friendship that binds us and of his exceptional erudition and polished eloquence—well, that if Quintianus here had had any birds 5 for dinner or, as they allege, had killed them for magical purposes, he would not have had a slave to sweep up the feathers and throw them out; and moreover that there was 6 such a cloud of smoke as to turn the walls black, and that Quintianus would have borne with that mess in his room as long as he stayed there! You're talking nonsense, Aemil- 7 ianus, it's not plausible, unless perhaps Crassus on his return went not to the room, but in his usual way straight to the stove.

And what made Crassus' slave suspect that it was par- 8 ticularly at night that the walls were covered in soot? The color of the soot? No doubt nighttime soot is darker and thus different from daytime soot. And why did so suspi- 9 cious and so careful a slave let Quintianus move out before he made the house clean again? Why did those feathers wait so long for Crassus' return, as if made of lead?[114] Crassus should not incriminate his slave: no, he himself 10 made up these lies about soot and feathers, since even in giving evidence he can't stray too far from the kitchen.

59. But why did you read the evidence from a document? Where on earth is Crassus himself? Has he got tired of home and scurried back to Alexandria? Is he washing down his walls? Or as is more likely, is the drunkard suffering from a hangover? I noticed him myself here in Sa- 2 bratha yesterday, in the middle of the forum, all too conspicuously belching in your face, Aemilianus. Question

[114] Wordplay on *pluma* (feather) and *plumbum* (lead).

ribus tuis, Maxime, quamquam est ille cauponibus quam
nomenclatoribus notior, tamen, inquam, interroga, an hic
3 Iunium Crassum Oeensem viderint; non negabunt. Ex-
hibeat nobis Aemilianus iuvenem honestissimum, cuius
testimonio nititur. Quid sit diei vides: dico Crassum iam
dudum ebrium stertere, aut secundo lavacro ad repotia
cenae obeunda vinulentum sudorem in balneo desudare.
4 Is tecum, Maxime, praesens per libellum loquitur, non
quin adeo sit alienatus omni pudore, ut etiam, sub oculis
tuis si foret, sine rubore ullo mentiretur, sed fortasse nec
tantulum potuit ebrius[62] sibi temperare, ut hanc horam
5 sobrie expectaret. Aut potius Aemilianus de consilio fecit,
6 ne eum sub tam severis oculis tuis constitueret, ne tu be-
luam illam vulsis maxillis foedo aspectu de facie impro-
bares, cum animadvertisses caput iuvenis barba et capillo
populatum, madentis oculos, cilia turgentia, rictum ‹restrictum›,[63] salivosa labia, vocem absonam, manuum tre-
7 morem, ructus popinam.[64] Patrimonium omne iam pridem abligurrivit, nec quicquam ei de bonis paternis
superest, nisi una domus ad calumniam venditandam,
quam tamen numquam carius quam in hoc testimonio
8 locavit; nam temulentum istud mendacium tribus milibus nummis Aemiliano huic vendidit, idque Oeae nemini
ignoratur.

60. Omnes hoc, antequam fieret, cognovimus, et potui

[62] ebrius *u*: ebria ω
[63] restrictum *add. Acidalius*
[64] ructus popinam *Pricaeus*: ructuspinam ω

your name slaves,[115] Maximus, though innkeepers are
more familiar with the man than name slaves are—still, I
repeat, ask them whether they saw Junius Crassus of Oea
here, and they will not deny it. Let Aemilianus show us   3
that fine young man on whose evidence he relies. You see
what time it is; I assure you, already Crassus has long been
snoring drunkenly, or is sweating wine in a bathhouse,
taking a second bath before he joins an after-dinner de-
bauch. Though here, Maximus, he addresses you through   4
a document; true, he is not so divorced from any sense of
shame as to be able to lie without a blush if he was before
your eyes, but perhaps the sot could not control himself
even a little so as to wait for this moment sober; or rather   5
Aemilianus has deliberately arranged so as not to put him
under your strict scrutiny, in case you condemned the   6
monster with his plucked chin and hideous appearance
merely by looking at him, when you observed the young
man with a head bereft of hair and beard, bleary eyes,
swollen eyelids, gaping grin, drooling lips, hoarse voice,
trembling hands, alcoholic belch. He has long since gulped   7
down all his legacy, and has none of his father's property
left other than a single house which he uses to hawk his
false testimony, which he never offered at so high a price
as with this deposition; for he sold Aemilianus here that   8
drunken lie for three thousand denarii, as everyone at Oea
knows.

60. All of us knew about this before it happened, and I
could have prevented it with a summons, except that I

[115] Literally, "name-callers" (*nomenclatores*), slaves whose
function was to recognize and to name their masters' acquaintances.

denuntiatione impedire, nisi scirem mendacium tam stultum potius Aemiliano, qui frustra redimebat, quam mihi,
qui merito contemnebam, obfuturum. Volui et Aemilianum damno adfici et Crassum testimonii sui dedecore
2 prostitui. Ceterum nudiustertius haudquaquam occulta
res acta est in Rufini cuiusdam domo, de quo mox dicam,
intercessoribus et depectoribus[65] ipso Rufino et Calpurniano. Quod eo libentius Rufinus perfecit, quod erat certus ad uxorem suam, cuius stupra sciens dissimulat, non
3 minimam partem praemii eius Crassum relaturum. Vidi te
quoque, Maxime, coitionem adversum me et coniurati-
onem eorum pro tua sapientia suspicatum, simul libellus
4 ille prolatus est, totam rem vultu aspernantem. Denique
quamquam sunt ‹in›solita[66] audacia et importuna impudentia praediti, tamen testimonium[67] Crassi, cuius ob-
oluisse faecem videbant, nec ipsi ausi sunt perlegere nec
5 quicquam eo niti. Verum ego ista propterea commemoravi, non quod pinnarum formidines et fuliginis maculam
te praesertim iudice timerem, sed ut ne impunitum Crasso
foret, quod Aemiliano, homini rustico, fumum vendidit.

61. Inde[68] etiam crimen ab illis, cum Pudentillae litteras legerent, de cuiusdam sigilli fabricatione prolatum est,
2 quod me aiunt ad magica maleficia occulta fabrica ligno
exquisitissimo comparasse et, cum sit sceleti forma turpe

65 depectoribus *Kronenberg*: deprecatoribus ω
66 ‹in›solita *Jahn*: solita ω
67 testimonium *Colvius*: testimonia ω
68 inde *Acidalius*: unde ω

116 "Feathers" and "soot" refer to Crassus' testimony (ch. 57),
but also to a hunting net with feathers attached, called a *formido*

knew that such a foolish lie would injure Aemilianus, who wasted money buying it, rather than me, who rightly despised it. I wanted Aemilianus to suffer a loss and at the same time Crassus to be pilloried for his shameful deposition. And yet the bargain was agreed two days ago quite 2 openly in the house of a certain Rufinus, whom I will discuss later, with Rufinus himself and Calpurnianus acting as intermediaries and arrangers. Rufinus was all the happier to settle it, knowing full well that his very own wife, whose adulteries he purposely overlooks, would recover no small part of the payment from Crassus. I noticed 3 that you too, Maximus, suspected their alliance and conspiracy against me, such is your sagacity, and that, the moment they produced this document, your expression showed your contempt for the whole business. In the end, 4 despite possessing unusual effrontery and tactless impudence, seeing that Crassus' evidence smelled of dregs, they neither dared to read it out themselves nor to put any reliance on it. I mention all this, not because I was afraid 5 to be trapped by feathers or smudged with soot, particularly with you as my judge, but so that Crassus would not go unpunished for blowing smoke in the eyes of that peasant, Aemilianus.[116]

61. After that, when reading out Pudentilla's letters they also brought a charge about the making of a certain statuette. So they allege, I bought it to perform harmful 2 magic; it was made in secret from the rarest wood, and though it is something hideous and dreadful in the shape

(terror). *Fumum vendere* (to sell smoke), which I have translated "to blow smoke in the eyes," was an expression for selling something of no value.

et horribile, tamen impendio colere et Graeco vocabulo
3   βασιλέα nuncupare. Nisi fallor, ordine eorum uestigia
persequor et singillatim apprehendens omnem calumniae
textum retexo.

4   Occulta fuisse fabricatio sigilli quod dicitis qui potest,
cuius vos adeo artificem non ignorastis, ut ei praesto ad-
5   esset denuntiaveritis? En adest Cornelius Saturninus arti-
fex, vir inter suos et arte laudatus et moribus comprobatus,
qui tibi, Maxime, paulo ante diligenter sciscitanti omnem
ordinem gestae rei summa cum fide et veritate percensuit:
6   me, cum apud eum multas geometricas formas e buxo
vidissem subtiliter et adfabre factas, invitatum eius artificio quaedam mechanica ut mihi elaborasset petisse, simul
et aliquod simulacrum cuiuscumque vellet dei, cui ex
more meo supplicassem, quacumque materia, dummodo
7   lignea, exculperet. Igitur primo buxeam temptasse. Interim dum ego ruri ago, Sicinium Pontianum privignum
meum, qui mihi ‹gratum›[69] factum volebat, impetratos
hebeni loculos a muliere honestissima Capitolina ad se
attulisse, ex illa potius materia rariore et durabiliore uti
faceret adhortatum; id munus cum primis mihi gratum
8   fore. Secundum ea se fecisse, proinde ut loculi suppete-
bant. Ita minutatim ex tabellis compacta crassitudine Mercuriolum expediri potuisse.

62. Haec ut dico omnia audisti. Praeterea a filio Capi-
tolinae probissimo adulescente, qui praesens est, sciscí-
tante te eadem dicta sunt: Pontianum loculos petisse,

---

[69] gratum *add. van der Vliet*

of an skeleton, still I worship it fervently and call it by a Greek name, "king." If I am not mistaken, I shall trace all 3 their steps in turn, and bit by bit unravel the whole fabric of their accusation.

You say that the statue was made in secret, but how 4 can that be? So far are you from not knowing who made it that you demanded his presence in court. Here indeed 5 is the maker, Cornelius Saturninus, a man whom his acquaintances both praise for his skill and commend for his character. You questioned him closely not long ago, Maximus, and he went through the whole history of the affair with the utmost reliability and honesty. I had seen many 6 geometrical figures in his shop, precisely and ingeniously made of boxwood. His skill was an inducement to ask him to make me certain mechanical devices, and at the same time to carve an image of any god he wished for me to worship in my usual way, using any material provided it was of wood. At first, therefore, he tried one in boxwood. 7 In the meanwhile, I was in the country when my stepson Sicinius Pontianus, who wanted to do me a kindness, begged some ebony boxes from that excellent woman Capitolina, brought them to him, and urged him to make it from that wood instead, being more rare and more durable; that would make a particularly welcome present. Saturninus followed his instructions as best he could with 8 the boxes available, and by fitting together bits and pieces of the panels, he was able to turn out a small Mercury in the round.

62. (*Addressing Maximus:*) You have heard all this just as I have said it, and moreover that excellent young man, Capitolina's son, who is here in court, said the same in answer to your interrogation; Pontianus asked for the boxes,

151

2   Pontianum Saturnino artifici detulisse. Etiam illud non
negatur, Pontianum a Saturnino perfectum sigillum rece-
3   pisse, postea mihi dono dedisse. His omnibus palam atque
aperte probatis quid omnino superest, in quo suspicio aliqua magiae delitescat? Immo quid omnino est, quod vos
4   manifesti mendacii non revincat? Occulte fabricatum esse
dixistis quod Pontianus, splendidissimus eques, fieri cura-
vit, quod Saturninus, vir gravis et probe inter suos cogni-
tus, in taberna sua sedens propalam exsculpsit, quod ornatissima matrona munere suo adiuvit, quod et futurum et
factum multi cum servorum tum amicorum qui ad me
5   ventitabant scierunt. Lignum a me toto oppido et quidem
oppido quaesitum non piguit vos commentiri, quem quidem[70] afuisse in eo tempore scitis, quem iussisse fieri
qualicumque materia probatum est.

    63. Tertium mendacium vestrum fuit macilentam, vel
omnino evisceratam formam diri cadaveris fabricatam,
2   prorsus horribilem et larvalem. Quodsi compertum habe-
batis tam evidens signum magiae, cur mihi ut exhiberem
non denuntiastis? An ut possetis in rem absentem libere
mentiri? Cuius tamen falsi facultas opportunitate quadam
3   meae consuetudinis vobis adempta est. Nam morem mihi
habeo, quoquo eam, simulacrum alicuius dei inter libellos
conditum gestare eique diebus festis ture et mero et ali-
4   quando victima supplicare. Dudum ergo cum audirem
sceletum perquam impudenti mendacio dictitari, iussi,
curriculo iret aliquis et ex hospitio meo Mercuriolum af-

---

[70] quem quidem *u*: quemquem ω

---

[117] A play on the double meaning of *oppido,* "in the town,"
and "exceedingly."

152

Pontianus brought them to the maker Saturninus. There 2
is also no dispute that Pontianus received the finished
statuette from Saturninus and gave it to me later as a present. Now that all this has been openly and clearly proved, 3
is there anything left with some hint of magic lurking in
it? Or rather is there anything at all that does not prove
you to be barefaced liars? You said that something ordered 4
by Pontianus, a most distinguished knight, was made clan-
destinely although Saturninus, a respectable man honorably known to his colleagues, carved it in full view sitting
in his workshop, although a lady of very high rank contrib-
uted a gift of her own to it, although many slaves and
friends who came to my house knew about it both before and after its creation. You shamelessly asserted that I 5
looked for the wood up and down the town,[117] though you
know I was away at the time, though it is a proven fact that
I ordered any kind of material to be used in making it.

63. Your third lie was that the finished object was an
emaciated, or rather completely skeletal image of a horrible corpse, something truly ghoulish and ghastly. But if 2
you had discovered such irrefutable proof of magic, why
did you not demand that I produce it? Was it so that you
could lie freely about something not here? But a certain
lucky habit of mine took away your chance to tell that lie.
For it is my practice to carry some god's image together 3
with my books everywhere I go, and to worship it on feast
days with incense, wine and the occasional sacrifice of an
animal. Well, when I heard a while ago that a shameless 4
lie was being repeated about a skeleton, I got someone to
run to my lodging and bring the miniature Mercury that

ferret, quem mihi Saturninus iste Oeae fabricatus est.
5 Cedo tu eum, videant, teneant, considerent. Em vobis,
quem scelestus ille sceletum nominabat. Auditisne recla-
mationem omnium qui adsunt? Auditisne mendacii vestri
damnationem? Non vos tot calumniarum tandem dispu-
6 det? Hiccine est sceletus, haeccine est larva, hoccine est
quod appellitabatis daemonium? Magicumne istud an sollemne et commune simulacrum est? Accipe quaeso, Maxime, et contemplare; bene tam puris et tam piis manibus
7 tuis traditur res consecrata. Em vide, quam facies eius
decora et suci palaestrici plena sit, quam hilaris dei vultus,
ut decenter utrimque lanugo malis deserpat, ut in capite
crispatus capillus sub imo pillei umbraculo appareat,
8 quam lepide super tempora pares pinnulae emineant,
quam autem festive circa humeros vestis substricta sit.
9 Hunc qui sceletum audet dicere, profecto ille simulacra
deorum nulla videt aut omnia neglegit. Hunc denique qui
larvam putat, ipse est larvatus.
    64. At tibi, Aemiliane, pro isto mendacio duit deus iste
superum et inferum commeator utrorumque deorum malam gratiam, semperque obvias species mortuorum, quidquid umbrarum est usquam, quidquid lemurum, quidquid
2 manium, quidquid larvarum, oculis tuis oggerat, omnia
noctium occursacula, omnia bustorum formidamina, omnia sepulchrorum terriculamenta, a quibus tamen aevo et
3 merito haud longe abes. Ceterum Platonica familia nihil
novimus nisi festum et laetum et sollemne et superum et
caeleste. Quin altitudinis studio secta ista etiam caelo ipso
sublimiora quaepiam vestigavit et in extimo mundi tergo

[118] A play on *scelestus* (villainous) and *sceletus* (skeleton).
[119] A play on *larva* (skeleton, ghost) and *larvatus* (deranged).

154

Saturninus made here in Oea. (*To a servant of the court:*)   5
You there, bring it and let them see, hold and examine it.
(*To the prosecution:*) Look at what that scoundrel called a
skeleton.[118] Don't you hear the outraged shouting of everyone present? Don't you hear them condemning your
lie? Is this a skeleton, is this a spook, is this what you kept   6
calling a demon? Is this something magical or is it an ordinary image of the usual kind? (*To Maximus:*) Take it,
please, Maximus, and look it over: it is right for innocent,
pious hands like yours to be entrusted with a hallowed
object. Just see how handsome and full of athletic bloom   7
the face is, how cheerful the god's expression, how becom-
ingly the down creeps over his cheeks, how the curly hair
on his head peeks out from under the brim of his cap, how   8
prettily the pair of feathers rises up over his temples, and
how gaily his cloak is tied around his shoulders. Surely   9
someone who dares to calls this a skeleton has either never
seen images of the gods or disregards them all. In short,
only a fool can think this one a ghoul.[119]

64. But as for you, Aemilianus, may that god, the inter-
mediary between the upper and lower worlds, repay you
for that lie with the ill will of the gods above and below;
may he ever bring dead men's forms to meet your eyes,
every shade, phantom, specter, ghost that ever was, every   2
apparition of the night, every horror of the pyre, every
terror of the graveyard, to all of which your age and just
deserts have brought you near. By contrast, we followers   3
of Plato know only what is festive, cheerful, sacred, exalted, heavenly. Yes, in its transcendental yearning this
school has studied certain matters more sublime even
than heaven itself and has stood on the very circumference

4 stitit. Scit me vera dicere Maximus, qui τὸν ὑπερουράνιον
5 τόπον et οὐρανοῦ νῶτον legit in Phaedro diligenter. Idem
Maximus optime intellegit, ut de nomine etiam vobis respondeam, quisnam sit ille non a me primo, sed a Platone
6 βασιλεύς nuncupatus: περὶ τὸν πάντων βασιλέα πάντ᾽
7 ἐστὶ καὶ ἐκείνου πάντα, quisnam sit ille basileus, totius
rerum naturae causa et ratio et origo initialis, summus
animi genitor, aeternus animantum sospitator, assiduus
mundi sui opifex, sed enim sine opera opifex, sine cura
sospitator, sine propagatione genitor, neque loco neque
tempore neque vice ulla comprehensus eoque paucis cogi-
8 tabilis, nemini effabilis. En ultro augeo magiae suspicionem: non respondeo tibi, Aemiliane, quem colam βασιλέα, quin si ipse proconsul interroget quid sit deus meus,
taceo.

65. De nomine ut impraesentiarum satis dixi. Quod
superest, nec ipse sum nescius quosdam circumstantium
cupere audire, cur non argento vel auro, sed potissimum
2 ex ligno simulacrum fieri voluerim, idque eos arbitror non
3 tam ignoscendi quam cognoscendi causa desiderare, ut
hoc etiam scrupulo liberentur, cum videant omnem suspi-
4 cionem criminis abunde confutatam. Audi igitur cui cura
cognoscere est, sed animo quantum potes erecto et at-
tento, quasi verba ipsa Platonis iam senis de novissimo
5 legum libro audituurs: Θεοῖσι δὲ ἀναθήματα χρεὼν ἔμ-
μετρα τὸν μέτριον ἄνδρα ἀνατιθέντα δωρεῖσθαι. γῆ μὲν
οὖν ἑστία τε οἰκήσεως ἱερὰ πᾶσι πάντων θεῶν· μηδεὶς
6 οὖν δευτέρως ἱερὰ καθιερούτω θεοῖς. Hoc eo prohibet, ut

---

120 Pl. *Phdr.* 247B–C.
121 Pl. *Ep.* 2.312E.
122 Pl. *Leg.* 12.955E. On the reading, see apparatus.

of the universe. Maximus knows that I speak the truth, 4
having attentively read about "the supracelestial region"
and "the heaven's back" in the *Phaedrus*.[120] And Maximus 5
also understands perfectly, just to answer your other question about the name, who that being is whom Plato, not I,
was the first to call "king"—"All is connected to the King 6
of All, and all exists because of him"[121]—exactly who that 7
"king" is, the cause, reason and prime source of all nature,
the sublime progenitor of soul, the eternal savior of living beings, the tireless craftsman of his universe, who yet
crafts without toil, preserves without anxiety, fathers without generation, limited neither by space, time, nor the
least change, and so conceivable by only a few, expressible
by none. Look, I will increase your suspicion of my magic 8
without your asking: I will not tell you, Aemilianus, what
"king" I worship; yes, were the proconsul himself to ask
about the nature of my god, my lips are sealed.

65. I have said enough about the name for the present.
Beyond that, I too am aware that certain bystanders wish
to hear why I especially wanted the statuette made of
wood, and not of silver or gold, and as I believe, they desire 2
it less to excuse than to understand it, and to be relieved 3
of this further uncertainty by seeing every suggestion of
criminality completely refuted. So anyone who cares to 4
understand may listen, but must listen with a mind as alert
and attentive as possible, since you are about to hear the
very words of the aged Plato from the last book of the
Laws: "Dedications to the gods that the moderate man 5
presents to them should be moderate. Now the earth and
the seat of habitation are sacred to all the gods in general;
therefore no one shall consecrate for a second time what
is already sacred."[122] The purpose of this prohibition is so 6

157

delubra nemo audeat privatim constituere, censet enim
satis esse civibus ad immolandas victimas templa publica.
7 Deinde subnectit: χρυσὸς δὲ καὶ ἄργυρος ἐν ἄλλαις
πόλεσιν ἰδίᾳ τε καὶ ἐν ἱεροῖς ἐστιν ἐπίφθονον κτῆμα,
ἐλέφας δὲ ἀπολελοιπότος ψυχὴν σώματος οὐκ εὐαγὲς[71]
ἀνάθημα, σίδηρος δὲ καὶ χαλκὸς πολέμων ὄργανα· ξύ-
λου δὲ μονόξυλον ὅτι ἂν ἐθέλῃ τις ἀνατιθέτω, καὶ λίθου
8 ὡσαύτως. Vt omnium assensus declaravit, Maxime quique
in consilio estis, competentissime videor usus Platone ut
vitae magistro, ita causae patrono, cuius legibus obedien-
tem me videtis.[72]

66. Nunc tempus est ad epistulas Pudentillae praeverti,
vel adeo totius rei ordinem paulo altius petere, ut omnibus
manifestissime pateat me, quem lucri cupiditate invasisse
Pudentillae domum dictitant, si ullum lucrum cogitarem,
2 fugere semper a domo ista debuisse; quin et in ceteris
causis minime prosperum matrimonium, nisi ipsa mulier
tot incommoda virtutibus suis repensaret, inimicum.
3 Neque enim ulla alia causa praeter cassam invidiam
repperiri potest, quae iudicium istud mihi et multa antea
pericula vitae conflaverit. Ceterum cur Aemilianus com-
moveretur, etsi vere magum me comperisset, qui non
modo ullo facto, sed ne tantulo quidem dicto meo laesus

[71] εὐαγές Clem. Al. Strom. 5.76.3, p. 377 Stählin; Euseb.
Praep. evang. 3.8.2, p. 125 Mras: εὐχερι ω   [72] Titulum Ego G.
CRISPVS SALVSTIVS EMENDAVI ROME FELIX. APVLEI PLATONICI
MADAVRENSIS PRO SE APVT CL. MAXIMVM PROCOS. DE MAGIA
LIB. I. EXPLICIT. INCIP. LIB. II. LEGE FELICITER praebet F

[123] Pl. Leg. 12.955 E–56A.
[124] Manuscript F here has an annotation, "I, Gaius Sallustius

that no one dare to establish private shrines, for he thinks it enough for citizens to perform animal sacrifice in public temples. He goes on to say this: "In other states gold and 7 silver, both at home and in shrines, are invidious possessions; and ivory, being taken from a body deprived of life, is not a pure dedication, while iron and bronze are instruments of war; as for wood, one may dedicate anything he wishes consisting of wood alone, and the same holds for stone."[123] As the general applause makes clear, Maximus, 8 and you who are here as his advisers, I think I have very fittingly adopted Plato as my guide in life and no less as my defender in court, and you see me obeying his laws.[124]

66. Now it is time to turn to Pudentilla's letters, or rather to trace the course of the whole business a fair way back, so that, even though they insist that I trespassed on Pudentilla's property in my desire for gain, it will be clearly evident to all that if profit had been in my mind, I ought rather to have shunned that house for ever; and further- 2 more that my marriage, far from fortunate for other reasons, would have been disadvantageous if the excellences of my wife herself had not made up for so many drawbacks.

For no reason other than baseless envy can be found 3 for concocting this lawsuit against me and the many dangers to my life that preceded it. Yet what incited Aemilianus, even if he had truly found me to be a magician, to suppose he had a just motive for revenge? I had not

Crispus, successfully corrected (this) at Rome. End of Book I of (the speech of) Apuleius, Platonist of Madauros, in his own defense before Claudius Maximus, proconsul, on (a charge of) magic. Beginning of Book II. Read it and good luck."

4   est, ut videretur se merito ultum ire? Neque autem gloriae
causa me accusat, ut M. Antonius Cn. Carbonem, C. Mucius A. Albucium, P. Sulpicius Cn. Norbanum, C. Furius

5   M. Aquilium, C. Curio Q. Metellum. Quippe homines
eruditissimi iuvenes laudis gratia primum hoc rudimentum forensis operae subibant, ut aliquo insigni iudicio
civibus suis noscerentur. Qui mos incipientibus adulescentulis ad illustrandum ingenii florem apud antiquos

6   concessus diu exolevit. Quod si nunc quoque frequens
esset, tamen ab hoc procul afuisset. Nam neque facundiae
ostentatio rudi et indocto neque gloriae cupido rustico et
barbaro neque inceptio patrociniorum capulari seni con-

7   gruisset; nisi forte Aemilianus pro sua severitate exemplum dedit et ipsis maleficiis infensus accusationem istam

8   pro morum integritate suscepit. At hoc ego Aemiliano,
non huic Afro, sed illi Africano et Numantino et praeterea
Censorio vix credidissem; ne huic frutici credam non
modo odium peccatorum sed saltem intellectum inesse.

    67. Quid igitur est? Cuivis clare dilucet[73] aliam rem
invidia nullam esse quae hunc et Herennium Rufinum,
impulsorem huius, de quo mox dicam, ceterosque inimi-
cos meos ad nectendas magiae calumnias provocarit.

2   Quinque igitur res sunt, quas me oportet disputare. Nam
si probe memini, quod ad Pudentillam attinet, haec ob-

3   iecere: una res est, quod numquam eam voluisse nubere
post priorem maritum, sed meis carminibus coactam

---

[73] clare dilucet *u*: claridilucet *ω*

---

[125] On the names in this section, see Appendix D.
[126] P. Cornelius Scipio Aemilianus "the Younger" captured
and destroyed Carthage in 146 and was censor in 142.

harmed him by the least word, let alone by any deed. For   4
it is not in order to enhance his reputation that he accuses
me, as Marcus Antonius accused Gnaeus Carbo, Gaius
Mucius Aulus Albucius, Publius Sulpicius Gnaeus Norba-
nus, Gaius Furius Manius Aquilius, Gaius Curio Quintus
Metellus.[125] Those learned young men began their ap-   5
prenticeship in forensic activity to win glory, and to get a
name among their fellow citizens for a striking legal victory. This practice, by which youthful beginners adver-
tised their budding talents, was permissible in our ancestors' time, but has become obsolete long since. But even   6
if it were still customary, it would have been quite mis-
placed in this man's case. A display of eloquence would
have not have sat well on a man inexperienced and ignorant, love of glory on a man rustic and uncouth, appren-
ticeship as a barrister on an old man next to the grave.
Unless perhaps Aemilianus, puritan that he is, has set us   7
an example, and in his hatred of crime itself has undertaken this suit to defend public morality. But I can scarcely   8
believe that Aemilianus would have done so, not this African, but the famous one, who was called Africanus, Nu-
mantinus, and Censor too:[126] still less can I believe that
this dolt has any hostility to wrongdoing, or even any idea
what it is.

67. What is it then? As anybody can clearly see, jealousy
and no other motive has prompted this man, his instigator
Herennius Rufinus, whom I will come to later, and my
other enemies to concoct these false charges of magic.
There are five things therefore that I must discuss, for if   2
my memory is correct, they made the following charges
with regard to Pudentilla. One was their assertion that she   3
never wanted to marry after losing her first husband, but

dixere; altera res est de epistulis eius, quam confessionem
magiae putant; deinde sexagesimo anno aetatis ad libidinem nupsisse, et quod in villa ac non in oppido tabulae
nuptiales sint consignatae, tertio et quarto loco obiecere;
4 novissima et eadem invidiosissima criminatio de dote fuit.
Ibi omne virus totis viribus adnixi effudere,[74] ibi maxime
angebantur, atque ita dixere me grandem dotem mox in
principio coniunctionis nostrae mulieri amanti remotis
5 arbitris in villa extorsisse. Quae omnia tam falsa, tam nihili, tam inania ostendam adeoque facile et sine ulla con-
troversia refutabo, ut medius fidius verear, Maxime quique
in consilio estis, ne submissum[75] et subornatum a me accusatorem putetis, ut invidiam meam reperta occasione pa-
6 lam restinguerem. Mihi credite, quod reapse intellegetur:
oppido quam mihi laborandum est, ne tam frivolam accusationem me potius callide excogitasse quam illos stulte
suscepisse existimetis.

68. Nunc dum ordinem rei breviter persequor et effi-
cio, ut ipse Aemilianus re cognita falso se ad invidiam
meam inductum et longe a vero aberrasse necesse habeat
confiteri, quaeso, uti adhuc fecistis vel si quo magis etiam
potestis, ipsum fontem et fundamentum iudicii huiusce
diligentissime cognoscatis.

2 Aemilia Pudentilla, quae nunc mihi uxor est, ex quodam Sicinio Amico, quicum antea nupta fuerat, Pontianum et Pudentem filios genuit eosque pupillos relictos in
potestate paterni avi—nam superstite patre Amicus de-

---

[74] effudere *u*: effundere ω
[75] submissum *Wowerius*: demissum ω

my spells forced her. A second concerns her letters, which
they think constitute an admission of magic. Next, they say
that she was sixty years old when she married to please
herself, and that the nuptial contract was signed in her
country house and not in town, these being their third and
fourth charges. Their last and also their most malicious ac-   4
cusation concerned the dowry. On this issue they spewed
all their venom at full force, this especially irked them;
hence they said that, in the first days of our marriage, I
promptly extorted a large dowry from my love-struck wife,
in a country house from which witnesses had been banished. All of this I will prove to be so false, so worthless,   5
so groundless, and so easily and so incontrovertibly will I
refute it, that by heaven, Maximus and you his advisers, I
am afraid you may think I set on and suborned the pros-
ecutor, just in order to dispel my unpopularity in public as
soon as I got the chance. Believe me, and the facts will   6
bear me out, that I must do my utmost to prevent your
supposing that so baseless an accusation was a crafty plot
of mine rather than a foolish undertaking of theirs.

68. I will now briefly set out the sequence of events,
and ensure that even Aemilianus, when the truth is known,
will be obliged to admit that he was led to dislike me by
an error, and that he has greatly mistaken the facts. I beg
you to listen carefully to the very source and foundation
of this suit just as you have hitherto, or even more so if you
can.

Aemilia Pudentilla, who is now my wife, had two sons,   2
Pontianus and Pudens, by a certain Sicinius Amicus, her
previous husband. When they were left as minors under
the guardianship of their paternal grandfather (Amicus
having died when his own father was still alive), for about

cesserat—per annos ferme quattuordecim memorabili
3 pietate sedulo aluit, non tamen libenter in ipso aetatis suae
4 flore tam diu vidua. Sed puerorum avus invitam eam
conciliare studebat [ceterum][76] filio suo Sicinio Claro eoque ceteros procos absterrebat; et praeterea minabatur, si
extrario nupsisset, nihil se filiis eius ex paternis eorum
5 bonis testamento relicturum. Quam condicionem cum
obstinate propositam videret mulier sapiens et egregie
pia, ne quid filiis suis eo nomine incommodaret, facit quidem tabulas nuptiales cum quo iubebatur, cum Sicinio
6 Claro, verum enimvero vanis frustrationibus nuptias elu-
dit eo ad dum puerorum avus fato concessit, relictis filiis
eius heredibus ita ut Pontianus, qui maior natu erat, fratri
suo tutor esset.

69. Eo scrupulo liberata cum a principibus viris in
matrimonium peteretur, decrevit sibi diutius in viduitate
non permanendum, quippe ut solitudinis taedium perpeti
posset, tamen aegritudinem corporis ferre non poterat.
2 Mulier sancte pudica, tot annis viduitatis sine culpa, sine
fabula, assuetudine coniugis torpens et diutino situ visce-
rum saucia, vitiatis intimis uteri saepe ad extremum vitae
3 discrimen doloribus obortis exanimabatur. Medici cum
obstetricibus consentiebant penuria matrimonii morbum
quaesitum, malum in dies augeri, aegritudinem ingraves-
cere; dum aetatis aliquid supersit, nuptiis valetudinem
4 medicandum. Consilium istud cum alii approbant, tum

[76] *ceterum* del. Novák

[127] Apuleius borrows from Plato's *Timaeus* (91C) his account
of the deleterious effects on a woman of abstinence from sex, as
he does his account of epilepsy (ch. 50).

fourteen years she raised them carefully and with extraordinary devotion, though reluctant to be so long a widow 3
when she herself was in her prime. But the boys' grandfa- 4
ther was eager to marry her off against her will to his own
son, Sicinius Clarus, and so he frightened other suitors
off. Moreover, he threatened that if she married outside
the family, he would leave her sons nothing from their
ancestral property in his will. Seeing how obstinately he 5
pressed the match, that sagacious and exceptionally devoted woman, not wanting to disadvantage her sons on
that account, signed a nuptial agreement with Sicinius
Clarus, as she had been bidden, but nevertheless, by var- 6
ious evasions she put off the wedding until the boy's grandfather had breathed his last; he had designated her sons as
his heirs on condition that the elder one, Pontianus, would
be his brother's guardian.

69. Once relieved of that concern, and because men of
the upper class were eager to marry her, she determined
to remain a widow no longer, for though she could endure
the tedium of loneliness, she could not bear her physical
illness. She was a woman of impeccable chastity, so many 2
years a widow without fault or rumor, but she was lethargic
from lack of conjugal intercourse and ill from her womb's
long inactivity, so that her inner uterus became infected,
and the resulting pains often exhausted her till her life
was in danger.[127] The doctors and the midwives agreed 3
that she had contracted her illness from deprivation of
conjugal life, that the danger was increasing with every
day and her pains getting more acute; while life was still
left to her, she should counteract her illness by marriage.
Everyone approved the plan and especially Aemilianus 4

165

maxime Aemilianus iste, qui paulo prius confidentissimo
mendacio adseverabat numquam de nuptiis Pudentillam
cogitasse, priusquam foret magicis maleficiis a me coacta,
me solum repertum, qui viduitatis eius velut quandam
5 virginitatem carminibus et venenis violarem. Saepe audivi
non de nihilo dici mendacem memorem esse oportere; at
tibi, Aemiliane, non venit in mentem, priusquam ego
Oeam venirem, te litteras etiam, uti nuberet, scripsisse ad
filium eius Pontianum, qui tum adultus Romae agebat.

6   Cedo tu epistulam, vel potius da ipsi: legat, sua sibi
7 voce suisque verbis sese revincat. Estne haec tua epistula?
   Quid palluisti? Nam erubescere tu quidem non potes.
8 Estne tua ista subscriptio? Recita quaeso clarius, ut omnes
   intellegant quantum lingua eius manu discrepet, quan-
   tumque minor illi sit mecum quam secum dissensio. (. . .)

   70. Scripsistine haec, Aemiliane, quae lecta sunt? "Nubere illam velle et debere scio, sed quem eligat nescio."
   Recte tu quidem: nesciebas; Pudentilla enim tibi, cuius
   infestam malignitatem probe norat, de ipsa re tantum,
2 ceterum de petitore nihil fatebatur. At tu dum eam putas etiamnum Claro fratri tuo denupturam, falsa spe inductus filio quoque eius Pontiano auctor adsentiendi
3 fuisti. Igitur si Claro nupsisset, homini rusticano et decre-
   pito seni, sponte eam diceres sine ulla magia iam olim
   nupturisse; quoniam iuvenem talem qualem dicitis elegit,
   coactam fecisse ais, ceterum semper nuptias aspernatam.

here, even though not long ago he lied in his teeth and said
that Pudentilla had had no thought of marriage before I
had forced her into it by malignant magic, and that only
I had ventured to deflower her virgin widowhood, so to
speak, by means of spells and poisons. As I have often   5
heard, not for nothing do they say a liar should have a good
memory, but it has slipped your mind, Aemilianus, that
before I came to Oea you had even written a letter to her
son Pontianus, who was then an adult living in Rome, urging that she marry.

(*To a clerk of the court:*) Here, bring the letter, or   6
rather give it to Aemilianus himself: let him read it and
refute himself in his own voice and in his own words. Is   7
this your letter? Why have you turned pale? Blushing is
certainly not in your power. Is this your signature? (*To the*   8
clerk:) Read it out very clearly, please, so that everyone
can see how his tongue is at variance with his hand, and
how much less he disagrees with me than with himself.
(*The letter is read out.*)

70. Did you write the words read out, Aemilianus? "I
know that she wants to marry and that she ought, but I
don't know whom she will choose." You're quite right, you
didn't know, since Pudentilla being fully aware of your
hateful malice talked only about her situation itself, but
said nothing about her suitor. You, however, believing   2
even then that she was going to marry your brother Clarus,
were led on by false hopes and urged her son Pontianus
to give his consent too. So if she had married Clarus, a clod   3
broken down with age, you would be saying that she had
long wanted to marry unprompted and without any magic;
but because she married someone you call a young man,
you say she was forced, and otherwise had always abhorred

4   Nescisti, improbe, epistulam tuam de ista re teneri, ne-
    scisti te tuomet testimonio convictum iri. Quam tamen
    epistulam Pudentilla testem et indicem tuae voluntatis,
    ut quae te levem et mutabilem nec minus mendacem et
    impudentem sciret, maluit retinere quam mittere.

5   Ceterum ipsa de ea re Pontiano suo Romam scripsit,
6   etiam causas consilii sui plene allegavit. Dixit illa omnia de
    valetudine: nihil praeterea esse, cur amplius deberet ob-
    durare, hereditatem avitam longa viduitate cum despectu
    salutis suae quaesisse, eandem summa industria auxisse;
7   iam deum voluntate ipsum uxori, fratrem eius virili togae
    idoneos esse; tandem aliquando se quoque paterentur so-
8   litudini suae et aegritudini subvenire; ceterum de pietate
    sua et supremo iudicio nihil metuerent; qualis vidua eis
    fuerit, talem nuptam futuram. Recitari iubebo exemplum
    epistulae huius ad filium missae. (. . .)

    71. Satis puto ex istis posse cuivis liquere Pudentillam
    non meis carminibus ab obstinata viduitate compulsam,
    sed olim sua sponte a nubendo non alienam [quam][77] me
2   fortasse prae ceteris maluisse. Quae electio tam gravis
    feminae cur mihi crimini potius quam honori danda sit,
    non reperio; nisi tamen miror quod Aemilianus et Rufinus
    id iudicium mulieris aegre ferant, cum hi, qui Pudentillam
    in matrimonium petiverunt, aequo animo patiantur me
3   sibi praelatum. Quod quidem illa ut faceret, filio suo pot-

    ---

    [77] quam *del. Novák.*

    ---

    [128] Hunink, *Apuleius of Madauros,* 184–85, suggests that Ae-
    milianus entrusted the letter to Pudentilla, on the assumption
    that she would know Pontianus' address in Rome, but on reading
    it herself she decided not to send it.

marriage. You scoundrel, you didn't know that your letter 4
on the subject was extant, you didn't know that you were
to be convicted by your very own testimony. That letter,
however, the witness and the proof of your agreement,
Pudentilla chose to retain rather than to send, knowing
that you were as shallow and changeable as you were un-
truthful and shameless.[128]

She herself, though, wrote to her son Pontianus in 5
Rome on the subject, and also set out in full the reasons
for her decision. She told that whole story of her illness; 6
there was no further reason for her to hold out any longer;
by her long widowhood and by neglecting her own health
she had obtained his grandfather's inheritance, and had
added to it by her own great efforts; now by the kindness 7
of the gods he for his part was of an age to marry, and his
brother to take the toga of manhood; at long last they must
also allow her to remedy her loneliness and illness; but in 8
the matter of her affection and her final dispositions they
need fear nothing; as a married woman she would be the
same person she had been to them as a widow. I shall order
a copy of this letter that she sent to her son to be read out.
(*The clerk reads the letter.*)

71. From all this I think anyone can clearly see that no
spells of mine drove Pudentilla from her long-maintained
widowhood; no, having been for a long time not disin-
clined to marry, she perhaps preferred me to others. Why 2
this choice on the part of so respectable a woman should
be counted against me as a crime rather than as a compliment I do not see: I merely wonder why Aemilianus and
Rufinus resent the lady's choice, while those who sought
Pudentilla's hand in marriage are resigned to her prefer-
ring me to them. In fact, in so doing she obeyed her son 3

ius quam animo obsecuta est. Ita factum nec Aemilianus
4 poterit negare; nam Pontianus acceptis litteris matris confestim Roma Oeam[78] advolavit metuens ne, si quem avarum virum nacta esset, omnia, ut saepe fit, in mariti do-
5 mum conferret. Ea sollicitudo non mediocriter animum
angebat, omnes illi fratrique divitiarum spes in facultati-
6 bus matris sitae erant. Avus modicum reliquerat, mater
sestertium quadragies possidebat, ex quo sane aliquantam
pecuniam nullis tabulis, sed, ut aequum erat, mera fide
7 acceptam filiis debebat. Hunc ille timorem mussitabat;
adversari propalam non audebat, ne videretur diffidere.

72. Cum in hoc statu res esset inter procationem matris
et metum fili, fortene an fato ego advenio pergens Alexan-
dream. Dixissem hercule "quod utinam numquam evenis-
2 set," ni me uxoris meae respectus prohiberet. Hiemps anni
erat. Ego ex fatigatione itineris advectus apud Appios istos
amicos meos, quos honoris et amoris gratia nomino, ali-
3 quam multis diebus decumbo. Eo venit ad me Pontianus.
Nam fuerat mihi non ita pridem [ante multos annos][79]
Athenis per quosdam communis amicos conciliatus et arto
4 postea contubernio intime iunctus. Facit omnia circa honorem meum observanter, circa salutem sollicite, circa
amorem callide. Quippe etenim videbatur sibi perido-
neum maritum matri repperisse, cui bono periculo totam
5 domus fortunam concrederet. Ac primo quidem volunta-
tem meam verbis inversis periclitabundus, quoniam me

78 Roma Oeam *Casaubon*: Romam ω
79 ante multos annos *del. Krüger*

rather than her inclination, as not even Aemilianus can deny. For when Pontianus received his mother's letter, 4 he immediately dashed from Rome to Oea, fearing that she might choose some avaricious man, and (as often happens) might transfer everything to her husband's estate. That concern gave him no slight anxiety, since his and his 5 brother's hopes of wealth depended entirely on his mother's property. His grandfather had left a modest sum, his 6 mother possessed four million sesterces; from that she owed her sons a certain amount, certainly, though the loan was not documented but made simply on faith, as was right and proper. He kept this fear of his unspoken, and 7 did not dare to object openly in case he seemed to distrust her.

72. So matters stood between the mother's marital prospects and her son's fears, when by chance or by destiny I arrived on my way to Alexandria. So help me, I would have said, "if only that had never happened," if consideration for my wife did not restrain me. It was the 2 winter season. I had arrived after an exhausting journey, and was laid up for a good number of days at the house of my friends here, the Appii, whom I name to show my esteem and affection. There Pontianus came to see me, 3 since not long before he had made my acquaintance at Athens through certain mutual friends, and thereafter we had shared lodgings together and become closely attached. In all he did he showed deference to my position, 4 concern for my health, shrewdness with regard to my affections; for, you see, he thought he had found the perfect husband for his mother, one in whose hands he could without any risk place the family's whole property. At first, 5 indeed, he tested my inclination by speaking indirectly,

171

viae cupidum et conversum ab uxoria re videbat, orat saltem paulisper manerem: velle se mecum proficisci; hie-
mem alteram propter Syrtis aestus et bestias opperien-
6 dam, quod illam mihi infirmitas exemisset. Multis etiam
precibus meis ⟨ab⟩[80] Appiis aufert, ut ad sese in domum
matris suae transferar: salubriorem mihi habitationem
futuram; praeterea prospectum maris, qui mihi gratissi-
mus est, liberius me ex ea fruiturum.

    73. Haec omnia adnixus impenso studio persuadet, ma-
trem suam suumque fratrem, puerum istum, mihi commendat. Non nihil a me in communibus studiis adiuvan-
2 tur, augetur oppido familiaritas. Interibi revalesco; dissero
aliquid postulantibus amicis publice; omnes qui aderant
ingenti celebritate basilicam, qui locus auditorii erat, com-
plentes inter alia pleraque congruentissima voce "insigni-
ter" adclamant petentes ut remanerem, fierem civis Oeen-
3 sium. Mox auditorio misso Pontianus eo principio me
adortus consensum publicae uocis pro divino auspicio
interpretatur aperitque consilium sibi esse, si ego non
nolim, matrem suam, cui plurimi inhient, mecum coniun-
gere; mihi quoniam soli ait rerum omnium confidere sese
4 et credere. Ni id onus recipiam, quoniam non formosa
pupilla, sed mediocri facie mater liberorum mihi offera-
tur,—si haec reputans formae et divitiarum gratia me ad

---

[80] ab *add. Hildebrand*

---

[129] The journey from Oea to Alexandria, if made by land,
would involve crossing the Great Syrtis, which for lack of roads
required orientation by the stars and was infested with snakes and
wild animals (Plin. *HN* 5.26).

since he saw that I was eager to set out, and was averse to
the married state, and he begged me to stay at least for a
while; he wanted to leave with me, but because of the heat
and the creatures in the Syrtes we should wait until the
next winter,[129] since my illness ruled out the present one.
By much entreaty, too, he got my friends the Appii to   6
agree that I should be transferred to him at his mother's
house; it would be a healthier place for me to stay, and
furthermore I would be better placed to see the sea from
there, which is one of my greatest pleasures.

73. By pressing all these points so insistently he convinced me, and entrusted his mother and the boy here, his
brother, to me. I helped them considerably in our joint
studies, and our intimacy greatly increased. Meanwhile I   2
recovered, and gave a public speech at the request of my
friends. The audience filled the town hall, where the lecture took place, in large numbers, and among other compliments gave a unanimous shout of "Bravo," begging me
to stay and to become a citizen of Oea.[130] Later, when the   3
audience had left, Pontianus made this his cue to influence
me, interpreting the unanimous public opinion as a sign
from heaven, and revealed that he had a scheme, if I had
no objection, to marry me to his mother, for whom many
men were lying in wait; since, so he said, I was the only
person whom he could trust and believe in every respect.
If I did not take on this burden, since the prospect was not   4
a pretty young ward but a homely mother of children—
if with that consideration in mind I was readying myself

[130] It was customary to offer honorary citizenship to distinguished performers such as orators and athletes.

aliam condicionem reservarem, neque pro amico neque
pro philosopho facturum.

5 Nimis multa oratio est, si velim memorare quae ego
6 contra responderim, quam diu et quotiens inter nos ver-
bigeratum sit, quot et qualibus precibus me aggressus
7 haud prius omiserit quam denique impetrarit, non quin
ego Pudentillam iam anno perpeti adsiduo convictu probe
spectassem et virtutium eius dotes explorassem, sed utpote peregrinationis cupiens impedimentum matrimoni
8 aliquantisper recusaveram. Mox tamen talem feminam
nihilo segnius volui quam si ultro appetissem. Persuaserat
idem Pontianus matri suae, ut me aliis omnibus mallet, et
9 quam primum hoc perficere incredibili studio avebat. Vix
ab eo tantulam moram impetramus, dum prius ipse uxorem duceret, frater eius virilis togae usum auspicaretur:
tunc deinde ut nos coniungeremur.

74. Utinam hercule possem quae deinde dicenda sunt
sine maximo causae dispendio transgredi, ne Pontiano, cui
errorem suum deprecanti simpliciter ignovi, videar nunc
2 levitatem exprobrare. Confiteor enim, quod mihi obiectum est, eum, postquam uxorem duxerit, a compecti fide
descivisse ac derepente animi mutatum quod antea nimio
studio festinarat pari pertinacia prohibitum isse, denique
ne matrimonium nostrum coalesceret, quidvis pati, quid-
3 vis facere paratum fuisse, quamquam omnis illa tam foeda
animi mutatio et suscepta contra matrem simultas non ipsi
vitio vertenda sit, sed socero eius eccilli Herennio Rufino,

---

131 At an age between fourteen and seventeen, boys put on
the "man's toga" (*toga virilis*) of pure white in a *rite de passage,*
marking their entry into manhood.

174

for another proposal in the hope of beauty and wealth, I would be acting neither as a friend nor as a philosopher.

It will take too long if I try to recount what I said in reply, our long and frequent conversations, the many different pleas he urged on me, not ending until he had finally made me yield. Certainly, I had not failed to observe Pudentilla closely in a full year of constant intimacy, and had tested the excellences by which she was adorned, but being eager for foreign travel, I had for some time avoided being tied down by marriage. Soon, however, my desire for so excellent a woman was no less keen than if I had sought her hand myself. Pontianus had also persuaded his own mother to make me her first choice, and was extraordinarily eager to settle the business as soon as possible. With difficulty we got his consent to a short delay, until he himself could take a wife and his brother could celebrate his taking of the man's toga;[131] only then should the two of us be united.

74. If only, by heaven, I could pass over what I must say next without very much weakening my case; I forgave Pontianus wholeheartedly when he asked my pardon for his error, and do not wish to seem to fault him now for irresponsibility. For I admit something that has been alleged against me: that after he had taken a wife, he broke the terms of our agreement and, suddenly changing his mind, began to prevent with no less pertinacity what he had previously urged with great energy; in short, that he would have been ready to undergo or do anything to prevent the consummation of our marriage. And yet all this shameful change of mind, and the quarrel he began with his mother, should not be blamed on him, but rather on his father-in-law here, Herennius Rufinus, who has abso-

qui unum neminem in terris viliorem se aut improbiorem
4 aut inquinatiorem reliquit. Paucis hominem, quam mo-
destissime potero, necessario demonstrabo, ne, si omnino
de eo reticuero, operam perdiderit, quod negotium istud
mihi ex summis viribus conflavit.

5   Hic est enim pueruli huius instigator, hic accusationis
auctor, hic advocatorum conductor, hic testium coemptor,
hic totius calumniae fornacula, hic Aemiliani huius fax et
flagellum, idque apud omnis intemperantissime gloriatur,
6 me suo machinatu reum postulatum. Et sane habet in istis
quod sibi plaudat. Est enim omnium litium depector,
omnium falsorum commentator, omnium simulationum
architectus, omnium malorum seminarium, nec non idem
libidinum ganearumque locus, lustrum, lupanar; iam inde
7 ab ineunte aevo cunctis probris palam notus, olim in pueritia, priusquam isto calvitio deformaretur, emasculatori-
bus suis ad omnia infanda morigerus, mox in iuventute
saltandis fabulis exossis plane et enervis, sed, ut audio,
indocta et rudi mollitia. Negatur enim quicquam histrionis
habuisse praeter impudicitiam.

    75. In hac etiam aetate qua nunc est—qui istum di
perduint! Multus honos auribus praefandus est—domus
eius tota lenonia, tota familia contaminata; ipse propudio-
2 sus, uxor lupa, filii similes. Prorsus diebus ac noctibus ludibrio iuventutis ianua calcibus propulsata, fenestrae canticis circumstrepitae, triclinium comisatoribus inquietum,

---

[132] "Pantomimes" (*pantomimi*), also known as "actors" (*histriones*), were in fact male ballet dancers noted for their extreme
suppleness and frequently considered effeminate (*molles*); their
art required extensive knowledge of ballet plots, whereas Herennius Rufinus was "ignorant and clumsy."

lutely no equal at all on earth for vileness, immorality and
depravity. I am obliged to characterize the man briefly, or   4
else, if I remain silent about him, he will have wasted his
time in using all his resources to bring this trouble on me.

For this is the man who incited this young boy, who   5
originated the suit, assembled the lawyers, bribed the witnesses; this is the one who cooked up all this slander, who
fired and whipped up Aemilianus here, and cannot restrain himself from boasting to all and sundry that *his*
contriving made me the accused defendant. And certainly   6
he has cause for self-congratulation in all this, since he
is the contriver of every lawsuit, the fabricator of every
lie, the hand behind every pretense, the seedbed of every wickedness, and at the same time the center, the
haunt, the brothel of lecheries and debaucheries, generally known for every vice from his earliest age. As a boy   7
long ago, before that baldness of his ruined his looks, he
complied with every unspeakable wish of those who made
a eunuch of him; then in his youth he danced ballets like
one entirely without sinew or bone, though I hear that he
did so like an ignorant and clumsy pansy; for they say there
was nothing of the dancer about him except lewdness.[132]

75. Moreover, now at his present age (may the gods
damn him! I beg your great indulgence for paining your
ears) his whole house is a brothel, the whole family degraded: he himself is shameless, his wife a whore, his sons
no different. Indeed his door rattles with the kicks of   2
rowdy youths day and night, his windows resound with
serenades, his dining room echoes with revelry, his bed-

cubiculum adulteris pervium. Neque enim ulli ad intro-
3 eundum metus est, nisi qui pretium marito non attulit, ita
ei lecti sui contumelia vectigalis est. Olim sollers suo, nunc
coniugis corpore vulgo meret. Cum ipso plerique—nec
mentior!—cum ipso, inquam, de uxoris noctibus paciscun-
4 tur. Hic iam illa inter virum et uxorem nota collusio: qui
amplam stipem mulieri detulerunt, nemo eos observat,
suo arbitratu discedunt; qui inaniores venere, signo dato
pro adulteris deprehenduntur, et quasi ad discendum ve-
nerint, non prius abeunt quam aliquid scripserint.

5   Quid enim faciat homo miser ampliuscula fortuna de-
volutus, quam tamen fraude patris ex inopinato invenerat?
Pater eius plurimis creditoribus defaeneratus maluit pe-
6 cuniam quam pudorem. Nam cum undique versum tabulis flagitaretur et quasi insanus ab omnibus obviis tenere-
7 tur, "pax" inquit, negat posse dissolvere, anulos aureos et
omnia insignia dignitatis abicit, cum creditoribus depacis-
8 citur. Pleraque tamen rei familiaris in nomen uxoris cal-
lidissima fraude confert. Ipse egens, nudus et ignominia
sua tutus reliquit Rufino huic—non mentior!—sestertium
XXX devorandum. Tantum enim ad eum ex bonis matris
liberum venit, praeter quod ei uxor sua cotidianis dotibus
9 quaesivit. Quae tamen omnia in paucis annis ita hic degu-
lator studiose in ventrem condidit et omnimodis collur-

---

133 That is, they are required to leave an IOU to avoid prosecution for adultery; Apuleius sarcastically compares them to
schoolboys made to finish a writing exercise before going home.
    134 Though the gold ring was a sign of free status (*ingenuitas*),
men could wear more than one ring (e.g., Hor. *Sat.* 2.7.9), and
Apuleius probably means that Herennius shed everything that
made him look rich.

room is thronged with adulterers. For anybody can enter
without fear so long as he brings a fee to the husband, so   3
much is the insult to his bed a paying concern. Formerly
he made money by skillful use of his own body, now he
does so openly by using his wife's. In person (and I am not
lying), I repeat, in person, he contracts with many men
about nights for them to spend with his wife. And yes,   4
there is that famous arrangement between husband and
wife: those who bring the woman a generous fee go unob-
served and leave when they choose, but if they come with
too little, at a given signal they find themselves trapped
like men caught in adultery, and as if they had come to
learn a lesson they leave only after writing something
first.[133]

For what was the poor man to do? He had been re-   5
duced from a good-sized fortune, though even that he got
unexpectedly through his father's fraud. Bankrupted by
his many creditors, his father chose money over reputation. For finding himself importuned with bills on every   6
side and stopped by everyone in the street like a madman,
he cried "enough," claimed he was insolvent, threw off his   7
gold rings and all emblems of his rank,[134] and settled with
his creditors. Nevertheless, by a very cunning fraud he   8
transferred most of possessions to his wife's name. Though
needy, penniless, and safe behind his own disgrace, he left
three million sesterces (this is no lie) for Rufinus here to
run through; yes, that was the amount that came to him
unencumbered from his mother's estate, in addition to
what his wife got for him by her daily dowries. All that   9
however in just a few years this guzzler rapidly buried in
his belly and squandered by gluttony of every kind; you

chinationibus dilapidavit, ut crederes metuere ne quid
10 habere ex fraude paterna diceretur. Homo iustus et morum ⟨proborum⟩[81] dedit operam, quod male partum erat
ut male periret, nec quicquam ei relictum est ex largiore
fortuna praeter ambitionem miseram et profundam gu-
lam.

76. Ceterum uxor iam propemodum vetula et effeta tot
2 iam domus[82] contumeliis abnuit. Filia autem per adules-
centulos ditiores invitamento matris suae nequicquam
circumlata, quibusdam etiam procis ad experiendum per-
missa, nisi in facilitatem Pontiani incidisset, fortasse an
3 adhuc vidua ante quam nupta domi sedisset. Pontianus ei
multum quidem dehortantibus nobis nuptiarum titulum
falsum et imaginarium donavit, non nescius eam paulo
ante quam duceret a quodam honestissimo iuvene, cui
4 prius pacta fuerat, post satietatem derelictam. Venit igitur
ad eum nova nupta secura et intrepida, pudore dispoliato,
flore exsoleto, flammeo obsoleto, virgo rursum post recens
repudium, nomen potius adferens puellae quam integri-
5 tatem. Vectabatur octaphoro; vidistis profecto qui adfuis-
tis, quam improba iuvenum circumspectatrix, quam inmo-
dica sui ostentatrix. Quis non disciplinam matris agnovit,
cum in puella videret immedicatum os et purpurissatas
6 genas et illices oculos? Dos erat a creditore omnis ad te-
runcium pridie sumpta et quidem grandior quam domus
exhausta et plena liberis postulabat.

[81] proborum *add. van der Vliet*
[82] tot iam domus *van der Vliet*: totam domum ω

[135] Cf. Plaut. *Cist.* 43–45, where the procuress says that her
daughter "marries a man every day . . . I have never let her go to
bed a widow."   [136] That is, a household so manifestly poor

would think he was afraid people might say he still had
some of his father's loot. This upright and principled char-   10
acter made sure that what evil had gained evil should lose,
and he had nothing left over from an ample fortune except
thwarted ambition and a deep stomach.

76. However, his wife, now almost a worn-out hag, at
last gave up these insults to the family. Their daughter,   2
though, they passed around among some rich youths,
whom her own mother invited in, but to no effect, and
they also gave her over to certain suitors for trial. If the
easygoing Pontianus had not fallen in her way, she might
still have been sitting at home, a widow before she was
a bride.[135] Despite our urgent representations Pontianus   3
gave her a false and imaginary claim to be married, even
though knowing that before he married her, a certain
young man of very good family, her previous fiancé, had
had his fill and then left her. And so she came to him as a   4
new bride, brazen and fearless, with her ruined honor,
faded bloom, threadbare veil, a virgin again after her recent divorce, a girl in name rather than in purity. She was   5
carried in an eight-man litter; all of you who were there
must have seen how boldly she surveyed the men, how
shamelessly she paraded herself. Who failed to recognize
the mother's training when they saw the daughter with
painted face, rouged cheeks, seductive eyes? Her whole   6
dowry down to the last penny had been got from a creditor
the day before, and indeed was larger than necessary for
a bankrupt household full of children.[136]

would not normally have been required to produce so large a
dowry; in this case, it had borrowed the money "with the expectation of preying on Pudentilla's fortune" to pay it back (Butler and
Owen, *Apulei Apologia*).

77. Sed enim iste, ut est rei modicus, spei immodicus,
pari avaritia et egestate totum Pudentillae quadragiens
praesumptione cassa devorarat eoque me amoliendum
ratus, quo facilius Pontiani facilitatem, Pudentillae solitu-
2 dinem circumveniret, infit generum suum obiurgare,
quod matrem suam mihi desponderat; suadet quam primum ex tanto periculo, dum licet, pedem referat, rem
matris ipse potius habeat quam homini extrario sciens
3 transmittat; ni ita faciat, inicit scrupulum amanti adules-
4 centulo veterator, minatur se filiam abducturum. Quid
multis? Iuvenem simplicem, praeterea novae nuptae ille-
5 cebris obfrenatum suo arbitratu de via deflectit. It ille ad
matrem verborum Rufini gerulus, sed nequicquam temp-
tata eius gravitate ultro ipse levitatis et inconstantiae in-
6 crepitus reportat ad socerum haud mollia: matri suae
praeter ingenium placidissimum immobili iram quoque
sua expostulatione accessisse, non mediocre pertinaciae
7 alimentum;[83] respondisse eam denique non clam se esse
Rufini exoratione secum expostulari; eo vel magis sibi
auxilium mariti adversum eius desperatam avaritiam com-
parandum.

78. Hisce auditis exacerbatus aquariolus iste uxoris
suae ita ira extumuit, ita exarsit furore, ut in feminam
sanctissimam et pudicissimam praesente filio eius digna
2 cubiculo suo diceret, amatricem eam, me magum et vene-

---

[83] alimentum *u*: aiumentum *vel* alumentum *ω*

---

[137] That is, he had already spent the four million that he expected to get by marrying his daughter to Pudentilla's son.
[138] Prostitutes had "water carriers" as servants, to wash them-

77. But in fact this man here, with his moderate means but immoderate hopes, with greed equal to his poverty, had already used up Pudentilla's four million in his fruitless expectation.[137] Accordingly, he decided he had to do 2 away with me so that he could more easily trick Pontianus' good nature and Pudentilla's loneliness, and so began to reproach his son-in-law for betrothing his own mother to me. He urged him to back out of this danger while he could, and to keep his mother's estate himself rather than deliberately making it over to a stranger; if he refused, the 3 old crook struck hesitation into the love-struck adolescent and threatened to take his daughter back. In brief, since 4 the youth was naïve, and moreover was in thrall to his new bride's seductions, he turned him from the straight and narrow to please himself. The youth went to his mother as 5 Rufinus' spokesman, but when he tried in vain to influence her steady character, instead he himself got a scolding for his vacillation and inconstancy, and brought back no pleasant message to his father-in-law: his mother, usually of 6 such a very placid nature, was immovable, and his request had actually moved her to anger, no small addition to her obstinacy. In a word, she replied that it was no secret to 7 her that this request came from Rufinus' instigation, and hence she had even more need of a husband to help her against his desperate greed.

78. Enraged at this news, this water carrier[138] for his wife so swelled with anger, so burned with fury, that in her son's presence he used language worthy of his own bedroom against that most proper and chaste lady; in the 2

selves off after intercourse: cf. Cic. *Cael.* 34 (Appius Claudius to Clodia), *ideo aquam adduxi ut ea tu inceste uterere*?

ficum clamitaret multis audientibus (quos, si voles, nomi-
3 nabo); se mihi sua manu mortem allaturum. Vix hercule
possum irae moderari, ingens indignatio animo oboritur.
Tene,[84] effeminatissime, tua manu cuiquam viro mortem
4 minitari? At qua tandem manu? Philomelae an Medeae
an Clytaemnestrae? Quas tamen cum saltas (tanta mollitia
animi, tanta formido ferri est), sine cludine saltas.

5   Sed ne longius ab ordine digrediar: Pudentilla postquam filium videt praeter opinionem contra suam esse
sententiam depravatum, rus profecta scripsit ad eum ob-
iurgandi gratia illas famosissimas litteras, quibus, ut isti
aiebant, confessa est sese mea magia in amorem inductam
6 dementire. Quas tamen litteras tabulario Pontiani praesente et contra scribente Aemiliano nudius tertius tuo
iussu, Maxime, testato descripsimus; in quibus omnia contra praedicationem istorum pro me reperiuntur.

     79. Quamquam, etsi destrictius magum me dixisset,
posset videri excusabunda se filio vim meam quam volun-
tatem suam causari maluisse. An sola Phaedra falsum epistolium de amore commenta est? At non omnibus mulieri-
bus haec ars usitata est, ut, cum aliquid eius modi velle
2 coeperunt, malint coactae videri? Quod si etiam animo ita
putavit, me magum esse, idcircone magus habear, quia
hoc scripsit Pudentilla? Vos tot argumentis, tot testibus,
tanta oratione magum me non probatis: illa uno verbo

---

[84] tene *Hildebrand*: tune ω

---

[139] Pantomimes danced themes taken from myth or tragedy
and sometimes carried stage props appropriate to their roles.
Philomela, Medea, and Clytaemnestra were all heroines who
committed murder.

hearing of many people (whom I will name if you wish),
he shouted that she was oversexed, I a magician and poisoner, and he would kill me by his own hand. I swear I   3
can scarcely control my anger; intense indignation is rising in my mind. You, you total effeminate, do you raise
your hand against any *man*? But whose hand, may I ask?   4
Philomela's, Medea's, or Clytemnestra's? Though when
you dance their roles, you dance with a stage sword, such
is your effeminate character and your fear of cold steel.[139]

But not to stray too far from the subject: Pudentilla,   5
seeing to her surprise that her son had been tricked into
contradicting his own advice, set off for the country and
wrote that celebrated letter of reproach in which she admitted, so those people alleged, that my magic had caused
her to fall madly in love. But I transcribed that letter two   6
days ago, with Pontianus' secretary present and with Aemilianus making his own copy, as you ordered, Maximus,
and before witnesses; everything in it will prove to be in
my favor and contrary to what they asserted.

79. And yet, even had she frankly called me a magician,
one might think that she preferred to allege compulsion
on my part when excusing herself to her son, rather than
consent on hers. Is Phaedra the only woman to have contrived a false love letter? Is this not the usual trick that all
women play, once they begin to want something like this,
to prefer to seem compelled to do so? Yet even if she had   2
believed in her heart that I was a magician, am I to be
thought one for that reason—Pudentilla's having said so in
writing? You with all your proofs, all your witnesses, all
your speeches cannot prove I am a magician, and was she

probaret? Et quanto tandem gravius habendum est quod
in iudicio subscribitur quam quod in epistula scribitur.
3 Quin tu me meismet factis, non alienis verbis revincis?
Ceterum eadem via multi rei cuiusvis maleficii postula-
buntur, si ratum futurum est quod quisque in epistula sua
4 vel amore vel odio cuiuspiam scripserit. "Magum te scripsit Pudentilla: igitur magus es." Quid si consulem me
scripsisset: consul essem? Quid enim si pictorem, si medi-
cum, quid denique, si innocentem? Num aliquid horum
5 putares idcirco, quod illa dixisset? Nihil scilicet. Atqui
periniurium est ei fidem in peioribus habere, cui in melio-
ribus non haberes, posse litteras eius ad perniciem, non
6 posse ad salutem. "Sed inquies[85] animi fuit, efflictim te
amabat." Concedo interim. Num tamen omnes qui aman-
tur magi sunt, si hoc forte qui amat scripserit? Credo nunc
quod Pudentilla me in eo tempore non amabat, siquidem
id foras scripsit, quod palam erat mihi obfuturum.

80. Postremo quid vis: sanam an insanam fuisse, dum
scriberet? Sanam dices? Nihil ergo erat magicis artibus
passa. Insanam respondebis? Nesciit ergo quid scripserit,
eoque ei fides non habenda est; immo etiam, si fuisset
2 insana, insanam se esse nescisset. Nam ut absurde facit qui
tacere se dicit, quod ibidem dicendo tacere sese non tacet
et ipsa professione quod profitetur infirmat, ita vel magis
hoc repugnant, "ego insanio," quod verum non est, nisi

---

[85] inquies *Hildebrand*: inquit *ω*

to prove it by a mere word? And yet how much more serious should one consider what is formally written in an
indictment than what is written in a letter. Why don't you 3
convict me by my own deeds, not by another's words?
Moreover, on that principle many people will be charged
as defendants for any crime at all, if something that someone puts in a letter out of love or hate for another is to
be thought an established fact. "Pudentilla wrote that you 4
were a magician, and therefore you are one." Suppose she
had written that I was consul, would I be consul? Or suppose she written that I was an artist, a doctor, or if it comes
to that, an innocent man? Would you believe any such
thing just on her say-so? Of course not. And yet it is the 5
height of injustice to believe her in an unfavorable sense
when you would not in a favorable one—for her letter to
be able to ruin a man and not to keep him safe. "Ah, but 6
she was not in her right mind, she loved you passionately."
I grant that for the moment. But surely not all those who
inspire love are magicians if their lover happens to say so
in writing? I believe now that Pudentilla did not love me
at the time, if she really wrote something for the eyes of
others that was to do me harm in public.

80. Finally, what is it that you are alleging—that she
was sane or insane when she wrote? "Sane," will you say?
Then she was not influenced by magic arts. "Insane," will
you reply? Then she did not know what she wrote and
therefore cannot be believed: or rather, if she had been
insane she would not have known that she was so. For just 2
as it is absurd for someone to say that he is not speaking, because merely to say he is not speaking means he is
speaking, and his very assertion disproves his assertion,
in the same way or even more so, "I am insane" is self-

sciens dicit. Porro sanus est, qui scit quid sit insania,
quippe insania scire se non potest, non magis quam caeci-
3 tas se videre; igitur Pudentilla compos mentis fuit, si com-
potem mentis se non putabat. Possum, si velim, pluribus,
sed mitto dialectica: ipsas litteras longe aliud clamantis et
quasi dedita opera ad iudicium istud praeparatas et ac-
commodatas recitabo. Accipe tu et lege, usque dum ego
interloquar.

4   Sustine paulisper quae sequuntur; nam ad deverticu-
5 lum rei ventum est. Adhuc enim, Maxime, quantum equidem animadverti, nusquam mulier magiam nominavit, sed
ordinem repetivit eundem, quem ego paulo prius, de longa
viduitate, de remedio valetudinis, de voluntate nubendi,
de meis laudibus, quas ex Pontiano cognoverat, de suasu
ipsius, ut mihi potissimum nuberet.

      81. Haec usque adhuc lecta sunt. Superest ea pars epis-
tulae, quae similiter pro me scripta in memet ipsum vertit
cornua, ad expellendum a me crimen magiae sedulo missa
memorabili fraude[86] Rufini vicem mutavit et ultro contra-
riam mihi opinionem quorundam Oeensium quasi mago
2 quaesivit. Multa fando, Maxime, audisti, etiam plura le-
gendo didicisti, non pauca experiendo comperisti, sed
enim versutiam tam insidiosam, tam admirabili scelere
3 conflatam negabis te umquam cognovisse. Quis Palamedes, quis Sisyphus, quis denique Eurybates aut Phrynon-

---

[86] fraude *Acidalius*: laude ω

refuting: it is not true unless said consciously. Further-more, a person is sane if he knows what insanity is, be-cause insanity cannot know itself any more than blindness can see itself; hence Pudentilla was of sound mind if she   3 thought herself not of sound mind. I could say more if I chose, but this is enough logic chopping. I will read the actual letter, which loudly proclaims something quite dif-ferent, and has been almost been deliberately prepared and adapted for use in this suit. (*To a servant of the court:*) Here you, take it and read until I interrupt you. (*The letter is read.*)

Stop before you read the rest, since we have come to   4 the heart of the matter. For up to this point, Maximus, as   5 far as *I* noticed, the lady nowhere mentioned sorcery, but went over the same course of events as I did just now, about her long widowhood, about curing her illness, about her desire to marry, about the praises of myself that she had heard from Pontianus, about his own urging that she should marry me and not someone else.

81. So far the part already read out: there remains the part which, though similarly written in my support, turned and gored me. Though expressly sent to clear me of the charge of magic, by a memorable maneuver of Ru-finus it changed its role, and furthermore tried to give certain citizens of Oea the opposite view of me, as a magi-cian. You have heard much in conversation, Maximus, you   2 have learned even more by reading, you have discovered a good many things by experience, but still you must admit that you have never met with a plot so crafty or con-cocted with such extraordinary wickedness. What Palam-   3 edes, what Sisyphus, or indeed what Eurybates or Phry-

4   das talem excogitasset? Omnes isti quos nominavi et si qui
praeterea fuerunt dolo memorandi, si cum hac una Rufini
fallacia contendantur, macci prorsus et buccones videbun-
5   tur. O mirum commentum! O subtilitas digna carcere et
robore! Quis credat effici potuisse, ut quae defensio fuerat, eadem manentibus eisdem litteris in accusationem
transverteretur? Est hercule incredibile. Sed hoc incredibile qui sit factum, probabo.

    82. Obiurgatio erat matris ad filium, quod me, talem
virum qualem sibi praedicasset, nunc de Rufini sententia
2   magum dictitaret. Verba ipsa ad hunc modum se habebant: "Ἀπολέϊος μάγος, καὶ ἐγὼ ὑπ᾽ αὐτοῦ μεμάγευμαι
3   καὶ ἐρῶ· ἐλθὲ τοίνυν πρὸς ἐμέ, ἕως ἔτι σωφρονῶ." Haec
ipsa verba Rufinus quae Graece interposui sola excerpta
et ab ordine suo seiugata quasi confessionem mulieris cir-
cumferens et Pontianum flentem per forum ductans vulgo
ostendebat, ipsas mulieris litteras illatenus qua dixi legen-
4   das praebebat, cetera supra et infra scripta occultabat.
Turpiora esse quam ut ostenderentur dictitabat; satis esse
5   confessionem mulieris de magia cognosci. Quid quaeris?
Verisimile omnibus visum. Quae purgandi mei gratia
scripta erant, eadem mihi immanem invidiam apud im-
6   peritos concivere. Turbabat impurus hic in medio foro
bacchabundus, epistulam saepe aperiens proquiritabat:
"Apuleius magus: dicit ipsa quae sentit et patitur. Quid

---

140 When Odysseus feigned madness in order to avoid going
to Troy, Palamedes used a trick to expose him, and became proverbial for cunning; Sisyphus cheated death in various ways until
he was condemned to eternal punishment in the underworld (cf.
Hom. *Od.* 11.593–600; Alcaeus fr. 38A Campbell); Eurybates and

nondas could have conceived such a thing?[140] All those I 4
have just mentioned, and any others memorable for their
craftiness, if they were set against this one ruse of Rufinus,
will seem absolute clowns and bumblers. What an incred- 5
ible scheme! What ingenuity, fit for prison and dungeon!
Who could believe it possible to arrange so that a previous
defense could be converted into an accusation with no
change in the wording? Incredible indeed it is, but how
this incredible thing was done, I will now demonstrate.

82. It was a mother's reproach to her son because,
though I was just such a man as he had described to her,
now at Rufinus' prompting he alleged I was a magician.
Her actual words were as follows: "Apuleius is a magician; 2
he has bewitched me and I am in love. So come to me
while I am still in my right mind." Rufinus excerpted only 3
the words I have quoted in Greek, detached them from
their context, and bandied them about as if they were the
lady's confession. He led the weeping Pontianus through
the town square, showed him to everybody, allowed the
lady's actual letter to be read only to the point I have in-
dicated, and suppressed everything written before and 4
after it. *That,* he insisted, was too disgraceful to be exhibited; it was enough that the lady's admission of magic
should be made known. What more can I say? Everyone 5
thought it plausible. The very words written to exculpate
me caused naïve folk to regard me with immense hostility.
This degenerate dashed around the middle of the town 6
square like one possessed; opening the letter over and
over, he called out, "Apuleius is a magician: the woman

Phrynondas are mentioned by Attic authors as stock tricksters,
e.g., Pl. *Prt.* 327D.

7 vultis amplius?" Nemo erat qui pro me staret[87] ac sic responderet: "Totam sodes epistulam cedo, sine omnia in-
8 spiciam, a principio ad finem perlegam. Multa sunt, quae
   sola prolata calumniae possint videri obnoxia. Cuiavis oratio insimulari potest, si ea quae ex prioribus nexa sunt
   principio sui defrudentur, si quaedam ex ordine scriptorum ad libidinem supprimantur, si quae simulationis
   causa dicta sunt adseverantis pronuntiatione quam expro-
9 brantis legantur." Haec et id genus ea quam merito tunc
   dici potuerunt! Ipse ordo epistulae ostendat.

   83. At tu, Aemiliane, recognosce, an et haec mecum
   testato descripseris: βουλομένην γάρ με δι᾽ ἃς εἶπον αἰ-
   τίας γαμηθῆναι, αὐτὸς ἔπεισας τοῦτον ἀντὶ πάντων
   γαμηθῆναι, θαυμάζων τὸν ἄνδρα καὶ σπουδάζων αὐτὸν
   οἰκεῖον ὑμῖν δι᾽ ἐμοῦ ποιεῖσθαι· νῦν δὲ ὡς κακήγοροι[88]
   ἡμῶν κακοήθεις σε ἀναπείθουσιν, αἰφνίδιον ἐγένετο
   Ἀπολέϊος μάγος, καὶ ἐγὼ ὑπ᾽ αὐτοῦ μεμάγευμαι καὶ
2 ἐρῶ· ἐλθὲ τοίνυν πρὸς ἐμέ ἕως ἔτι σωφρονῶ. Oro te, Maxime, si litterae, ita ut partim vocales dicuntur, etiam pro-
   priam vocem usurparent, si verba, ita ut poetae aiunt,
3 pinnis apta vulgo volarent, nonne, cum primum epistulam
   istam Rufinus mala fide excerperet, pauca legeret, multa
   et meliora sciens reticeret, nonne tunc ceterae litterae

87 staret *Stewechius*: ferret ω
88 κακήγοροι *Helm*: μακάριοι vel μοχθηροί ω

141 *Litterae* means both "a letter" and "letters (of the alpha-
bet)," and the Latin for vowels (*vocales*) also means "vocal"; there
may be an additional allusion to the idea that letters were a conversation conducted by other means (e.g., Demetrius, *On Style*
223).   142 The Homeric "winged words," e.g., *Il.* 1.201.

herself says what she feels and suffers; what more do you want?" There was no one to take my side and say in reply: 7
"Give me the entire letter, please, let me examine the whole thing, let me read it from start to finish. Often words 8 quoted by themselves can seem liable to misrepresentation; any utterance you like can be impugned if words attached to previous ones are robbed of their introduction, if words are arbitrarily omitted from their written context, if expressions intended ironically are read in a tone of assertion rather than of reproach." This and more of the kind 9 could very justifiably have been said at that time: let the actual text of the letter prove it.

83. Now, Aemilianus, check whether this too was copied by you and me together before witnesses: "I wanted to marry for the reasons I said, and you yourself persuaded me to choose him rather than anyone, since you admired the man and wanted to link him with our family through me. But now that our accusers are maliciously persuading you otherwise, suddenly Apuleius has become a magician; he has bewitched me and I am in love. So come to me while I am still in my right mind." I ask you, Maximus: if 2 a letter, some components of which are called "vowels,"[141] were also to speak in its own voice, if words, as the poets say, were to be fitted with wings and fly everywhere,[142] then surely, as soon as Rufinus treacherously excerpted 3 that letter, reading out just a bit and deliberately suppressing the much longer and more favorable part, would not the other letters have cried out that they were being

sceleste se detineri proclamassent, verba suppressa de
Rufini manibus foras evolassent, totum forum tumultu
4 complessent? "Se quoque a Pudentilla missas, sibi etiam
quae dicerent mandata; improbo ac nefario homini per
alienas litteras falsum facere temptanti nec auscultarent,
5 sibi potius audirent; Apuleium magiae non accusatum a
6 Pudentilla, sed accusante Rufino absolutum." Quae omnia
etsi tum dicta non sunt, tamen nunc, cum magis prosunt,
luce illustrius apparent. Patent artes tuae, Rufine, fraudes
7 hiant, detectum mendacium est. Veritas olim interversa
nunc se effert[89] et velut alto barathro calumnia se mergit.

84. Ad litteras Pudentillae provocastis: ⟨his⟩[90] litteris
vinco, quarum si vultis extremam quoque clausulam audire, non invidebo. Dic tu, quibus verbis epistulam finierit
2 mulier obcantata, vecors, amens, amans: ἐγὼ οὔτε μεμάγευμαι οὔτ᾽ ἐρῶ. Τὴν εἱμαρμένην †ΕΚΦ†.[91] Etiamne amplius? Reclamat vobis Pudentilla et sanitatem suam a ves-
3 tris calumniis quodam praeconio vindicat. Nubendi autem
seu rationem seu necessitatem fato adscribit, a quo multum magia remota est vel potius omnino sublata. Quae
enim relinquitur vis cantaminibus et veneficiis, si fatum
rei cuiusque veluti violentissimus torrens neque retineri
4 potest neque impelli? Igitur hac sententia sua Pudentilla
non modo me magum, sed omnino esse magiam negavit.
5 Bene, quod integras epistulas matris Pontianus ex more
adservavit; bene, quod vos festinatio iudicii antevertit, ne

[89] effert *u*: fert ω   [90] his *add. Sauppe*
[91] ΕΚΦ *varie suppleverunt edd.*: ἐκφεύγειν οὐκ ἔξεστιν *Helm*
(*malim* ἐ. ο. ἔνι)

[143] I translate Helm's supplement.

wickedly imprisoned? Would not the suppressed words have flown from Rufinus' hands and filled the whole town square with their shouting? "They too had been sent by 4 Pudentilla, they too had had been entrusted with her words; no one should listen to an unscrupulous crook trying to use another's letter to perpetrate a lie, but should hear themselves instead; Pudentilla did not accuse Apuleius of magic—Rufinus accused him and she acquitted him." Though no one said all that at the time, still now, 6 when it is more helpful, it shines brighter than daylight. Your tricks are revealed, Rufinus, your frauds are exposed, your lie is detected. Truth, once hoodwinked, now rises up 7 and emerges from slander as from a deep abyss.

84. You appealed to Pudentilla's letter: with this letter I win my case, and if you want to hear the very last sentence as well, I will not object. (*To a servant of the court:*) You, read out the words with which the lady closed her letter when she was bewitched, maddened, raving, doting. "I have neither been bewitched nor am I in love. One can- 2 not escape fate."[143] Isn't that enough? Pudentilla cries out against you all, she practically issues a proclamation to assert her sanity against your false charges. But she as- 3 cribes her reason or, if you like, her need for marriage to fate, which is a very far thing from magic, or rather is totally unconnected with it. What power can spells and potions still have, if the destiny of everything is like the most violent torrent, which one can neither hold back nor hurry forward? Thus by her very own statement Pudentilla not 4 only denied that I was a magician, but that magic existed at all. It is a lucky thing that Pontianus habitually kept 5 complete copies of his mother's letters; a lucky thing too that your hurry to bring on the trial prevented you from

195

6 quid in istis litteris ex otio novaretis. Tuum hoc, Maxime,
   tuaeque providentiae beneficium est, quod a principio
   intellectas calumnias, ne corroborarentur tempore, prae-
7 cipitasti et nulla impertita mora subnerviasti. Finge nunc
   aliquid matrem filio secretis litteris de amore, uti adsolet,
   confessam. Hocine verum fuit, Rufine, hoc non dico pium,
   sed saltem humanum, provulgari eas litteras et potissi-
8 mum fili praeconio publicari? Sed sumne ego inscius, qui
   postulo ut alienum pudorem conserves qui tuum perdide-
   ris?

   85. Cur autem praeterita conqueror, cum non sint
   minus acerba praesentia? Hocusque a vobis miserum istum puerum depravatum, ut matris suae epistulas, quas
2 putat amatorias, pro tribunali proconsulari recitet apud
   virum sanctissimum Cl. Maximum, ante has imperatoris
   Pii statuas filius matri suae pudenda exprobret stupra et
3 amores obiectet. Quis tam est mitis quin exacerbescat?
   Tune, ultime, parentis tuae animum in istis scrutaris, oculos observas, suspiritus numeras, adfectiones exploras, ta-
4 bulas intercipis, amorem revincis? Tune quid in cubiculo
   agat perquiris, ‹tibi›ne[92] mater tua non dico amatrix, sed
   ne omnino femina est? ‹Nihil›ne[93] tu in ea cogitas nisi
5 unam parentis religionem? O infelix uterum tuum, Pudentilla, o sterilitas liberis potior, o infausti decem menses,

---

[92] tibi *add. Haupt*
[93] nihil *add.* Helm: *locus conclamatus*

---

[144] Antoninus Pius, emperor from 138 to 160. Apuleius plays
on the emperor's title of *Pius*, "Dutiful," earned by his loyalty to
his adoptive father, Hadrian, as a contrast with the undutiful conduct of Pudentilla's son Pudens.

in any way tampering with this letter at your leisure. This 6
is thanks to you, Maximus, and to your foresight: recogniz-
ing the false charges right away, you forced them along so
that they should not grow stronger with time, and you
hamstrung them by refusing an adjournment. Well, sup- 7
pose that the mother admitted something in a private letter to her son about being in love, as often happens. Was
it honest, Rufinus, was it—I do not say dutiful, but at any
rate humane, to advertise that letter and to make her son
of all people trumpet it in public? But no doubt it is naïve 8
of me to expect you to protect someone else's reputation
after ruining your own.

85. But why do I deplore the past, when the present is
just as painful? To think that you have corrupted this poor
boy so much that he reads out his mother's letter, thinking
it a love letter, doing so before the proconsul's bench and 2
before the most honorable Claudius Maximus—that beneath these statues of the emperor Pius he charges his
mother with shameful sexual exploits, and reproaches her
for having affairs.[144] Who is so forgiving as not to feel fury? 3
You monster, do you pry into your mother's thoughts in
these matters, watch her eyes, count her sighs, investigate
her feelings, intercept her papers, condemn her love? Do 4
you investigate what she does in her bedroom? In your
eyes is your mother, I will not say "oversexed,"[145] not even
a woman? Do you only think of her as owing the duty of a
mother? How unlucky was your womb, Pudentilla! How 5
much better would sterility have been than childbirth!
How ominous were your nine months, how ill-rewarded

[145] This was a term allegedly applied to Pudentilla by Rufinus,
78.1.

197

o ingrati XIIII anni viduitatis! Vipera, ut audio, exeso matris utero in lucem proserpit atque ita parricidio gignitur;
at enim tibi a filio iam adulto acerbiores morsus viventi et
6 videnti offeruntur. Silentium tuum laniatur, pudor tuus
carpitur, pectus tuum foditur, viscera intima protrahuntur.
7 Hascine gratias bonus filius matri rependis ob datam vitam, ob acquisitam hereditatem, ob XIIII annorum longas
alimonias? Hiscine te patruus disciplinis erudivit, ut, si
compertum habeas filios tibi similes futuros, non audeas
8 ducere uxorem? Est ille poetae versus non ignotus:

"odi puerulos praecoqui sapientia."

Sed enim malitia praecoqui puerum quis non aversetur
atque oderit, cum videat velut monstrum quoddam prius
robustum scelere quam tempore, ante nocentem quam
9 potentem, viridi pueritia, cana malitia, vel potius hoc magis noxium, quod cum venia perniciosus est et nondum
poenae, iam iniuriae sufficit—iniuriae dico? Immo enim
sceleri adversum parentem nefando, immani, impetibili.

86. Athenienses quidem propter commune ius huma-
nitatis ex captivis epistulis Philippi Macedonis hostis sui
unam epistulam, cum singulae publice legerentur, recitari
prohibuerunt, quae erat ad uxorem Olympiadem conscripta. Hosti potius pepercerunt, ne maritale secretum
divulgarent, praeferendum rati fas commune propriae
2 ultioni. Tales hostes adversum hostem; tu qualis filius adversum matrem? Vides quam similia contendam. Tu ta-

---

146 From an unknown comedy (Ribbeck, *Comicorum Romanorum Fragmenta*[3] [151 no. 78]).

your fourteen years of widowhood! The viper, so I hear, gnaws through its mother's womb before it crawls into the daylight, and so murders its parent at birth: but your full-grown son gnaws *you* more painfully while you still live and breathe. Your discretion is ravaged, your honor at- 6 tacked, your heart pierced, your very innards ripped out. Is this the gratitude that a good son shows to the mother 7 who gave you life, who increased your inheritance, who raised you for fourteen long years? Are these the lessons your uncle taught you, so that you would feel certain of having sons like yourself and would not dare to marry? There is a well known line of the poet, 8

"I dislike boys prematurely wise,"[146]

but who would not shun and abhor a boy prematurely wicked, when one sees a sort of prodigy hardened by crime and not yet by time, dangerous and not yet adult, with the greenness of youth and the gray hairs of malice? Or rather a boy all the more dangerous because pardon- 9 ably pernicious, not yet of an age to do time but already of an age to do harm? Did I say "to do harm"? No, to commit an unspeakable, monstrous, insufferable crime against his parent.

86. Now the Athenians observed the common laws of humanity when they had intercepted their enemy Philip's letters. They had each of them read out in public, but prohibited the reading of one that he had written to his wife Olympias. They spared their enemy rather than exposing conjugal privacy, thinking that a general right ranked higher than personal revenge. That is how enemies 2 dealt with an enemy: what kind of son were you in dealing with your mother? You see how close my comparison is!

199

men filius matris epistulas de amore, ut ais, scriptas in isto coetu legis, in quo si aliquem poetam lasciviorem iubereris legere, profecto non auderes: pudore tamen aliquo

3 impedirere. Immo enim nunquam matris tuae litteras attigisses, si ullas alias litteras attigisses.

4 At quam ⟨nequiter⟩[94] ausus es tuam ipsius epistulam legendam dare, quam nimis irreverenter, nimis contumeliose et turpiter de matre tua scriptam, cum adhuc in eius sinu alerere, miseras clanculo ad Pontianum, scilicet ne semel peccasses ac tam bonum tuum factum oblivio[95] ca-

5 pesseret. Miser, non intellegis idcirco patruum tuum hoc fieri passum, quod se hominibus purgaret, si ex litteris tuis nosceretur te etiam prius quam ad eum commigrasses, etiam cum matri blandirere, tamen iam tum vulpionem et impium fuisse. 87. Ceterum nequeo in animum inducere tam stultum Aemilianum esse, ut arbitretur mihi litteras pueri et eiusdem accusatoris mei offuturas.

2 Fuit et illa commenticia epistula neque mea manu scripta neque verisimiliter conficta, qua videri volebant blanditiis a me mulierem sollicitatam. Cur ego blandirem,

3 si magia confidebam? Qua autem via ad istos pervenit epistula, ad Pudentillam scilicet per aliquem fidelem

4 missa, ut in re tali accurari solet? Cur praeterea tam vitiosis verbis, tam barbaro sermone ego scriberem, quem idem dicunt nequaquam Graecae linguae imperitum? Cur

---

[94] ⟨nequiter⟩ *add. Vulcanius*
[95] oblivio *Casaubon*: obtutu ω

---

[147] *Litterae* means both "a letter" and "literature"; Apuleius implies that Pudens would never have acted as he did if he had had any proper education.

Though a son, you read what you call your mother's love letters in this assembly, and yet if you were told to read some rather risqué poet before it, you would certainly not dare: some sense of decency would restrain you even yet. Or rather, you would never have read your mother's letters 3 if you had had any other reading.[147]

But how wicked it was of you to give your very own 4 letter to be read! How very disrespectful, insulting and shameful was that letter you wrote about your own mother! She was still raising you under her protection when you secretly sent it to Pontianus, no doubt so that you would not do wrong only once, or let such a kind deed be buried in oblivion. Poor fool, don't you see that your uncle al- 5 lowed all this to happen—to excuse himself to the world when it became known from your letter that even before you moved in with him, even while you were fawning on your mother, you were already deceitful and unfilial. 87. Still, I cannot bring myself to believe that Aemilianus is so stupid as to suppose *I* will be harmed by the letter of a boy who is also my accuser.

There was also that fraudulent letter, neither in my 2 handwriting nor a plausible forgery, in which they wanted it to seem that I had wooed the lady by complimenting her. Why compliment her if I put my trust in magic? And by 3 what route did the letter get into their hands? For I would surely have sent it to Pudentilla by some trusted agent, the usual precaution in such an affair. And why should I write 4 in such uneducated language, such barbarous style, when these same people say I have no slight acquaintance with

autem tam absurdis tamque tabernariis blanditiis subigi-
tarem, quem idem aiunt versibus amatoriis satis scite lasci-
5 vire? Sic est profecto, cuivis palam est: hic, qui epistulam
Pudentillae Graecatiorem legere non potuerat, hanc ut
suam facilius legit et aptius commendavit.

6 Sed iam de epistulis satis dictum habebo, si hoc unum
addidero: Pudentillam, quae scripserat dissimulamenti
causa et deridiculi: ἐλθὲ τοίνυν ἕως ἔτι σωφρονῶ, post
hasce litteras evocasse ad se filios et nurum, cum his ferme
7 duobus mensibus conversatam. Dicat hic pius filius, quid
in eo tempore sequius agentem vel loquentem matrem
suam propter insaniam viderit; neget eam rationibus villi-
conum et upilionum et equisonum sollertissime subscrip-
8 sisse; neget fratrem suum Pontianum graviter ab ea mo-
nitum, ut sibi ab insidiis Rufini caveret; neget vere
obiurgatum, quod litteras, quas ad eum miserat, vulgo
9 circumtulisset nec tamen bona fide legisset; neget post ista
quae dixi matrem suam mihi apud villam iam pridem
10 condicto loco nupsisse. Quippe ita placuerat, in suburbana
villa potius ut coniungeremur, ne cives denuo ad sportulas
convolarent, cum haud pridem Pudentilla de suo quinquaginta milia nummum ‹in›⁹⁶ populum expunxisset ea die,
qua Pontianus uxorem duxit et hic puerulus toga est invo-
11 lutus, praeterea, ut conviviis multis ac molestiis superse-
deremus, quae ferme ex more novis maritis obeunda sunt.

⁹⁶ in *add. u*

¹⁴⁸ Pudens had read out his mother's letter in court but (according to Apuleius) had represented it as a love letter (ch. 85.1).
¹⁴⁹ Presents (*sportulae,* "little baskets") were commonly given
out on all kinds of occasions, either in kind or in cash, but big

Greek? And why should I ply her with such absurd, bar-room compliments when these same people call me quite clever at writing risqué love poems? In short, the fact is this, as anyone can see: this man, who could not read Pudentilla's letter in idiomatic Greek, was more at ease reading one of his own and more skillful at communicating it.

But I will soon have done with letters when I have added this one point. Pudentilla had written, "So come while I am still of sound mind" in a spirit of irony and jest; and after writing this letter she invited her sons and daughter-in-law to join her, and spent about two months with them. Now let her dutiful son mention anything untoward he saw his mother do or say at that time because of insanity. Let him deny that she most meticulously audited the account books of her stewards, herdsmen, and grooms. Let him deny that that she strongly advised his brother Pontianus to beware of Rufinus' treacheries. Let him deny that she quite properly scolded him because he had publicly circulated a letter she had sent him, and even so had not read it in good faith.[148] Let him deny, after all I have said, that his mother married me at her country house, a place we had long since arranged. For we had agreed to prefer a house outside of town for our marriage, so that the citizenry would not flock there again in hope of wedding favors.[149] Not long before, Pudentilla had paid out fifty thousand sesterces of her own money to the people on the day Pontianus married and the boy here assumed the toga. Moreover, we wanted to dispense with the many banquets and nuisances that newlyweds usually have to go through according to custom.

events such as weddings could involve such gifts to hundreds of people.

88. Habes, Aemiliane, causam totam, cur tabulae nuptiales inter me ac Pudentillam non in oppido sint sed in villa suburbana consignatae: ne quinquaginta milia nummum denuo profundenda essent nec tecum aut apud te

2 cenandum. Estne causa idonea? Miror tamen, quod tu a villa tantopere abhorreas, qui plerumque rure versere.

3 Lex quidem Iulia de maritandis ordinibus nusquam sui ad hunc modum interdicit: "uxorem in villa ne ducito."

4 Immo, si verum velis, uxor ad prolem multo auspicatius in villa quam in oppido ducitur, in solo uberi quam in loco

5 sterili, in agri caespite quam in fori silice. Mater futura in ipso materno sinu nubat, in segete adulta, super fecundam glebam, vel enim sub ulmo marita cubet, in ipso gremio terrae matris, inter suboles herbarum et propagines vitium

6 et arborum germina. Ibi et ille celeberrimus in comoediis versus de proximo congruit:

παίδων ἐπ᾿ ἀρότῳ γνησίων ἐπὶ σπορᾷ.

7 Romanorum etiam maioribus Quinctiis et Serranis et multis aliis similibus non modo uxores, verum etiam consulatus et dictaturae in agris offerebantur. Cohibeo[97] me in

---

[97] cohibeo *van der Vliet*: cohibebam ω

---

[150] In 18 BC Augustus passed the *lex Iulia de maritandis ordinibus* in order to promote marriage and increase the population.

[151] "Mother's arms" refers to the earth as mother (cf. Suet. *Iul.* 7.2). Vines were trained on, and thus "married" to, elm trees (*OLD marito* 4): Catullus' exploits the same idea in one of his wedding poems, 62.49–55.

88. There you have the entire reason, Aemilianus, why
Pudentilla and I signed our marriage contact together in
a house outside of town rather than in town: to avoid having to lavish fifty thousand sesterces a second time or to
dine with you or at your house. Isn't that a good enough
reason? I am surprised, though, that you have such horror 2
of a country house, when you spend most of your time in
the country. At no point does the Julian Law for Marriage 3
in the Social Orders make any such ban as this: "Let him
not take a wife in a country house."[150] No, if you want 4
the truth, for a woman to have children it is much more
auspicious for her to be married in a country house than
in town, on fertile ground rather than on a barren spot,
on country greensward than on the stone of the public
square. Let a mother-to-be marry in the very arms of her 5
mother, amid ripe grain, on lush turf; or indeed let her lie
beneath the wedded elm, in the very bosom of Mother
Earth, amid the growing grass, the spreading vines, the
budding trees.[151] That is also where the well-known verse 6
of comedy fits most closely:

> For the tilling of legitimate offspring, for the sowing
>   of children.[152]

The Romans of olden days too, the Quinctii, the Serrani, 7
and many others like them, had not only their wives but
even their consulates and dictatorships offered to them in

---

[152] This line does not occur in any extant play but combines
several different phrases from Menander; Apuleius may have run
separate phrases into one line.

tam prolixo loco, ne tibi gratum faciam, si villam lauda-
vero.

89. De aetate vero Pudentillae, de qua post ista satis
confidenter mentitus es, ut etiam sexaginta annos natam
diceres nupsisse, de ea tibi paucis respondebo: nam
⟨non⟩[98] necesse est in re tam perspicua pluribus dispu-
2 tare. Pater eius natam sibi filiam more ceterorum professus est. Tabulae eius partim tabulario publico, partim
3 domo adservantur, quae iam tibi ob os obiciuntur. Porrige
tu Aemiliano tabulas istas: linum consideret, signa quae
impressa sunt recognoscat, consules legat, annos compu-
4 tet, quos sexaginta mulieri adsignabat. Probet quinque et
quinquaginta: lustro mentitus sit. Parum hoc est, libera-
lius agam, nam et ipse Pudentillae multos annos largitus
est. Redonabo igitur vicissim decem annos: Mezentius
cum Ulixe erravit. Quinquaginta saltem annorum mulierem ostendat.

5 Quid multis? Ut cum quadruplatore agam, bis duplum
quinquennium faciam, viginti annos simul[99] detraham.
Iube, Maxime, consules computari. Nisi fallor, invenies
nunc Pudentillae haud multo amplius quadragensimum
6 annum aetatis ire. O falsum audax et nimium! O mendacium viginti annorum exilio puniendum! Dimidio tanta,

---

[98] non *add. Novák*   [99] simul *Bosscha*: semel ω

---

[153] The persons referred to are L. Quinctius Cincinnatus, dic-
tator in 458, and Atilius Serranus in the First Punic War (above,
10.2), both of whom were called from the plow to hold military
commands.   [154] The document was on a sheet of papyrus
tied with a thread and contained the names and seals of the witnesses and the consular date.

206

the fields.[153] But I refrain from pursuing so broad a topic, not wanting to gratify you by praising a country house.

89. Now about Pudentilla's age you went on to tell such a barefaced lie as to say that she married at sixty. On this matter my answer will be brief, since there is no call for lengthy argument when the facts are so clear. Like other 2 fathers, her father registered his daughter's birth. The records are kept both in the public record office and at home, and they are now being brought for you to see. (*To* 3 *the servant of the court:*) You, hand those records to Aemilianus; let him examine the thread, acknowledge the stamped seals, read the names of the consuls, calculate the years, of which he bestowed sixty on the lady.[154] If he ac- 4 knowledged fifty-five, his lie would be five years off, but that is not enough. I will be more generous, since he himself lavished many years on Pudentilla, so in turn I will give him back ten. Mezentius has been off ten years with Ulysses:[155] let him show the lady to be at least fifty.

Do I need to say more? I am dealing with a four- 5 folder,[156] so I will multiply five years by four and subtract a total of twenty years. Have the consuls counted up, Maximus, and if I am not mistaken, you will find that Pudentilla is barely past her fortieth year. What a bold, ex- 6 travagant falsehood! What a lie, worth a penalty of twenty

[155] That is, Aemilianus as a second Mezentius (cf. 56.7) will be off by ten years if he makes Pudentilla fifty, as Odysseus wandered for ten years after the sack of Troy.

[156] A "fourfolder" (*quadruplator*) was either a professional accuser in cases involving a quadruple penalty (*quadruplum*) or (less probably) one who received a quarter of the accused's estate in case of a successful prosecution.

Aemiliane, mentiris, falsa audes sesquealtera. Si triginta annos pro decem dixisses, posses videri computationis gestu errasse, quos circulare debueris digitos aperuisse.[100]

7 Cum vero quadraginta, quae facilius ceteris porrecta palma significantur, ea quadraginta tu dimidio auges, non potes digitorum gestu errasse, nisi forte triginta annorum Pudentillam ratus binos cuiusque anni consules numerasti.

90. Missa haec facio: venio nunc ad ipsum stirpem accusationis, ad ipsam causam maleficii. Respondeat Aemilianus et Rufinus, ob quod emolumentum, etsi maxime magus forem, Pudentillam carminibus et venenis ad ma-

2 trimonium pellexissem. Atque ego scio plerosque reos alicuius facinoris postulatos, si fuisse quaepiam causae probarentur, hoc uno se tamen abunde defendisse, vitam suam procul ab huiusmodi sceleribus abhorrere nec id sibi obesse debere, quod videantur quaedam fuisse ad malefi-

3 ciendum invitamenta; non enim omnia quae fieri potuerint pro factis habenda, rerum vices varias evenire; certum indicem cuiusque animum esse; qui semper eodem ingenio ad virtutem vel malitiam moratus firmum argumentum est accipiendi criminis aut respuendi.

4 Haec ego quamquam possim merito dicere, tamen vo-

---

[100] aperuisse *u*: adperisse ω

---

[157] That is, twenty is half of forty, and one-third of sixty.

[158] On the practice of signifying numerals by configurations of the hand, see the commentaries of Butler-Owen and Hunink. Since there were two "ordinary" consuls each year, Apuleius affects to suppose that Aemilianus had counted each of thirty years twice to arrive at sixty.

years' exile! Your lie is off by half, Aemilianus, you are adding an imaginary third.[157] If you had said thirty years instead of ten, one might think you had made the wrong gesture in calculating, and that you had spread your fingers when you should have made a circle of them. But since the sign for forty is an open palm, an easier one than for other numbers, and you are adding half forty to forty, you cannot have mistaken the position of the fingers, unless perhaps you thought Pudentilla was thirty, and counted both consuls for each year.[158]

90. I will leave all this aside, and now come to the actual root cause of the charge, to the actual motive for using magic. I wish Aemilianus and Rufinus would tell me what I had to gain, even if I really were a sorcerer, by using spells and potions to trick Pudentilla into marriage. And yet *I* know that many men named as defendants on a criminal charge, even when it could be proved that possible motives existed, have fully cleared themselves by this one argument: that their way of life was wholly inconsistent with such crimes, and it should not count against them if there seemed to have been certain factors tempting them to do wrong. Not everything that might be a fact ought to be considered fact, and different situations can have different outcomes. The sure clue is each man's mind: if its constant nature accustoms it to do good or evil, that is a powerful argument for inferring or rejecting a criminal charge.

All this I could justly say, but I waive it for your benefit,

bis condono, nec satis mihi duco, si me omnium quae in-
simulastis abunde purgavi, si nusquam[101] passus sum vel
5 exiguam suspicionem magiae consistere. Reputate vobiscum, quanta fiducia innocentiae meae quantoque despectu vestri agam: si una causa vel minima fuerit inventa,
cur ego debuerim Pudentillae nuptias ob aliquod meum
commodum appetere, si quamlibet modicum emolumen-
6 tum probaveritis, ego ille sim Carmendas vel Damigeron
vel his ‹maiores›[102] Moses vel Iohannes vel Apollobex vel
ipse Dardanus vel quicumque alius post Zoroastren et
Hostanen inter magos celebratus est.

91. Vide quaeso, Maxime, quem tumultum suscitarint,
quoniam ego paucos magorum nominatim percensui.
2 Quid faciam tam rudibus, tam barbaris? Doceam rursum
haec et multo plura alia nomina in bibliothecis publicis
apud clarissimos scriptores me legisse? An disputem longe
aliud esse notitiam nominum, aliud artis eiusdem communionem, nec debere doctrinae instrumentum et erudi-
3 tionis memoriam pro confessione criminis haberi? An,
quod multo praestabilius est, tua doctrina, Claudi Maxime, tuaque perfecta eruditione fretus contemnam stultis
4 et impolitis ad haec respondere? Ita potius faciam; quid
illi existiment, nauci non putabo. Quod institui pergam
disputare: nullam mihi causam fuisse Pudentillam venefi-
5 ciis ad nuptias prolectandi. Formam mulieris et aetatem

---

[101] si nusquam *u*: sinus quam *ω*
[102] maiores *add. Helm: locus conclamatus*

---

[159] Carmendas is unknown; Damigeron is mentioned as the
author of a book on stones; Iohannes, or Iannes, is one of the
magicians who opposed Moses and Aaron at the court of Pharaoh

and I am not satisfied just to have cleared myself fully of all your allegations against me, to have allowed not even a slight suspicion of sorcery to stand in any respect. Just 5 observe carefully what assurance of my own innocence, what contempt for you I am about to show: if a single reason can be found, however slight, why I should have tried to marry Pudentilla for some advantage to myself, then call me the famous Carmendas or Damogeron, or 6 their predecessors Moses, Iohannes, Apollobex, Dardanus himself, or any other celebrated magician since Zoroaster and Ostanes.[159]

91. I ask you, Maximus: see what a hubbub they have started just because I listed the names of a few magicians. How shall I manage such peasants, such boors? Shall I tell 2 them yet again that I have read these names and very many more in public libraries and in the best known authors? Or shall I argue that knowing names is a far different thing from sharing the same profession, and that to be supplied with knowledge and to recall one's learning should not be counted as tantamount to confessing a crime? Or, as is more desirable, shall I rely on your knowl- 3 edge and your peerless erudition, and not deign to answer stupid, uncivilized folk on these subjects? Yes, I will rather 4 do that: I will not care a rap for what they think, but continue as I had begun and maintain that I had no motive to use potions to lure Pudentilla into marriage. They them- 5

(*Exodus* 7:8–12; 2 Timothy 3:8); for Apollobex, Plin. *HN* 30.9, and *Papyri Magicae Graecae* 2.66, 12.121; Dardanus is the legendary ancestor of the kings of Troy, also known as a magician (E. Wellmann, *RE* 4 [1901]: 2180, Dardanos 11); for Zoroaster, 25.11; for (H)ostanes, 27.2.

ipsi ultro improbaverunt idque mihi vitio dederunt, talem
uxorem causa avaritiae concupisse atque adeo primo dotem in congressu grandem et uberem rapuisse.

6   Ad haec, Maxime, longa oratione fatigare te non est
consilium. Nihil verbis opus est, cum multo disertius ipsae
tabulae loquantur, in quibus omnia contra quam isti ex sua
rapacitate de me quoque coniectaverunt facta impraesen-

7 tiarum et provisa in posterum deprehendis: iam primum
mulieris locupletissimae modicam dotem neque eam da-

8 tam, sed tantum modo ‹promissam›;[103] praeter haec ea
condicione factam coniunctionem, nullis ex me susceptis
liberis ‹si›[104] vita demigrasset, uti dos omnis apud filios
eius Pontianum et Pudentem maneret, sin vero uno unave
superstite diem suum obisset, uti tum dividua pars dotis
posteriori filio, reliqua prioribus cederet.

92. Haec, ut dico, tabulis ipsis docebo. Fors fuat an ne
sic quidem credat Aemilianus sola trecenta milia nummum scripta eorumque repetitionem filiis Pudentillae

2 pacto datam. Cape sis ipse tu manibus tuis tabulas istas,
da impulsori tuo Rufino: legat, pudeat illum tumidi animi
sui et ambitiosae mendicitatis. Quippe ipse egens, nudus
CCCC milibus nummum a creditore acceptis filiam dota-

3 vit; Pudentilla locuples femina trecentis milibus dotis fuit
contenta, et maritum habet et multis saepe et ingentibus
dotibus spretis inani nomine tantulae dotis contentum,

4 ceterum praeter uxorem suam nihil computantem, om-

---

[103] promissam *add. u*
[104] si *add. u*

---

[160] That is, a child fathered by Apuleius.

selves have gratuitously criticized the lady's appearance
and age, and alleged to my discredit that I wanted such a
wife for reasons of avarice, and in addition that on our very
first meeting I extorted a large and lavish dowry from her.

On these points, Maximus, it is not my intention to   6
tire you with a long speech. Words are unnecessary when
the marriage contract itself speaks much more eloquently.
There, contrary to what their own rapacity made them
infer about me as well, you will find everything settled for
the present and arranged for the future: first of all, a very   7
rich woman's modest dowry, and one not given but merely
promised; further, an agreement made on this condition,   8
that if she departed this life without having children by
me, the entire dowry should remain with her sons Pontianus and Pudens; if however she passed away with one son
or daughter surviving,[160] then half the dowry should go to
the later child and the rest to the earlier ones.

92. All this, I repeat, I shall prove from the contract itself. It may well be that even so Aemilianus will not believe
that a mere three hundred thousand sesterces were speci-
fied, and that Pudentilla's sons were formally given the
reversion of them. (*To Aemilianus:*) Take that contract in   2
your own hands, please, give it to your instigator, Rufinus:
let him read it and blush for his presumptuous thoughts
and self-serving beggary. For, needy and destitute as he is,
he personally borrowed four hundred thousand sesterces
from a creditor for his daughter's dowry, while Pudentilla,   3
a lady of wealth, was satisfied with a dowry of three hundred thousand. And she has a husband who often turned
down many large dowries and was satisfied with such a
small, merely nominal one; other than that, he consid-   4

nem supellectilem cunctasque divitias in concordia coniugii[105] et multo amore ponentem.

5 Quamquam quis omnium vel exigue rerum peritus cul-
pare auderet, si mulier vidua et mediocri forma, at non
aetate mediocri, nubere volens larga[106] dote et molli condicione invitasset iuvenem neque corpore neque animo
6 neque fortuna paenitendum? Virgo formosa etsi sit oppido
pauper, tamen abunde dotata est; affert quippe ad maritum novum animi indolem, pulchritudinis gratiam, floris
rudimentum. Ipsa virginitatis commendatio iure meri-
7 toque omnibus maritis acceptissima est. Nam quodcumque aliud in dotem acceperis, potes, cum libuit, ne sis
beneficio obstrictus, omne ut acceperas retribuere: pecuniam renumerare, mancipia restituere, domo demigrare,
praediis cedere; sola virginitas cum semel accepta est,
reddi nequitur, sola apud maritum ex rebus dotalibus re-
8 manet. Vidua autem qualis nuptiis venit, talis divertio di-
greditur. Nihil affert inreposcibile, sed venit iam ab alio
praeflorata, certe tibi ad quae velis minime docilis, non
minus suspectans novam domum quam ipsa iam ob unum
9 divertium suspectanda; sive illa morte amisit maritum, ut
scaevi ominis mulier et infausti coniugii minime appe-
10 tenda, seu repudio digressa est, utramvis habens culpam
mulier, quae aut tam intolerabilis fuit ut repudiaretur, aut
11 tam insolens ut repudiaret. Ob haec et alia viduae dote

[105] coniugii *Casaubon*: coniugis ω
[106] larga *Stewechius*: longa ω

ered his wife to be all that counted, and that all appurtenances and all riches consisted in marital concord and mutual love.

And yet is there anyone, even someone with only slight 5 experience of life, who would dare to find fault if a widowed woman, of middling looks but not middling age, and inclined to marry, had attracted a grown man of no slight attractiveness, character, or fortune, thanks to her ample dowry and easy terms? A beautiful virgin may be very 6 poor, but still is amply endowed, since she brings to her new husband the cast of her thoughts, the charm of her beauty, the freshness of her bloom. The state of virginity in itself is a very agreeable recommendation to any husband, and deservedly so. For with anything else you re- 7 ceive as dowry, if you do not wish to be bound by an act of generosity, you can return it entire in the condition you received it—repay the cash, return the servants, move out of the house, give up the estates. Virginity is the one thing that cannot be returned once it has been received; of all the dowry goods, it alone remains with the husband. A 8 widow, however, is the same woman entering marriage and leaving it by divorce. She brings nothing that cannot be revoked, but she comes already deflowered by another. She is decidedly slow to learn your wishes, and is just as suspicious of the new household as it is suspicious of her because of her one separation. If she lost her husband by 9 death, she is a woman of ill omen and unprosperous marriage, and so very undesirable; or if she left her husband 10 by divorce, she is a woman with one of two faults: either she was so unbearable that *he* divorced *her*, or she was so headstrong that *she* divorced *him*. For these and other 11

aucta procos sollicitant. Quod Pudentilla quoque in alio
marito fecisset, si philosophum spernentem dotis non rep-
perisset.

93. Age vero, si avaritiae causa mulierem concupissem,
quid mihi utilius ad possidendam domum eius fuit quam
simultatem inter matrem et filios serere, alienare ab eius
animo liberorum caritatem, quo liberius et artius desola-
2   tam mulierem solus possiderem? Fuitne hoc praedonis,
quod vos fingitis? Ego vero quietis et concordiae et pieta-
tis auctor, conciliator, favisor non modo nova odia non
3   serui, sed vetera quoque funditus extirpavi. Suasi uxori
meae, cuius, ut isti aiunt, iam universas opes transvora-
ram, suasi, inquam, ac denique persuasi, ut filiis pecuniam
suam reposcentibus (de quo supra dixeram) ut eam pecuniam sine mora redderet in praediis uili aestimatis et
4   quanto ipsi volebant, praeterea ex re familiari sua fructuo-
sissimos agros et grandem domum opulente ornatam mag-
namque vim tritici et hordei et vini et olivi ceterorumque
fructuum, servos quoque haud minus CCCC, pecora am-
5   plius neque pauca neque abiecti pretii donaret, ut eos et
ex ea parte quam tribuisset securos haberet et ad cetera
6   hereditatis bona spe[i] invitaret. Haec ergo ab invita Pudentilla—patietur enim me, uti res fuit, ita dicere—aegre
extudi, ingentibus precibus invitae et iratae extorsi, matrem filiis reconciliavi, privignos meos primo hoc vitrici
beneficio grandi pecunia auxi.

reasons widows tempt suitors by their ample dowries, and Pudentilla would have done so with another husband, if her choice had not fallen on a philosopher who cared nothing about a dowry.

93. But think: if avarice was why I desired the lady, what better way was there to take over her estate than by sowing discord between the mother and her sons, banishing motherly affection from her heart, so as to have freer and tighter possession of the lady when she was isolated? Was that like a robber, as you pretend I am? In fact I constantly promoted, reconciled, and supported peace, concord, and family feeling, and so far from sowing new hatreds I even tore old ones out by the roots. Though these people say I had already swallowed up my wife's entire fortune, I urged her, I repeat, I urged and finally persuaded her, when her sons demanded the return of the money I mentioned earlier, to return it immediately in the form of lands, valued cheaply and at the price they wanted. Furthermore, I urged her to draw on her own property and grant them very fertile estates, a large town house richly furnished, a great quantity of wheat, barley, wine, olive oil and other produce, no less than four hundred slaves as well, and in addition a good many cattle of no small value. In that way she would make them sure of the part that she had granted them, and encourage them to expect the remainder of their legacy in full confidence. Well, Pudentilla was reluctant (for she will not mind my stating the actual facts), but with great difficulty I wrung these concessions from her; I made endless entreaties to extract them when she was angry and reluctant; I reconciled the mother to the sons, and by this first service as a stepfather I enriched my stepsons with a large amount of money.

217

94. Cognitum hoc est tota civitate. Rufinum omnes
2 execrati me laudibus tulere. Venerat ad nos, priusquam
ista[107] donationem perficeret, cum dissimili isto fratre suo
Pontianus, pedes nostros advolutus veniam et oblivionem
praeteritorum omnium postularat, flens et manus nostras
osculabundus ac dicens paenitere quod Rufino et simili-
3 bus auscultarit. Petit postea suppliciter, uti se Lolliano
quoque Avito clarissimo viro purgem, cui haud pridem
4 tirocinio orationis suae fuerat a me commendatus. Quippe
compererat ante paucos dies omnia me, ut acta erant, ad
5 eum perscripsisse. Id quoque a me impetrat. Itaque acceptis litteris Carthaginem pergit, ubi iam prope exacto
proconsulatus[108] sui munere Lollianus Avitus te, Maxime,
6 opperiebatur. Is epistulis meis lectis pro sua eximia humanitate gratulatus Pontiano, quod cito errorem suum cor-
rexisset, rescripsit mihi per eum quas litteras, di boni, qua
doctrina, quo lepore, qua verborum amoenitate simul et
7 iucunditate, prorsus ut "vir bonus dicendi peritus." Scio
te, Maxime, libenter eius litteras auditurum, et quidem
8 ipse legam,[109] mea voce pronuntiabo. Cedo tu Aviti epistulas, ut quae semper ornamento mihi fuerunt, sint nunc
9 etiam saluti. At tu licebit aquam sinas fluere; namque
optimi viri litteras ter et quater aveo quantovis temporis
dispendio lectitare.

107 ista *Hildebrand*: istam ω
108 proconsulatus *scripsi*: consulatus ω
109 ipse legam *Rohde*: si praelegam *ut videtur* ω

161 On Lollianus, see n. 55 and also Appendix E.
162 A definition of the true orator attributed to the elder Cato,
e.g., by Quint. *Inst.* 12.1.1.

94. The whole city learned about this. One and all cursed Rufinus and praised me to the skies. Even before my wife had completed her gift, Pontianus had come to us together with this brother who so little resembles him, thrown himself at our feet, and begged us to forgive and forget everything that had passed; he wept, kissed our hands, and apologized for listening to Rufinus and those like him. Next, he begged and prayed me to clear him also with his excellency Lollianus Avitus,[161] to whom I had recently recommended him at the start of his speaking career; for he had found out that I had written a full and detailed statement of the facts to him a few days earlier. This too he persuaded me to do. And so after getting my letter he left for Carthage, where Lollianus, being almost at the end of his duties as proconsul, was awaiting yourself, Maximus. On reading my letter, as the extraordinarily kind person he is, he congratulated Pontianus on having promptly corrected his mistake, and through him he sent back such a letter to me—heavens above—so cultivated, so elegant, in language both so charming and so pleasant, absolutely like "the good man skilled in speech" he is.[162] I know, Maximus, that you will be glad to hear his letter, and indeed I will read it myself, I will recite it in my own voice. (*To the servant of the court:*) You there, Avitus' letter, please, which has always been an honor to me and is now a vindication too. (*To another* [?] *servant of the court:*) You there, you may keep the clock going,[163] since I am quite ready to read His Excellency's letter three or four times over, whatever it costs of my time.

[163] Literally, "allow the water to flow," referring to the action of the water clock.

95. Non sum nescius debuisse me post istas Aviti litteras perorare. Quem enim laudatorem locupletiorem,
quem testem vitae meae sanctiorem producam, quem
2 denique advocatum facundiorem? Multos in vita mea
Romani nominis disertos viros sedulo cognovi, sed sum
3 aeque neminem admiratus. Nemo est hodie, quantum
4 mea opinio fert, alicuius in eloquentia laudis et spei, quin
Avitus esse longe malit, si cum eo se remota invidia velit
conferre. Quippe omnes fandi virtutes paene diversae in
5 illo viro congruunt. Quamcumque orationem struxerit
Avitus, ita illa erit undique sui perfecte absoluta, ut in illa
neque Cato gravitatem requirat neque Laelius lenitatem
nec Gracchus impetum nec Caesar calorem nec Hortensius distributionem nec Calvus argutias nec parsimoniam
6 Sallustius nec opulentiam Cicero. Prorsus, inquam, ne
omnis persequar, si Avitum audias, neque additum quicquam velis neque detractum neque autem aliquid com-
mutatum.
7 Video, Maxime, quam benigne audias, quae in amico
tuo Avito recognosces. Tua me comitas, ut vel pauca dice-
8 rem de eo, invitavit. At non usque adeo tuae benevolentiae
indulgebo, ut mihi permittam iam propemodum fesso in
causa prorsus ad finem inclinata de egregiis virtutibus eius
nunc demum incipere, quin potius eas integris viribus et
tempori libero servem. 96. Nunc enim mihi, quod aegre

---

164 The orators referred to are (1) M. Porcius Cato "the Elder"
(n. 44), (2) C. Laelius (n. 50), (3) either Tib. Sempronius Gracchus, tribune in 133, or his younger brother Gaius, tribune in 123
and 122 (cf. Cic. *Brut.* 103, 125), (4) C. Julius Caesar, a distinguished orator as well as a general and statesman, (5) C. Licinius
Calvus, friend of Catullus and Cicero, poet and famously vehe-

95. I know full well that I should have followed this letter with my summation. For what more generous eulogist, more unimpeachable witness to my way of life, in short more eloquent advocate could I produce? In the 2 course of my life I have closely observed many eloquent men among citizens of Rome, but there is none I have so much admired. There is no one today, in my opinion, who 3 has some repute and promise as an orator, and yet would 4 not far prefer to be Avitus, if he chose to put aside envy and compare himself with him; since all the oratorical virtues, almost irreconcilable as they are, come together in him alone. Any speech composed by Avitus will be so 5 perfectly finished in every way that Cato could not ask for more solemnity, Laelius more smoothness, Gracchus more force, Caesar more warmth, Hortensius more structure, Calvus more animation, Sallust more economy, Cicero more richness.[164] In sum, I repeat, not to name every 6 orator, after once hearing Avitus you would want nothing added, nothing removed, and indeed nothing altered.

I notice, Maximus, with what goodwill you heard the 7 qualities you will recognize in your friend Avitus; your courtesy prompted me to speak just briefly about him. But 8 I will not so far encroach on your goodwill, being almost exhausted in a case already near its end, as to allow myself to begin only now on his extraordinary excellences, but instead will save them for when my powers are restored and my time is free. 96. For now, much against my inclina-

---

ment orator, (6) Q. Hortensius Hortalus, consul in 69, Cicero's predecessor as the leading Roman orator, (7) C. Sallustius Crispus, tribune in 52 and Roman historian, and (8) M. Tulllius Cicero, consul in 63 and Rome's greatest orator, though criticized by some such as Calvus for excessive richness of style.

fero, a commemoratione tanti viri ad pestes istas oratio revolvenda est.

2   Audesne te ergo, Aemiliane, cum Avito conferre? Quemne ille bonum virum ait, cuius animi dispositionem[110] tam plene suis litteris collaudat, eum tu magiae

3 ‹et›[111] maleficii criminis insectabere? An invasisse me domum Pudentillae et concipilare bona eius tu magis dolere debes quam doluisset Pontianus, qui mihi ob paucorum dierum vestro scilicet instinctu ortas simultates etiam absenti apud Avitum satisfecit, qui mihi apud tantum virum gratias egit?

4   Puta me acta apud Avitum, non litteras ipsius legisse. Quid posses vel tu vel quisquis[112] in isto negotio accusare? Pontianus ipse quod a matre donatum acceperat meo muneri acceptum ferebat, Pontianus me vitricum sibi

5 contigisse intimis affectionibus laetabatur. Quod utinam incolumis Carthagine revertisset! Vel, quoniam sic ei fuerat fato decretum, utinam tu, Rufine, supremum eius iudicium non impedisses! Quas mihi aut coram aut denique in

6 testamento gratias egisset! Litteras tamen, quas ad me Carthagine[m] vel iam adveniens ex itinere praemisit, quas adhuc validus, quas iam aeger, plenas honoris, plenas

7 amoris, quaeso, Maxime, paulisper recitari sinas, ut sciat frater eius, accusator meus, quam in omnibus minor vitae[113] curriculum cum fratre optimae memoriae viro currat.

110 dispositionem *Fuluius*: disputationem ω
111 et *add. Bosscha*
112 tu vel quisquis *van der Vliet*: quas q(ui)s ω
113 minor vitae *Lennep*: minerve ω (*locus vix sanus*)

165 A Roman will often contained the testator's final tribute to

tion, from recalling that great man my speech must revert to these scoundrels.

Well, Aemilianus, do you dare to oppose Avitus? When 2 *he* calls someone a good man, and praises his cast of mind so highly in his letter, will you attack that man with a charge of magic and poisoning? Ought *you* to complain 3 that I have broken into Pudentilla's home and plundered her property more than Pontianus would have done— Pontianus who apologized to me before Avitus, though I was absent, because of a few days' quarrel which you of course had caused, and who thanked me before that great man?

Suppose I had read the records before Avitus and not 4 Pontianus' own letter. What ground for accusation could you or anyone find in the affair? Pontianus himself considered his mother's gift as a present from me; Pontianus rejoiced with the deepest affection for the luck of having me for a stepfather. If only he had returned alive from 5 Carthage! Or rather, since that was how it had to be, if only you, Rufinus, had not thwarted his final testimony! What thanks he would have expressed to me either in person or at least in his will![165] Yet the letters he sent ahead to me 6 from Carthage or on the road while returning, some when in good health, some when already ill, full of respect, full of love—I beg you, Maximus, let them be read out briefly, so that his brother, my accuser, may see how in every re- 7 spect he falls short of his dearly missed brother as he runs the course of life. (*The letters are read out.*)

his or her heirs and legatees. As emerges below, Pontianus had presumably written his last valid will at the time of his estrangement from his stepfather, and Rufinus had in some way prevented or dissuaded him from completing a later one.

97. Audistine vocabula, quae mihi Pontianus frater
tuus tribuerat, me parentem suum, me dominum, me magistrum cum saepe alias, tum in extremo tempore vitae
2 vocans, post quam[114] tuas quoque paris epistulas prome-
rem, si vel exiguam moram tanti putarem. Potius testamentum illud recens tui fratris quamquam imperfectum
tamen proferri cuperem, in quo mei officiosissime et ho-
3 nestissime meminit. Quod tamen testamentum Rufinus
neque comparari neque perfici passus est pudore perditae
hereditatis, quam ⟨praemium⟩[115] paucorum mensium,
quibus socer Pontiani fuit, magno quidem pretio noctium
4 computarat. Praeterea nescio quos Chaldaeos consolue-
rat, quo lucro filiam collocaret; qui, ut audio (utinam illud
non vere respondissent!) primum eius maritum in paucis
mensibus moriturum. Cetera enim de hereditate, ut ad-
solent, ad consulentis votum confinxerunt.
5 Verum, ut dii voluere, quasi caeca bestia in cassum
hiavit. Pontianus enim filiam Rufini mali[116] compertam
non modo heredem non reliquit, sed ne honesto quidem
6 legato impertivit, quippe qui ei ad ignominiam lintea ad-
scribi ducentorum fere denariorum iusserit, ut intelle-
geretur iratus potius aestimasse eam quam oblitus prae-
7 terisse. Scripsit autem heredes tam hoc testamento quam
priore, quod lectum est, matrem cum fratre; cui, ut vides,
admodum puero eandem illam filiae suae machinam Rufi-

---

[114] post quam (sc. epistulam) *Ellis, CR (1901), 49*: postquam ω   [115] praemium *add. Helm*
[116] mali *Casaubon*: male ω

---

[166] Apuleius assumes that anything Pontianus left to Rufinus
and his daughter was a costly payment for his nights with his wife.

97. (*Addressing Pudens:*) Did you hear the terms that your brother used for me, "father," "sir," "teacher," in the last hours of his life as at many other times? After that letter I could produce similar ones from you too, if I thought them worth even a brief pause. Instead I would have liked to have your brother's recent will exhibited, even unfinished though it is, since he mentions me with the greatest respect and honor in it. That will, though, Rufinus did not let him either draw up or finish, embarrassed at losing the legacy he had expected as payment for the few months he had been Pontianus' stepfather, a high price for his nights with his daughter.[166] Besides that, he had inquired of some Chaldeans[167] what profit he would get from marrying off his daughter; and as I hear (I only wish their answer had been wrong), they replied that her first husband would die within a few months; as for the rest about the inheritance, they made it up to suit their client's hopes, as they usually do.

However, so it pleased the gods, like a blind animal he opened his jaws to no effect. For after finding the worst about Rufinus' daughter, Pontianus did not even leave her a decent legacy, let alone make her his heir: for to mark her infamy he directed that she receive napkins worth about two hundred denarii, thus making clear that he had judged her in anger, and not omitted her by mistake. Now both in this will and in the previous one that was read out, he appointed his mother as his heir together with his brother; and, as you see, Rufinus is bringing that same

---

[167] "Chaldeans" was a generic term for fortune-tellers, because of the reputation of Babylonia as a source of astronomical and astrological knowledge.

nus admovet ac mulierem aliquam multo natu maiorem, nuperrime uxorem fratris, misero puero obicit et obsternit.

98. At ille, puellae meretricis blandimentis et lenonis patris illectamentis captus et possessus, exinde ut frater eius animam edidit, relicta matre ad patruum commigra-
2 vit, quo facilius remotis nobis coepta perficerentur. Favet enim Rufino Aemilianus et proventum cupit. Ehem, recte vos admonetis: etiam suam spem bonus patruus temperat in isto ac fovet, qui sciat intestati pueri legitimum magis
3 quam iustum heredem futurum. Nollem hercule hoc a me profectum: non fuit meae moderationis tacitas omnium suspiciones palam abrumpere. Male vos, qui suggessistis!
4 Plane quidem, si verum[117] velis, multi mirantur, Aemiliane, tam repentinam circa puerum istum pietatem tuam, postquam frater eius Pontianus est mortuus, cum antea tam ignotus illi fueris, ut saepe ne in occursu quidem fi-
5 lium fratris tui de facie agnosceres. At nunc adeo patientem te ei praebes itaque eum indulgentia corrumpis, adeo ei nulla re adversare, ut per haec suspicacioribus fidem facias. Investem a nobis accepisti; vesticipem ilico
6 reddidisti. Cum a nobis regeretur, ad magistros itabat; ab iis nunc magna fugela in ganeum fugit, amicos serios as-

---

[117] verum *u*: puerum *ω*

---

[168] As Pudens' guardian, Aemilianus would be the default heir (*heres legitimus*) though not the heir appointed by will (*heres iustus*).

[169] Apuleius hints that Aemilianus played the passive role in sex with his ward, just as he more openly accuses Aemilianus' collaborator Rufinus of having been a "pansy" (74.7).

siege engine, his daughter, to bear on that very young boy,
and though a much older woman and lately his brother's wife, he is throwing her at the poor lad and beneath
his feet.

98. So he was trapped and ensnared by the charms of
a young prostitute and the lures of her pimping father, and
as soon his brother had breathed his last, he left his mother
and moved in with his uncle, so that the scheme could be
carried out more easily with us out of the way. For Aemil- 2
ianus is supporting Rufinus and wants him to succeed. (*To
the bystanders:*) Ah yes, thank you for the reminder: as a
kindly uncle, he is also using the boy to advance and foster
his own hopes, knowing that if he dies intestate he himself will be the legal heir, though not the proper one.[168] I 3
would not have wanted to start this idea; my self-restraint
did not allow me to blurt out openly what all suspect silently. Shame on you for suggesting it! Yet the fact is, if 4
you want to hear the truth, Aemilianus, that many people
wonder at your sudden family feeling for this boy after
his brother Pontianus' death. Hitherto you were such a
stranger to him that you often did not recognize the face of
your own brother's son even when you met. Now, though, 5
you show yourself so compliant with him, you so spoil him
with your indulgence, you so grant his every wish, that by
so doing you confirm the belief of anyone at all suspicious.
You got him from us in boy's clothes, you soon put man's
clothes on him.[169] Under our guidance he went to school, 6
while now he runs far away into taverns, shuns his studi-

pernatur, cum adulescentulis postremissimis inter scorta
7 et pocula puer hoc aevi convivium agitat. Ipse domi tuae
rector, ipse familiae dominus, ipse magister convivio. In
ludo quoque gladiatorio frequens visitur;[118] nomina gla-
diatorum et pugnas et vulnera plane quidem ut puer ho-
8 nestus ab ipso lanista docetur. Loquitur nunquam nisi
Punice et si quid adhuc a matre graecissat; enim Latine
9 loqui neque vult neque potest. Audisti, Maxime, paulo
ante (pro nefas!) privignum meum, fratrem Pontiani, di-
serti iuvenis, vix singulas syllabas fringultientem, cum ab
eo quaereres donassetne illis mater quae ego dicebam me
adnitente donata.

99. Testor igitur te, Claudi Maxime, vosque, qui in consilio estis, vosque etiam, qui tribunal mecum adsistitis,
haec damna et dedecora morum eius patruo huic et can-
2 didato illo socero adsignanda meque posthac boni consul-
turum, quod talis privignus curae meae iugum cervice
excusserit, neque postea pro eo matri eius supplicaturum.
3 Nam, quod paenissime oblitus sum, nuperrime cum testamentum Pudentilla post mortem Pontiani filii sui in mala
valetudine scriberet, diu sum adversus illam renisus, ne
hunc ob tot insignis contumelias, ob tot iniurias exhereda-
4 ret. Elogium gravissimum iam totum medius fidius per-
scriptum ut aboleret, impensis precibus oravi. Postremo,
ni impetrarem, diversurum me ab ea comminatus sum;
mihi hanc veniam tribueret, malum filium beneficio vin-
5 ceret, me invidia omni liberaret. Nec prius destiti quam
ita fecit. Doleo me huncce scrupulum Aemiliano demp-

[118] visitur *u*: visitor *ω*

ous friends and associates with the most depraved youths while still a boy, feasting among whores and goblets. He 7 and he alone runs your household, owns your slaves, leads the revels. As a frequent visitor to the gladiatorial school, he hears the names of the gladiators, their fights and injuries from the trainer himself, this virtuous boy. He never 8 talks except in Punic and in the little Greek he still has from his mother; Latin he neither wishes to speak, nor can he. Maximus, just now (shocking as it is!) you heard how 9 my stepson, the brother of that young orator Pontianus, scarcely stammered out one syllable at a time when you asked if their mother had made them the presents that I said I had urged her to make.

99. I call you to witness, therefore, Claudius Maximus, you, his fellow judges, and you who are supporting me before the judgment seat. These blemishes and stains on his character should be imputed to his uncle and would-be father-in-law here. Henceforth I shall be fully content that 2 a stepson like this has shaken the yoke of my protection off his back, and in future I shall not plead for him with his mother. For, as I had nearly forgotten, when Puden- 3 tilla, though very ill, was recently writing her will after her son Pontianus' death, she wanted to disinherit this boy here because of all his flagrant insults and all his outrages, but for a long time I opposed her. She had already written 4 out a very damning codicil, I swear, but I urgently pleaded with her to cancel it. In the end, I threatened to leave her if I could not persuade her; I asked her to do me this favor, to win over her wicked son by an act of kindness, and to spare me from any kind of unpopularity. I desisted only 5 when she did so. I am sorry to have taken this worry off

sisse, tam inopinatam rem ei indicasse. Specta quaeso
Maxime, ut hisce auditis subito obstipuerit, ut oculos ad
6 terram demiserit. Enim longe sequius ratus fuerat, nec
immerito: mulierem filii contumeliis infectam, meis officiis
devinctam sciebat. De me quoque fuit quod timeret: quivis vel aeque ut ego spernens hereditatis tamen vindicari
7 de tam inofficioso privigno non recusasset. Haec praecipue sollicitudo eos ad accusationem mei stimulavit: hereditatem omnem mihi relictam falso ex sua avaritia con-
iectavere. Solvo vos in praeteritum isto metu. Namque
animum meum neque hereditatis neque ultionis occasio
8 potuit loco demovere. Pugnavi cum irata matre pro privigno malo vitricus, veluti pater pro optimo filio adversus
novercam, nec satis fuit, ni bonae uxoris prolixam liberalitatem circa me nimio plus aequo coercerem.

100. Cedo tu testamentum iam inimico filio a matre
factum me, quem isti praedonem dicunt, verba singula
2 cum precibus praeeunte. Rumpi tabulas istas iube, Maxime: invenies filium heredem, mihi vero tenue nescio quid
honoris gratia legatum, ne, si quid ei humanitus atti-
gisset, nomen maritus in uxoris tabulis non haberem.
3 Cape istud[119] matris tuae testamentum, vere hoc quidem inofficiosum, quidni? In quo obsequentissimum maritum exheredavit, inimicissimum filium scripsit heredem,
4 immo enimvero non filium, sed Aemiliani spes et Rufini
nuptias, sed temulentum illud collegium, parasitos tuos.

---

[119] istud *Casaubon*: ista ut ω

---

[170] That is, by saying that he begged Pudentilla not to disinherit Pudens, Apuleius has proved that he will not try to make her
cut Pudens out of her will.

230

Aemilianus' mind,[170] and to have informed him of something so unexpected. Just see, if you please, Maximus, how this news has made him suddenly go silent and turn his eyes to the ground. For what he had supposed was very 6 different, and for good reason; he knew that the son had smeared the lady with insults, while I had endeared her by kindness. He had reason to fear me too: anyone, even one so indifferent to legacies as I am, might still not have shrunk from avenging himself on so undutiful a stepson. It was this worry above all that prompted them to prose- 7 cute me: their own greed made them guess that I had been left the whole estate. (*To Aemilianus and his supporters:*) As to the past, let me relieve you of that fear, for neither the chance of receiving a legacy nor of getting my revenge could have swayed me. As a stepfather, I fought for a 8 wicked stepson against his angry mother, as a father would for the best of sons against a stepmother, and I did not rest until I had restrained my kind wife's lavish generosity to me to a far greater degree than was fair.

100. (*To a servant of the court:*) You there, bring the will made by a mother whose son was now her enemy; they call me a burglar, and yet I dictated every word, mingling them with my pleas. Order that document unsealed, Max- 2 imus: you will find that she made her son her heir, while leaving me some modest legacy as a mark of respect, so that if anything happened to her in the course of nature, I as her husband should not go unmentioned in my wife's will. (*To Pudens:*) Take your mother's will there, which in 3 one way really is undutiful, and that is this: she disinherited so indulgent a husband and made so hostile a son her heir—or rather not her son, but Aemilianus' hopes, Rufi- 4 nus' marriage, and that drunken fraternity of your hang-

5 Accipe, inquam, filiorum optime, et positis paulisper epistulis amatoriis matris, lege potius testamentum. Si quid quasi insana scripsit, hic reperies et quidem mox a principio: "Sicinius Pudens filius meus mihi heres esto." Fateor,
6 qui hoc legerit insanum putabit. Hicine filius heres, qui te in ipso fratris sui funere advocata perditissimorum iuvenum manu voluit excludere e domo quam ipsa donaveras, qui te sibi a fratre coheredem relictam graviter et acerbe
7 tulit, qui confestim te cum tuo luctu et maerore deseruit
8 et ad Rufinum et Aemilianum de sinu tuo aufugit, qui tibi plurimas postea contumelias dixit coram et adiuvante patruo fecit, qui nomen tuum pro tribunalibus ventilavit, qui pudorem tuum tuismet litteris conatus est publice
9 dedecorare, qui maritum tuum, quem elegeras, quem, ut
10 ipse obiciebat, efflictim amabas, capitis accusavit? Aperi quaeso, bone puer, aperi testamentum: facilius insaniam matris sic probabis.

101. Quid abnuis, quid recusas, postquam sollicitudinem de hereditate materna reppulisti? At ego hasce tabulas, Maxime, hic ibidem pro pedibus tuis abicio testorque me deinceps incuriosius habiturum, quid Pudentilla testa-
2 mento suo scribat. Ipse iam, ut libet, matrem suam de
3 cetero exoret: mihi, ut ultra pro eo deprecer, locum non reliquit. Ipse iam, ut sui potens ac vir, acerbissimas litteras matri dictet, iram eius deleniat: qui potuit perorare, poterit exorare. Mihi iam dudum satis est, si non modo crimina obiecta plenissime dilui, verum etiam radicem iudicii huius, id est hereditatis quaesitae invidiam, funditus sustuli.

---

171 Cf. 85.1, where Apuleius accuses Pudens of making his mother's letters of affection public.

ers-on. I repeat, take it, you model son, put away your 5
mother's love letters for a moment[171] and read her will. If
anything in it seems written by a madwoman, you will find
it here, in fact just in the opening words: "Let my son Sicinius Pudens be my heir." I admit it, anyone reading this
will think it mad. (*To Pudentilla:*) Is this son your heir? 6
Why, even at his brother's funeral he summoned a gang of
young desperadoes, and tried to shut you out of the house
that you yourself had given him. He was furious and re-
sentful because you had made his brother his coheir. He 7
immediately deserted you in your grief and sorrow, and
fled from your protection to Rufinus and Aemilianus. He 8
hurled many insults at you with his uncle present and assisting him. He bandied your name about the law courts.
He used your very own letters in trying to dishonor you
with the public. He brought a capital charge against your 9
chosen husband, whom you loved devotedly, as he himself
rebuked you for doing. Open, if you please, you loving son, 10
open the will: that way you will more easily prove your
mother insane.

101. Why do you decline, why refuse, now that you have
shed your worry about your mother's bequest? Meanwhile
I, Maximus, throw this will here before your feet, and call
you to witness that from now on I will be quite indifferent
to what Pudentilla writes in her will. Now let him plead 2
his own case to his mother as he pleases; he has left me no 3
motive to make further pleas on his behalf. Let him, as his
own master and a grown man, write letters full of bitter-
ness to his mother, and try to assuage her anger: he could
plead in court, he can surely plead for himself. By now I
have long been satisfied not just with rebutting the alleged
crimes in full, but also with tearing out the root cause of
this trial, which is resentment over a hoped-for legacy.

4   Illud etiam, ne quid omnium praeteream, priusquam peroro, falso obiectum revincam. Dixistis me magna pecunia mulieris pulcherrimum praedium meo nomine emisse.

5   Dico exiguum herediolum LX milibus nummum, id quoque non me, sed Pudentillam suo nomine emisse, Pudentillae nomen in tabulis esse, Pudentillae nomine pro eo

6   agello tributum dependi. Praesens est quaestor publicus, cui depensum est, Corvinius Celer, vir ornatus. Adest etiam tutor auctor mulieris, vir gravissimus et sanctissimus, omni cum honore mihi nominandus, Cassius Lon-

7   ginus. Quaere, Maxime, cuius emptionis auctor fuerit, quantulo pretio mulier locuples agellum suum praestinarit.

    [Testimonium Cassi Longini tutoris et Corvini Clementis quaestoris.][120]

8   Estne ita ut dixi? Uspiam in hac emptione nomen meum ascriptum est? Num ipsum heredioli pretium invidiosum est, num vel hoc saltem in me collatum?

    102. Quid etiam est, Aemiliane, quod non te iudice refutaverim? Quod pretium magiae meae repperisti? Cur ergo Pudentillae animum veneficiis flecterem? Quod ut ex ea commodum caperem? Uti dotem mihi modicam potius

2   quam amplam diceret? O praeclara carmina! An ut eam dotem filiis suis magis restipularetur quam penes me sine-

3   ret? Quid addi ad hanc magiam potest? An uti rem fami-

---

[120] Testimonium . . . qR *del. Acidalius*

---

[172] A married woman needed a temporary guardian (*tutor*) other than her husband when conducting certain kinds of business.

Since I do not wish to leave anything out, I will rebut 4
that other false charge before I close. You said that I used
a large amount of my wife's money to buy a splendid property on my own account. I contend that it was a small farm 5
worth sixty thousand sesterces, and that it too was bought
by Pudentilla, not by me, that Pudentilla's name is on the
deed, and the tax on that estate is paid in Pudentilla's
name. The public treasurer is here, Corvinius Celer, a 6
distinguished gentleman, to whom the tax has been paid.
Here too is Cassius Longinus, the guardian responsible for
my wife,[172] a thoroughly dependable and honorable gentleman, whom I should name with the highest respect. Ask 7
him, Maximus, what purchase he authorized, and how low
a price my wealthy wife paid for her little plot.

[Testimony of Cassius Longinus, guardian, and Corvinius Clemens, treasurer.][173]

Is it not just as I said? Is my name written anywhere in 8
this deed of purchase? Surely the price of the plot is nothing to be jealous of, and surely not even that was conveyed
to me?

102. What else is there, Aemilianus, that I have failed
to refute, in your opinion? What reward for my magic have
you uncovered? Why then should I have used magic to
change Pudentilla's mind? What good did I intend to get
from her? That she should promise me a modest dowry,
not a large one? Fine spells I must have used. Was it that 2
she should give her sons the reversion of the dowry and
not leave it with me? What better magic than that could
there be? Was it that at my urging she should make most 3

[173] This clause appears to be interpolated; it is unclear why
the treasurer is given the name Clemens instead of Celer.

liarem suam meo adhortatu pleramque filiis condonasset,
quae nihil illis ante me maritum fuerat largita, mihi ‹nihil›[121] quicquam impertiret? O gratum[122] veneficium di-
4 cam an ingratum beneficium! An ut testamento, quod irata
filio scribebat, filium potius, cui offensa erat, quam me, cui
devincta, heredem relinqueret? Hoc quidem multis cantaminibus difficile impetravi.

5   Putate vos causam non apud Cl. Maximum agere, virum aequum et iustitiae pertinacem, sed alium aliquem
pravum et saevum iudicem substituite, accusationum fau-
6 torem, cupidum condemnandi: date ei quod sequatur,
ministrate vel tantulam verisimilem occasionem secundum vos pronuntiandi. Saltim fingite aliquid, eminiscimini
7 quod respondeatis, qui vos ita rogarit. Et quoniam omnem
conatum necesse est quaepiam causa praecedat, respon-
dete qui Apuleium dicitis animum Pudentillae magicis
8 illectamentis adortum, quid ex ea petierit, cur fecerit. Formam eius voluerat? Negatis. Divitias saltem concupierat?
Negant tabulae dotis, negant tabulae donationis, negant
tabulae testamenti, in quibus non modo non cupide appe-
tisse, verum etiam dure reppulisse liberalitatem suae ux-
9 oris ostenditur. Quae igitur alia causa est? Quid obmutuis-
tis? Quid tacetis? Ubi illud libelli vestri atrox principium
nomine privigni mei formatum: "hunc ego, domine Maxime, reum apud te facere institui"?

      103. Quin igitur addis: "reum magistrum, reum vitri-
cum, reum deprecatorem"? Sed quid deinde? "Plurimo-
rum maleficiorum et manifestissimorum." Cedo unum de

---

[121] nihil *add. Pricaeus*
[122] gratum *Kronenberg*: grave ω

of her own property over to her sons, when she had made them no present before our marriage, and should allow me nothing at all? Gratitude for sorcery, shall I call it, or ingratitude for kindness? Or was it that she should write 4 her will while angry with her son, and yet she should make an heir of her son, with whom she had quarreled, rather than of me, to whom she was devoted? Even with many spells, it was hard to persuade her of that.

Suppose that you were not pleading your case before 5 Claudius Maximus, a man of fairness and unwavering justice, but replace him with some other judge, corrupt and cruel, favorable to accusations and eager to condemn. Give him something to follow up, provide him with a plau- 6 sible excuse, however slight, to declare in your favor. At least devise something. Think up what to reply if he happens to ask you. And since every effort must be preceded 7 by some motive or other, tell him how you maintain that Apuleius worked on Pudentilla's heart with magic charms, what he wanted from her and what his motive was. Did 8 he want her beauty? "No," you say. Well, at least did he want her wealth? "No," says the dowry deed, "no" says the deed of gift, "no" say the pages of her will: they show that, so far from greedily hankering after his wife's generosity, in actual fact he firmly refused it. What other motive is 9 there, then? Why are you dumbstruck? Why are you silent? What has become of that formidable opening of your writ, which you drew up in my stepson's name: "My lord Maximus, I formally accuse this man before you"?

103. Why not add, then: "I accuse my teacher, I accuse my stepfather, I accuse my intercessor"? But what comes next? "Of most numerous and flagrant crimes." Let us have one of the "numerous" crimes, let us have a vague or

plurimis, cedo dubium vel saltem obscurum de manifes-
2 tissimis. Ceterum ad haec, quae obiecistis, numera an
binis verbis respondeam. "Dentes splendidas": ignosce
munditiis. "Specula inspicis": debet philosophus. "Versus
facis": licet fieri. "Pisces exploras": Aristoteles docet. "Lig-
3 num consecras": Plato suadet. "Uxorem ducis": leges
iubent. "Prior natu'st":[123] solet fieri. "Lucrum sectatu's":[124]
dotalis accipe, donationem recordare, testamentum lege.

4   Quae si omnia affatim retudi, si calumnias omnes refu-
tavi, si me in omnibus non modo criminibus, verum etiam
maledictis procul a culpa magiae[125] tutus sum, si philosophiae honorem, qui mihi salute mea antiquior est, nusquam minui, immo contra ubique si cum septem pennis
5 eum tenui: si haec, ut dico, ita sunt, possum securus existimationem tuam revereri quam potestatem vereri, quod
minus grave et verendum mihi arbitror a proconsule dam-
nari quam si a tam bono tamque emendato viro improbarer.[126]

     Dixi.[127]

[123] natu'st (*i.e.,* natu est) *Butler ad loc.*: natu is est ω
[124] sectatu's *Purser, Hermathena 14 (1907), 394*: sectatus es ω
[125] magiae *Acidalius*: philosophiae ω
[126] improbarer *Salmasius*: improber ω
[127] *Titulum* APVLEI PLATONICI MADAVRENSIS PROSAE DE
MAGIA LIB. II. EXPL(ICIT). EGO SALVSTIVS EM(EN)DAVI ROME
FELIX *praebet* φ

APOLOGIA

at least an obscure crime from among the "most flagrant"
ones. At any rate, in answer to what you *have* alleged,   2
count to see if two words are enough for my reply. "You
polish your teeth." Excusable cleanliness. "You examine
mirrors." Philosophic duty. "You write poetry." Allowable
activity. "You study fish." Aristotelian doctrine. "You consecrate wood." Platonic precept. "You marry a wife." Legal   3
requirement. "She was older than you." Nothing unusual.
"You were after profit." Take the document, recall the gift,
read the will.

If I have sufficiently demolished all these charges, if I   4
have refuted all their false accusations; if after all their
charges, and likewise all their insults, I am safe from the
charge of magic; if I have in no way lessened the dignity
of Philosophy, which I value more than my own preservation, but rather upheld it on all points and with flying
colors: if this is so, I repeat, I can respect your judgment   5
with more confidence than I fear your authority. For a
proconsul's guilty verdict is less grave or dreadful, I think,
than the disapproval of a man so virtuous and so upright.[174]

I have finished.[175]

[174] That is, an innocent man can be guilty before the law, for
example Socrates, but for a philosopher it would be worse to seem
guilty in the eyes of someone such as Maximus.

[175] Manuscript φ has an annotation, "Book II of the (speech
in) prose on magic of Apuleius, Platonist of Madauros, ends. I,
Sallustius, corrected it at Rome with good luck."

FLORIDA

INTRODUCTION

As noted in the General Introduction, the work called *Florida* in the manuscripts consists of a series of Apuleian excerpts, though one or two of them may be entire speeches. The title perhaps denotes a bouquet of highly wrought passages, imagined as especially colorful or perfumed; the selection was presumably made not by Apuleius but by someone later. The selections represent a variety of literary genres, principally the encomium and the *prolalia,* a short preface designed to win over the audience and often consisting of an anecdote or an exercise in yet another genre, the *ecphrasis.*

The whole work comes down in two distinct parts. The larger part is contained in Laurentianus 68.2 (F), where it follows the *Apologia* and the *Metamorphoses.* Unlike those two works, it lacks subscriptions by Sallustius and was perhaps not part of the manuscript that he corrected in 395 and 397, but was joined to the other two works at a later stage of transmission. F and its descendant φ divide this part into four short books of approximately equal length, but editors divide it into twenty-three chapters. The other part consists of five "orphan chapters," here numbered with an asterisk, which come down by a separate line of transmission.

The main part of the *Florida* presents many problems.

It is not always clear where one excerpt ends and another begins, for example, between chapters 3 and 4, both of which concern famous players on the *aulos*. Some chapters open with particles that might imply a lost beginning, such as *at non* or *enim* (chs. 2, 5, 8, 11, 13), others break off in midsentence (11, 22). Some seem highly polished, others give the impression of improvisation (e.g., 16.33–34), though this might be deliberate, as in a musical *impromptu*.[1]

The whole twenty-eight chapters also vary in length and subject. Chapter 1, for example, is a mere paragraph, while the encomiastic chapters (9, 16, 17, 18, and 20) each take several pages. Apart from these encomia, other themes stand out: accounts of past philosophers (Crates, chs. 14 and 22; Pythagoras, 15; Protagoras and Thales, 18), descriptions or *ecphrases* (the eagle's flight, 2; a parrot, 12; the statue of a musician in Samos, 15), myths or stories (Marsyas, 3; Crates' "marriage" with Hipparche, 14; the death of Philemon, 16, an exceptionally fine passage; Pythagoras' failed bet with his pupil Euathlus, 18; Asclepiades' resuscitation of a man apparently dead, 19; 4*, the vixen and the crow).

The five "orphan chapters" of the *Florida* are transmitted in the manuscripts of *De deo Socratis* as the opening of that work. These chapters are unconnected with each other, though all in different ways are concerned with public speaking. The last is about switching from Greek to Latin in the course of a speech and may in fact be a preface to the *De deo Socratis*.

---

[1] On the problems of the *Florida,* see Hilton's introduction in Harrison et al.,*Apuleius,* 123–28; Lee, *Apuleius' Florida:* 13–20.

APULEIUS

The subjects of all twenty-eight chapters are as follows:

1. On the custom of leaving gifts at roadside sanctuaries
2. On the superiority of mental to ocular vision in human beings
3. The myth of Marsyas' flaying at the hands of Apollo
4. Antigenidas the piper and the application of the same word to objects differing in kind
5. A brief address to an audience
6. The customs of the Indians
7. Alexander the Great's allowing only chosen artists to portray him
8. Virtue matters more than rank
9. Encomium of the proconsul Severianus Honorinus
10. On Providence
11. Criticism of a plagiarist
12. Description of a parrot
13. Comparison of birdsongs with a philosopher's speech
14. Crates the Cynic
15. Samos and its native son Pythagoras
16. Apuleius' sprained ankle; the comic-poet Philemon; Apuleius' reception of an honorific statue
17. Encomium of the proconsul Scipio Orfitus
18. Encomium of Carthage; Protagoras and his pupil Euathlus; comparison of Protagoras with Thales
19. Asclepiades the doctor and his resuscitation of a man supposedly dead
20. Apuleius' education and praise of the culture of Carthage

‹ FLORIDA ›[1]

1. Ut ferme religiosis viantium moris est, cum aliqui lucus
aut aliqui locus sanctus in via oblatus est, votum postulare,
2 pomum apponere, paulisper adsidere, ita mihi ingresso
sanctissimam istam civitatem, quamquam oppido festi-
nem, praefanda venia et habenda oratio et inhibenda pro-
3 peratio est. Neque enim iustius religiosam moram viatori
obiecerit aut ara floribus redimita aut spelunca frondibus
inumbrata aut quercus cornibus onerata aut fagus pellibus
4 coronata, vel enim colliculus saepimine consecratus vel
truncus dolamine effigiatus vel caespes libamine umigatus
5 vel lapis unguine delibutus. Parva haec quippe et quamquam paucis percontantibus adorata, tamen ignorantibus
transcursa.

2. At non itidem maior meus Socrates, qui cum deco-
rum adulescentem et diutule tacentem conspicatus foret,
2 "ut te videam," inquit, "aliquid et loquere." Scilicet Socrates tacentem hominem non videbat; etenim arbitrabatur
homines non oculorum, sed mentis acie et animi obtutu

---

[1] *Titulum* APVLEI PLATONICI FLORIDORVM LIB. I *praebet* φ

< FLORIDA >[1]

1. It is generally the custom of pious travelers to offer a prayer, leave some fruit, and make a brief halt if their path brings them to some grove or some hallowed place. So I 2 too as I enter this most venerable city, though pressed for time, must beg your indulgence, make a speech, and slacken my haste. For nothing can more fittingly present 3 a traveler with a pious reason to linger—not an altar garlanded with flowers, a cave shaded by branches, an oak hung with antlers, a beech hung with hides, or even a 4 hillock consecrated by a fence, a tree stump carved into an image, an altar of turf moistened by a libation,[2] or a stone smeared with unguent. For these things are humble, 5 and though they are venerated by the few who inquire about them, the uninformed pass them by.

2. But not so my master Socrates. Whenever he had noticed a handsome youth keeping silent for a while, he would say, "If I am to see you, you must also say something." Clearly, Socrates did not see a silent person, think- 2 ing that one needed sharpness of intellect, not of vision,

---

[1] On the titles given in the principal manuscripts here and at 9.15, 16.1, 18.1, 1.1*, and 5.1*, see General Introduction.

[2] For such turf altars, Hor. *Carm.* 1.19.13, with the note of Nisbet and Hubbard; *OLD* sv *caespes* 3b.

3 considerandos. Nec ista re cum Plautino milite congru-
ebat, qui ita ait:

"Pluris est oculatus testis unus quam auriti decem."

4 Immo enimvero hunc versum ille ad examinandos homines converterat:

"Pluris est auritus testis unus quam oculati decem."

5 Ceterum si magis pollerent oculorum quam animi iudi-
cia, profecto de sapientia foret aquilae concedendum.
6 Homines enim neque longule dissita neque proxime assita
possumus cernere, verum omnes quodam modo caecuti-
7 mus: ac si ad oculos et obtutum istum terrenum redigas et
hebetem, profecto verissime poeta egregius dixit velut
nebulam nobis ob oculos offusam, nec cernere nos nisi
8 intra lapidis iactum valere. Aquila enimvero cum se nubium tenus altissime sublimavit, evecta alis totum istud
spatium, qua pluitur et ninguitur, ultra quod cacumen nec
fulmini nec fulguri locus est, in ipso, ut ita dixerim, solo
9 aetheris et fastigio hiemis—cum igitur eo sese aquila extulit, nutu clementi laevorsum vel dextrorsum tanta mole
corporis labitur, velificatas alas quo libuit advertens mo-
10 dico caudae gubernaculo; inde cuncta despiciens, ibidem
pinnarum remittens indefessa remigia, ac paulisper cunc-
tabundo volatu paene eodem loco pendula circumtuetur,
et quaerit quorsus potissimum in praedam superne sese
11 ruat fulminis vicem; de caelo improvisa, simul campis
pecua, simul montibus feras, simul homines urbibus uno

---

3 *Truculentus* 489.
4 *Il.* 3.10–12.

and the mind's eye, to observe humanity. On that point he   3
differed from the soldier in Plautus who says,[3]

"One witness with eyes is better than ten with ears."

No, in order to examine human beings, Socrates had re-   4
versed this line:

"One witness with ears is better than ten with eyes."

Besides, if visual judgment were superior to intellec-   5
tual, no doubt we would have to yield the primacy for
wisdom to the eagle. We humans cannot make out things   6
placed far off or brought very close, but all of us are to
some extent blind. When it comes down to the eyes and   7
our dull, earth-bound vision, what the great poet said is
surely very true—that a kind of fog is spread before our
eyes, and we do not have the capacity to see beyond a
stone's throw.[4] An eagle, by contrast, when he has risen   8
high, high up to the clouds, soaring on his wings above this
space where rain and snow fall, up to a height beyond
which there is no room for thunderbolt or lightning flash,
to the very floor of heaven and the roof of the storm cloud,
so to speak—well, when the eagle climbs that far, by a   9
gentle inclination he glides left or right with the great
mass of his body, and turns his wings like sails in any direction he chooses, his tail serving as a small rudder; from   10
there he looks down on everything, tirelessly plying his
outspread wings and, briefly suspended with a lazy motion
in almost the same place, he gazes around and wonders
where best to swoop down from above on his prey like
a thunderbolt; unnoticed from above, he simultaneously   11
observes cattle in the fields, wild beasts on the mountains,
human beings in the cities, in one sweep of a single glance

obtutu sub eodem impetu cernens, unde rostro transfodiat, unde unguibus inuncet vel agnum incuriosum vel leporem meticulosum vel quodcumque esui animatum vel laniatui fors obtulit . . .

3. Hyagnis fuit, ut fando accepimus, Marsyae tibicinis pater et magister; rudibus adhuc musicae saeculis solus ante alios catus[2] canere, nondum quidem tam flexanimo sono nec tam pluriformi modo nec tam multiforatili tibia;

2 quippe adhuc ars ista repertu novo commodum oriebatur. Nec quicquam omnium est quod possit in primordio sui perfici, sed in omnibus ferme ante est spei rudimentum

3 quam rei experimentum. Prorsus igitur ante Hyagnin nihil aliud plerique callebant quam Vergilianus upilio seu busequa,

stridenti miserum stipula disperdere carmen.

4 Quod si quis videbatur paulo largius in arte promovisse, ei quoque tamen mos fuit una tibia velut una tuba personare.

5 Primus Hyagnis in canendo manus discapedinavit, primus duas tibias uno spiritu animavit, primus laevis et dexteris foraminibus, acuto tinnitu et gravi bombo, concentum musicum miscuit.

6 Eo genitus Marsyas cum in artificio patrissaret tibicinii, Phryx cetera et barbarus, vultu ferino, trux, hispidus, inlutibarbus, spinis et pilis obsitus, fertur—pro nefas—cum Apolline certavisse, taeter cum decoro, agrestis cum eru-

7 dito, belua cum deo. Musae cum Minerua dissimulamenti gratia iudices adstitere, ad deridendam scilicet monstri

---

[2] catus *Colvius*: cantus ω

looking for the place where to impale with his beak or grasp with his talons an unsuspecting lamb, a cowering hare, or whatever living thing chance has offered for him to devour or dismember.

3. Hyagnis, so tradition tells us, was the father and teacher of the piper Marsyas. In what were still the early ages of music, he surpassed all others for his skill in playing, not yet indeed with such seductive notes or such varied modes or with so many stops to his pipe, for this newly invented art was as yet just coming into being. And indeed nothing at all can be perfect at its first stage, but hopeful aspiration usually precedes practical application in every field. Indeed, before Hyagnis most musicians had no skill beyond that of Virgil's shepherd or cowherd,[5]

To ruin a poor tune with a shrill reed.

But if anyone seemed a little further along in the art, still he too customarily played on a single pipe as if on a single trumpet. Hyagnis was the first to use both hands independently in playing, the first to use a single breath to animate two pipes, the first to compose a harmonious melody with left- and right-hand stops, from a high treble to a low bass.

Though his son Marsyas followed his father in the art of piping, in every other respect he was a Phrygian and a barbarian, with a brutish face, savage and shaggy, with dirty beard, covered with prickly stubble. They say (dreadful thought) that he competed with Apollo, an ugly being versus a lovely one, a rustic versus an expert, an animal versus a god. The Muses and Minerva presided as judges, so they pretended, but really to mock that mon-

[5] *Ec.* 3.27.

APULEIUS

illius barbariam nec minus ad stoliditatem puniendam.
8 Sed Marsyas, quod stultitiae maximum specimen, non intellegens se deridiculo haberi, priusquam tibias occiperet inflare, prius de se et Apolline quaedam deliramenta barbare effutivit, laudans sese, quod erat et coma relicinus et barba squalidus et pectore hirsutus et arte tibicen et for-
9 tuna egenus: contra Apollinem (ridiculum dictu) adversis virtutibus culpabat, quod [Apollo]³ esset et coma intonsus et genis gratus et corpore glabellus et arte multiscius et
10 fortuna opulentus. "Iam primum," inquit, "crines eius praemulsis antiis et promulsis caproneis anteventuli et propenduli, corpus totum gratissimum, membra nitida, lingua fatidica, seu soluta⁴ oratione seu versibus malis,
11 utrubique facundia aequipari. Quid quod et vestis textu tenuis, tactu mollis, purpura radians? Quid quod et lyra eius auro fulgurat, ebore candicat, gemmis variegat? Quid
12 quod et doctissime et gratissime cantilat? Haec omnia" inquit "blandimenta nequaquam virtuti decora, sed luxuriae accommodata": contra corporis sui qualitatem prae se
13 maximam speciem ostentare. Risere Musae cum audirent hoc genus crimina sapienti exoptanda Apollini obiectata, et tibicinem illum certamine superatum velut ursum bipedem corio exsecto nudis et laceris visceribus reliquerunt.
14 Ita Marsyas in poenam cecinit et cecidit. Enimvero Apollinem tam humilis victoriae puditum est.

4. Tibicen quidam fuit Antigenidas, omnis voculae melleus modulator et idem omnimodis peritus modificator,

³ Apollo *secl. Krüger*   ⁴ soluta *Heinsius*: tute ω

⁶ Antigenidas of Thebes, celebrated player and teacher of the double pipe (*aulos*) in the early fourth century.

ster's uncouthness and at the same time to punish his stupidity. But the clearest evidence of Marsyas' folly was his   8
failing to see that he was considered ridiculous, and before
blowing on his pipes he first blurted out some inarticulate ravings about himself and Apollo. He praised himself for having spiky hair, a dirty beard, a hairy chest, with
only a piper's skill and humble status, while by contrast   9
(ridiculous as it is to say) he blamed Apollo for the opposite qualities—for having long hair, graceful cheeks,
smooth body, with many skills and a glorious position.
"First of all," said he, "his hair with its combed tresses   10
and smoothed locks dangles over his brow and hangs before his face, his whole body is grace itself, his limbs are
sleek, his tongue prophetic; if you want prophecies either
in prose or verse, he is just as expressive in both. Not to   11
mention that his clothing too is light in texture, soft to the
touch and of dazzling purple, and that his lyre too glitters
with gold, glistens with ivory, and sparkles with precious
stones. Not to mention that he warbles with extraordinary
skill and charm. All of these," says he, "are fripperies that   12
in no way suit virtue, but are adapted for indulgence": by
contrast his own physical attributes, he said, exhibited the
greatest beauty. Such charges, which a wise man would   13
pray for, made the Muses laugh when hurled at Apollo,
and when that piper had lost the contest, they left him
looking like a two-footed bear, with his hide peeled away
and his innards exposed and mangled. Thus Marsyas both   14
sang and sank to his own perdition, while so cheap a victory made Apollo blush.

4. There was a certain piper, Antigenidas,[6] who played
every note with sweetness and employed every mode with

seu tu velles Aeolium simplex sive Iastium varium seu
Lydium querulum seu Phrygium religiosum seu Dorium
2 bellicosum. Is igitur cum esset in tibicinio adprime nobilis,
nihil aeque se laborare et animo angi et mente dicebat,
quam quod monumentarii ceraulae "tibicines" dicerentur.
3 Sed ferret aequo animo hanc nominum communionem, si
mimos spectavisset: animadverteret illic paene simili pur-
4 pura alios praesidere, alios vapulare; itidem si munera
nostra spectaret: nam illic quoque videret hominem praesidere, hominem depugnare; togam quoque parari et voto
et funeri, item pallio cadavera operiri et philosophos ami-
ciri.

5. Bono enim studio in theatrum convenistis, ut qui
sciatis non locum auctoritatem orationi derogare, sed cum
primis hoc spectandum esse, quid in theatro deprehendas.
2 Nam si mimus est, riseris, si funerepus, timueris, si comoedia est, faveris, si philosophus, didiceris.

6. Indi, gens populosa cultoribus et finibus maxima,
procul a nobis ad orientem siti, prope oceani reflexus et
solis exortus, primis sideribus, ultimis terris, super Aegyp-
tios eruditos et Iudaeos superstitiosos et Nabataeos mer-
catores et fluxos vestium Arsacidas et frugum pauperes
2 Ityraeos et odorum divites Arabas—eorum igitur Indo-
rum non aeque miror eboris strues et piperis messes et
cinnami merces et ferri temperacula et argenti metalla et

---

7 At athletic and musical contests, the presiding official wore
purple, as did competitors in musical events; mimes were farces
in which one or more of the actors could get a beating.

8 Nabataea had been an Arabian kingdom and was now a Roman province; the Arsacids were the ruling dynasty of Parthia;
Ituraea lies between the Libanos and Antilibanos ranges of southern Lebanon.

skill, whether it was the simple Aeolian you wanted, the
varied Ionian, the plaintive Lydian, the solemn Phrygian
or the martial Dorian. Well, since he was outstandingly 2
famous as a piper, he used to say that nothing pained
him so much or gave him such anguish of soul and mind
as when funeral trumpeters were called "pipers." But he 3
would not have minded others sharing this name, had he
ever observed mimes. There he would have noticed that
those who take the chair and those who take a beating are
dressed in nearly identical purple robes;[7] and similarly 4
if he had observed our public games, for there too he
would have seen one man presiding and one man fighting
it out; and also that togas are worn both for prayer and for
mourning, and again that a cloak is used to hide corpses
and to clothe philosophers.

5. For you have gathered at the theater in high expectation, knowing that a speech loses nothing from its setting: the chief consideration is what you expect to find *in*
the theater. For if it is a mime you will laugh, if a rope- 2
walker, shiver, if a comedy, applaud, if a philosopher, learn.

6. The people of India, a land of many inhabitants and
huge extent, are situated far from us to the east, near
to where the Ocean ebbs and the sun rises, where the
stars begin and the land ends, beyond the learned Egyp-
tians, the superstitious Jews, the mercantile Nabataeans,
the Arsacids with their flowing robes, the Ituraeans poor
in crops,[8] the Arabs rich in spices—well, among the pos- 2
sessions of these Indians I do not so much admire their
heaps of ivory, their harvests of pepper, their cargoes of
cinnamon, their iron foundries, their silver mines, their

3 auri fluenta, nec quod Ganges apud eos unus omnium amnium maximus

> Eois regnator aquis in flumina centum
> discurrit, centum valles illi oraque centum,
> oceanique fretis centeno iungitur amni,

4 nec quod isdem Indis ibidem sitis ad nascentem diem tamen in corpore color noctis est, nec quod apud illos immensi dracones cum immanibus elephantis pari periculo 5 in mutuam perniciem concertant: quippe lubrico volumine indepti revinciunt, ut illis expedire gressum nequeuntibus vel omnino abrumpere tenacissimorum serpentium squameas pedicas necesse sit ultionem a ruina molis suae petere ac retentores suos toto corpore oblidere. 6   Sunt apud illos et varia colentium genera (libentius ego de miraculis hominum quam naturae disseruerim); est apud illos genus, qui nihil amplius quam bubulcitare no-7 vere, ideoque agnomen illis bubulcis inditum. Sunt et mutandis mercibus callidi et obeundis proeliis strenui vel sagittis eminus vel ensibus comminus. Est praeterea ge-8 nus apud illos praestabile, gymnosophistae vocantur. Hos ego maxime admiror, quod homines sunt periti non propagandae vitis nec inoculandae arboris nec proscindendi soli; non illi norunt arvum colere vel aurum colare vel equum domare vel taurum subigere vel ovem vel capram 9 tondere vel pascere. Quid igitur est? Unum pro his omnibus norunt: sapientiam percolunt tam magistri senes quam discipuli iuniores. Nec quicquam aeque penes illos

---

9 These lines are usually attributed to Clemens, the friend of Apuleius mentioned in *Flor.* 7.3 as the author of a poem on Alexander: thus Courtney, *FLP* 401, Blänsdorf[2] 364–65.

gold-bearing rivers, nor the fact that their Ganges, that   3
greatest of all rivers,

> Ruler of the eastern waters, he divides into a
>   hundred rivers,
> A hundred valleys he has and a hundred mouths,
> With a hundredfold stream he meets Ocean's waters.[9]

Nor do I admire the fact that those same Indians, though   4
situated in the same region toward sunrise, even so have
bodies with the color of night, nor that they have huge
snakes that struggle with monstrous elephants, with equal
risk to both and for their mutual destruction; for the   5
snakes tangle the elephants in their slimy coils, so that they
cannot free their feet or in any way break the scaly fetters
of those tenacious serpents, but must get their revenge by
bringing their own bulk down and crushing their captors
with their whole bodies.

Among the Indians there are various classes of inhabi-   6
tant (I am happier to talk about human than natural wonders). They have a class that knows only how to herd cattle,
and have consequently earned the name of "herdsmen."
Some are shrewd dealers in merchandise or valiant fight-   7
ers of battles, where they either shoot arrows from a distance or wield swords at close quarters. They also have a
preeminent class of so-called "gymnosophists." These I   8
admire most of all, because they are men with no skill to
train a vine, graft a branch or plow the earth; *they* have no
idea how to till a field, sieve gold, break a horse, tame a
bull, or shear or pasture a sheep or a goat. What then is the   9
reason? They know one thing worth all the rest: they study
philosophy, both the old men as teachers and the young as
pupils. And there is nothing about them that I praise so

10 laudo, quam quod torporem animi et otium oderunt. Igitur ubi mensa posita, priusquam edulia apponantur, omnes adulescentes ex diversis locis et officiis ad dapem con-
veniunt; magistri perrogant, quod factum a lucis ortu ad
11 illud diei bonum fecerint. Hic alius se commemorat inter
duos arbitrum delectum, sanata simultate, reconciliata
gratia, purgata suspicione amicos ex infensis reddidisse;
12 itidem alius sese parentibus quaepiam imperantibus oboe-
disse, et alius aliquid meditatione sua repperisse vel alterius demonstratione didicisse, denique ‹cetera›[5] ceteri
commemorant. Qui nihil habet afferre cur prandeat, im-
pransus ad opus foras extruditur.

7. Alexandro illi, longe omnium excellentissimo regi,
cui ex rebus actis et auctis cognomentum magno inditum
est, ne vir unicam gloriam adeptus sine laude umquam
2 nominaretur (nam solus a condito aevo, quantum hominum memoria exstat, inexsuperabili imperio orbis auctus
fortuna sua maior fuit, successusque eius amplissimos et
provocavit ut strenuus et aequiperavit ut meritus et supe-
3 ravit ut melior, solusque sine aemulo clarus, adeo ut nemo
eius audeat virtutem vel sperare, fortunam vel optare),
4 eius igitur Alexandri multa sublimia facinora et praeclara
edita fatigaberis admirando vel belli ausa vel domi provisa,
quae omnia adgressus est meus Clemens, eruditissimus et
suavissimus poetarum, pulcherrimo carmine illustrare.
5 Sed cum primis Alexandri illud praeclarum, quod imagi-

---

[5] cetera *add. van der Vliet*

---

[10] On Clemens see above, on 6.3.

much as their abhorrence of a dull, vacant mind. Conse- 10
quently, when the table is laid and the food not yet served,
all the young men gather from their different places and
occupations to dine, and their teachers ask what good
deed they have done from early dawn until that hour of
the day. At this, one reports that he was chosen to arbitrate 11
between two people, and has turned enemies into friends
by patching up their quarrel, restoring their goodwill, and
allaying their suspicions. Similarly, another reports that he 12
has obeyed certain orders of his parents, and another that
he has made some discovery from his own meditation or
from another's explanation, and after that the others mention other matters. If anyone cannot produce a reason why
he should dine, he is driven outdoors to work without his
dinner.

7. The famous Alexander, by far the greatest king that
ever was, whose deeds and achievements earned him the
title of "Great," so that as a man who had achieved unex-
ampled glory he could never be named without praise
(for from the beginning of time, so far as human memory 2
records, he alone, the possessor of an unparalleled empire, was greater than his own Fortune, and challenged
her greatest successes by his energy, equaled them by his
merit, and exceeded them by his superiority, and is the 3
only man famous without peer, so that no one dares either
to hope for his valor or pray for his Fortune)—well, one 4
might tire himself out praising this Alexander's extraordinary deeds and famous achievements, whether ventured
in war or planned in peace (and all of them my friend
Clemens, the most learned and melodious of poets, has
undertaken to glorify in a most beautiful poem).[10] But one 5
thing about Alexander is especially memorable. To ensure

nem suam, quo certior posteris proderetur, noluit a multis
6 artificibus vulgo contaminari, sed edixit universo orbi suo,
ne quis effigiem regis temere assimularet aere, colore,
caelamine, quin [saepe][6] solus eam Policletus aere duceret, solus Apelles coloribus deliniaret, solus Pyrgoteles
7 caelamine excuderet; praeter hos tris multo nobilissimos
in suis artificiis si quis uspiam reperiretur alius sanctissi-
mae imagini regis manus admolitus, haud secus in eum
8 quam in sacrilegum vindicaturum. Eo igitur omnium
metu factum, solus Alexander ut ubique imaginum simil-
limus esset, utique omnibus statuis et tabulis et toreumatis
idem vigor acerrimi bellatoris, idem ingenium maximi
honoris, eadem forma viridis iuventae, eadem gratia reli-
cinae frontis cerneretur.

9   Quod utinam pari exemplo Philosophiae edictum vale-
ret, ne qui imaginem eius temere assimularet, uti pauci
boni artifices, idem probe eruditi omnifariam sapientiae
10 studium contemplarent, neu rudes, sordidi, imperiti pallio
tenus philosophos imitarentur et disciplinam regalem tam
ad bene dicendum quam ad bene vivendum repertam
11 male dicendo et similiter vivendo contaminarent. Quod
utrumque scilicet perfacile est. Quae enim facilior res
quam linguae rabies et vilitas morum, altera ex aliorum
12 contemptu, altera ex sui? Nam viliter semet ipsum colere

---

[6] saepe *del. Wowerius et Scioppius*

---

[11] The mention of Polyclitus is a blunder, since he worked in
the later fifth century; Apelles is the most famous of Greek paint-
ers, but the gem-carver Pyrgoteles is known only from the elder
Pliny (*HN* 7.125, naming Apelles, Pyrgoteles, and Lysippus in the
same context, and 37.8) and this passage.

that future generations should inherit as faithful as pos- sible a likeness of him, he refused to have it generally muddled by a multiplicity of artists, but issued an edict to 6 his whole world that no one should dare to reproduce the royal likeness in bronze, color, or relief; only Polycleitus should mold it in bronze, Apelles trace it in colors, Pyr- goteles carve it in relief.[11] Apart from these three, out- 7 standingly famous in their fields, if anyone else should be found trying his hand on the sacred royal image, he would punish the offender for nothing less than sacrilege. This 8 general threat had the result that only Alexander looked exactly the same in all his portraits everywhere, and that every statue, painting, or relief showed the same vigor of the relentless warrior, the same stamp of the highest birth, the same beauty of fresh youth, and the same charm of brow with its upswept hair.[12]

Now if only an edict of similar type was in force for 9 Philosophy, to the effect that no one should venture to copy her portrait at will, and that only a few good crafts- men, also outstanding in every field of knowledge, should survey the field of wisdom; and that uncouth, grubby, un- 10 educated people should not play the philosopher as far as wearing the cloak, and not debase the queen of disci- plines, which was invented for the art of good speaking and good living, by evil speech and a life to match. Both 11 of these two are of course very easy. For what is more easily obtainable than a rabid tongue and a vile character, the first of which comes from contempt of others and the second from contempt of self? For vile conduct is con- 12

[12] An allusion to the famous *anastolê,* or ridge of hair above Alexander's forehead.

sui contemptus est, barbare alios insectari audientium
contumelia est. An non summam contumeliam vobis
imponit, qui vos arbitratur maledictis optimi cuiusque
gaudere, qui vos existimat mala et vitiosa verba non in-
13 tellegere aut, si intellegatis, boni consulere? Quis ex rupi-
conibus, baiolis, tabernariis tam infans est, ut, si pallium
accipere velit, ⟨non⟩[7] disertius maledicat?

8. Hic enim plus sibi debet quam dignitati, quamquam
nec haec illi sit cum aliis promiscua; nam ex innumeris
2 hominibus pauci senatores, ex senatoribus pauci nobiles
genere et ex iis ⟨pauci consulares, ex⟩[8] consularibus pauci
boni et adhuc ex bonis pauci eruditi. Sed ut loquar de solo
honore, non licet insignia eius vestitu vel calceatu temere
usurpare.

9. Si quis forte in hoc pulcherrimo coetu ex illis inviso-
2 ribus meis malignus sedet (quoniam, ut in magna civitate,
hoc quoque genus invenitur, qui meliores obtrectare malint quam imitari et, quorum similitudinem desperent,
eorundem affectent simultatem, scilicet uti, qui suo no-
3 mine obscuri sunt, meo innotescant), si qui igitur ex illis
lividulis[9] splendidissimo huic auditorio velut quaedam
4 macula se immiscuit, velim paulisper suos oculos per
hunc incredibilem consessum circumferat contemplatus-
que frequentiam tantam, quanta ante me in auditorio phi-
5 losophi numquam visitata est, reputet cum animo suo,

---

[7] non *add. van der Vliet*   [8] ex iis pauci consulares *add.*
Helm (ex iis pauci consulares et ex *iam Gronovius*)
[9] lividulis *Thomas*: libidinis ω

---

[13] If the amended text is correct, a false philosopher with the
gift of the gab can outtalk a true one.

tempt of self, gross attacks on others are an insult to your audience. For are you not subjected to the gravest insult if someone supposes you to enjoy hearing slanders aimed at the best people—if he thinks that you do not understand bad, faulty language, or if you do, that you do not mind it? What lout, what porter, what innkeeper is so inarticulate that, if he chose to don the cloak, he would not insult more fluently?[13]

8. For this man is more indebted to his own self than to his rank, although even *that* is not something that he shares with others, since in all of countless humanity few are senators, and of senators few are noble by descent, of those few are consulars, and of consulars rank few are good men, and moreover of the good few are scholars. But to speak only of his rank, one may not casually usurp its insignia in one's dress or footwear.[14]

9. If perhaps in this most illustrious assembly some ill-wisher is sitting, one of those who envy me (for this being a large city, people of that type are also found—ones who prefer to criticize their betters rather than to imitate them, and pretend to have a feud with those they despair of resembling, doubtless hoping that, obscure as they are on their own account, they may attract notice on mine), well, if any of that spiteful crowd has penetrated this most distinguished audience like a kind of stain, I would ask him briefly to turn his eyes around this extraordinary assembly, to observe this huge crowd, larger than any ever seen in a philosopher's audience before my time, and think carefully how much someone not used to being despised

[14] Senators wore a broad stripe on their undergarment (*tunica*), and distinctive boots.

quantum periculum conservandae existimationis hic adeat
qui contemni non consuevit, cum sit arduum et oppido
difficile vel modicae paucorum exspectationi satisfacere,
6 praesertim mihi, cui et ante parta existimatio et vestra de
me benigna praesumptio nihil, non quicquam, sinit negle-
genter ac de summo pectore hiscere.

7   Quis enim vestrum mihi unum soloecismum ignoverit?
Quis vel unam syllabam barbare pronuntiatam donaverit?
Quis incondita et vitiosa verba temere quasi delirantibus
oborientia permiserit blaterare? Quae tamen aliis facile et
8 sane meritissimo ignoscitis. Meum vero unumquodque
dictum acriter examinatis, sedulo pensiculatis, ad limam
et lineam certam redigitis, cum torno et coturno vero com-
paratis: tantum habet vilitas excusationis, dignitas difficultatis.

9   Agnosco igitur difficultatem meam, nec deprecor quin
sic existimetis. Nec tamen vos parva quaedam et prava
similitudo falsos animi habeat, quoniam quaedam, ut
10 saepe dixi, palliata mendicabula obambulant. Praeco proconsulis et ipse tribunal ascendit, et ipse togatus illic videtur, et quidem perdiu stat aut ambulat aut plerumque
11 contentissime clamitat; enimvero proconsul ipse mode-
rata voce rarenter et sedens loquitur et plerumque de ta-
12 bella legit; quippe praeconis vox garrula ministerium est,
proconsulis autem tabella sententia est, quae semel lecta

---

15 Literally, "the lathe and the tragic boot," i.e., as if resulting
from the expertise of a craftsman or a tragic poet: Apuleius plays
on the similarity of *torno* and *coturno* to produce a bold zeugma.
16 Apuleius' comparison looks forward to the praise of the
proconsul Severianus with which the speech concludes.

risks the maintenance of his reputation here. For it is hard, indeed very difficult, to satisfy even the modest expectations of a few listeners, and especially for me; the reputation I have already acquired, and your kindly preconceptions about me, do not allow me to utter anything, anything at all, unthinkingly or on the spur of the moment. 6

For would any of your number pardon me for a single 7 solecism? Would anyone overlook just a single syllable ignorantly pronounced? Would anyone allow me to stammer out confused and wrongly formed words at random, like ones issuing from a lunatic? Yet you readily and indeed quite properly pardon them in other people. The 8 least word of mine, however, you examine closely, ponder carefully, test it for smoothness and evenness, and measure it against the lathe and the stage.[15] So much indulgence attaches to vulgarity, and so much difficulty to eminence.

I acknowledge my difficulty, therefore, and do not ask 9 you to judge otherwise. Even so, do not let a kind of slight, vulgar similarity lead you into a mistake, since, as I have said several times, there are certain beggars going around in cloaks. Even the herald of the proconsul actually as- 10 cends the platform, even he actually appears there with the toga in person, and moreover he stands there for a long time, or walks back and forth, or very often shouts at the top of his voice, while by contrast the actual proconsul 11 speaks in a subdued voice now and then and from his chair, and often reads from a document.[16] For the herald's wag- 12 ging tongue is a mere instrument, while a proconsul's document is a decision, and once read may neither be

neque augeri littera una neque autem minui potest, sed
utcumque recitata est, ita provinciae instrumento refertur.

13   Patior et ipse in meis studiis aliquam pro meo captu
similitudinem; nam quodcumque ad vos protuli, excep-
tum ilico et lectum est, nec revocare illud nec immutare[10]

14   nec emendare mihi inde quicquam licet. Quo maior reli-
gio dicendi habenda est, et quidem non in uno genere
studiorum, plura enim mea exstant in Camenis quam Hip-
piae in opificiis [operibus].[11] Quid istud sit, si animo atten-
datis, diligentius et accuratius disputabo.[12]

15   Et Hippias e numero sophistarum est, artium multitudine prior omnibus, eloquentia nulli secundus; aetas illi
cum Socrate, patria Elis; genus ignoratur, gloria vero
magna, fortuna modica, sed ingenium nobile, memoria

16   excellens, studia varia, aemuli multi. Venit Hippias iste
quondam certamine Olympio Pisam, non minus cultu

17   visendus quam elaboratu mirandus. Omnia secum quae
habebat, nihil eorum emerat, sed suis sibi manibus confe-
cerat—et indumenta, quibus indutus, et calciamenta, quibus erat inductus, et gestamina, quibus erat conspicatus.

18   Habebat indutui ad corpus tunicam interulam tenuissimo
textu, triplici licio, purpura duplici: ipse eam sibi solus

19   domi texuerat. Habebat cinctui balteum, quod genus pic-
tura Babylonica miris coloribus variegatum: nec in hac

---

[10] immutare *Vulcanius*: a me mutare ω
[11] operibus *del. Vulcanius*   [12] *Titulum* APVLEI PLATONICI
FLORIDORVM LIB. I EXPLIC. INCIP. II *add.* F

---

[17] Hippias of Elis was a sophist contemporary with Socrates,
who appears in several Platonic dialogues; Apuleius' description

lengthened nor yet shortened by a single letter, but is placed on the provincial record just as it was read out.

Something rather similar happens to me too, in a hum- 13 bler way, in my field of knowledge; for whatever I pronounce in your presence is immediately noted down and read, and I cannot retract it, or indeed change or correct a single thing thereafter. Hence I must be all the more 14 scrupulous in my choice of words, and indeed not just in one branch of knowledge, for I have more works of literature to my name than Hippias had inventions.[17] What I mean, if you will give me your attention, I will explain fully and precisely.

Hippias too is counted among the sophists, superior to 15 them all in the variety of his skills and second to none of them in eloquence. He was a contemporary of Socrates, and his native city was Elis. His ancestors are unknown and yet his fame is great; his means were modest but his talent famous, his memory excellent, his fields of study various, his rivals many. This Hippias once came to Pisa 16 during the Olympic games, and drew as much notice for his appearance as amazement for his elegance. For of all 17 the things he had about him not one had he bought, but had made them with his very own hands—the clothes on his body, the shoes on his feet, and the accessories that caught the eye. The clothing next to his body was an un- 18 dergarment of the lightest material, with triple thread and twice-dyed purple, which he himself had woven alone and unassisted at home. As a belt he wore a sash, of a kind 19 decorated with wonderful colors of Babylonian embroi-

of his self-made clothing and other articles (9.17–23) is an expansion of a passage in the *Hippias minor* ascribed to Plato (368B–C).

20 eum opera quisquam adiuverat. Habebat amictui pallium
candidum, quod superne circumiecerat: id quoque pal-
21 lium comperior ipsius laborem fuisse. Etiam pedum tegi-
menta crepidas sibimet compegerat; etiam anulum in
laeva aureum faberrimo signaculo quem ostentabat, ipse
eius anuli et orbiculum circulaverat et palam clauserat et
22 gemmam insculpserat. Nondum omnia eius commemoravi. Enim non pigebit me commemorare quod illum non
puditum est ostentare, qui magno in coetu praedicavit,
fabricatum semet sibi ampullam quoque oleariam, quam
gestabat, lenticulari forma, tereti ambitu, pressula rotun-
23 ditate, iuxtaque honestam strigileculam, recta fastigatione
cymulae, flexa tubulatione ligulae, ut et ipsa in manu ca-
pulo moraretur et sudor ex ea rivulo laberetur.
24 Quis autem non laudabit hominem tam numerosa arte
multiscium, totiugi scientia magnificum, tot utensilium
peritia daedalum? Quin et ipse Hippian laudo, sed ingenii
eius fecunditatem malo doctrinae quam supellectilis mul-
25 tiformi instrumento aemulari, fateorque me sellularias
quidem artes minus callere, vestem de textrina emere,
26 baxeas istas de sutrina praestinare, enimvero anulum nec
gestare, gemmam et aurum iuxta plumbum et lapillos nulli
aestimare, strigilem et ampullam ceteraque balnei utensi-
27 lia nundinis mercari. Prorsum enim non eo infitias nec
radio nec subula nec lima nec torno nec id genus ferramen-
tis uti nosse, sed pro his praeoptare me fateor uno charta-
rio calamo me reficere poemata omnigenus apta virgae,
28 lyrae, socco, coturno, item satiras ac griphos, item histo-

---

[18] Compare the headband (*tainia*) embroidered by Persinna
in Heliod. *Aeth.* 10.14.1.   [19] Literally, "suitable for the staff
[and] the lyre." Rhapsodes reciting the poems of Homer were
supposed to do so while holding a staff (*rhabdos*).

dery, and no one had helped him to make this either.[18] His   20
dress was a white mantle thrown over the rest; that too, I
find, was his own work. Moreover, he had cobbled his own   21
boots to cover his feet; and as for the gold ring on his left
hand which he flaunted with its exquisite seal stone, he
himself had molded the band, enclosed the bezel, and
carved the intaglio. I have not yet mentioned all that he   22
had, since I will not be shy to mention something he was
not shy to display: he announced to a large crowd that he
had also crafted for himself the oil flask that he was carrying, elliptical in shape, with smooth edges and slightly
convex sides, and in addition a handsome little strigil, with   23
a straight-sided, tapering grip and a curved, grooved blade,
so that the grip made the strigil steady in the hand, and
the channel allowed the sweat to run off.

Now who will not praise a man deeply versed in so   24
many trades, extraordinary for his encyclopedic knowledge, the dexterous maker of so many useful things? Why,
I too praise Hippias, but I prefer to imitate his fertile talent by having a multifarious stock of learning rather than
of accessories, and I confess to being none too skilled in   25
the sedentary arts: I buy my clothing from a weaver's shop,
buy these sandals from a cobbler's, while a ring is some-   26
thing I do not even wear, gems and gold I value as highly
as lead and pebbles, and purchase my strigil, oil flask and
other bathing equipment at the market. What is more, I   27
admit to not knowing how to use a shuttle, awl, file, lathe,
or other metal implements of the kind; instead of these, I
confess I prefer using simple pen and paper to recreate
poetry of every sort in the genres of rhapsody,[19] lyric, comedy, tragedy, and similarly satires and riddles, histories on   28

29 rias varias rerum nec non orationes laudatas disertis nec
non dialogos laudatos philosophis, atque haec et alia eiusdem modi tam Graece quam Latine, gemino uoto, pari
studio, simili stilo.

30 Quae utinam possem equidem non singillatim ac dis-
cretim, sed cunctim et coacervatim tibi, proconsul [ut][13]
optime, offerre ac praedicabili testimonio tuo ad omnem
31 nostram Camenam frui! Non hercule penuria laudis, quae
mihi dudum integra et florens per omnes antecessores
tuos ad te reservata est, sed quoniam nulli me proba-
tiorem uolo, quam quem ipse ante omnis merito probo.
Enim sic Natura comprobatum est, ut eum quem laudes
etiam ames, porro quem ames etiam laudari te ab illo velis.
32 Atque ego me dilectorem tuum profiteor, nulla tibi privatim, sed omni publicitus gratia obstrictus, nihil quippe a
33 te impetravi, quia nec postulavi. Sed Philosophia me docuit non tantum beneficium amare sed etiam maleficium,
magisque iudicio impertire quam commodo inservire et
quod in commune expediat malle quam quod mihi. Igitur
34 bonitatis tuae diligunt plerique fructum, ego studium. Idque facere adortus sum dum moderationem tuam in pro-
vincialium negotiis contemplor, qua effectius te amare
debeant experti propter beneficium, expertes propter

---

[13] ut *del. Krüger*

[20] The proconsul who, together with his son, forms the subject
of the rest of the speech is Cocceius Severianus Honorinus (*PIR*
C 1230), proconsul probably in 161/2. His son, Cocceius Honorinus (*PIR* C 1218), served as his legate and was now praetor designate; it is not known whether he ever reached the proconsulate
anticipated by Apuleius (ch. 40). See further below, on 18.36.

various subjects, speeches praised by orators, dialogues praised by philosophers, and these and other works of the same kind both in Greek and in Latin, with twofold ambition, equal application, and similar style. | 29

I only wish I could offer them to you, most excellent proconsul, not individually and separately, but jointly and cumulatively, and could have your invaluable esteem for all my literary works.[20] Not, I swear, for want of fame, since I have long preserved my fame, complete and fresh, under all your predecessors up to you, but because there is no one whose approval I want more than someone whom I rightly approve above all others. For it is a rule laid down by nature that if you praise someone you also cherish him, and further if you cherish someone you also want his praise.[21] And indeed I profess myself your affectionate friend, as one obliged to you not by some personal kindness, but by every sort of public one, for I have never obtained anything from you, having never requested one. Yet philosophy has taught me not only to cherish a kindness but also an unkindness, to value justice rather than to serve my own advantage, and to prefer the general good to my own. Hence it is that while most cherish your goodness for the benefits it brings, *I* cherish you for pursuing it. And I began to do so when I observed your balanced way of dealing with provincial affairs, so that you have made those who have experienced it bound to cherish you for your favor, and those who have not to cher- | 30, 31, 32, 33, 34

[21] The thought seems to be: "I would like your approval of everything I have written so far, not because I have failed to win approval hitherto, but because my reputation has waited for you to set the seal on it."

35 exemplum. Nam et beneficio multis commodasti et exemplo omnibus profuisti. Quis enim a te non amet discere
quanam moderatione obtineri queat tua ista gravitas
iucunda, mitis austeritas, placida constantia blandusque
vigor?

36 Neminem proconsulum, quod sciam, provincia Africa
magis reverita est, minus verita: nullo nisi tuo anno ad
coercenda peccata plus pudor quam timor valuit. Nemo
te alius pari potestate saepius profuit, rarius terruit, nemo
similiorem virtute filium adduxit. Igitur nemo Carthagini

37 proconsulum diutius fuit. Nam etiam eo tempore, quo
provinciam circumibas, manente nobis Honorino, minus
sensimus absentiam tuam, quamquam[14] te magis deside-

38 raremus: paterna in filio aequitas, senilis in iuvene [aucto-
ritas][15] prudentia, consularis in legato auctoritas, prorsus
omnis virtutes tuas ita effingit ac repraesentat, ut medius
fidius admirabilior esset in iuvene quam in te patre[16] laus,

39 nisi eam tu talem dedisses. Qua utinam perpetuo liceret
frui! Quid nobis cum istis proconsulum vicibus, quid cum
annis brevibus et festinantibus mensibus? O celeres bonorum hominum dies, o praesidum optimorum citata curricula! Iam te, Severiane, tota provincia desideramus.

40 Enimvero Honorinum et honos suus ad praeturam vocat
et favor Caesarum ad consulatum format et amor noster

[14] quamquam *Lipsius*: quam ω
[15] auctoritas *om. u*
[16] patre *Brantius*: parta ω

---

[22] That is, Honorinus, remaining behind in the capital of the
province while his father was on his judicial tour, so exactly re-

ish you for your example. For you have at the same time   35
obliged many by your favor, and profited all by your example. For who would not be glad to learn from you what
sort of moderation can give a man that affable gravity of
yours, your tempered severity, your calm steadiness, your
gentle energy?

No proconsul to my knowledge has been more revered   36
and less feared by the province of Africa; in no year other
than yours has self-respect been more able than fear to
check wrongdoing. No one other than you in the same
position of power has more often done good, more rarely
struck terror, no one has brought with him a son more like
him in virtue, and hence no proconsul was ever longer in
Carthage.[22] For even at the time when you were touring   37
the province, because Honorinus remained with us we felt
your absence less, though we missed you all the more. The   38
son has his father's fairness, the youth has an old man's
prudence, the legate has a consular's authority. So much
does he embody and reproduce all your virtues that, I
swear, one might rather admire the excellence of the youth
than of you his father, except that you passed it without
alteration on to him. If only we could enjoy it for ever!   39
What do we want with those changes of proconsuls, those
short years and those fleeting months? How swift are the
days when good men are here, how rapid are the terms of
the best governors! Already, Severianus, our whole province misses you. And yet his rank promises Honorinus   40
the praetorship, and the emperors' favor prepares him

produced his father's virtues that the Carthaginians missed Severianus all the more.

impraesentiarum tenet, et spes Carthaginis in futurum
spondet, uno solacio freta exempli tui, quod qui legatus
mittitur, proconsul ad nos cito reversurus est.

   10. Sol qui candentem candido[17] curru atque equis
     flammam citatis fervido ardore explicas,

itemque luminis eius Luna discipula nec non quinque
2 ceterae vagantium potestates: Iovis benefica, Veneris vo-
luptifica, pernix Mercuri, perniciosa Saturni, Martis ignita.
3 Sunt et aliae mediae deum potestates, quas licet sentire,
non datur cernere, ut Amoris ceterorumque id genus,
4 quorum forma invisitata, vis cognita. Item in terris, utcumque providentiae ratio poscebat, alibi montium ar-
duos vertices extulit, alibi camporum supinam planitiem
coaequavit, itemque ubique distinxit amnium fluores, pra-
torum virores, item dedit volatus avibus, volutus serpen-
tibus, cursus feris, gressus hominibus.

   11. Patitur enim, quod qui herediolum sterile et agrum
scruposum, meras rupinas et senticeta miseri colunt: quoniam nullus in tesquis suis fructus est nec ullam illic aliam
2 frugem vident, sed

   infelix lolium et steriles dominantur avenae.

---

[17] candido *Acc. fr. 555 Dangel*: feruido ω

[23] Marcus Aurelius and Lucius Verus.
[24] That is, just as Severianus had previously been a legate, so
his son, now a legate, will one day be proconsul.
[25] From Accius' *Phoenissae,* quoted by the grammarian
Priscian with slightly different wording (*ROL* 2.524; *Accius,* ed.
J. Dangel [Budé], lines 555–56).

for the consulate,[23] while our affection keeps him here for the present, and the hope of Carthage promises him in future, having its sole consolation in the precedent you have set, that one sent as legate will shortly return to us as proconsul.[24]

10. Sun, who with bright chariot and speeding steeds in burning heat display your brilliant flame.[25]

and in addition Moon, the acolyte of that radiance, and as well the powers of the five other planets[26]—beneficent in Jupiter's case, voluptuous in Venus', swift in Mercury's, destructive in Saturn's, fiery in Mars'. There are other, intermediate divine powers, whom we sense but may not behold, such as Love and the other gods like him, whose form we do not see but whose strength we feel. So also on earth, as the design of Providence required, in one place she raised the lofty peaks of mountains and in another smoothed the level expanse of plains, and so too she everywhere divided the flowing rivers and the green fields, and similarly gave the means of flying to birds, of slithering to reptiles, of running to animals and of walking to humans.[27]

11. The same happens to him as to those unfortunates who till an infertile and stony property, mere hollows and thickets; their badlands give them no yield, and they see no other growth there, but

Gloomy darnel and barren oats prevail.[28]

[26] The moon, not having a fixed place in the sky, was regarded as a planet ("wanderer").   [27] This passage is inspired by one in Cic. *Nat. D.* 2.98.   [28] Verg. *G.* 1.154.

Suis frugibus indigentes aliena furatum eunt et vicinorum flores decerpunt, scilicet ut eos flores carduis suis misceant; ad eundem modum qui suae virtutis sterilis est . . .

12. Psittacus [avis][18] Indiae avis est, instar illi minimo minus quam columbarum, sed color non columbarum: non enim lacteus ille vel lividus vel utrumque, subluteus aut sparsus est, sed color psittaco viridis et intimis plumulis et extimis palmulis, nisi quod sola cervice distinguitur.

2 Enimvero cervicula eius circulo mineo velut aurea torqui pari fulgoris circumactu cingitur et coronatur. Rostri prima duritia: cum in petram quampiam concitus altis-

3 simo uolatu praecipitat, rostro se velut ancora excipit. Sed et capitis eadem duritia quae rostri. Cum sermonem nostrum cogitur aemulari, ferrea clavicula caput tunditur, imperium magistri ut persentiscat; haec discenti ferula est.

4 Discit autem statim pullus usque ad duos aetatis suae annos, dum facile os, uti conformetur, dum tenera lingua, uti convibretur; senex autem captus et indocilis est et obli-

5 viosus. Verum ad disciplinam humani sermonis facilior est psittacus glande qui vescitur et cuius in pedibus ut homi-

6 nis quini digituli numerantur. Non enim omnibus psittacis id insigne, sed illud omnibus proprium, quod eis lingua latior quam ceteris avibus; eo facilius verba hominis arti-

7 culant patentiore plectro et palato. Id vero, quod didicit, ita similiter nobis canit vel potius eloquitur, ut, vocem si audias, hominem putes: nam ‹corvum›[19] quidem si audias,

8 id est crocitare,[20] non loqui. Verum enimvero et corvus et

[18] avis *del. Philomathes*
[19] corvum *add. Helm*
[20] id est crocitare *Helm* (id est *iam Fuluius*): idem conate φ

Lacking crops of their own, they go stealing others' property and pluck their neighbors' flowers, no doubt hoping to mix those flowers with their own thistles. So also someone who brings forth no virtue of his own . . .

12. The parrot is a Indian bird, in size ever so slightly smaller than a dove, though not of a dove's color; it is not milky white or grayish blue or both together, it is not pale yellow or mottled: no, the parrot is green from where its feathers begin to the end of its wings, with a difference only on its neck. For its neck has a scarlet ring like a golden 2 collar, that encircles and crowns it all around with unvarying brilliance. Its beak is of extreme hardness; when it darts swiftly down from above onto some rock, it catches itself with its beak as if with an anchor. But its head is no 3 less hard than its beak. When you force it to learn our language, you rap it on the head with an iron key to make it feel its master's command: this acts as a stick does on a pupil.

Well, it learns from when it is a chick up to two years 4 old, while its mouth is malleable enough to be formed, its tongue soft enough to vibrate, but if you catch it when old, it is unteachable and forgetful. But the parrot is more eas- 5 ily taught human language if fed on acorns and if the toes on each foot number five, as in humans. Not all parrots 6 have that feature, you see, but one thing they all have in common: their tongue is broader than that of other birds, so that they more easily articulate human speech, having a broader tongue and palate. Now what it has learned it 7 sings, or rather speaks, in a way so like ours that if you hear its voice, you might think it human: while if you hear a crow, that is squawking, not talking. But all the same, both 8

psittacus nihil aliud quam quod didicerunt pronuntiant. Si
convicia docueris, conviciabitur diebus ac noctibus per-
strepens maledictis: hoc illi carmen est, hanc putat can-
9 tionem. Ubi omnia quae didicit maledicta percensuit,
denuo repetit eandem cantilenam. Si carere convicio velis,
lingua excidenda est aut quam primum in silvas suas re-
mittendus est.

13. Non enim mihi Philosophia id genus orationem
largita est, ut Natura quibusdam avibus brevem et tem-
porarium cantum commodavit, hirundinibus matutinum,
cicadis meridianum, noctuis serum, ululis vespertinum,
2 bubonibus nocturnum, gallis antelucanum; quippe haec
animalia inter se vario tempore et vario modo occinunt et
occipiunt carmine, scilicet galli expergifico, bubones ge-
mulo, ululae querulo, noctuae intorto, cicadae obstrepero,
3 hirundines perarguto. Sed enim philosophi ratio et oratio
tempore iugis est et auditu venerabilis et intellectu utilis
et modo omnicana.

14. Haec atque hoc genus alia partim cum audiret a
Diogene Crates, alia ipse sibimet suggereret, denique in
forum exsilit, rem familiarem abicit velut onus stercoris
magis labori quam usui, dein coetu facto maximum excla-
2 mat: "Crates" inquit "Cratetem manu mittit":[21] et exinde
non modo solus, verum nudus et liber omnium, quoad
vixit, beate vixit. Adeoque eius cupiebatur, ut virgo nobilis,

---

[21] Cratetem manumittit *Fulvius*: Crates te manumittes ω

---

[29] Crates of Thebes (ca. 365–ca. 285), celebrated Cynic philosopher, pupil of Diogenes of Sinope (d. 323), who founded the
Cynic school; Crates became the teacher of Zeno of Citium (ca.
334–262), the founder of Stoicism.

a crow and a parrot articulate only what they have learned. If you teach a parrot to abuse, it will abuse by cussing loudly night and day; this is its idea of song, this it thinks is melody. When it has exhausted its whole repertory of cusswords, it repeats the same old tune all over again. If you want to be free of its abuse, you must cut out its tongue or pack it off to its native woods at the first opportunity.

13. For it was not that kind of speech that Philosophy bestowed on me, as Nature has lent certain birds a brief, temporary song—the morning for swallows, midday for cicadas, afternoon for little owls, evening for tawny owls, night for horned owls, dawn for cockerels. For these creatures differ from each other in the time and the way they break into and introduce their songs: for instance, rousing in the case of cockerels, tremulous in horned owls, plaintive in tawny owls, subdued in little owls, insistent in cicadas, high-pitched in swallows. But by contrast the philosopher's reasoning and speaking are continuous in time, solemn to the ear, profitable to the mind, and polyphonous in tone.

14. Crates heard these maxims and others like them from Diogenes,[29] while others he thought out himself. Then he burst into the forum, threw away his property as if it were a load of dung, more burdensome than useful, and then with a crowd gathered around him he shouted in a loud voice, "Crates liberates Crates."[30] From then on, not just alone but naked and totally free, he lived happily for the rest of his life. And he was so desirable that a virgin

[30] L. Paquet, *Les Cyniques grecs* (Paris, 1975), 114, Crates fr. 20.

spretis iunioribus ac ditioribus procis, ultronea eum sibi
3 optaverit. Cumque interscapulum Crates retexisset, quod
erat aucto gibbere, peram cum baculo et pallium humi
posuisset eamque supellectilem sibi esse puellae profite-
4 retur eamque formam, quam viderat: proinde sedulo con-
suleret, ne post querelae causam[22] caperet; enimvero Hip-
5 parche condicionem accipit. Iam dudum sibi provisum
satis et satis consultum respondit, neque ditiorem maritum neque formosiorem uspiam gentium posse invenire;
6 proinde duceret quo liberet. Duxit Cynicus in porticum;
ibidem, in loco celebri, coram luce clarissima accubuit,
coramque virginem imminuisset paratam pari constantia,
ni Zeno proiectu[23] palliastri circumstantis coronae obtutu
magistri secretum[24] defendisset.

15. Samos Icario in mari modica insula est exadversum
Mileto,[25] ad occidentem eius sita nec ab ea multo pelagi
dispescitur; utramuis clementer navigantem dies alter in
2 portu sistit. Ager frumento piger, aratro irritus, fecundior
oliveto, nec vinitori nec holitori culpatur.[26] Ruratio omnis
in sarculo ei surculo, quorum proventu magis fructuosa
3 insula est quam frugifera. Ceterum et incolis frequens et
hospitibus celebrata. Oppidum habet, nequaquam pro
gloria, sed quod fuisse amplum semiruta moenium multi-
4 fariam indicant. Enimvero fanum Iunonis antiquitus fami-
geratum; id fanum secundo litore, si recte recordor viam,
5 viginti haud amplius stadia oppido abest. Ibi donarium

---

[22] querelae causam *Colvius*: querelam eam ω
[23] proiectu *Fulvius*: procinctu ω
[24] secretum *scripsi, alii alia*: in secreto ω
[25] Mileto *Scioppius*: Miletos ω
[26] culpatur *Rohde*: scalpit(ur) ω

of high birth rejected younger and richer suitors and chose him for herself of her own free will. Crates bared the space 3 between his shoulder blades where there was a protruding hump, put his bag, stick and cloak on the ground, and assured the girl that she had seen his entire accessories and his entire appearance, and should therefore think carefully and not have reason to complain later; and yet 4 Hipparche accepted the deal. She had already planned 5 enough, she replied, and thought enough, and she could find no husband either richer or better looking anywhere in the world; so he could take her wherever he liked. The 6 Cynic took her to a portico, and then, in a busy spot, he bedded her in public and in broad daylight, and would have deflowered the virgin in public, she being ready and just as determined, except that Zeno used his cloak as a cover to preserve the Master's privacy from the gaze of the crowd standing around.

15. Samos is an island of middling size in the Icarian sea opposite Miletus, and lying to its west, and separated from it only by a strait of no great width; a gentle sail in either direction brings you to port on the next day. The 2 soil is slow to yield grain and unprofitable for the plow, but is more fertile for the olive grove, and neither wine nor vegetable growers find fault with it. The hoe and the sapling make up all its husbandry, the products of which make the island rich in fruits rather than in grain. Moreover, it 3 is full of inhabitants and thronged with visitors. The town is far short of its reputation, but was once large, as the half-collapsed walls amply show. Yet the shrine of Juno has 4 been famous from ancient times; if my memory of the route is correct, this shrine is not more than twenty stades from the town if you follow the shore. There the goddess 5

deae perquam opulentum: plurima auri et argenti ratio
in lancibus, speculis, poculis et huiuscemodi utensilibus.

6 Magna etiam vis aeris vario effigiatu, veterrimo et specta-
bili opere; vel inde ante aram Bathylli statua a Polycrate
tyranno dicata, qua nihil videor effectius cognovisse; qui-

7 dam Pythagorae eam falso existimant. Adulescens est
visenda pulchritudine, crinibus ⟨a⟩[27] fronte parili sepa-
ratu per malas remulsis, pone autem coma prolixior inter-
lucentem cervicem scapularum finibus obumbrat; cervix
suci plena, malae uberes, genae teretes, at medio mento

8 lacunatur;[28] eique prorsus citharoedicus status: deam
conspiciens, canenti similis, tunicam picturis variegatam
deorsus ad pedes deiectus ipsos, Graecanico cingulo, chla-
myde velat utrumque brachium ad usque articulos pal-

9 marum, cetera decoris striis dependent; cithara balteo
caelato apta strictim sustinetur; manus eius tenerae, pro-
cerulae: laeva distantibus digitis nervos molitur, dextra
psallentis gestu pulsabulum citharae admovet, ceu parata

10 percutere, cum vox in cantico interquievit; quod interim
canticum videtur ore tereti semihiantibus in conatu label-
lis eliquare.

11   Verum haec quidem statua esto cuiuspiam puberum,
qui Polycrati tyranno dilectus Anacreonteum amicitiae

12 gratia cantilat. Ceterum multum abest Pythagorae philosophi statuam esse; et natu Samius et pulchritudine

[27] a *add. Oudendorp*
[28] lacunatur *Puteanus*: laculat(ur) ω

[31] Bathyllus, often mentioned by the lyric poet Anacreon, was
the boy lover (*paidika*) of Polycrates, tyrant of Samos in the sixth

has an extremely rich treasury—a huge amount of gold
and silver in dishes, mirrors, cups and similar utensils, and   6
furthermore a large and varied collection of bronze statues, of very ancient and admirable make. One of them, for
instance, is a statue of Bathyllus before the altar, dedicated
by the tyrant Polycrates,[31] more perfect than anything I
ever remember seeing; some wrongly think it shows Pythagoras. It is a young man of striking beauty, his hair in   7
front brushed back to fall evenly about his cheeks, while
his flowing hair behind shades his neck gleaming between
his shoulder blades; his neck is rosy and full, his cheeks
round, his jaws smooth, he has a cleft in the middle of his
chin, and his posture is exactly that of a citharode. He faces   8
the goddess as if he were singing; he has a tunic embroidered with various figures coming down to his very feet;
his belt is in Greek style; his cloak covers each arm up to
the wrist bones, the rest hangs down in lovely pleats. His   9
lyre hangs close to his body by an ornamental strap; his
hands are soft and tapering; his left hand plies the strings
with outspread fingers, while his right hand touches the
quill to the cithara in the attitude of one playing, as if about
to strike up when his voice has paused from its song; up to   10
then he seems to be pouring forth a melody from his ten-
der mouth, his lips half-open in the effort.

But let us grant that this is the statue of some un-   11
known youth, a lover of the tyrant Polycrates, who is singing a song of Anacreon in virtue of their friendship: still,   12
that is far different from its being a statue of the philosopher Pythagoras. He was Samian by birth and of extremely

century: Campbell, *Greek Lyric* 2 (Loeb Classical Library), 27
no. 4, 31 no. 11.

adprime insignis et psallendi musicaeque omnis multo
doctissimus ac ferme id aevi, quo Polycrates Samum poti-
ebatur, sed haudquaquam philosophus tyranno dilectus
13 est. Quippe eo commodum dominari orso profugit ex insula clanculo Pythagoras, patre Mnesarcho nuper amisso,
quem comperio inter sellularios artifices gemmis faber-
rime sculpendis laudem magis quam opem quaesisse.
14 Sunt qui Pythagoran aiant eo temporis, inter captivos
Cambysae regis Aegyptum cum adveheretur, doctores
habuisse Persarum magos ac praecipue Zoroastren, omnis
divini arcani antistitem, posteaque eum a quodam Gillo
15 Crotoniensium principe reciperatum. Verum enimvero
celebrior fama obtinet sponte eum petisse Aegyptias disciplinas atque ibi a sacerdotibus caerimoniarum incredundas potentias, numerorum admirandas vices, geometriae
16 sollertissimas formulas ‹didicisse›;[29] nec his artibus animi
expletum mox Chaldaeos atque inde Bracmanos (hi sapientes viri sunt, Indiae gens est)—eorum ergo Bracma-
17 num gymnosophistas adisse. Chaldaei sideralem scien-
tiam, numinum vagantium statos ambitus, utrorumque
varios effectus in genituris hominum ostendere nec non
medendi remedia mortalibus latis pecuniis terra caeloque
18 et mari conquisita; Bracmani autem pleraque philoso-

---

[29] didicisse *add. u*

---

[32] Cambyses: son and successor of Cyrus the Great as king of
Persia, and conqueror of Egypt. Zoroaster: see on *Apol.* 26.1.
Gillus is otherwise unknown but could be the Tarentine men-
tioned by Hdt. 3.138. Croton is a Greek colony in southeast Italy,
where Pythagoras settled with a group of his followers about 530
BC.

striking beauty, expert at the lyre and in every branch of music. He lived about the same time as Polycrates ruled Samos, but the philosopher was in no way the tyrant's beloved. In fact, just when Polycrates began to be tyrant, Pythagoras secretly escaped from the island, his father Mnesarchus having lately died (he, I find, was a sedentary artist, who sought praise rather than profit by his great skill as a gem cutter). Some say that about that time Pythagoras became a captive of King Cambyses during his Egyptian expedition, and studied with the Persian magi, notably Zoroaster, the master of every divine mystery, and was later ransomed by one Gillus, a leading citizen of Croton.[32] Nonetheless, according to the better-known account he went by his own choice in search of Egyptian lore, and he there learned from the priests the extraordinary power of their rituals, the marvelous properties of numbers, the subtlest geometrical theorems; but, his intellect not being satisfied with these sciences, he next went to the Chaldeans and thereafter to the Brahmins (these are an Indian race of wise men)—well, to those of the Brahmins who were gymnosophists.[33] The Chaldeans, they say, showed him the science of the stars, the fixed revolutions of the wandering powers,[34] the influences of both of these on human horoscopes, and in addition medicines to cure mortals that they themselves had gathered from earth, sky and sea at considerable expense; while the Brahmins contrib-

13

14

15

16

17

18

---

[33] Chaldeans are Babylonians, famous for their astronomical skill, cf. *Apol.* 97.4; the Brahmins, the priestly class of India, were identified or confused with the Gymnosophists ("naked wise men") from the late Hellenistic period onward.

[34] That is, the planets (*planêtai*, "wanderers").

phiae eius contulerunt, quae mentium documenta, quae
corporum exercitamenta, quot partes animi, quot vices
vitae, quae diis manibus pro merito suo cuique tormenta

19 vel praemia. Quin etiam Pherecydes Syro ex insula oriundus, qui primus versuum nexu repudiato conscribere ausus est passis verbis, soluto locutu, libera oratione, eum quoque Pythagoras magistrum coluit et infandi morbi putredine in serpentium scabiem solutum religiose huma-

20 vit. Fertur et penes Anaximandrum Milesium naturabilia commentatus nec non et Cretensem Epimeniden inclitum

21 fatiloquum et piatorem disciplinae gratia sectatus, itemque Leodamantem Creophyli discipulum, qui [Creophylus][30] memoratur poetae Homeri hospes et aemulator canendi fuisse.

22 Tot ille doctoribus eruditus, tot tamque multiiugis calicibus disciplinarum toto orbe haustis, vir praesertim ingenio ingenti ac profecto super captum hominis animi au-

23 gustior, primus philosophiae nuncupator et conditor, nihil prius discipulos suos docuit quam tacere, primaque apud eum meditatio sapienti futuro linguam omnem coercere, verbaque, quae volantia poetae appellant, ea verba detractis pinnis intra murum candentium dentium premere.

24 Prorsus, inquam, hoc erat primum sapientiae rudimen-

---

[30] Creophylus *del. Kronenberg*

---

[35] Pherecydes, a cosmologist and allegedly the first Greek
writer of prose, flourished circa 544; Anaximander (died soon
after 547) was a noted cosmologist; Epimenides was a holy man
of the late seventh century about whom many fabulous stories
collected; Creophylus was alleged to be a friend of Homer and
an early epic poet; Leodamas is unknown, and the name is per-

uted most of his philosophy—all their lessons for the mind and exercises for the body, all the parts of the soul, all the stages of life, and those torments or rewards that await the spirits of the dead in accordance with their deserts. Furthermore, Pherecydes, born on the isle of Syros, who was the first to reject the interconnected lines of verse and dared to write in ordinary speech, in prose style and in unconstricted language, was another teacher whom Pythagoras followed, and whom he buried reverently when a dreadful, purulent disease had reduced his skin to the scaliness of a snake. He is also said to have studied natural phenomena under Anaximander of Miletus, and in addition to have followed Epimenides of Crete, a famous soothsayer and a master of expiatory rites, and also Leodamas the pupil of Creophylus, who according to tradition was a host of the poet Homer and his rival in song.[35]

Educated by so many masters, and after draining so many cups of knowledge of such different kinds throughout the world, that master of truly great genius, more venerable than the human mind can encompass, the first to give a name and foundation to philosophy, made silence the first lesson he taught his students, and the first exercise of the would-be philosopher in his school was to suppress all speech and, stripping the feathers from those words that poets call "winged," to imprison them within "the wall of shining teeth."[36] This, I repeat, was absolutely their first

19

20

21

22

23

24

haps a slip for Hermodamas, a descendant of Creophylus whom Pythagoras is said to have met in Samos (Diog. Laert. 8.2)

[36] "Feathered words" and "barrier of the teeth" are both frequent expressions in Homer.

25 tum: meditari condiscere, loquitari dediscere. Non in totum aevum tamen vocem desuescebant, nec omnes pari
tempore elingues magistrum sectabantur, sed gravioribus
viris brevi spatio satis videbatur taciturnitas modificata,
loquaciores enimvero ferme in quinquennium velut exsi-
26 lio vocis puniebantur. Porro noster Plato, nihil ab hac secta
vel paululum devius, pythagorissat in plurimis; aeque ut[31]
ipse in nomen eius a magistris meis adoptarer, utrumque
meditationibus academicis didici, et, cum dicto opus est,
impigre dicere, et, cum tacito opus est, libenter tacere.
27 Qua moderatione videor ab omnibus tuis antecessoribus
haud minus oportuni silentii laudem quam tempestivae
vocis testimonium consecutus.[32]

16. Priusquam vobis occipiam, principes Africae viri,
gratias agere ob statuam, quam mihi praesenti honeste
postulastis et absenti benigne decrevistis, prius volo causam vobis allegare, cur aliquam multos dies a conspectu
2 auditorii afuerim contulerimque me ad Persianas aquas,
gratissima prorsus et sanis natabula et aegris medicabula
3 (quippe ita institui omne vitae meae tempus vobis probare, quibus me in perpetuum firmiter dedicavi, ⟨ut⟩[33]

[31] ut *Hildebrand*: et ω
[32] *Titulum* APVLEI PLATONICI FLORIDORVM LIB. II EXPLIC.
INCIP. III *add.* F
[33] ut *addidi*

---

[37] The audience is the Carthaginian senate, consisting of the
foremost citizens; it was customary for cities, acting through their
representative bodies, to vote statues to persons of distinction.
Oddly, in sections 10 and 43, Apuleius speaks as if he were addressing the Carthaginians in general.

exercise in philosophy—to learn meditation and to un-
learn chatter. Yet it was not for the rest of their lives that   25
they lost the use of speech, and they were not all voiceless
at the same time as they followed the master: for the more
serious, a limited silence for a short time was thought
enough, while the more talkative were punished with a
sort of vocal exile for about five years. Further, my master   26
Plato, who deviates from this school only slightly if at all,
is a Pythagorean in very many ways. Similarly, in order for
my teachers to take myself on as his follower, I learned two
things from the practices of the Academy: to be prompt to
speak when speech is required, and also to be willing to
be silent when silence is required. By this middle course,   27
I think I have caused your predecessors to praise me for
opportune silence as much as to commend me for timely
speech.

16. Before I begin to give thanks to you, notables of
Africa,[37] for my statue that you honorably proposed in my
presence and kindly voted in my absence, I first want to
lay before you the reason why I avoided the sight of an
audience for a good many days, and took myself off to the   2
baths of Perseus,[38] which is a very pleasant swimming pool
for the healthy to swim in and for the sick to be cured (for   3
I have so determined to make sure that every moment of
my life is approved by you, to whom I have steadfastly
devoted myself, that I do nothing so large, nothing so

[38] An inscription found at Hammam Lif, a coastal town about
twenty kilometers southeast of Carthage (Tunis), shows that a
certain T. Iulius Perseus made a dedication there to Asclepius: he
must be the founder of the baths mentioned here (CIL 8.997; *PIR*
I 456) and is probably mentioned in 19.39ff.

nihil tantum, nihil tantulum faciam, quin eius vos et gnaros
4 et iudices habeam)—quid igitur ‹me›[34] de repentino ab
5 hoc splendidissimo conspectu vestro distulerim. Exemplum eius rei paulo secus simillimum memorabo, quam
improvisa pericula hominibus subito oboriantur, de Phile-
mone comico. De ingenio eius qui satis nostis, de interitu
paucis cognoscite. An etiam de ingenio pauca vultis?
6 Poeta fuit hic Philemon, mediae comoediae scriptor,
fabulas cum Menandro in scaenam dictavit certavitque
cum eo, fortasse impar, certe aemulus, namque eum etiam
7 vicit saepenumero (pudet dicere). Reperias tamen apud
ipsum multos sales, argumenta lepide inflexa, agnitus lu-
cide explicatos, personas rebus competentes, sententias
vitae congruentes, ioca non infra soccum, seria non usque
8 ad coturnum. Rarae apud illum corruptelae, tuti errores,
9 concessi amores. Nec eo minus et leno periurus et amator
fervidus et servulus callidus et amica illudens et uxor in-
hibens et mater indulgens et patruus obiurgator et sodalis
opitulator et miles proeliator, sed et parasiti edaces et
parentes tenaces et meretrices procaces.
10 Hisce laudibus diu in arte comoedica nobilis, forte
recitabat partem fabulae, quam recens fecerat, cumque
iam in tertio actu, quod genus in comoedia fieri amat, iu-
cundiores affectus moveret, imber repentino coortus, ita
ut mihi ad vos venit usus nuperrime, differri auditorii coe-
11 tum et auditionis coeptum coegit: reliquum tamen, variis

[34] me *add. van der Vliet*

[39] Philemon (ca. 365–ca. 265) is usually considered a leading
poet of New, not Middle, Comedy.

290

small, that I would not want you to know of and to
judge)—in short, why all of a sudden I disappeared from   4
the sight of this most honorable body of yours. I will men-   5
tion an example, very close to my situation or nearly so,
of how unexpected the dangers are that suddenly befall
people. It is about the comic poet Philemon. His genius
you are well aware of, so let me give you a brief account
of his death, unless perhaps you want a few words about
his genius too.

This Philemon was a poet, a writer of Middle Comedy,   6
who wrote plays for the stage in Menander's time and
competed with him, perhaps with less talent, but certainly
with as much success, since he actually defeated him many
times, I am sorry to say.[39] Nonetheless, you will find much   7
wit in his works, plots cleverly constructed, recognitions
brilliantly contrived, characters fitting the situation, senti-
ments applicable to life, jokes not too low for comedy,
solemnity not high enough for tragedy. The rapes in his   8
works are few, the mistakes slight, the love affairs respectable. Even so, you also find the perfidious pimp, the ar-   9
dent lover, the cunning slave, the coy girlfriend, the pos-
sessive wife, the indulgent mother, the reproachful uncle,
the helpful friend, the battle-scarred warrior, as well as the
gluttonous parasites, stingy parents and brazen mistresses.

He had long been famous and praised in the field of   10
comedy when he once happened to be giving a recital of
part of a play he had recently written. He had got to the
third act and, as happens in comedy, was arousing great
pleasure, when suddenly a shower began, just as happened
to me recently in your presence, and this forced the assembled audience and the unfinished recital to be put off;
though at various people's request, he said he would finish   11

291

postulantibus, sine intermissione deincipiti die perlectu-
rum. Postridie igitur maximo studio ingens hominum fre-
12 quentia convenere; sese quisque exadversum quam proxime collocat; serus adveniens amicis adnuit, locum sessui
13 impertiant; extimus quisque excuneati queruntur; farto
toto theatro, ingens stipatio, occipiunt inter se queri; qui
non affuerant percontari ante dicta, qui affuerant recor-
dari audita, cunctisque iam prioribus gnaris sequentia ex-
spectare.
14   Interim dies ire, neque Philemon ad condictum venire;
quidam tarditatem poetae murmurari, plures defendere.
Sed ubi diutius aequo sedetur nec Philemon uspiam comparet, missi ex promptioribus qui accierent, atque eum
15 in suo sibi lectulo mortuum offendunt. Commodum ille
anima edita obriguerat, iacebatque incumbens toro, similis cogitanti: adhuc manus volumini implexa, adhuc os
lecto[35] libro impressum, sed enim iam animae vacuus, libri
16 oblitus et auditorii securus. Stetere paulisper qui introie-
rant, perculsi tam inopinatae rei, tam formonsae mortis
17 miraculo. Dein regressi ad populum renuntiavere Phile-
monem poetam, qui exspectaretur qui in theatro fictum
argumentum finiret, iam domi veram fabulam consum-
masse; enimvero iam dixisse rebus humanis valere et plau-
18 dere, suis vero familiaribus dolere et plangere; hesternum
illis imbrem lacrimas auspicasse; comoediam eius prius ad
funebrem facem quam ad nuptialem venisse; proin, quo-

---

[35] lecto *Colvius*: recto ω

---

[40] The description is hard to visualize, and the text may be
corrupt.   [41] Some plays of New Comedy ended with a wedding procession in which torches were carried.

the reading with nothing omitted on the day after. On the next day, therefore, a huge crowd assembled, agog with expectation; everybody sat as close as possible facing the stage; latecomers nodded to their friends and asked for a place to sit; those at the end complained at being pushed off their seats; the whole theater being packed, there was a terrible crush and people began complaining to each other; those who had been absent asked what had been said previously, those who had been present recalled what they had heard, and when at last when all the earlier matter was known they awaited the sequel.

Meanwhile the day passed and Philemon did not keep his appointment; some grumbled at the poet's lateness, but most excused it. But when they had been sitting unduly long and Philemon was nowhere to be seen, some volunteers were sent to fetch him, and these found him dead in his very own bed. He had just breathed his last and grown stiff, and lay reclining on his couch as if deep in thought; he still had his hand wrapped in the roll, and his face still pressed against the book he had read,[40] but was now devoid of life, oblivious of his book and unmindful of his audience. Those who had entered stood for a moment, marveling at so unexpected an event, so beautiful a death. Then they went back to the people and announced that the poet Philemon, who was expected to finish his fictitious plot in the theater, had already ended a true play at home; indeed, he had said goodbye to the world and asked for its applause, while telling his household to grieve and mourn; yesterday's shower had foreshadowed the people's tears; his play had ended with a funerary torch before a nuptial one;[41] and so, since the

niam poeta optimus personam vitae deposuerit, recta de
auditorio eius exsequias eundum, legenda eius esse nunc
ossa, mox carmina.

19   Haec ego ita facta, ut commemoravi, olim didiceram,
sed hodie sum e meo periculo recordatus. Nam, ut memi-
nistis profecto, cum impedita esset imbri recitatio, in pro-
pinquum diem vobis volentibus protuli, et quidem Phile-
20   monis exemplo paenissime; quippe eodem die in palaestra
adeo vehementer talum inverti, ut minimum afuerim,
quin articulum etiam a crure defringerem; tamen articu-
21   lus loco concessit exque eo luxu adhuc fluxus est. Et iam
dum eum ingenti plaga reconcilio, iamiam sudoro affatim
22   corpore diutule obrigui; inde acerbus dolor intestinorum
coortus modico ante sedatus est, quam me denique vio-
lentus exanimaret et Philemonis ritu compelleret ante
letum abire quam lectum, potius implere fata quam fanda,
23   consummare potius animam quam historiam. Cum primum igitur apud Persianas aquas leni temperie nec minus
24   utili[36] quam blando fomento gressum receperavi, nondum
quidem ad innitendum idonee, sed quantum ad vos festi-
nanti satis videbatur, veniebam redditum quod pepige-
ram, cum interim vos mihi beneficio vestro non tantum
clauditatem dempsistis, verum etiam pernicitatem addi-
distis.

25   An non properandum mihi erat, ut pro eo honore vobis
multas gratias dicerem, pro quo nullas preces dixeram?

---

[36] utili *u*: uti *ω*

294

great poet had laid aside the mask of life, they should go straight from the theater to his funeral, and should collect his bones now and his works in future.[42]

This version of these events I heard long ago, but my 19 own danger reminded me of it today. As you surely remember, when a shower interrupted my recitation, I postponed it to the next day with your consent, and indeed very nearly with Philemon as a precedent. For that same 20 day I twisted my ankle so badly in the wrestling ground that I very nearly quite broke the joint from the leg; as it was, the joint was dislocated and has been unsteady ever since that sprain. And next, when I used a heavy blow to 21 set it, my body was immediately bathed in sweat and for a while I was paralyzed; then a sharp pain in my stomach 22 came on, and after a short remission its violence finally made me faint, and as happened to Philemon it began to set me on my way to the bier quicker than my bed, to complete my span before my speech, to finish my life before my story.[43] So just as soon as I had recovered the 23 use of my leg in Perseus' Spa, thanks to its gentle warmth and a compress both effective and mild, not yet indeed 24 enough for me to lean on it but sufficiently, as it seemed to me in my hurry to see you, I was on my way to keep my agreement, when you not only cured my lameness by your generosity but even gave wings to my feet.

Was I not right to hurry to thank you heartily for an 25 honor that I had no way begged from you? Not that the

---

[42] *legere* means both to "gather," i.e., to collect the cremated bones of the dead, and "to read"; the pun is untranslatable.

[43] Apuleius plays on the similarity of *letum* and *lectum, fata* and *fanda, animam* and *historiam.*

Non quin magnitudo Carthaginis mereatur etiam ⟨a⟩[37] philosopho precem pro honore, sed ut integrum et intemeratum esset vestrum beneficium, si nihil ex gratia eius petitio mea defregisset, id est, ut usque quaque esset gra-

26 tuitum. Neque enim aut levi mercede emit qui precatur, aut parvum pretium accipit qui rogatur, adeo ut omnia

27 utensilia emere velis quam rogare. Id ego arbitror praecipue in honore observandum; quem qui laboriose exoraverit, sibi debet unam gratiam, quod impetrarit; qui vero sine molestia ambitus adeptus est, duplam gratiam praebentibus debet, et quod non petierit et quod acceperit.

28 Duplam igitur vobis gratiam debeo, immo enimvero multiiugam, quam ubique equidem et semper praedicabo.

29 Sed nunc impraesentiarum libro isto ad hunc honorem mihi conscripto, ita ut soleo, publice protestabor. Certa est enim ratio, qua debeat philosophus ob decretam sibi pu-

30 blice statuam gratias agere, a qua paululum demutabit liber quem Strabonis Aemiliani excellentissimus honor flagitat, quem librum sperabo me commode posse conscribere, si is eum hodie vobiscum probarit.[38]

31 Est enim tantus in studiis, ⟨ut⟩[39] praenobilior sit proprio ingenio quam patricio consulatu. Quibusnam verbis tibi, Aemiliane Strabo, vir omnium, quot umquam fuerunt

---

[37] a *add. u*
[38] si is . . . probarit *Colvius*: scitis . . . probare *ω*
[39] ut *add. u*

---

[44] That is, you incur a heavy burden of obligation if you beg for something, but no obligation if you buy it.

[45] Strabo Aemilianus was consul in 156 (*PIR* S 923), and his family may have been elevated to patrician rank, though the term

great city of Carthage does not deserve that even a philosopher should beg for an honor, but so that your act of generosity should be entire and unimpaired, with none of its spontaneity diminished by a request from me; that is, so that it should be spontaneous to the highest degree. For 26 one who begs buys at no trifling price, and the one whom he asks for something gets no small payment, which is why one generally prefers to buy all one's necessaries rather than to borrow them.[44] That rule I think is especially to 27 be followed in the matter of honor. One who takes trouble to obtain it is indebted only to himself if he receives it; but one who achieves it without the trouble of petitioning owes a double debt to the givers, because he both made no request and at the same time was the recipient. I owe 28 you therefore a double debt, indeed I may say a multiple one, which for my part I will proclaim everywhere and always. For the moment, though, by means of the present 29 work on the subject of this honor, I will make a public declaration in my usual way. For there is a fixed course that a philosopher must follow when giving thanks for a statue voted to him by the people: though the written ver- 30 sion required by a man of Aemilianus Strabo's outstanding dignity will slightly depart from it, a version that I will hope to be able to compose easily, if I have his approval and yours for it today.

For he is so eminent as a scholar as to be more con- 31 spicuous for his own talent than for his patrician consulate.[45] With what words, Aemilianus Strabo, a man who of

"patrician consulate" (ch. 31) was not an official one. See further below, on ch. 40.

aut sunt aut etiam erunt, inter optimos clarissime, inter
32 clarissimos optime, inter utrosque doctissime, quibus tandem verbis pro hoc tuo erga me animo gratias habitum et
commemoratum eam, qua digna ratione tam honorificam
benignitatem tuam celebrem, qua remuneratione dicendi
33 gloriam tui facti aequiperem, nondum hercle reperio. Sed
quaeram sedulo et conitar,

dum memor ipse mei, dum spiritus hos regit artus.

Nam nunc impraesentiarum (neque enim diffitebor) laetitia facundiae obstrepit et cogitatio voluptate impeditur;
ac mens occupata delectatione mavult impraesentiarum
34 gaudere quam praedicare. Quid faciam? Cupio gratus videri, sed prae gaudio nondum mihi vacat gratias agere.
Nemo me, nemo ex illis tristioribus velit in isto vituperare,
quod honorem meum non minus vereor[40] quam intellego,
quod clarissimi et eruditissimi viri tanto testimonio ex-
35 sulto. Quippe testimonium mihi perhibuit in curia Carthaginiensium non minus splendidissimum quam benignis-
simum; vir consularis, cui etiam notum esse tantummodo
summus honor est, is etiam laudator mihi apud principes
36 Africae viros quodam modo astitit. Nam, ut comperior,
nudius tertius libello misso, per quem postulabat locum
celebrem statuae meae, cum primis commemoravit inter
nos iura amicitiae a commilitio studiorum eisdem magistris honeste inchoata; tunc postea vota omnia mea se-

[40] vereor *ed. Aldina*: mereor ω

[46] Verg. *Aen.* 4.336.   [47] For statues to be set up in public places, the local council had to give permission and specify the

all men past, present or indeed future are as famous as
the best, as good as the most famous, as learned as either—with what words can I begin to give and to express   32
my thanks for your feelings toward me? How can I ade-
quately celebrate this conspicuous act of such flattering
kindness? With what payment in words can I equal the
splendor of your deed? Truly, I cannot yet see a way, but   33
I will think carefully and will strive,

> While conscious of myself, while breath rules these
> limbs.[46]

For just at this moment, as I cannot deny, joy overwhelms
my power of speech and pleasure impedes my delibera-
tion; my mind is overwhelmed with delight, and prefers
for the moment to exult rather than to praise. What can I   34
do? I want to show my gratitude, but in my joy I am not
yet free to express my thanks. May no one, no one, of that
gloomy crowd try to fault me for revering my honor as
much as I feel it, for exulting in such a tribute from a most
eminent and erudite personage. For the tribute that he   35
bestowed on me in the senate house of Carthage was both
very glowing and very generous; a man of consular rank,
whose notice even is the highest of honors, yes, he in a
way actually supported me by singing my praises before
the dignitaries of Africa. For, so I find, two days ago he   36
sent a petition for my statue to be put in a busy place,[47] in
which he particularly recalled the bonds of friendship between us, honorably inaugurated in our joint study under
the same teachers; and next he recounted all my prayers

site, choosing a much frequented one for a person especially
honored: see also below, ch. 41.

37 cundum dignitatis suae gradus recognovit. Iam illud primum beneficium, quod condiscipulum se meminit. Ecce
et hoc alterum beneficium, quod tantus diligi se ex pari
praedicat. Quin etiam commemoravit et alibi gentium et

38 civitatium honores mihi statuarum et alios decretos. Quid
addi potest ad hoc praeconium viri consularis? Immo
etiam docuit argumento suscepti sacerdotii summum mihi
honorem Carthaginis adesse. Iam hoc praecipuum beneficium ac longe ante ceteros excellens, quod me vobis lo-

39 cupletissimus testis suo etiam suffragio commendat. Ad
summam pollicitus est se mihi Carthagini de suo statuam
positurum, vir, cui omnes provinciae quadriiuges et sei-
uges currus ubique gentium ponere gratulantur. Quid igitur superest ad honoris mei tribunal et columen, ad laudis

40 meae cumulum? Immo enimvero, quid superest? Aemilianus Strabo, vir consularis, brevi votis omnium futurus
proconsul, sententiam de honoribus meis in curia Carthaginiensium dixit, omnes eius auctoritatem secuti sunt.
Nonne videtur hoc vobis senatus consultum esse?

41   Quid quod et Carthaginienses omnes, qui in illa sanc-
tissima curia aderant, tam libenter decreverunt locum
statuae,[41] ut illos scires idcirco alteram statuam, quantum

---

[41] statuae *Colvius*: statuere ω

---

[48] Augustine (*Ep.* 138.19) states that Apuleius was *sacerdos provinciae,* which should mean the chief priest of the imperial cult for the province: that is probably the priesthood mentioned here.   [49] That is, statues of Strabo driving a chariot with four or six horses. This is an evident exaggeration: even four-horse chariots were now granted only to members of the imperial house: K. Schneider, *RE* 24 (1963): 684–85.

of gratitude for each step of his career. That indeed was 37
the first favor, that he mentions himself as my fellow student. And here is a second one: that so great a man proclaims our affection as one between equals. What is more,
he recalled that in other lands and cities too I have been
voted honorific statues and other distinctions. What can 38
be added to such a proclamation from a man of consular
rank? Moreover, he cited the priesthood I have undertaken as proof that Carthage's supreme honor had fallen
to me.[48] But now his principal kindness, far surpassing the
others, is that this most trustworthy of witnesses recom-
mends me to you by his personal support. To crown it all, 39
he promised to set up my statue in Carthage at his own
expense—he, a man to whom every province throughout
the world joyfully sets up four- and six-horse chariots.[49]
What can be added to this monument and summit of my
honor, the culmination of my glory? I say again: what can
be added? Aemilianus Strabo, of consular rank, soon by 40
the prayers of all to be proconsul,[50] presented a motion in
the Carthaginian council house that I should be honored,
and all assented to his proposal. Do you not think this a
senatorial decree?[51]

Moreover, all the Carthaginians present in that most 41
venerable council house appointed a site so gladly as to
make clear that they deferred a second statue to the next

[50] As consul in 156, Strabo would have been eligible to be
proconsul of Africa about 172/3; if *brevi* is not an optimistic exaggeration, this would date the present speech about 170.

[51] That is, a proposal made by someone so authoritative as
Strabo is equivalent to a decree of the Roman senate.

42   spero, in sequentem curiam protulisse, ut salva venerati-
one, salva reverentia consularis sui viderentur factum eius
non aemulati, sed secuti, id est ut integro die beneficium
43   ad me publicum perveniret. Ceterum meminerant, optimi
magistratus et benivolentissimi principes, mandatum sibi
a vobis quod volebant. Id egone scirem ac praedicare ces-
44   sarem? Ingratus essem. Quin etiam universo ordini vestro
pro amplissimis erga me meritis quantas maximas possum
gratias ago atque habeo, qui me in illa curia honestissimis
acclamationibus decoravere, in qua curia vel nominari
tantummodo summus honor est.

45   Igitur, quod difficile factu erat quodque re vera ⟨erat⟩[42]
arduum, non existimabatur: gratum esse populo, placere
ordini, probari magistratibus et principibus, id (praefas-
46   cine dixerim) iam quodam modo mihi obtigit. Quid igitur
superest ad statuae meae honorem, nisi aeris pretium et
artificis ministerium? Quae mihi ne in mediocribus quidem civitatibus umquam defuere, nedum[43] Carthagini
desint, ubi splendidissimus ordo etiam de rebus maioribus
47   iudicare potius solet quam computare. Sed de hoc tum ego
perfectius, cum vos effectius. Quin etiam tibi, nobilitas
senatorum, claritudo civium, dignitas amicorum, mox ad
dedicationem statuae meae libro etiam conscripto plenius
48   gratias canam eique libro mandabo, uti per omnis provin-
cias eat totoque abhinc orbe totoque abhinc tempore laudes benefacti tui ubique gentium, semper annorum re-
praesentet.

[42] erat *add. Krüger*
[43] nedum *Stewechius*: ne ut ω

[52] That is, Apuleius is sure that the council of Carthage, a rich
city, will spare no expense in having his statue made.

session, so I hope, in order that, without detracting from   42
their reverence or from their respect for their consular
citizen, it could be seen that they had not rivaled his action
but seconded it—in other words, so that this honor from
the people should be reserved for a full day. Moreover, the   43
excellent magistrates and kindly dignitaries recalled that
what you had ordered them to do was their very own wish.
Could I know that and not proclaim it? I would be un-
grateful. On the contrary, I express and I feel the warmest   44
possible thanks to your whole legislature for its enormous
kindnesses to me. You have honored me by most handsome acclamations in a council house where the mere
mention of one's name is a high honor.

And so, hard as it was to do, difficult in reality and not   45
merely in appearance—to please the populace, satisfy the
legislature, gain the approval of the magistrates and the
dignitaries—in this (if I may say so without boasting) I
have now in a way succeeded. What therefore is left to   46
complete the honor of my statue, other than determining
the price of the bronze and the service of the sculptor?
Things that have never been refused me even in lesser
cities can hardly be denied me in Carthage, where even in
connection with weightier issues the most distinguished
senate is more used to making decisions than calculations.[52] But on that subject my speech will be more pol-   47
ished when your plan is more advanced. Yes, to you, noble
senators, distinguished citizens, honorable friends, soon,
when my statue is dedicated I will also sing a hymn of
thanks in a written work, and I will give that work a mis-
sion: to travel through every province, and thereafter   48
through the whole world, and for all future time, to renew
my praise of your kindness in every land and down all the
years.

17. Viderint quibus mos est oggerere se negotiosis[44] praesidibus, ut impatientia linguae commendationem ingenii quaerant et affectata amicitiae vestrae specie glorientur. Utrumque enim a me, Scipio Orfite, longe abest.

2 Nam et quantulumcumque ingenium meum iam pridem pro captu suo hominibus notius est quam ut indigeat novae commendationis, et gratiam tuam tuorumque similium malo quam iacto, magisque sum tantae amicitiae cupitor quam gloriator, quoniam cupere nemo nisi vere [putem][45] potest, potest autem quivis falso gloriari.

4 Ad hoc ita semper ab ineunte aevo bonas artes sedulo colui, eamque existimationem morum ac studiorum cum in provincia nostra tum etiam Romae penes amicos tuos quaesisse me tute ipse locupletissimus testis es, ut non minus vobis amicitia mea capessenda sit quam mihi vestra

5 concupiscenda. Quippe non prompte veniam impertire rarenter adeundi assiduitatem eius requirentis est, summumque argumentum amoris frequentibus delectari, cessantibus obirasci, perseverantem celebrare, desinentem desiderare, quoniam necesse est ⟨gratam praesentiam⟩[46] eiusdem esse cuius angat absentia.

6 Ceterum vox cohibita silentio perpeti non magis usui erit quam nares gravedine oppletae, aures spurcitie obse-

7 ratae, oculi albugine obducti. Quid si manus manicis restringantur, quid si pedes pedicis coartentur, iam rector

---

[44] negotiosis *Stewechius*: et otiosis ω
[45] putem *del. Contarenus*
[46] gratam praesentiam *add. Helm post Colvium*

---

[53] Ser. Cornelius Scipio Salvidienus Orfitus, proconsul of Africa in 163/4 (*PIR* C 1447). Sections 5 and 19 suggest that Apu-

17. Let that be the concern of those who have a way of thrusting themselves on busy governors, so that by their unwillingness to keep silent they may earn praise for their talent, and may pride themselves on a false appearance of having your friendship; since both practices are not my way at all, Scipio Orfitus.[53] For my talent, however slight, 2 has long been too well known to the world, as far as my abilities allow, to need further commendation; and I would 3 rather possess than flaunt the favor of you and those like you, and I prefer to aspire to such a lofty friendship rather than to boast about it, since no one can aspire without sincerity, but anyone may boast without truth.

Furthermore, I have always from my earliest youth 4 devoted myself tirelessly to liberal studies; and both in our province and among your friends at Rome, I have earned such a reputation for character and learning, as you yourself are more qualified than anyone to testify, that all of you must covet my friendship no less than I must wish for yours. For being reluctant to excuse someone for the rar- 5 ity of his visits is a sign that you miss his attentions, and the highest proof of affection is to be pleased by regular visitors and to be vexed by infrequent ones, to praise the faithful friend and to miss the one who no longer comes; since inevitably one who gives pleasure by his presence also pains by his absence.

But still, a voice locked in perpetual silence will be no 6 more useful than nostrils filled with mucus, ears blocked with dirt, eyes dimmed by cataract. What happens when 7 hands are pinioned with handcuffs, feet are locked to-

leius had been slow to appear before him, rather as Aelius Aristides was with Marcus Aurelius (Philostratus, *Lives of the Sophists* 2.9, p. 216 Wright).

nostri animus aut somno solvatur aut vino mergatur aut
8 morbo sepeliatur? Profecto ut gladius usu splendescit, situ
robiginat, ita vox in vagina silentii condita diutino torpore
hebetatur. Desuetudo omnibus pigritiam, pigritia veter-
num parit. Tragoedi adeo ni cottidie proclament, claritudo
arteriis obsolescit; igitur identidem boando purgant ra-
vim.
9   Ceterum ipsius vocis hominis exercendae[47] cassus la-
10 bor; supervacaneo studio plurifariam superatur, si quidem voce hominis et tuba rudore torvior et lyra concentu
variatior et tibia questu delectabilior et fistula susurru
11 iucundior et bucina significatu longinquior. Mitto dicere
multorum animalium immeditatos sonores distinctis pro-
prietatibus admirandos, ut est taurorum gravis mugitus,
luporum acutus ululatus, elephantorum tristis barritus,
equorum hilaris hinnitus nec non avium instigati clan-
12 gores, nec non leonum indignati fremores ceteraeque id
genus voces animalium truces ac liquidae, quas infesta
rabies vel propitia voluptas ciant.
13   Pro quibus homini vox divinitus data angustior quidem, sed maiorem habet utilitatem mentibus quam auri-
14 bus delectationem. Quo magis celebrari debet frequentius
usurpata, et quidem non nisi in auditorio, tanto viro prae-
sidente, in hac excellenti celebritate multorum erudito-
rum, multorum benignorum. Equidem et si fidibus adprime callerem, non nisi confertos homines consectarer.
15 In solitudine cantilavit

    Orpheus in silvis, inter delphinas Arion,

[47] exercendae *Oudendorp*: exercendi ω

---

[54] Verg. *Ecl.* 8.56.

gether with chains, or indeed our ruling principle, the mind, is either relaxed in sleep, drowned in wine, or deadened by disease? Clearly, just as a sword gleams with use, 8 but grows rusty with disuse, so a voice buried in a sheath of silence grows dull from long inactivity. Disuse always engenders lethargy, and lethargy engenders paralysis. Why, tragic actors have to declaim every day, or else they lose the resonance of their vocal cords, which is why they clear a hoarse throat by constantly declaiming.

Though to exercise the *human* voice is to waste energy 9 in superfluous effort; it is a lost cause many times over, since the trumpet has a fiercer blare than the human voice, 10 the lyre a more varied harmony, the pipe a more pleasing moan, the flute a more charming delicacy, the horn carries its signal further. I pass over the fact that the artless sounds 11 of many animals are admirable for their different qualities, for example the loud bellowing of bulls, the piercing howl of wolves, the fearful trumpeting of elephants, the cheerful whinnying of horses, and the alarmed cries of birds too, 12 the angry growl of lions, and other such animal sounds, whether harsh or melodious, whether provoked by hostile fury or friendly pleasure.

In compensation, heaven has given mankind a voice 13 that, while narrower in range, still is more advantageous to the intellect than charming to the ears. All the more 14 reason for it to be exercised by more frequent use, and indeed only before an audience, with so great a man presiding, in this honorable throng of many connoisseurs and many well-wishers. For myself, even were I a lyre player of consummate skill, my aim would be a packed house. It 15 was in solitude that

Orpheus in the woods, Arion among the dolphins,[54]

APULEIUS

quippe, si fides fabulis, Orpheus exsilio desolatus, Arion
navigio praecipitatus, ille immanium bestiarum delenitor,
hic misericordium beluarum oblectator, ambo miserrimi
cantores, quia non sponte ad laudem, sed necessario ad
16 salutem nitebantur. Eos ego impensius admirarer, si hominibus potius quam bestiis placuissent. Avibus haec secre-
taria utiquam magis congruerint, merulis et lusciniis et
17 oloribus. Et merulae in remotis tesquis ‹cantilenam pueritiae›[48] fringulliunt, lusciniae in solitudine arcana[49] canticum adulescentiae garriunt, olores apud avios fluvios
18 carmen senectae meditantur. Enimvero qui pueris et adu-
lescentibus et senibus utile carmen prompturus est, in
mediis milibus hominum canat, ita ut hoc meum de virtu-
19 tibus Orfiti carmen est, serum quidem fortasse, sed serium, nec minus gratum quam utile Carthaginiensium
20 pueris et iuvenibus et senibus, quos indulgentia sua praecipuus omnium proconsul sublevavit temperatoque desi-
derio et moderato remedio dedit pueris saturitatem, iuve-
21 nibus hilaritatem, senibus securitatem. Metuo quidem,
Scipio, quoniam laudes tuas attigi, ne me impraesentiarum
refrenet vel tua generosa modestia vel mea ingenua vere-
22 cundia. Sed nequeo quin ex plurimis, quae in te meritissimo admiramur, ex his plurimis quin vel paucissima attingam. Vos ea mecum, cives ab eo servati, recognoscite.[50]

18. Tanta multitudo ad audiendum convenistis, ut potius gratulari Carthagini debeam, quod tam multos erudi-
tionis amicos habet, quam excusare, quod philosophus

[48] cantilenam pueritiae *add. Kronenberg*
[49] arcana *Haupt, Opuscula 3.326*: Africana ω
[50] *Titulum* APVLEI PLATONICI FLORIDORVM LIB. III EXPLIC.
INCIPIT IIII *praebet* F

308

sang their songs, if the myths are true, since Orpheus was left in lonely exile, Arion was tossed from a ship, the first a tamer of monstrous beasts, the second a charmer of sympathetic sea creatures, both of them the most wretched of singers in that they did not strive for praise of their own will, but for survival under duress. I would admire them 16 more heartily had they charmed humans rather than animals; those lonely spots would have been in every way better suited to birds such as blackbirds, nightingales, and swans. Blackbirds too chirp their tune in remote thick- 17 ets like children, nightingales warble their melody in hidden solitude like youths, swans rehearse their song on solitary rivers like old men. And yet one who hopes to 18 produce a song useful to children, youths, and old men should sing before humans in their thousands, as is this song of mine about Orfitus' virtues—tardy perhaps, but 19 yet heartfelt, and as pleasing as it is profitable for the children, youths, and old men of Carthage. All of these 20 this proconsul without peer has supported by his kindliness, and by his moderate wishes and gentle correction he has brought abundance to children, joyfulness to the young, security to the old. Indeed, Scipio, now that I have 21 touched on your praises, I fear that either your gentlemanly modesty or my natural reserve may constrain me for the present. But many are the qualities for which we 22 most deservedly admire you, and I cannot help touching on a very few from among those many. My fellow citizens who owe him your preservation, let us recall them together.

18. You have come in such crowds to hear me that I ought rather to congratulate Carthage for having so many friends of learning than ask pardon for not declining to

2   non recusaverim dissertare. Nam et pro amplitudine civitatis frequentia collecta et pro magnitudine frequentiae
3   locus delectus est. Praeterea in auditorio hoc genus spectari debet non pavimenti marmoratio nec proscaenii con-
tabulatio nec scaenae columnatio, sed nec culminum
eminentia nec lacunarium refulgentia nec sedilium cir-
4   cumferentia, nec quod hic alias mimus halucinatur, co-
moedus sermocinatur, tragoedus vociferatur, funerepus
periclitatur, praestigiator furatur, histrio gesticulatur cete-
rique omnes ludiones ostentant populo quod cuiusque
5   artis est, sed istis omnibus supersessis nihil amplius spectari debet quam convenientium ratio et dicentis oratio.

6   Quapropter, ut poetae solent hic ibidem varias civitates
substituere, ut ille tragicus, qui in theatro dici facit:

Liber, qui augusta haec loca Cithaeronis colis,

7   item ille comicus:

perparvam partim postulat Plautus loci
de vostris magnis atque amoenis moenibus,
Athenas quo sine architectis conferat,

8   non secus et mihi liceat nullam longinquam et transmari-
nam civitatem hic, sed enim ipsius Carthaginis vel curiam

---

55 Apuleius is speaking in the theater of Carthage, not a place
where a philosopher would normally appear.

56 Much of the theater is preserved and corresponds closely
to Apuleius' description: F. Sear, *Roman Theatres: An Architec-
tural Study* (Oxford, 2006), 277–78.

57 For *histriones,* dancers on mythic subjects, *Apol.* 74.7.

58 Poet unknown (Ribbeck, *Tragicorum Romanorum Fragmenta*[3] [1897] 310 no. 119).   59 Plaut. *Truculentus* 1–3.

lecture, philosopher though I am.[55] For the assembled   2
multitude is proportionate to the grandeur of the city, and
the chosen venue to the size of the audience. Moreover,   3
in a setting such as this, what deserves observation is not
the marble of the floor, the boards of the proscenium, the
columns of the stage, the loftiness of the roof, the brilliance of the ceiling panels, or the curvature of the seat-
ing,[56] nor the fact that this is the place where at other times   4
the mime rambles, the comic actor prattles, the tragic one
declaims, the acrobat risks his neck, the conjurer picks
purses, the dancer gesticulates,[57] and all the other artists
display their own particular skill to the populace. Putting   5
all of that aside, nothing deserves observation so much as
the quality of the assembled audience and the words of
the speaker.

And so, just as poets in this very place often conjure up   6
different cities, for instance that tragic poet who writes
these words to be spoken in the theater:

> Bacchus, that livest in these solemn haunts of
>   Cithaeron,[58]

and similarly the famous writer of comedies,[59]   7

> Within your great and charming town
> Plautus asks just a little space
> without the help of architects
> to transfer Athens to this place,

just so I hope I may conjure up here, not a distant city   8
across the sea, but Carthage's own council house or library.

9 vel bibliothecam substituere. Igitur proinde habetote, si
   curia digna protulero, ut si in ipsa curia me audiatis, si
10 erudita fuerint, ut si in bibliotheca legantur. Quod utinam
   mihi pro amplitudine auditorii prolixa oratio suppeteret ac
   non hic maxime clauderet, ubi me facundissimum cupe-
11 rem. Sed verum verbum est profecto, qui aiunt nihil quicquam homini tam prosperum divinitus datum, quin ei
   tamen admixtum sit aliquid difficultatis, ut etiam in am-
   plissima quaque laetitia subsit quaepiam vel parva queri-
   monia, coniugatione quadam mellis et fellis: ubi uber, ibi
   tuber.
12   Id ego cum [in]⁵¹ alias, tum etiam nunc impraesentiarum usu experior. Nam quanto videor plura apud vos
   habere ad commendationem suffragia, tanto sum ad di-
13 cendum nimia reverentia vestri cunctatior, et qui penes
   extrarios saepenumero promptissime disceptavi, idem
   nunc penes meos haesito ac ⟨mirum dictum⟩ ipsis illecebris deterreor et stimulis refrenor et incitamentis cohi-
14 beor. An non multa mihi apud vos adhortamina suppetunt,
   quod sum vobis nec lare alienus nec pueritia invisitatus
   nec magistris peregrinus nec secta incognitus nec voce
15 inauditus nec libris inlectus improbatusve? Ita mihi et
   patria in concilio Africae, id est vestro, et pueritia apud vos
   et magistri vos et secta, licet Athenis Atticis confirmata,

---

⁵¹ in *del. Floridus*

---

⁶⁰ No such proverb is known, but the meaning must be similar
to Jane Austen, *Mansfield Park,* ch. 28, "Her happiness on this
occasion was very much à la mortal, *finely checkered.*"

Accordingly, please imagine, if what I produce is worthy 9
of the council, that you are hearing me in the council
house itself, if it is scholarly, that I am reading it in the
library. I only wish, considering the size of the audience, 10
that I had a copious speech at my command and not a lame
one, here above all where I would wish to be most eloquent. But it is certainly a true saying: heaven gives no 11
man success without some difficulty mixed in,[60] so that
even in the greatest joy there lurks ever so slight a draw-
back, a sort of combination of honey and vinegar: the
richer the plot, the more the rot.

That has happened to me on other occasions, and on 12
this one too. For the more assurances of your approval I
seem to have, the more my great respect for you makes
me hesitant to speak; and though I have very often been 13
very ready to lecture before strangers, yet now before my
fellow citizens I waver, and (strange to say) I am deterred
precisely by the inducements, restrained by the promptings, and checked by the incentives. And yet I surely have 14
many grounds for encouragement in your city, since I am
not alien to you by origin, unknown to you from boyhood,
taught by foreign teachers, obscure as a philosopher, unfamiliar as a speaker, unread or unappreciated as a writer.
Witness the fact that my native city is part of the Council 15
of Africa, to which you too belong,[61] my boyhood was
spent among you, you were my teachers, my philosophical studies, though matured in Attic Athens, neverthe-

[61] Like most of the Roman provinces, Africa had a delibera-
tive council to which the separate districts (*dioceses*) sent repre-
sentatives, and Carthage, the capital of the province, was its seat.

16 tamen hic inchoata est, et vox mea utraque lingua iam
vestris auribus ante proximum sexennium probe cognita,
quin et libri mei non alia ubique laude carius censentur
17 quam quod iudicio vestro comprobantur. Haec tanta ac
totiuga invitamenta communia non minus vos ad audiendum prolectant quam me ad audendum retardant, faciliu-
que laudes vestras alibi gentium quam apud vos praedica-
rim: ita apud suos cuique modestia obnoxia est, apud
18 extrarios autem veritas libera. Semper adeo et ubique vos
quippe ut parentis ac primos magistros meos celebro mer-
cedemque vobis rependo, non illam, quam Protagora sophista pepigit nec accepit, sed quam Thales sapiens nec
pepigit et accepit. Video quid postuletis: utramque nar-
rabo.

19   Protagora, qui sophista fuit longe multiscius et cum
primis rhetoricae repertoribus perfacundus, Democriti
physici civis aequaevus—inde ei suppeditata doctrina
20 est—, eum Protagoran aiunt cum suo sibi discipulo
Evathlo mercedem nimis uberem condicione temeraria
pepigisse, uti sibi tum demum id argenti daret, si primo
21 tirocinio agendi penes iudices vicisset. Igitur Evathlus,
postquam cuncta illa exorabula iudicantium et decipula
adversantium et artificia dicentium, versutus alioqui et
22 ingeniatus ad astutiam, facile perdidicit, contentus scire
quod concupierat, coepit nolle quod pepigerat, sed callide
nectendis moris frustrari magistrum diutuleque nec agere

---

62 Protagoras of Abdera (ca. 490–420 BC), celebrated early
sophist; Democritus of Abdera, born about 460 BC, famous above
all as the inventor of the atomic theory. Aul. Gell. *NA* 5.10 tells
the same story about Protagoras' Athenian pupil, Euathlus, in
very similar language.

less began here, and my mastery of both languages has 16
been thoroughly familiar to your ears for the past six years.
What is more, nowhere do my books receive a more valuable mark of esteem than your considered approval. In- 17
ducements so great and so various, shared between us,
invite you to hear me as much as they deter me from
making the attempt, and I could sound your praises anywhere in the world more easily than before you, so much
are we all restrained by modesty among friends, though
free to speak truth before strangers. Indeed, I praise you 18
everywhere and always as my parents and my first teachers, and I pay you a fee, not such a fee as the sophist
Protagoras set and was not paid, but as the philosopher
Thales was paid and did not set. I see what you are asking,
and will tell you about both.

Protagoras was a sophist of encyclopedic knowledge 19
and, as one of the first inventors of rhetoric, highly eloquent, a fellow citizen and contemporary of the natural
philosopher Democritus, from whom he derived his stock
of learning.[62] Well, this Protagoras is said to have agreed 20
with his very own pupil Euathlus on a very fat fee, but one
with an ill-considered clause: that Euathlus would pay him
the agreed sum only if he won his case before a jury on his
first appearance in court. Well, once Euathlus had easily 21
mastered all the usual pleas to the jurors, traps for the
opposing counsel, and tricks of rhetoric, being generally
clever and naturally cunning, satisfied that he knew all that 22
he had wanted, he began to refuse to fulfill his side of the
bargain and, by cleverly inventing reasons for delay, to
elude his teacher and for a long time not to want either to

23 velle nec reddere, usque dum Protagoras eum ad iudices
provocavit, expositaque condicione, qua docendum rece-
24 perat, anceps argumentum ambifariam proposuit. "Nam
sive ego vicero," inquit, "solvere mercedem debebis ut
condemnatus, seu tu viceris, nihilo minus reddere debebis
ut pactus, quippe qui hanc causam primam penes iudices
25 viceris. Ita, si vincis, in condicionem incidisti; si vinceris,
26 in damnationem." Quid quaeris? Ratio conclusa iudicibus
acriter et invincibiliter videbatur. Enimvero Evathlus, utpote tanti veteratoris perfectissimus discipulus, biceps il-
27 lud argumentum retorsit. Nam "si ita est," inquit, "neutro
modo quod petis debeo. Aut enim vinco et iudicio dimit-
tor, aut vincor et pacto absolvor, ex quo non debeo mercedem, si hanc primam causam fuero penes iudices victus.
Ita me omni modo liberat sententia,[52] si vinco, condicio,
28 si vincor." Nonne vobis videntur haec sophistarum argumenta obversa invicem vice spinarum, quas ventus convol-
verit, inter se cohaerere, paribus utrimque aculeis, simili
29 penetratione, mutuo vulnere? Atque ideo merces Prota-
gorae tam aspera, tam senticosa versutis et avaris re-
linquenda est: cui scilicet multo tanta praestat illa altera
merces, quam Thalen memorant suasisse.

30 Thales Milesius ex septem illis sapientiae memoratis
viris facile praecipuus (enim geometriae penes Graios primus repertor et naturae rerum certissimus explorator et
astrorum peritissimus contemplator) maximas res parvis
31 lineis repperit: temporum ambitus, ventorum flatus, stel-

---

[52] sententia *huc transpos. Helm*: *post* vincor *habet* ω

---

[63] Thales (fl. 585 BC) was universally held the earliest of the

plead or to pay up. Finally Protagoras appealed the case 23
to a jury, and after explaining the contract under which he
had agreed to teach him, proposed a double-edged argument in the form of a dilemma: "For if *I* win," said he," 24
you will have to pay the fee on losing your case, or if *you*
win, you will have to pay up as agreed, having won this first
case before a jury. So, if you win, you are bound by the 25
contract: if you lose, by the condemnation." As you can 26
imagine, the argument seemed to the jury tightly and incontrovertibly framed. Nonetheless Euathlus, as the star
pupil of so great a casuist, turned that double-edged argument around. "Well, if that's so," said he, "in neither case 27
do I owe what you ask. For either I win and the verdict
acquits me, or I lose and the contract absolves me, since
according to that I owe no fee if I lose this first case in
court. So either way the contract acquits me if I lose, and
the verdict does if I win." Don't you think that these argu- 28
ments between two sophists are like tumbleweeds rolled
together by the wind? They cling to each other, both of
them equally prickly, similarly piercing, mutually wound-
ing? And so Protagoras' bargain, though so sharp and 29
thorny, should be left to cheats and misers: better by far,
undoubtedly, is that other fee that Thales is said to have
proposed.

Thales of Miletus was easily the first among the famous 30
Seven Wise Men, for he was the first discoverer of geometry among the Greeks, the most accurate investigator of
nature, the most skilled observer of the stars.[63] He used
small lines to find the greatest truths: the circuit of the 31

Seven Wise Men: he is credited with many scientific theories and
discoveries.

larum meatus, tonitruum sonora miracula, siderum obli-
qua curricula, solis annua reverticula, itidem lunae vel
nascentis incrementa vel senescentis dispendia vel delin-
32 quentis obstiticula. Idem sane iam proclivi senectute divinam rationem de sole commentus est, quam equidem non
didici modo, verum etiam experiendo comprobavi, quotiens sol magnitudine sua circulum quem permeat metia-
33 tur. Id a se recens inuentum Thales memoratur edocuisse
Mandrolytum[53] Prienensem, qui nova et inopinata cogni-
tione impendio delectatus optare iussit quantam vellet
34 mercedem sibi pro tanto documento rependi. "Satis," inquit, "mihi fuerit mercedis," Thales sapiens, "si id quod a
me didicisti, cum proferre ad quospiam coeperis, tibi
non[54] asciveris, sed eius inventi me potius quam alium
35 repertorem praedicaris." Pulchra merces prorsum ac tali
viro digna et perpetua; nam et in hodiernum ac dein semper Thali ea merces persolvetur ab omnibus nobis, qui
eius caelestia studia vere cognovimus.

36   Hanc ego vobis mercedem, Carthaginienses, ubique
gentium dependo pro disciplinis, quas in pueritia sum
apud vos adeptus. Ubique enim me vestrae civitatis alum-
num fero, ubique vos omnimodis laudibus celebro, vestras
disciplinas studiosius percolo, vestras opes gloriosius prae-
37 dico, vestros etiam deos religiosius veneror. Nunc quoque

---

53 Mandrolytum *Crusius, Philologus 49 (1890), 677*: Man-
draytum ω
54 tibi non *u*: non tibi *secunda manu φ*

---

64 Literally, "how many times the sun by its size measures the
circle through which it moves." Thales is said to have shown that
the diameter of the sun was 1/720th of its 24-hour circuit.

seasons, the direction of the winds, the courses of the stars, the portentous crash of thunder, the oblique paths of the planets, the annual revolutions of the sun, and similarly the phases of the moon as it waxes when new, wanes when old, or disappears when eclipsed. And moreover, in his final years Thales formed an inspired theory about the sun, which I have both learned and confirmed by experiment, concerning the sun's diameter as a fraction of the circuit through which it moves.[64] Soon after making this discovery, they record that Thales imparted it to Mandrolytus of Priene,[65] and he, completely thrilled by this new and unexpected knowledge, told him to name any fee he wished for teaching him such a lesson. "It will be fee enough for me," said the wise Thales, "if you do not claim what you have learned from me as your own when you begin to pass it on to anyone, and instead name me and not someone else as the discoverer." A fine fee indeed, worthy of such a man and everlasting: for to this day and for evermore this is the fee paid to Thales by all of us who really know his study of the heavens.

This is the fee, men of Carthage, that I pay you across the world for the teachings that I received among you in my boyhood. For everywhere I advertise myself as your city's adoptive son, everywhere I celebrate you with praise of every kind, I follow your teachings scrupulously, I proclaim your resources with pride, and I also venerate your gods with fervor. Now too, therefore, with you as my audi-

32

33

34

35

36

37

[65] Known only from this anecdote, and the name is corrupted in the manuscripts: see O. Kern, *RE* 14 (1928): 1041, Mandrolytos 2.

igitur principium mihi apud vestras auris auspicatissimum
ab Aesculapio deo capiam, qui arcem nostrae Carthaginis
38 indubitabili numine propitius respicit. Eius dei hymnum
Graeco et Latino carmine vobis ecce iam canam[55] illi a me
dedicatum. Sum enim non ignotus illi sacricola nec recens
cultor nec ingratus antistes, ac iam et prorsa et vorsa fa-
39 cundia veneratus sum, ita ut etiam nunc hymnum eius
utraque lingua canam, cui dialogum similiter Graecum et
Latinum praetexui, in quo sermocinabuntur Sabidius Se-
40 verus et Iulius Persius, viri et inter se mutuo et vobis [et][56]
utilitatibus publicis merito amicissimi, doctrina et eloquentia et benivolentia paribus, incertum modestia qui-
etiores an industria promptiores an honoribus clariores.
41 Quibus cum sit summa concordia, tamen haec sola aemu-
latio et in hoc unum certamen est, uter eorum magis Carthaginem diligat, atque summis medullitus viribus conten-
42 dunt ambo, vincitur neuter. Eorum ego sermonem ratus
et vobis auditu gratissimum et mihi compositu congruen-
tem et ⟨deo⟩[57] dedicatu religiosum, in principio libri facio
quendam ex his, qui mihi Athenis condidicerunt, percontari a Persio Graece quae ego pridie in templo Aesculapi
43 disseruerim, paulatimque illis Severum adiungo, cui
interim Romanae linguae partes dedi. Nam et Persius,
quamvis et ipse optime possit, tamen hodie vobis atticis-
sabit.

---

[55] iam canam *Helm*: canam iam ω
[56] et *seclusi*   [57] deo *add. Kronenberg*

---

[66] Carthage had a notable cult of Asclepius; an inscription
(CIL 8.24535) shows that Cocceius Honorinus (above, 9, 36) con-
ferred some benefit on the temple.

ence I will make the most auspicious of beginnings with the god Asclepius, whose indisputable power makes him the benevolent guardian of our Carthage's citadel.[66] See,   38 I will now sing you a hymn to that god in Greek and Latin, dedicated to him by me. For I am not a devotee unknown to him, no recent votary or unwelcome priest, and I have worshipped him before now with eloquence in prose and verse. Similarly, I will sing him a hymn in both languages   39 on this occasion too, and I have prefaced it with a dialogue that is similarly both in Greek and in Latin. The speakers will be Sabidius Severus and Julius Perseus,[67] men who are the closest of friends to each other and to   40 you too, as well they should be for their public services. They are matched in learning, eloquence and benevolence, and it is an open question whether they are more unobtrusively modest, energetically zealous, or conspicuously distinguished. Though on the best of terms, still they   41 have just one source of rivalry and compete only on one point—which of them loves Carthage the more; both contend with every ounce of their strength and neither loses. Thinking that a conversation between them would be   42 most pleasing for you to hear, suitable for me to compose, and acceptable as an offering to the god, I begin the work with one of my fellow students at Athens asking Perseus in Greek what was the subject of my lecture the day before in the temple of Asclepius. Gradually I bring Severus into   43 the discussion, giving him the part of the Latin speaker for the occasion. For Perseus himself could very well speak Latin too, but for you today he will talk the purest Greek.

---

[67] Severus is unknown, while Perseus is probably the builder of the Baths of Perseus, to which Apuleius went for a cure (16.2).

19. Asclepiades ille, inter praecipuos medicorum si
unum Hippocratem excipias, ceteris princeps, primus
etiam vino repperit aegris opitulari, sed dando scilicet in
tempore: cuius rei observationem probe callebat, ut qui
diligentissime animadverteret venarum pulsus inconditos
2 vel praevaros. Is igitur cum forte in civitatem sese reci-
peret et rure suo suburbano rediret, aspexit in pomeriis
civitatis funus ingens locatum plurimos homines ingenti
multitudine, qui exsequias venerant, circumstare, omnis
3 tristissimos et obsoletissimos vestitu. Propius accessit,
utine cognosceret more ingenii ‹humani›[58] quisnam esset, quoniam percontanti nemo responderat, an vero ut
ipse aliquid in illo ex arte deprehenderet.[59] Certe quidem
4 iacenti homini ac prope deposito fatum abstulit.[60] Iam
miseri illius membra omnia aromatis perspersa, iam os
ipsius unguine odoro delibutum, iam eum pollinctum, iam
5 ‹igni›[61] paene paratum contemplatus [enim],[62] diligentissime quibusdam signis animadversis, etiam atque etiam
pertrectavit corpus hominis et invenit in illo vitam la-
6 tentem. Confestim exclamavit vivere hominem: procul
igitur faces abicerent,[63] procul ignes amolirentur, rogum
demolirentur, cenam feralem a tumulo ad mensam re-
7 ferrent. Murmur interea exortum; partim medico creden-
dum dicere, partim etiam irridere medicinam. Postremo
propinquis etiam omnibus[64] invitis, quodne iam ipsi hereditatem habebant, an quod adhuc illi fidem non habebant,
8 aegre tamen ac difficulter Asclepiades impetravit brevem

58 humani add. u
59 deprehenderet Wowerius: reprehenderet ω
60 abstulit Wowerius: attulit ω
61 ‹igni› add. Novák

19. The famous Asclepiades, the greatest of physicians with the sole exception of Hippocrates, and superior to all the rest, was also the first to find how to treat the sick with wine, of course only by giving it at the right time, a juncture he was highly skilled at observing, since he could detect an uneven or an irregular pulse very precisely. Well, he happened to be returning to the city from 2 his suburban estate when he noticed a large funeral prepared outside the city boundary, and a huge crowd of people standing around to attend the last rites, all of them very downcast and in very shabby clothing. He came 3 closer, either from a human curiosity to learn who it might be, since he had inquired and got no reply, or else to observe something in the man for himself by his expertise. Actually, though the man was laid out and almost buried, he canceled his doom. For after surveying all the poor 4 man's body when it was already sprinkled with perfumes, his face already daubed with fragrant ointment, his body already washed, already all but prepared for the flames, and after carefully observing certain signs, he ran his 5 hands several times over the man's body and found hidden life in it. Immediately he shouted, "The man is alive, so 6 throw away the torches, scatter the fire, dismantle the pyre, move the funeral banquet from the grave to the table." Meanwhile mutterings arose: some said that a medi- 7 cal man deserved belief, some even mocked the art of medicine. Finally, though all the relatives objected too, either because they already had a legacy, or as yet had no trust in him, even so Asclepiades with painful difficulty 8

---

62 enim *seclusi*   63 abicerent *Stewechius*: abigerent
64 omnibus *Stewechius*: hominibus ω

mortuo dilationem atque ita vispillonum manibus extortum velut ab inferis postliminio domum rettulit confestimque spiritum recreavit, confestim animam in corporis latibulis delitiscentem quibusdam medicamentis provocavit.

20. Sapientis viri super mensam celebre dictum est: "Prima," inquit, "creterra ad sitim pertinet, secunda ad hilaritatem, tertia ad voluptatem, quarta ad insaniam." 2 Verum enimvero Musarum creterra versa vice quanto crebrior quantoque meracior, tanto propior ad animi sani- 3 tatem. Prima creterra litteratoris ruditatem[65] eximit, secunda grammatici doctrina instruit, tertia rhetoris elo- 4 quentia armat. Hactenus a plerisque potatur: ego et alias creterras Athenis bibi—poeticae conditam,[66] geometriae limpidam, musicae dulcem, dialecticae austerulam, iam vero universae philosophiae inexplebilem scilicet ⟨et⟩[67] 5 nectaream. Canit enim Empedocles carmina, Plato dialogos, Socrates hymnos, Epicharmus comoedias,[68] Xeno- 6 phon historias, Crates satiras: Apuleius vester haec omnia novemque Musas pari studio colit, maiore scilicet voluntate quam facultate, eoque propensius fortasse laudandus est, quod omnibus bonis in rebus conatus in laude, effec- 7 tus in casu est, ita ut contra in maleficiis etiam cogitata scelera, non perfecta adhuc vindicantur, cruenta mente, 8 pura manu. Ergo sicut ad poenam sufficit meditari pu-

[65] ruditatem *Bechichemus*: ruato ω
[66] conditam *Scioppius*: comtam ω
[67] et *add. Colvius*
[68] comoedias *Teuffel in RE 1.2² (1866), 1349 (Kassel-Austin, Poet. Com. Gr. 1.13, no. 25)*: modos ω

obtained a brief delay for the deceased, and, having thus
wrested him from the hands of the undertakers, brought
him home like one restored from the underworld, and
immediately used certain medicines to revive the life hiding in the recesses of the body.

20. There is a famous saying of a wise man over dinner:
"The first bowl," said he, "is for thirst, the second for
cheer, the third for pleasure, the fourth for delirium."[68]
Not so the Muses' bowl: the more often drunk and the 2
more strongly mixed, the more it promotes the health of
the mind. The first bowl is the writing master's, and re- 3
moves ignorance; the second is the schoolmaster's and
provides learning; the third is the rhetorician's and arms
with eloquence. Most drink no more than that: but *I* have 4
drunk other bowls too in Athens—the aromatic one of
poetry, the clear one of geometry, the sweet one of music,
the slightly sharp one of dialectic, and of course the in-
exhaustible and sweet one of universal philosophy. For 5
Empedocles sings in poetry, Plato in dialogues, Socrates
in hymns, Epicharmus in comedies, Xenophon in histories, Crates in satires.[69] All of these and all nine Muses 6
your fellow citizen Apuleius reveres with equal ardor, and
no doubt with more aspiration than ability. That perhaps
makes him all the more praiseworthy, since with every
good pursuit the attempt wins praise, but success depends
on luck, just as with bad pursuits crimes are punished 7
when they are planned and not yet performed, when the
mind is bloody and the hands clean. And so, just as con- 8
templating a punishable act is sufficient for punishment,

[68] A similar saying is attributed to the Scythian sage Anacharsis (Diog. Laert. 1.103).   [69] On Crates' poetry, *Apol.* 22.4.

9   nienda, sic et ad laudem satis est conari praedicanda. Quae autem maior laus aut certior, quam Carthagini benedicere, ubi tota civitas eruditissimi estis, penes quos omnem disciplinam pueri discunt, iuvenes ostentant, senes do-

10   cent? Carthago provinciae nostrae magistra venerabilis, Carthago Africae Musa caelestis, Carthago Camena togatorum.

    21. Habet interdum et necessaria festinatio honestas moras, saepe uti malis interpellatam voluntatem: quippe

2   et illis, quibus curriculo confecta via opus est, adeo uti praeoptent pendere equo quam carpento sedere, propter molestias sarcinarum et pondera vehiculorum et moras

3   orbium et salebras orbitarum (adde et lapidum globos et

4   caudicum toros et camporum rivos et collium clivos), hisce igitur moramentis omnibus qui volunt devitare ac vectorem sibimet equum deligunt diutinae fortitudinis, vivacis pernicitatis, id est et ferre validum et ire rapidum,

    qui campos collesque gradu perlabitur uno,

5   ut ait Lucilius; tamen cum eo equo per viam concito pervolant, si quem interea conspicantur ex principalibus viris nobilem hominem, bene consultum, bene cognitum,

6   quamquam oppido festinent, tamen honoris eius gratia cohibent cursum, relevant gradum, retardant equum et ilico in pedes desiliunt, fruticem, quem verberando equo gestant, eam virgam in laevam manum transferunt,

---

70 The Camenae, here translated in the singular as "Latin Muse," were originally water goddesses and were identified with the Greek Muses; the toga was the distinctive dress of Roman male citizens. Apuleius praises Carthage as a center of both Greek and Roman culture.

so also making a praiseworthy effort is enough to win praise. Well, what higher or more assured praise could there be than for speaking well of Carthage, where every citizen is a scholar, where boys acquire knowledge of every kind, grown men display it, and elders teach it? Carthage is the venerable teacher of our province, Carthage is the divine Muse of Africa, Carthage is the Latin Muse of all who wear the toga.[70]

21. Even when obliged to rush, one sometimes has honorable excuses for delay, and hence he often prefers to have his intention impeded. Why, even those who need to finish a journey speedily, to such a degree that they would rather be perched on a horse than seated in a carriage, since luggage is bothersome, vehicles cumbrous, wheels cause delay, and ruts jolt, not to mention heaps of stones, bulky tree trunks, streams in plains and slopes on hills—well, some who want to avoid all these obstacles choose to be carried by a horse of untiring strength and brisk pace, that is, a sturdy mount and a fast pacer,

That glides o'er hill and dale with single stride,

to quote Lucilius.[71] But still, even when with such a horse they are flying fast on their way, if meanwhile they catch sight of some leader of society, someone well respected and well regarded, even though very pressed for time they still check their progress to pay him their respects; they slacken their pace, rein in their horse, jump down at once, and transfer to their left hand the switch that they carry as

[71] Lucilius, fr. 1278 Marx, *ROL* 3.160, fr. 506.

7   itaque expedita dextra adeunt ac salutant et, si diutule ille
quippiam percontetur, ambulant diutule et fabulantur,
denique quantumvis morae in officio libenter insumunt.

      22. Crates ille Diogenis sectator, qui ut lar familiaris
2   apud homines aetatis suae Athenis cultus est—nulla domus ⟨ei⟩[69] umquam clausa erat nec erat patris familias
tam absconditum secretum, quin eo tempestive Crates
interveniret, litium omnium et iurgiorum inter propin-
3   quos disceptator atque arbiter. Quod Herculem olim poetae memorant monstra illa immania hominum ac ferarum
virtute subegisse orbemque terrae purgasse, similiter adversum iracundiam et invidiam atque avaritiam atque libidinem ceteraque animi humani monstra et flagitia philo-
4   sophus iste Hercules fuit: eas omnes pestes mentibus
exegit, familias purgavit, malitiam perdomuit, seminudus
et ipse et clava insignis, etiam Thebis oriundus, unde Her-
5   culem fuisse memoria exstat. ⟨Is⟩[70] igitur, priusquam
plane Crates factus, inter proceres Thebanos numeratus
est, lectum genus, frequens famulitium, domus amplo or-
6   nata vestibulo, ipse bene vestitus, bene praediatus. Post
ubi intellegit nullum sibi in re familiari praesidium legatum, quo fretus aetatem agat, omnia fluxa infirmaque esse,
quicquid sub caelo divitiarum est, eas omnis ad bene vivendum ⟨nihil⟩[71] quicquam esse . . .

      23. Sicuti navem bonam, fabre factam, bene intrinse-
cus compactam, extrinsecus eleganter depictam, mobili
clavo, firmis rudentibus, procero malo, insigni carchesio,
splendentibus velis, postremo omnibus armamentis ido-
2   neis ad usum et honestis ad contemplationem, eam navem
si aut gubernator non agat aut tempestas agat, ut facile

---

[69] ei *add. u*   [70] is *add. Rohde*   [71] nihil *add. van der Vliet*

a whip. After freeing their right hand that way they come   7
up, offer greetings, and if he briefly asks some question,
they briefly walk and chat. In short, they gladly spend any
amount of delay to pay their respects.

22. The famous Crates, the follower of Diogenes, was
worshiped at Athens like a household god by his contem-
poraries. No home was ever closed to him, no household-   2
er's study was so private that Crates could arrive at the
wrong time to mediate and arbitrate any lawsuit or quarrel
between relatives. Just as poets say that Hercules once   3
subdued those fearsome monsters, both human and animal, by his courage, and cleared the face of the earth, in
the same way *he* was a Hercules against anger, jealousy,
avarice, lust, and the other monsters and iniquities of the
human heart. He drove all those sicknesses from people's   4
minds, cleaned households, subdued malice. He too was
half-naked and conspicuous for his club, and moreover he
was a native of Thebes, which tradition names as Hercules'
birthplace. Well, before he fully became Crates, he was   5
counted among the leading men of Thebes, of high birth,
the master of many slaves; his house was graced by a large
entrance hall, the master had fine clothing and a fine estate. In due course he realized that nothing he had inher-   6
ited among his possessions was a reliable support for living
his life, that everything was transitory and unstable, and
that all the wealth in the world had nothing to do with a
life of virtue.

23. A ship may be good, skillfully built, securely planked
inside, trimly painted outside, with responsive tiller, strong
rigging, tall mast, proud masthead, dazzling sails, in short
with all its tackle good for use and splendid to observe;
and yet if either the pilot does not steer the ship or a storm   2

cum illis egregiis instrumentis aut profunda hauserint aut
3 scopuli comminuerint! Sed et medici cum intraverint ad
aegrum, uti visant, nemo eorum, quod tabulina perpul-
chra in aedibus cernant et lacunaria auro oblita et gre-
gatim pueros ac iuvenes eximia forma in cubiculo circa
4 lectum stantis, aegrum iubet uti sit animo bono; sed, ubi
iuxtim consedit, manum hominis prehendit, eam pertrec-
tat, venarum pulsum et momenta captat: si quid illic
turbatum atque inconditum offendit, illi renuntiat male
5 morbo haberi. Dives ille cibo interdicitur; ea die in sua sibi
copiosa domo panem non accipit, cum interea totum eius
servitium hilares sunt atque epulantur, nec in ea re quicquam efficit condicio.[72]

1.*[73] Qui me voluistis dicere ex tempore, accipite rudimentum post experimentum. Quippe prout mea opinio
est, bono periculo periculum faciam, postquam mire[74]
probata meditata sunt, dicturus incogitata. Neque enim
metuo ne in frivolis displiceam, qui in gravioribus placui.
2 Sed ut me omnifariam noveritis, etiam in isto, ut ait Lucilius, "schedio . . . et incondito," experimini an idem sim
repentinus qui praeparatus, si qui tamen vestrum nondum
subitaria ista nostra cognostis, quae scilicet audietis pari
labore quo scribimus, venia propensiore quam legimus.
3 Enim sic ferme assolet apud prudentes viros esse in ope-

[72] condicio *Floridus*: condicione ω   [73] *Titulum* APVLEI
PLATONICI MADAVRENSIS INCIPIT DE DEO SOCRATIS FELICITER
praebent BM   [74] mire *Goldbacher*: re ω

[72] Lucilius, fr. 1279 Marx, *ROL* 3.366, fr. 1131; a word such
as *rudi* (rough) has fallen out.
[73] Presumably meaning that this is an improvised sketch for

does, how quickly do the waves swallow it or the rocks shatter it and all its fine tackle! So also when doctors too 3 enter a sick man's room to examine him, not one of them, even if he sees dazzling galleries in the house, ceilings inlaid with gold, and boys and youths of great beauty standing in crowds around the bed in the sickroom—still, no doctor tells the patient to cheer up, but instead he sits 4 beside him, takes the man's hand, feels it, and observes the pulse and its fluctuation. If he finds any disturbance or irregularity there, he advises the man that he is seriously ill. This Croesus is allowed no food; that day he takes no 5 bread in his own well-stocked house, while in the meanwhile his whole household makes merry and dines well, and at such a pass his rank is of no help to him.

1.* For those of you who wanted me to speak extempore, here is a draft coming after a final version. For so it seems to me, I run little risk in giving an improvised speech when my prepared one has been wonderfully admired, and moreover I am not afraid I may displease you on lighthearted subjects after pleasing you on serious ones. But to give you a complete idea of myself, even in 2 this "— and hasty sketch," as Lucilius says,[72] I ask you to judge whether I am as good extempore as I am after preparation, in case, that is, that any of you are still unfamiliar with these sketches of mine. You will surely listen to them with as much effort as I used in writing them, and with greater indulgence than I use in reading them.[73] For discerning critics tend to be more severe when judging works 3

which Apuleius requires the listeners' help in order to improve it; cf. ch. 4: they will therefore be more forgiving of its faults than he himself will be as he reads it aloud.

ribus elaboratis iudicatio restrictior, in rebus subitariis venia prolixior. Scripta enim pensiculatis et examinatis, repentina autem noscitis simul et ignoscitis; nec iniuria.

4 Illa enim quae scripta legimus, etiam tacentibus vobis, talia erunt, qualia illata sunt: haec vero, quae impraesentiarum et quasi vobiscum parienda sunt, talia erunt qualia 5 vos illa favendo feceritis. Quanto enim . . . exinde orationi modificabor . . . vos animadverto libenter audire. Proinde in vestra manu situm est vela nostra sinuare †etiam mittere,†[75] ne pendula et flaccida neve restricta et caperrata sint.

2.* At ego, quod Aristippus dixit, experiar. Aristippus ille Cyrenaicae sectae repertor, quodque malebat ipse, Socratis discipulus, eum quidam tyrannus rogavit, quid ille philosophiae studium tam impensum tamque diutinum 2 profuisset. Aristippus respondit, "ut cum omnibus," inquit, "hominibus secure et intrepide fabularer."

3.* Verbo subito sumpta sententia est, quia de repentino oborta est, quasi velut in maceria lapides temerario iniectu poni necesse est, neque interiecto intrinsecus pondere neque colliniato pro fronte situ neque conventi- 2 bus ad regulam lineis, quippe qui structor orationis huius egomet non e meo monte lapidem directim caesum afferam, probe omnifariam complanatum, laeviter extimas 3 oras ad unguem coaequatum, sed cuique operi accommodem vel inaequalitate aspera vel levitate lubrica vel angulis eminula vel rotunditate volubilia, sine regulae correctione et mensurae parilitate et perpendiculi sollertia.

[75] etiam (et iam) mittere ω, *damnavit Thomas; an* et summittere?

that are polished, and to be more ready to forgive the results of improvisation. A written speech you weigh and evaluate, an improvised one is forgiven as fast as it is given, and rightly too. For whatever we first write and then read 4 will stay exactly as it was committed to paper, even if you remain silent: but the present speech, which I must come up with on the spot and almost with your assistance, will be whatever your goodwill has made it into. For as much 5 . . . and thereafter I will revise the speech . . . I notice that you are listening with pleasure. Hence it is up to you both to spread my sails and also to brail them in such a way that they are neither loose and slack, nor wrinkled and furled.

2.* But *I* shall test Aristippus' dictum.[74] The celebrated Aristippus, founder of the Cyrenaic school, or as he himself preferred, the disciple of Socrates, was asked by a certain tyrant what good he had got from such deep and prolonged study of philosophy. Aristippus replied, "The 2 ability to talk to anybody calmly and fearlessly."

3.* I expressed my idea by speaking impromptu, since it came to me suddenly; almost as with a rough-set wall, one must lay the stones in a random order, without building an interior core, smoothing them with a plumb line, or aligning them with string. As the builder of this speech, I 2 certainly bring no stone from my quarry precisely squared, nicely chiseled all around, its outer surfaces smoothly and exactly evened. No, into each of my works I put things that 3 are sharp and uneven, or smooth and slippery, or protruding and angular, or round and unstable, not made straight with a rod, equal with a measure, or perpendicular with a

---

[74] Aristippus of Cyrene (ca. 430–355 BC), founder of the "Cyrenaic," or Hedonist, sect.

4 Nulla enim res potest esse eadem festinata simul et exa-
minata, nec est quicquam omnium, quod habere possit[76]
et laudem diligentiae simul et gratiam celeritatis.

4.* Praebui me quorundam voluntati, qui oppido quam
2 a me desiderabant ut dicerem ex tempore! At est hercule
formido ne id mihi evenerit, quod corvo suo evenisse
Aesopus fabulatur, id erit ne, dum hanc novam laudem
capto, parvam illam quam ante peperi cogar amittere. Sed
de apologo quaeritis: non pigebit aliquid fabulari.

3 Corvus et vulpes unam offulam simul viderant eamque
raptum festinabant pari studio, impari celeritate, vulpes
cursu, corvus volatu. Igitur ales bestiam praevenit et secundo flatu propassis utrimque pinnis praelabitur et anti-
cipat, atque ita praeda simul et victoria laetus, sublime
evectus, in quadam proxima quercu in summo eius cacu-
4 mine tutus sedit. Eo quoque tamen vulpes, quia lapidem
nequibat, dolum iecit. Namque eandem arborem succes-
sit, et subsistens, cum superne raptorem praeda ovantem
5 videret, laudare astu adorta est: "Ne ego inscita, quae cum
alite Apollinis frustra certaverim, quippe cui iam pridem
corpus tam concinnum est, ut neque oppido parvum neque nimis grande sit, sed quantum satis ad usum deco-
6 remque, pluma mollis, caput argutum, rostrum validum;
iam ipse alis persequax, oculis perspicax, unguibus perti-
7 nax. Nam de colore quid dicam? Nam cum duo colores
praestabiles forent, piceus et niveus, quibus inter se nox

---

[76] possit *Vincentius Bellov. et mss. quidam*: *omittunt mss. cett.*

---

[75] The fable of The Fox and the Crow survives in several ver-
sions: Aesop no. 124 Perry, Babrius no. 77, Phaedrus no. 1.13; it
is also the second of La Fontaine's 239 Fables.

plumb line. For nothing can be both hasty and polished,   4
and nothing exists that can both win praise for careful
preparation and give pleasure by speedy execution.

4.* I have yielded to certain people's wish—how they
wanted me to give an extempore speech! Yet, so help me,   2
I greatly fear that what befell the crow in Aesop's fable may
befall me, and that aiming at this novel sort of praise may
oblige me to lose the little praise I have earned up to now.
But since you ask about the fable, I am not ashamed to
ramble a little.[75]

A crow and a vixen both at the same time noticed a   3
single scrap of food, and rushed to seize it with equal
greed but unequal speed, the vixen running and the crow
flying. And so the bird outraced the beast, and with a following wind and with both wings outspread it swooped on
ahead and got in first. So, pleased with both its booty and
its victory, it flew high up and perched safely at the very
top of a certain oak nearby. Even that far, however, the   4
vixen could not send a stone but could send a trick. For
she came beneath that same tree, stood there, and when
she saw the robber up above gloating over his prize, she
began craftily to praise him. "What a fool I am, in a point-   5
less competition with Apollo's own bird! For he has always
had a body so trim as to be neither very small nor overly
large, but just the right size to be practical and beautiful.
He has soft feathers, a chiseled profile, a hard beak, and   6
he is swift in flight, keen of sight, and has talons that hold
tight. And as for his color, words fail me! For since there   7
were two colors superior to all the rest, pitch black and

cum die differunt, utrumque colorem Apollo suis alitibus
8 condonavit, candidum olori, nigrum corvo. Quod utinam
sicuti cygno cantum indulsit, ita huic quoque vocem tribuisset, ne tam pulchra ales, quae ex omni avitio longe
praecellit, voce viduata, deliciae facundi dei, muta viveret
9 et elinguis!" Id vero ubi corvus audit, hoc solum sibi prae
ceteris deesse, dum vult clarissime clangere, ut ne in hoc
10 saltem olori concederet, oblitus offulae, quam mordicus
retinebat, toto rictu hiavit atque ita, quod volatu pepere-
rat, cantu amisit; enimvero vulpes, quod cursu amiserat,
11 astu recuperavit. Eandem istam fabulam in pauca coga-
mus, quantum fieri potest cohibiliter: corvus ut se vocalem
probaret, croccire adortus praedae, quam ore gestabat,
inductricem compotivit.[77]

5.* Iamdudum scio quid hoc significatu flagitetis: ut
cetera Latine materiae persequamur. Nam et in principio
vobis diversa tendentibus ita memini polliceri, ut neutra
pars vestrum, nec qui Graece nec qui Latine petebatis,
2 dictionis huius expertes abiretis. Quapropter, si ita videtur,
satis oratio nostra atticissaverit; tempus est in Latium demigrare de Graecia. Nam et quaestionis huius ferme media tenemus, ut, quantum mea opinio est, pars ista poste-
rior, prae illa Graeca quae antevertit, nec argumentis sit
effetior nec sententiis rarior nec exemplis pauperior nec
oratione defectior.

[77] *Titulum* EXPLICIT PRAEFATIO, INCIPIT DISPVTATIO DE
DEO SOCRATIS FELICITER *praebent BMV*

snow white, different from each other as night and day,
Apollo gave both to his birds, white to the swan and black
to the crow. Now just as he presented the swan with the 8
power of song, if only he had given a voice to the crow too,
so that such a lovely bird, far superior to all birdland,
would not live mute and tongue-tied, vacant of voice yet
the pet of the god of speech!" Well, when the crow heard 9
that, that this was his only defect compared to the other
birds, he wanted to produce the loudest cry he could, and
not yield to the swan on this point either. So forgetting the 10
scrap he held in his mouth, he opened his beak to its wid-
est, and thus lost by singing what he had won by flying;
whereas the vixen regained by cunning what she had lost
by running. Let me put this same story in few words, as 11
concisely as I can: to prove that he had a voice, which the
vixen pretended was the one thing his great beauty lacked,
the crow tried to croak, and made over to the trickster the
prize he had carried in his beak.

5.* I have long since seen from your hints what it is that
you request—that I finish what remains of my subject in
Latin. When I began, you all tugged in contrary directions,
and I remember promising you that neither side, neither
those who wanted Greek nor those who wanted Latin,
should leave without a part of my speech. So if you agree, 2
my speech has perhaps spent enough time in Attic Greek:
it is time to move from Greece to Latium. For I am about
midway through my inquiry, and, in my opinion at least,
compared to its Greek predecessor this second part will
be no weaker in argument, poorer in illustrations, or infe-
rior in eloquence.

DE DEO SOCRATIS

INTRODUCTION

According to St. Augustine, Apuleius himself chose (*voluit*) the title *De Deo Socratis* (*Civ. Dei* 8.14), and the same title appears in the two principal manuscripts. Yet just as Augustine is almost certainly wrong in saying that Apuleius gave the title *Asinus Aureus* to the work that the manuscripts call the *Metamorphoses* (*Civ. Dei* 18.18), his testimony might be doubted here too. The *De Deo Socratis* is as much a treatise on the unity of Plato's ideas about the *daimôn* as it is about "Socrates' god" (though some have held that it lacks an original preface, conclusion, or both), and it mentions Socrates only toward the end (14.7). Moreover, Apuleius usually refers to Socrates' guiding spirit as his *daemon,* though also calling it Socrates' "own" god (*deus suus,* 17.1, cf. 18.5). A more accurate title, whether or not Apuleius would have chosen it, might have been *De daemone Platonis*.

The work unites two strains of Greek speculation, one of them general and the other specific to Socrates. The word *daimôn,* which Apuleius is the first to use in its Latin form *daemon,* etymologically means "one who divides or assigns," and in Homer is used both of the Olympian gods and of divine power in general, sometimes with a sense close to "destiny." By a long process of evolution, it acquired the sense of "malignant unseen being," which by way of its use in Jewish and Christian texts became the modern "demon." To this evolution, Plato gave a powerful impetus by treating the *daimones* as beings intermediate between heaven and earth, whereas a transcendent God was beyond direct contact with humanity.[1]

The other strain of thought began with Plato's characterization of Socrates as having an invisible guide and protector, not called a *daimôn* but *to daimonion,* in which the definite article *to* implies a particular entity, and *daimonion* is a noun formed from the adjective *daimonios,* "the heaven-sent *or* miraculous (one)." In Plato this entity serves only to warn Socrates against taking certain actions, but later speculation, some of it expounded in the pseudo-Platonic *Epinomis* and *Theages,* represented him as prompted by his *daimonion* to warn other people against particular actions, or even to predict the outcome of public events.[2] There were also theories that the *daimonion* was an everyday omen, such as a sneeze. Apuleius combines the two Platonic doctrines, that of the intermediate position of the *daemones* and the private, monitory role of Socrates' *daimonion,* into a single exposition, and

[1] F. Andres, *RE* Suppl. 3 (1918): 307–10; H. W. Versnel, *OCD*, 410. The basic text for this conception of the *daimones* is *Symp.* 202E–3A.

[2] On the *daimonion* in the *Apology* and the dialogues, J. Burnet, ed., *Plato's* Euthyphro, Apology of Socrates, *and* Crito (Oxford, 1924), index sv δαιμονίον. For later theorizing on the subject, C. Zintzen, in *Reallexikon für Antike und Christentum* 9 (1976): 640–68.

to reinforce his point he uses the same term, *daemon,* for both of Plato's entities.[3]

Extant works by two Platonists, one from the previous generation to Apuleius and the other his own close contemporary, are devoted to Socrates' *daimonion.* Plutarch's *On the daimonion of Socrates* is a dialog taking place in Athens soon after the Boeotians' recovery of Thebes in 379; this frames a narrated conversation that occurred at the very time of the Theban assault. There are four speakers, and though their conversation starts from Socrates' *daimonion,* it broadens out into an investigation of what the *daimones* are and of their role as guides of humans through life; here Plutarch's views resemble those of Apuleius.[4] The eighth lecture, or *dialexis,* of Maximus of Tyre is closer to Apuleius. The *daimones* are intermediaries between gods and men, having some of the same nature as both; they adhere closely to virtuous men, such as Socrates, but also to others, such as Plato and Pythagoras. Maximus' ninth lecture concerns the nature of *daimones* in general, and here too there are resemblances with Apuleius, as on the mixed nature of *daimones,* partly human and partly divine; but the only examples he gives are im-

[3] Contrast *Apol.* 27.3, 63.6, where Apuleius uses *daemonion,* a word hitherto used only by Cicero, *Div.* 1.122 (where modern editors have restored the Greek form). In my translation, I have rendered *daemon* as "demon," despite its Christian connotations.

[4] Plut. *Mor.* 575A–98F. On this work, H. G. Nesselrath, ed., *Plutarch: On the* daimonion *of Socrates: Human Liberation, Divine Guidance, and Philosophy* (Tübingen, 2010), especially the synopsis by D. M. Russell, ibid. 4–12.

mortalized humans, such as Asclepius and Heracles, who retain the power to sympathize with humans, and he does not mention Socrates.

Apuleius' work takes the form of a speech to multiple hearers, in whom he does not assume a knowledge of Platonic or indeed of any philosophy. He adapts his exposition to a cultured, Latin-speaking audience by drawing almost exclusively on Latin literature and history for his illustrations, though he assumes a knowledge of Homer (17.3, 20.4). The work is situated midway between Apuleius the orator and Apuleius the philosopher, and though some have dismissed it as trivial, others will sympathize with Augustine's judgment: *copiosissima et disertissima oratio*.[5] The date of the work and its place of delivery (if in fact there was a spoken version) are unknown.[6]

The work is structured as follows:

1–3.6	Plato's threefold division of animate beings into gods, *daemones*, humans: the various kinds of god
3.7–5.8	The sublime nature of the gods requires their separation from humans

[5] *Civ. Dei* 8.19. Even Rohde, *Kleine Schriften*, 1.xix n. 1, despite his contempt for the *philosophica*, allowed some merit to the *De Deo Socratis*, "eine besonders barocke Probe einer rhetorisch-philosophischen διάλεξις." (A singularly baroque attempt at a rhetorico-philosophical *dialexis*.)

[6] Harrison in Harrison et al., *Apuleius*, 187–88, suggests a date in the 160s or 170s and a Carthaginian audience.

⟨DE DEO SOCRATIS⟩[1]

1. Plato omnem naturam rerum, quod eius ad animalia praecipua pertineat, trifariam divisit censuitque esse summos deos. Summum, medium et infimum fac intellegas non modo loci disclusione verum etiam naturae dignitate, quae et ipsa neque uno neque gemino modo sed pluribus

2 cernitur. Ordiri tamen manifestius fuit a loci dispositione. Nam proinde ut maiestas postulabat, diis immortalibus caelum dicavit, quos quidem deos caelites partim visu

3 usurpamus, alios intellectu vestigamus. Ac visu quidem cernimus

> . . . uos, o clarissima mundi
> lumina, labentem caelo quae ducitis annum;

4 nec modo ista praecipua: diei opificem lunamque, solis aemulam, noctis decus, seu corniculata seu dividua seu protumida seu plena sit, varia ignium face, quanto longius facessat a sole, tanto largius conlustrata, pari incremento itineris et luminis, mensem suis auctibus ac dehinc pari-

5 bus dispendiis aestimans; sive illa proprio sibi[2] perpeti

---

[1] *Titulum ex Aug.* Civ. Dei *8, 14 suppl. edd.*
[2] sibi *Rohde:* seu ω

---

[1] In fact, Plato recognized a fourfold division of higher beings: gods, demons, heroes, and humans: cf. Beaujeu, *Apulée,* 203.

ON SOCRATES' GOD

1. Plato divided all of nature, at least as it pertains to the principal animate beings, into three parts, and held the gods to be the highest.[1] But by "highest, "middle," and "lowest" you must understand that he meant not only spatial separation but also natural status, which in turn is divided not just into one or two parts but into more. Still, it 2 was clearer for him to start from the disposition in space. For as their majesty required, he assigned the heaven to the immortal gods, that is, the gods of heaven of whom we apprehend some visually, while others we study intellectually. Now visually we distinguish 3

> . . . you, O brightest lights
> of the universe, who guide through the sky the
> gliding year,[2]

but not only those principal ones—the one who creates 4 day and the moon, the sun's rival, the glory of night, which according as it is crescent, halved, waxing or full, varies the brightness of its light, more brightly illuminated the further it proceeds from the sun, as its path and its light increase together, measuring the month by its growth and thereafter with its equal diminution. Either by its particu- 5

[2] Verg. G. 1.5–6.

347

candore pollens,[3] ut Chaldaei arbitrantur, parte luminis
compos, parte altera cassa fulgoris, pro circumversione
6 oris discoloris multiiuga speciem sui variat, seu tota pro-
prii candoris expers, alienae lucis indigua,[4] denso corpore
sed levi ceu quodam speculo radios solis obstipi[5] vel ad-
versi usurpat et, ut verbis utar Lucreti,

notham iactat de corpore lucem.

2. Utra[6] harum vera sententia est (nam hoc postea vi-
dero), tamen neque de luna neque de sole quisquam
2 Graecus aut barbarus facile cunctaverit deos esse, nec
modo istos, ut dixi, verum etiam quinque stellas, quae
vulgo vagae ab imperitis nuncupantur, quae tamen inde-
flexo et certo et stato cursu meatus longe ordinatissimos
3 divinis vicibus aeterno efficiunt. Varia quippe curriculi sui
specie, sed una semper et aequabili pernicitate, tunc pro-
gressus, tunc vero regressus mirabili vicissitudine assimu-
lant pro situ et flexu et instituto[7] circulorum, quos probe
4 callet qui signorum ortus et obitus comperit. In eodem
visibilium deorum numero cetera quoque sidera, qui cum
Platone sentis, locato:

Arcturum pluviasque Hyadas geminosque Triones

aliosque itidem radiantis deos, quibus caeli chorum comp-

---

[3] pollens *hic transpos. Thomas*: *post* multiiuga *habent* ω
[4] indigua *Hildebrand*: indicia ω
[5] obstipi *Ribbeck*: exstitit *vel* obsistit ω
[6] utra *Mercerus*: utraque ω
[7] instituto *Novák*: abstituto ω

lar but not constant brightness, as the Chaldeans think, in one half possessing light, in another lacking brilliance, it changes its appearance according to the many revolutions of its variegated face; or being entirely without its own 6
radiance and dependent on another's light, its dense and yet smooth mass resembling a kind of mirror, it borrows the rays of the oblique or facing sun and, to use the words of Lucretius,

> throws from its mass a spurious light.[3]

2. Whichever of these two opinions is true, a question I shall go into later, still neither of the sun nor of the moon would any Greek or barbarian readily hesitate to say that they are gods, and not just those two, as I have said, but 2
also the five stars, which the ignorant generally call "planets": these in fact, in an undeviating, certain and fixed path, eternally pursue their ordered courses in heavenly sequence.[4] For though their circuits look different, never- 3
theless it is at a single, even speed that they appear now to proceed and now to regress in wonderful alternation according to the place, curvature and law of their orbits, which anyone who has mapped the rising and setting of these signs fully understands. In the same company of the 4
visible gods those who share Plato's view must place

> Arcturus and the rainy Hyades and the two Triones[5]

and the other no less brilliant gods, whom in clear weather

---

[3] Lucr. 5.575.   [4] That is, the "planets" do not wander as their name (*planêtai*) implies, but follow a fixed course; though in *Flor.* 10.1, Apuleius calls the moon and the five planets "wanderers" (*vagantes*).   [5] Verg. *Aen.* 3.516.

⁵ tum et coronatum suda tempestate visimus, pictis nocti-
bus severa gratia, torvo decore, suspicientes in hoc per-
fectissimo mundi, ut ait Ennius, clipeo miris fulguribus
variata caelamina.

⁶ Est aliud deorum genus, quod natura visibus nostris
denegavit, nec non tamen intellectu eos rimabundi con-
⁷ templamur, acie mentis acrius contemplantes. Quorum in
numero sunt illi duodecim [numero][8] situ nominum in
duo versus ab Ennio coartati:

Iuno, Vesta, Minerua, Ceres, Diana, Venus, Mars,
Mercurius, Iovis, Neptunus, Vulcanus, Apollo,

⁸ ceterique id genus, quorum nomina quidem sunt nostris
auribus iam diu cognita, potentiae vero animis coniectatae
per varias utilitates in vita agenda animadversas in iis rebus, quibus eorum singuli curant.

3. Ceterum profana philosophiae turba imperitorum,
vana sanctitudinis, priva verae rationis, inops religionis,
impos veritatis, scrupulosissimo culto, insolentissimo
spretu deos neglegit, pars in superstitione, pars in con-
² temptu timida vel tumida. Hos namque cunctos deos in
sublimi aetheris vertice locatos, ab humana contagione
procul discretos, plurimi sed non rite venerantur, omnes
³ sed inscie metuunt, pauci sed impie diffitentur. Quos deos
Plato existimat naturas incorporalis, animalis, neque fine

---

[8] numero *del. Baehrens*

---

[6] Ennius, fr. 96 (d) Jocelyn (from the *Iphigeneia*).
[7] Enn. *Ann.* 240–41 Skutsch.
[8] "Ether" (*ether*) corresponds roughly to the stratosphere, a

we see adorning and crowning the heavenly chorus, sternly
graceful and fiercely beautiful in the tapestry of night,
when we raise our eyes to the variegated figures mar- 5
velously glowing on what Ennius calls this most perfect
"shield of heaven."[6]

There are gods of another kind whom nature has with- 6
held from our sight, and yet whom we contemplate by in-
tellectual inquiry, contemplating them all the more clearly
by our keenness of mind. In their number are those twelve 7
that Ennius, by his arrangement of their names, packed
into two lines:[7]

Juno, Vesta, Minerva, Ceres, Diana, Venus, Mars,
Mercury, Jupiter, Neptune, Vulcan, Apollo,

and the others of that sort, whose names indeed have long 8
since been familiar to our ears, but whose powers in those
areas that each of them individually governs are inferred
by our intellects as we pass our lives.

3.But the ignorant masses, uninitiated in philosophy,
devoid of piety, lacking true reason, deficient in religion,
ignorant of truth, neglect the gods by their extremes of
scrupulous veneration or insolent neglect, some made
timid by superstition, others proud by contempt. You see, 2
all these gods dwell at the highest level of ether,[8] far removed from human contact, and many worship them,
though incorrectly, all fear them, though ignorantly, few
despise them, though impiously, These gods Plato con- 3
ceives as incorporate but animate beings, animate, with

realm of pure air suitable only for the gods, as opposed to "air"
(*aer*), the lower air beneath the moon; to mark the distinction, I
have translated the two words as "ether" and "air."

ullo neque exordio, sed prorsus ac retro aeviternas, ⟨a⟩[9]
corporis contagione suapte natura remotas, ingenio ad
summam beatitudinem perfecto, nullius extrarii boni participatione sed ex sese bonas et ad omnia competentia sibi
4 promptu facili, simplici, libero, absoluto. Quorum parentem, qui omnium rerum dominator atque auctor est, solutum ab omnibus nexibus patiendi aliquid gerendive, nulla
vice ad alicuius rei munia obstrictum, cur ego nunc dicere
5 exordiar, cum Plato caelesti facundia praeditus, aequipe-
rabilia diis immortalibus disserens, frequentissime prae-
dicet hunc solum maiestatis incredibili quadam nimietate
et ineffabili non posse penuria sermonis humani quavis
6 oratione vel modice comprehendi, vix sapientibus viris,
cum se vigore animi, quantum licuit, a corpore remove-
runt, intellectum huius dei, id quoque interdum, velut in
artissimis tenebris rapidissimo coruscamine lumen candidum intermicare?
7 Missum igitur hunc locum faciam, in quo non mihi
[quidem][10] tantum, sed ne Platoni quidem meo quiverunt
ulla verba pro amplitudine rei suppetere, ac iam rebus
mediocritatem meam [in][11] longe superantibus receptui
canam tandemque orationem de caelo in terram devo-
8 cabo. In qua praecipuum animal homines sumus, quamquam plerique se incuria verae disciplinae ita omnibus
erroribus ac piacularibus depravaverint, sceleribus im-
buerint, et prope exesa mansuetudine generis sui immane
efferarint, ut possit videri nullum animal in terris homine

[9] a add. Lütjohann
[10] quidem del. Colvius
[11] in del. Goldbacher

neither beginning nor end, but eternal through the whole
length of time, by their very nature distanced from the
contamination of materiality, by their innate perfection
supremely blessed, partaking in no external good but good
in themselves and with easy, simple, free and complete
communication with everything within their sphere. As   4
for their father, the ruler and creator of all things, remote
from all links of passive or active contact, not bound by
reciprocity to perform any function, why should I now
begin to speak of him, when Plato, who was endowed with   5
heavenly eloquence, and discoursed in language match-
ing the immortal gods, frequently proclaims that this god
alone, having a kind of extraordinary and inexpressible
magnitude, cannot be even slightly defined by any utterance because of the poverty of human language? Even for   6
philosophers, who have detached themselves as best they
can from the body by their power of intellect, the conception of this god scarcely does more than flash, and even so
only now and then, like a bright light gleaming for the
shortest time in the deepest darkness.

So I will omit this topic, for which not only I, but not   7
even my master Plato can find words appropriate for the
immensity of the subject, and since the matter already far
surpasses my modest ability, I will now sound the retreat
and finally bring my speech down from heaven to earth.
On earth we humans are the supreme living beings, even   8
though many in their indifference to true learning have so
debased themselves by errors and abominations of every
kind, have so plunged into crime, and have so almost cor-
roded the natural kindness of their species, have grown so
monstrously bestial, that one might think no creature on

9 postremius. Sed nunc non de errorum disputatione, sed
   de naturae distributione disserimus.

      4. Igitur homines ratione gaudentes,[12] oratione pol-
   lentes, immortalibus animis, moribundis membris, levi-
   bus et anxiis mentibus, brutis et obnoxiis corporibus, dis-
   similimis moribus, similibus erroribus, pervicaci audacia,
2 pertinaci spe, casso labore, fortuna caduca, singillatim
   mortales, cunctim tamen [universo genere][13] perpetui, vicissim sufficienda prole mutabiles, volucri tempore, tarda
   sapientia, cita morte, querula vita, terras incolunt.
3   Habetis interim bina animalia: deos ab hominibus plurimum differentis loci sublimitate, vitae perpetuitate, naturae perfectione, nullo inter se propinquo communicatu,
4 cum et habitacula summa ab infimis tanta intercapedo
   fastigii dispescat et vivacitas illic aeterna et indefecta sit,
   hic caduca et subsiciva, et ingenia illa ad beatitudinem
5 sublimata sint, haec ad miserias infimata. Quid igitur?
   Nullone conexu natura se vinxit, sed in divinam et humanam partem ⟨hiul⟩cam[14] se et interruptam ac veluti debi-
6 lem passa est? Nam, ut idem Plato ait, nullus deus misce-
   tur hominibus, sed hoc praecipuum eorum sublimitatis
   specimen est, quod nulla adtrectatione nostra contami-
7 nantur. Pars eorum tantummodo obtutu hebeti visuntur,
   ut sidera, de quorum adhuc et magnitudine et coloribus
   homines ambigunt, ceteri autem solo intellectu neque
8 prompte noscuntur. Quod quidem mirari super diis im-

12 gaudentes *Aug.* Civ. Dei 9.8: plaudentes ω
13 universo genere *del. Novák*
14 ⟨hiul⟩cam se *Thomas*: cam se *vel* campse *mss.*

9 *Symp.* 203A.

earth lower than the human one. But for now the subject   9
of my discourse is not a discussion of error, but the disposition of the natural world.

4. Well, human beings who have the enjoyment of reason and the power of speech, immortal souls, perishable
bodies, nimble and inquiring minds, heavy and cumbrous
bodies, very dissimilar characters, similar errors, obstinate
audacity, unwavering hope, futile struggle, uncertain des-   2
tiny, who are mortal as individuals and yet immortal as a
whole, changing with the repeated replacement of generations, fleeting in duration and late in wisdom, quick to
die, fretful in life—these are the inhabitants of the earth.

So far, then, you have two classes of animate beings: 3
gods utterly different from humans in the loftiness of their
station, the perpetuity of their existence, the perfection of
their nature, with no ready communication between the
two, both because so lofty a distance between highest and   4
lowest separates their habitations from ours, and since
with them enjoyment of life is eternal and unfailing,
whereas with us it is uncertain and fragmentary, and their
natures are elevated to blessedness, ours sunk in misery.
Well then, is there no link by which Nature has kept her-   5
self connected? Has she instead allowed herself to become two separate parts, gaping, discontinuous, and as it
were disabled? For as again Plato says,[9] no god consorts   6
with humans, but the supreme sign of their sublimity is
this—that they are not defiled by any contact with us. Only   7
some of them are visible to our weak sight, for example
the stars, whose size and colors humans debate even now,
while the other gods are apprehended solely and not easily by intellect. This is not something that should surprise   8

355

mortalibus nequaquam congruerit, cum alioquin et inter
homines, qui fortunae munere opulenti elatus et usque ad
regni nutabilem suggestum et pendulum tribunal evectus
est, raro aditu sit, longe remotis arbitris in quibusdam dig-
9 nitatis suae penetralibus degens: parit enim conversatio
contemptum, raritas conciliat admirationem.

5. "Quid igitur, orator," obiecerit aliqui, "post istam
caelestem quidem sed paene inhumanam tuam sententiam faciam, si omnino homines a diis immortalibus procul
2 repelluntur atque ita in haec terrae tartara relegantur, ut
omnis sit illis adversus caelestes deos communio denegata,
nec quisquam eos e caelitum numero velut pastor vel
equiso vel busequa ceu balantium vel hinnientium vel
mugientium greges intervisat, qui ferocibus moderetur,
3 morbidis medeatur, egenis opituletur? Nullus, inquis,
deus humanis rebus intervenit: cui igitur preces allegabo?
4 Cui votum nuncupabo? Cui victimam caedam? Quem
miseris auxiliatorem, quem fautorem bonis, quem adver-
satorem malis in omni vita ciebo? Quem denique, quod
5 frequentissimum est, iuri iurando arbitrum adhibebo? An
ut Vergilianus Ascanius

per caput hoc iuro, per quod pater ante solebat?"

At enim, o Iule, pater tuus hoc iure iurando uti poterat
inter Troianos stirpe cognatos et fortasse an inter Graecos
proelio cognitos; at enim inter Rutulos recens cognitos si
nemo huic capiti crediderit, quis pro te deus fidem dicet?

us at all about the immortal gods, since in fact on the human plane too, if a man is elevated by the rich generosity of fortune and carried to the unsteady throne and precarious platform of royalty, he is infrequent of access, banishes observers far off and lives as it were in the inner sanctum of his rank; for familiarity breeds contempt, while aloofness earns admiration.

5. "What then, speaker," someone might object, "am I to do, after this opinion of yours, heavenly indeed and yet almost inhumane, if humans are driven far off from the immortal gods and so far banished to this underworld of earth that they are denied all communion with the gods above, and not one of the heavenly host comes to visit them as a shepherd, groom or cowherd visits their bleating, neighing or lowing charges so as to calm the violent, heal the sick, help the needy? No god, you say, intervenes in human affairs. To whom then shall I address my prayers? To whom shall I offer a vow? For whom shall I slaughter a victim? Whom shall I call on to help the downcast, support the good, confront the wicked at every stage of life? And finally, whom shall I summon to witness an oath, the most frequent need of all? Or shall I do as Virgil's Ascanius did, and

Swear by this head, that once my father swore by?"

But, Iulus, your father was able to use this oath when among the Trojans, who were related to him by blood, and perhaps among the Greeks, who were known to him in battle: but if none of the Rutulians whom you have only recently come to know believes in this head, what god will

6 An ut [se][15] ferocissimo Mezentio dextra et telum? Quippe
haec sola advenerat, quibus propugnabat:

Dextra mihi deus et telum, quod missile libro.

7 Apage sis tam cruentos deos, dextram caedibus fessam
telumque sanguine robiginosum: utrumque idoneum non
est propter quod adiures, neve per ista iuretur, cum sit
summi deorum hic honor proprius. Nam et ius iurandum
8 Iovis [iurandum][16] dicitur, ut ait Ennius. Quid igitur
censes? Iurabo per Iovem lapidem Romano vetustissimo
ritu? Atque si Platonis vera sententia est, numquam se
deum cum homine communicare, facilius me audierit lapis quam Iuppiter.

  6. "Non usque adeo," responderit enim Plato pro sententia sua mea voce, "non usque adeo," inquit, "seiunctos
et alienatos a nobis deos praedico, ut ne vota quidem nostra ad illos arbitrer pervenire; neque enim illos a cura
2 rerum humanarum, sed contrectatione sola removi. Ceterum sunt quaedam divinae mediae potestates inter summum aethera et infimas terras in isto intersitae aeris
spatio, per quas et desideria nostra et merita ad eos com-
3 meant." Hos Graeci nomine daemonas nuncupant, inter

---

[15] se *del. ed. Rom.*   [16] iurandum *del. Lütjohann*

---

[10] In Verg. *Aen.* 9.296–302, Aeneas' son Iulus, also called Ascanius, swears by this oath that he will pay to Euryalus' mother
and family the reward that he had previously promised to Euryalus.   [11] In Verg. *Aen.* 10.773–76, Mezentius, the *contemptor divum* (see on *Apol.* 56.7) swears by this oath that he will dress
his son Lausus in the armor of the dead Aeneas: his impiety is
punished when Aeneas kills Lausus and Mezentius in turn.

be your sponsor?[10] Will it be your right hand and spear, as   6
it was for that savage Mezentius? For he reveres only the
things that he uses to fight:

> My god is my right hand and the flying spear I
>   brandish.[11]

Let us have none of these bloodstained gods, please—a   7
hand weary from slaughter, a spear ruddy with blood: neither of them is proper for you to swear by, and do not
swear by them, since that is an honor reserved for the
supreme god. For indeed an oath is said to be "Jupiter's
oath," to quote Ennius.[12] What therefore do you suggest?   8
Shall I swear by the Jupiter stone, following the ancient
Roman custom?[13] Indeed, if Plato's doctrine is correct,
and no god communicates with a human, a stone will hear
me more readily than will Jupiter.

   6. "I do not" (supposing Plato was using my voice to
defend his views),"I do not assert that the gods are so far
separated and estranged from us as to think that not even
our prayers can reach them; for I did not dissociate them
from concern for human affairs, but only from contact
with them. Now there are certain intermediate, godlike   2
powers, who are placed between the highest level, the
ether, and the lowest, the earth, in this region of air, and
they carry both our desires and our good deeds to the
gods." These the Greeks call "demons," who traveling be-   3

---

[12] Ennius, fr. 184 (b), ed. Jocelyn (uncertain play).

[13] As late as Cicero's time, oath takers swore while holding a
stone consecrated to Jupiter: Wissowa, "Lapis (2)," *RE* 12 (1924):
779–82.

⟨terricolas⟩[17] caelicolasque vectores hinc precum hinc
donorum, qui ultro citro portant hinc petitiones inde suppetias ceu quidam utrisque interpretes et salutigeri. Per
hos eosdem, ut Plato in Symposio autumat, cuncta denun-
tiata et magorum varia miracula omnesque praesagiorum
4 species reguntur. Eorum quippe de numero praediti curant singuli [eorum],[18] proinde ut est cuique tributa provincia, vel somniis conformandis vel extis fissiculandis vel
praepetibus gubernandis vel oscinibus erudiendis vel
vatibus inspirandis vel fulminibus iaculandis vel nubibus
coruscandis ceterisque adeo, per quae futura dinoscimus.
5 Quae cuncta caelestium voluntate et numine et auctoritate, sed daemonum obsequio et opera et ministerio fieri
arbitrandum est.

7. Horum enim munus atque opera atque cura est, ut
Hannibali somnia orbitatem oculi comminentur, Flaminio
extispicia periculum cladis praedicant, Attio Navio augu-
2 ria miraculum cotis addicant; item ut nonnullis regni fu-
turi signa praecurrant, ut Tarquinius Priscus aquila obum-
bretur ab apice, Seruius Tullius flamma colluminetur a

17 terricolas *add. secunda manus in* B
18 eorum *del. Goldbacher*

14 *Symp.* 202E.
15 Divination by the examination of entrails (*extispicium*),
borrowed by the Romans from the Etruscans, involved opening
the sacrificial animal (*hostia*) and looking for clefts (*fissa*) in its
entrails to predict the future.
16 When Hannibal was planning to commit sacrilege against
Juno, a dream warned him that he would lose the sight of his one

tween those on earth and those in heaven convey prayers
from here and gifts from there, and go back and forth
carrying requests from here and help from there, as it
were ambassadors and goodwill messengers for both.
These same beings, as Plato declares in the *Symposium*,[14]
supervise all predictions, the various miracles of magicians, and every type of omen. For particular members of   4
their company are appointed, according to the area assigned to each, to see that dreams are formed, entrails are
cloven,[15] that birds are guided to fly propitiously and made
to sing prophetically, that thunderbolts are hurled, clouds
made to flash, and all the other signs by which we foretell
the future. We must believe that all such things occur   5
through the will, power and authority of the heavenly gods,
but also by the compliance, service and agency of the
demons.

7. For it is their duty, task and concern to ensure that
dreams threaten Hannibal with the loss of his eye, that
entrails warn Flaminius of the risk of disaster, that bird
omens promise Attius Navius the miracle of the whetstone;[16] similarly to ensure that some receive prior tokens   2
of their future reigns—the eagle that overshadowed Tarquinius Priscus' cap, the halo of fire around Servius Tul-

good eye (Cic. *Div.* 1.24.48); when C. Flaminius was sacrificing a
calf to inaugurate his consulship in 217, the calf broke away and
spattered the bystanders with blood, an omen of his future defeat
at Lake Trasimene (Livy 21.63.13; Apuleius follows a different
version); Attius Navus, a famous augur, was challenged by the
king Tarquinius Priscus to split a whetstone with a razor, and he
successfully did so (Livy 1.36.3–4).

capite; postremo cuncta hariolorum praesagia, Tuscorum
piacula, fulguratorum bidentalia, carmina Sibyllarum.
3 Quae omnia, ut dixi, mediae quaepiam potestates inter
homines ac deos obeunt. Neque enim pro maiestate deum
caelestium fuerit, ut eorum quisquam vel Hannibali som-
nium fingat,[19] vel Flaminio hostiam corruget,[20] vel Attio
Navio avem velificet, vel Sibyllae fatiloquia versificet, vel
Tarquinio velit apicem rapere sed reddere, Servio vero
4 inflammare verticem nec exurere. Non est operae diis
superis ad haec descendere: mediorum divorum ista sortitio est, qui in aeris plagis terrae conterminis nec minus
confinibus caelo perinde versantur, ut in quaque parte
naturae propria animalia, in aethere volventia, in terra
gradientia.

8. Nam cum quattuor sint elementa notissima, veluti
quadrifariam natura magnis partibus disterminata, sint-
que propria animalia terrarum, ‹aquarum›,[21] flammarum,
2 siquidem Aristoteles auctor est in fornacibus flagrantibus
quaedam [propria][22] animalia pennulis apta volitare to-
tumque aevum suum in igne deversari, cum eo exoriri
3 cumque eo extingui, praeterea cum totiuga sidera, ut iam
prius dictum est, sursum in aethere, id est in ipso liquidis-
4 simo ignis ardore, compareant, cur hoc solum quartum

19 fingat *Salmasius*: pingat ω
20 corruget (conruget) *Ellis*: conroget ω
21 aquarum *add. Mercerus*
22 propria *del. Ribbeck*

17 An eagle snatched the cap from Tarquinius Priscus' head
while he was still a private citizen and then replaced it, a omen of
his future kingship (Livy 1.34.8); flames enveloped the head of

lius' head,[17] and finally all the prophecies of soothsayers, the expiations of the Etruscans, the sacred enclosures of lightning prophets, the songs of the Sibyls. All these, as I 3 have said, are the tasks of certain powers intermediate between men and gods, for it would not be consonant with the majesty of the gods that one of them should invent a dream for Hannibal, seam a victim for Flamininus,[18] guide a bird's path for Attius Navus, versify the prophecies of the Sibyl, or agree to snatch and then return Tarquinius' cap, and moreover make fire play around Servius' head without scorching it. It is not worth the supreme gods' trouble to 4 descend to such tasks: that is the role of the intermediate divinities, who move in regions of the air that border on the earth and at the same time touch the sky, so that each part has its own living beings—those who circle through heaven and those who tread the earth.

8. For since there are four very well-known elements, nature being so to speak divided into four major parts, and since earth, water, and fire each have their own particular beings (for Aristotle states that in blazing furnaces there 2 are certain winged creatures that fly about in fire and spend their entire lives there, arising with it and dying with it);[19] and since moreover so many stars of every kind, 3 as I have already said, appear above us in the ether, that is, just where the heat of fire is the most intense, why then 4 should nature leave only this fourth element of air, which

Servius Tullius, when still a child, while he slept, a similar omen of kingship (Livy 1.39.1–2)

[18] That is, introduce clefts (see n. 15), which signified imminent defeat.

[19] *Hist. an.* 5.19 (552B).

elementum aeris, quod tanto spatio intersitum est, cassum
ab omnibus, desertum a cultoribus suis natura pateretur,
quin in eo quoque aeria animalia gignerentur, ut in igni
5 flammida, in unda fluxa, in terra glebulenta? Nam quidem
qui aves aeri attribuet, falsum sententiae meritissimo dix-
eris, quippe [quae aves][23] nulla earum ultra Olympi verti-
6 cem sublimatur, qui cum excellentissimus omnium per-
hibeatur, tamen altitudinem perpendiculo si metiare, ut
geometrae autumant, ⟨decem⟩[24] stadia altitudo fastigii
non aequiperat, cum sit aeris agmen immensum usque ad
citimam lunae helicem, quae porro aetheris sursum versus
7 exordium est. Quid igitur tanta uis aeris, quae ab humilli-
mis lunae anfractibus usque ad summum Olympi verticem
interiacet? Quid tandem? Vacabitne animalibus suis atque
8 erit ista naturae pars mortua ac debilis? Immo enim si
sedulo advertas, ipsae quoque aves perterrestre[25] animal,
non aerium rectius perhibeantur. Enim semper illis uictus
omnis in terra, ibidem pabulum, ibidem cubile; tantum
quod aera proximum terrae volitando transverberant, ceterum cum illis fessa sunt remigia pinnarum, terra ceu
portus est.

9. Quod si manifestum flagitat ratio debere propria
animalia etiam in aere intellegi, superest ut, quae tandem
et cuiusmodi ea sint, disseramus. Igitur terrena nequaquam, devergant enim pondere, sed nec flammida, ne

23 quae aves *del. Mercerus*
24 decem *add. Colvius*
25 perterrestre *ω*: terrestre *B²* *et edd. plerique*

20 About 6,000 feet; Olympus is about 9,500 feet measured
from sea level.

occupies so large a middle space, to be entirely void and empty of its own inhabitants? Why should not aerial beings come into being in air too, as fiery ones do in fire, aquatic ones in sea, earthy ones on earth? For indeed if 5 anyone were to attribute the air to birds, one would be quite right in calling him mistaken. No bird soars above the summit of Olympus; though it is rightly believed to be 6 the highest of all mountains, yet if you could measure its height perpendicularly, so the surveyors tell us, the height of its summit is less than ten stades,[20] whereas there is an immeasurable volume of air up to the nearest orbit of the moon, where the ether merely begins its upward expanse. What then of this great volume of air, which lies between 7 the lowest revolutions of the moon and the highest peak of Olympus? What indeed? Will it have no being of its own, and will that part of the natural order be dead and defective? Why, on a careful consideration, it would be 8 more correct to count even birds as fully terrestrial beings rather than aerial ones, for they pass their whole existence on earth, their sustenance is there, their nest there, except that they fan the air closest to earth in flying through it. Moreover, when their feathered oars grow weary, the earth is as it were their harbor.

9. But if logic manifestly requires that we understand the air too as containing beings peculiar to itself, it remains for us to discuss just what they are and of what kind. Now they are certainly not terrestrial, since gravity would pull them down, and yet not fiery, since heat would carry

2 sursum versus calore rapiantur. Temperanda est ergo nobis pro loci medietate media natura, ut ex regionis ingenio
sit etiam cultoribus eius ingenium. Cedo igitur mente for-
memus et gignamus animo id genus corporum texta, quae
neque tam bruta quam terrea neque tam levia quam
3 aetheria, sed quodam modo utrimque seiugata vel enim
utrimque commixta sint, sive amolita seu modificata utri-
usque rei participatione: sed facilius ex utroque quam ex
4 neutro intellegentur. Habeant igitur haec daemonum corpora et modicum ponderis, ne ad superna inscendant,
⟨et⟩26 aliquid levitatis, ne ad inferna praecipitentur.

10. Quod ne vobis videar poetico ritu incredibilia
confingere, dabo primum exemplum huius libratae me-
dietatis, neque enim procul ab hac corporis subtilitate
2 nubes concretas videmus; quae si usque adeo leves forent
ut ea quae omnino carent pondere, numquam infra iuga,
ut saepenumero animadvertimus, gravatae caput editi
3 montis ceu quibusdam curvis torquibus coronarent: porro
si suapte natura spissae tam graves forent ut nulla illas
vegetioris levitatis admixtio sublevaret, profecto non secus
quam plumbi raudus et lapis suopte nisu caducae terris
4 inliderentur. Nunc enimvero pendulae et mobiles huc
atque illuc vice navium in aeris pelago ventis gubernan-
tur, paululum immutantes proximitate et longinquitate.
5 Quippe si aliquo umore fecundae sunt, veluti ad fetum
edendum deorsus degrassantur, atque ideo umectiores
humilius meant aquilo agmine, tractu segniore; sudis
vero sublimior cursus est, cum lanarum velleribus similes

26 et *add. B*³

366

them upward. We must therefore compound a intermedi- 2
ate nature appropriate to their intermediate position, so
that the nature of the region suits the nature of its inhabitants. So come, let us mentally shape and imaginatively
create bodily textures not as coarse as earthly ones, and
yet not as light as ethereal ones, but in some way distinct 3
from both, or indeed compounded from both, according
as they have either no portion of either element or a mixed
one (though they are more easily imagined as consisting
of both than of neither). Let therefore these demonic bod- 4
ies have both a modicum of weight to prevent them from
rising to the heavens, and a certain lightness to prevent
them from plunging to the depths.

10. But so that you do not think I am fabricating what
is impossible to believe, as a poet does, I will give a first
example of this balanced middle state. You see, this fineness of volume is not much different from what we see in
the composition of clouds. If these were as light as things 2
entirely weightless, they would never sink below the highest peaks, as we often observe them doing, and they would
not wreathe the summit of a lofty mountain with a kind
of circular collar. Furthermore, if their inherent density 3
made them so heavy that no admixture of active lightness
sustained them, their own gravity would surely bring them
crashing down to earth like stones or lumps of lead. As it 4
is, they are in fact floating and mobile, steered this way
and that by the winds like ships in the sky's expanse, gradually changing as they get closer together or more distant. For if they are pregnant with any moisture, they bear 5
down as if to discharge their offspring, and hence being
more moist they move in a dark mass gradually advancing;
if dry, however, they fly higher, driven along like flocks of

6 aguntur, cano agmine, volatu perniciore. Nonne audis,
quid super tonitru Lucretius facundissime disserat?

> Principio tonitru quatiuntur caerula caeli
> propterea quia concurrunt sublime volantes
> aetheriae nubes contra pugnantibus ventis.

11. Quod si nubes sublime volitant, quibus omnis et
exortus est terrenus et retro defluxus in terras, quid tandem censes daemonum corpora, quae sunt concretio[27]
2 multo tanta subtilior? Non enim ex hac faeculenta nube-
cula et umida caligine conglobata, sicuti nubium genus
est, sed ex illo purissimi[28] aeris liquido et sereno elemento
coalita eoque nemini hominum temere visibilia, nisi divi-
3 nitus speciem sui offerant, quod nulla in illis terrena soli-
ditas locum luminis occuparit, quae nostris oculis possit
obsistere, qua soliditate necessario offensa acies immore-
4 tur, sed fila corporum possident rara et splendida et tenuia
usque adeo ut radios omnis nostri tuoris et raritate trans-
mittant et[29] splendore reverberent et subtilitate frustren-
5 tur. Hinc est illa Homerica Minerva, quae mediis coetibus
Graium cohibendo Achilli intervenit. Versum Graecum, si
paulisper opperiamini, Latine enuntiabo—atque adeo hic
sit impraesentiarum: Minerva igitur, ut dixi, Achilli mode-
rando iussu Iunonis advenit:

> soli perspicua est, aliorum nemo tuetur.

[27] concretio *Kronenberg*: concreta ω   [28] purissimi *scripsi*:
purissimo ω   [29] et *omittunt mss. plerique*

---

[21] Lucr. 6.96–98. All of chapter 10, on the nature and move-
ment of clouds, draws on this passage of Lucretius.

[22] Apuleius here assumes a theory of vision by which rays are

wool, in a white mass swiftly flying. Do you not hear Lu- 6
cretius' very expressive description of thunder?[21]

> First of all, thunder shakes the blue heavens
> Because the ethereal clouds that fly on high
> Collide when winds make battle.

11. But if clouds fly on high, though they arise entirely from the earth and shed their moisture back onto
the earth, whatever do you suppose the bodies of spirits
to be, when their substance is so very much finer? For they 2
are not compounded from this dirty, dank, dark fog, as is
the nature of clouds, but coalesce out of that clear, calm
element of the purest air, and hence are not readily visible
to any human unless by divine favor they permit themselves to be seen; since they do not have an earthly solidity 3
that provides a place to catch the light, a solidity that will
necessarily meet our gaze and make it linger. Rather, their 4
bodies are made of such sparse, bright, fine strands that
their sparsity transmits all the rays of our vision,[22] their
brightness dazzles them, their fineness eludes them. This 5
explains Homer's famous Minerva, who passed though the
middle of the Greek army to check Achilles. If you wait a
moment, I will cite the Greek verse in Latin, and indeed
here it is right away. Minerva then, as I said, comes on
Juno's orders to calm Achilles:

> Only to him is she clear, no other man beholds her.[23]

emitted from the eyes and reflected back from solid objects: cf.
Apol. 15.13–15.

[23] Translation of Hom. *Il.* 1.198; Maximus of Tyre uses the
same incident to illustrate Socrates' *daimonion, Diss.* 8.5.

6 Hinc et illa Vergiliana Iuturna, quae mediis milibus aux-
iliabunda fratri conversatur

  miscetque viris neque cernitur ulli,

prorsus quod Plautinus miles super clipeo suo gloriatur,

  praestringens oculorum aciem hostibus.

12. Ac ne ceteros longius persequar, ex hoc ferme daemonum numero poetae solent haudquaquam procul a
veritate osores et amatores quorundam hominum deos
2 fingere: hos prosperare et evehere, illos contra adversari
et affligere; igitur et misereri et indignari et angi et laetari
omnemque humani animi faciem pati, simili motu cordis
et salo mentis ad omnes cogitationum aestus fluctuare.
3 Quae omnes turbelae tempestatesque procul a deorum
caelestium tranquillitate exulant; cuncti enim caelites
semper eodem statu mentis aeterna aequabilitate potiun-
4 tur, qui numquam illis nec ad dolorem versus nec ad voluptatem finibus suis pellitur, nec quoquam a sua perpetua
secta ad quempiam subitum habitum demovetur—nec
alterius vi, nam nihil est deo potentius, neque suapte na-
5 tura,[30] nam nihil est deo perfectius. Porro autem qui potest videri perfectus fuisse, qui a priore statu ad alium
rectiorem statum migrat, cum praesertim nemo sponte
capessat nova, nisi quem paenituit priorum? Non potest
enim subsequi illa mutata ratio sine praecedentium infir-

[30] natura *mss. AGRP,* sponte *ceteri*

---

[24] *Aen.* 1.440, on Aeneas visiting Carthage while remaining
invisible. Apuleius is thinking of Turnus' sister Juturna, who in

This also explains the famous Juturna in Virgil, who when   6
aiding her brother amid a vast throng addresses him,

> And mingles with men and yet is seen by none,[24]

exactly as the soldier in Plautus boasts about his shield,

> Dazzling the sight of the enemy's eyes.[25]

12. But not to go on and enumerate the rest, this is
more or less the class of demons on which poets usually
draw, not without a certain truth, when they depict gods
as hating or loving certain humans, and say that they sup-   2
port and exalt some men, while by contrast they oppose
and crush others, and hence that they feel pity, resentment, sorrow, joy, and every state of the human mind, and
when their hearts are moved and their minds in turmoil
like ours, they waver with every surge of thought. But all   3
these billows and storms are far removed from the tran-
quility of the heavenly gods, since all the heavenly ones
forever enjoy the same state of mind in an eternal invari-
ability. This state of theirs is never driven from its limits   4
into either pain or pleasure, and nothing diverts it from
its everlasting course into any sudden state—neither external force, for nothing is more powerful than godhead,
nor their own choice, for nothing is more perfect than
godhead. And indeed how can anyone be thought perfect   5
from the moment of his creation if he shifts from a previous state to another, higher one, especially since no one
consciously desires what is new unless he disavows what
is past? For such a change of mind cannot occur without

---

fact appears to her brother in the guise of Metiscus, his charioteer
(*Aen.* 12.222–37).   [25] Plaut. *Mil.* 4.

6 matione. Quapropter debet deus nullam perpeti vel odii
vel amoris temporalem perfunctionem, et idcirco nec indignatione nec misericordia contingi, nullo angore con-
trahi, nulla alacritate gestire, sed ab omnibus animi pas-
sionibus liber nec dolere umquam, nec aliquando laetari,
nec aliquid repentinum velle vel nolle.

13. Sed et haec cuncta et id genus cetera daemonum
mediocritati rite congruunt. Sunt enim inter nos ac deos
ut loco regionis ita ingenio mentis intersiti, habentes com-
munem cum superis immortalitatem, cum inferis passio-
2 nem. Nam proinde ut nos, pati possunt omnia animorum
placamenta vel incitamenta, ut et ira incitentur et misericordia flectantur et donis inuitentur et precibus leniantur
et contumeliis exasperentur et honoribus mulceantur, ali-
3 isque omnibus ad similem nobis modum varient. Quippe,
ut fine comprehendam, daemones sunt genere animalia,
ingenio rationabilia, animo passiva, corpore aeria, tempore aeterna. Ex his quinque, quae commemoravi, tria a
principio eadem quae nobis sunt,[31] quartum proprium,
postremum commune cum diis immortalibus habent, sed
4 differunt ab his passione. Quae propterea passiva non
absurde, ut arbitror, nominavi, quod sunt iisdem, quibus
nos, turbationibus mentis obnoxii.

14. Unde etiam religionum diversis observationibus et
sacrorum variis suppliciis fides impertienda est, esse nonnullos ex hoc divorum numero, qui nocturnis vel diurnis,
promptis vel occultis, laetioribus vel tristioribus hostiis vel
2 caerimoniis vel ritibus gaudeant, uti Aegyptia numina

---

[31] nobis sunt *Erdmann*: nobiscum *mss.*

repudiation of all that precedes. It must therefore be that 6
a god experiences no transitory access of either hatred or
love, and therefore is not touched either by resentment or
by pity, nor depressed by any sorrow or uplifted by any joy,
but is free from all passions of the mind, neither once
grieves nor occasionally rejoices, and never feels a sudden
desire or aversion.

13. On the other hand, all such feelings and all like
them precisely suit the intermediate position of demons.
For just as they are placed between us and the gods in
their physical location, so they are in their mental nature,
having immortality in common with those above, but emotionality with those below. For just as we are, they are 2
capable of experiencing everything that calms or irritates
the mind, so that anger rouses them, pity moves them,
gifts attract them, prayers mollify them, abuse infuriates
them, honors appease them, and they change with every
other such stimulus just as we do. For, to define them 3
comprehensively, demons are living beings by species, rational ones by nature, emotional in mind, aerial in body,
eternal in time. Of these five qualities that I have mentioned, the first three they share with us, the fourth is
peculiar to them, the last they share with the gods, though
they differ from these in respect to emotionality. The term 4
I have used for these beings, "emotional," is not inappro-
priate, I think, since they are subject to the same fluctua-
tions of mind as we are.

14. For this reason, we should also accept what the
diversity of religious observances and the variety of sacred
offerings tell us—that some in this category of divine beings take pleasure in sacrifices, in ceremonies or rites that
are performed by night or by day, openly or secretly, in
joy or in sorrow. For instance, Egyptian divinities gener- 2

ferme plangoribus, Graeca plerumque choreis, barbara
autem strepitu cymbalistarum et tympanistarum et cho-
3 raularum. Itidem pro regionibus et cetera in sacris differunt longe varietate: pomparum agmina, mysteriorum
silentia, sacerdotum officia, sacrificantium obsequia, item
deorum effigiae et exuviae, templorum religiones et
4 regiones, hostiarum cruores et colores. Quae omnia pro
cuiusque more loci sollemnia et rata sunt, ut plerumque
somniis et vaticinationibus et oraculis comperimus saepenumero indignata numina, si quid in sacris socordia vel
5 superbia neglegatur. Cuius generis mihi exempla adfatim
suppetunt, sed adeo celebrata et frequentata sunt ut nemo
ea commemorare adortus sit, quin multo plura omiserit
6 quam recensuerit. Idcirco supersedebo impraesentiarum
in his rebus orationem occupare, quae si non apud omnis
certam fidem, at certe penes cunctos notitiam promis-
7 cuam possident. Id potius praestiterit Latine dissertare,
varias species daemonum philosophis perhiberi, quo liqui-
dius et plenius de praesagio Socratis deque eius amico
numine cognoscatis.

15. Nam quodam significatu et animus humanus etiam
nunc in corpore situs daemon nuncupatur:

. . . Dine hunc ardorem mentibus addunt,[32]
‹Euryale, an sua cuique deus fit dira cupido?›[33]

2 Igitur et bona cupido animi bonus deus est. Unde nonnulli
arbitrantur, ut iam prius dictum est, "eudaemonas" dici

---

[32] mentibus addunt *ms. P²*: M. A. (*sic*) *mss. ceteri*
[33] Euryale . . . cupido *add. ed. Rom.*

---

[26] Players on the *diaulos* (*Flor.* 3.5) accompanied by a chorus.
[27] Verg. *Aen.* 9.184–85.

ally take pleasure in lamentation, Greek ones usually in dances, but barbarian ones in the noise of cymbal players, drummers, and choral pipers.[26] So also in the matter of 3 rites there is a great diversity by region—in the formation of processions, the silence of mysteries, the duties of priests, the rules of sacrifice, and similarly in the images and ornaments of gods, the liturgy and placement of temples, the blood and the color of sacrificial victims. All these 4 things are traditional and determined according to the custom of each place, and hence we usually learn from dreams, prophecies and oracles that divine powers often feel anger if carelessness or disdain causes any detail of their rites to be neglected. I could cite an abundance of 5 such examples, but they are so well known and so familiar that no one undertaking to list them could fail to omit many more than he included. For the moment, therefore, 6 I will refrain from spending more of my speech on these topics, which do not carry conviction for everyone, but at least are generally known everywhere. It will perhaps 7 be better to discuss in Latin how philosophers represent the various types of demons, to give you a clearer and fuller understanding of Socrates' foreknowledge and of the power that befriended him.

15. In a certain sense the human soul too, even when still residing in the body, is called a *daemon:*

Is it the gods that so inflame our minds,
Euryalus, or do we each create
Our own god from our terrible desire?[27]

It follows that a good desire of the soul is also a good god, 2 which is why some people think, as I have already said,

beatos, quorum daemon bonus, id est animus, virtute per-
3 fectus est. Eum nostra lingua, ut ego interpretor, haud
sciam an bono, certe quidem meo periculo, poteris "genium" vocare, quod is deus, qui est animus sui cuique,
quamquam sit immortalis, tamen quodam modo cum ho-
4 mine gignitur, ut eae preces, quibus genium et genua pre-
camur, coniunctionem nostram nexumque videantur mihi
obtestari, corpus atque animum duobus nominibus com-
prehendentes, quorum communio et copulatio sumus.
5   Est et secundo significatu species daemonum animus
humanus emeritis stipendiis vitae corpori³⁴ suo abiurans;
hunc vetere Latina lingua reperio "Lemurem" dictitatum.
6 Ex hisce ergo Lemuribus qui posterorum suorum curam
sortitus placato et quieto numine domum possidet, Lar
7 dicitur familiaris; qui vero ob adversa vitae merita nullis
[bonis]³⁵ sedibus, incerta vagatione ceu quodam exilio pu-
nitur, inane terriculamentum bonis hominibus, ceterum
8 malis noxium, id genus plerique Larvas perhibent. Cum
vero incertum est, quae cuique eorum sortitio evenerit,
utrum Lar sit an Larva, nomine Manem deum nuncupant.
9 Scilicet et honoris gratia dei vocabulum additum est,
quippe tantum eos deos appellant, qui ex eodem numero
iuste ac prudenter curriculo vitae gubernato pro numine

³⁴ corpori *ms. Pb*: corpore *mss. ceteri*
³⁵ bonis *del. Markland*

---

28 *Genius* is properly an innate principle of human males,
expressing the power of generation and regarded as a kind of
personal guardian, with *Juno* as its female counterpart. Apuleius
argues that since we pray to the *genius* and pray by clutching

that the term *eudaimones* is applied to those blessed ones
who have a good *daemon,* that is, a mind of perfect virtue.
In our language, to give a translation that is perhaps not   3
the best, but at any rate one I will venture to give, you
could call a *daemon* a "genius," because the god that is
everyone's soul, though immortal, nevertheless is jointly
"engendered" with him as a human being. Hence those   4
prayers that people address to the "genius" and to the
knees seem to me to prove our interconnection and our
link, since they use two nouns to cover soul and body, of
which we are the combined and linked expression.[28]

There is also a class of demons in a second sense—the   5
human soul that has renounced its body after doing its
years of service in life; in early Latin I find this called a
"lemur." Well, in this class of "lemurs" the one who is as-   6
signed responsibility for his descendants, and inhabits the
home with his serene and untroubled influence, is called
the "household lar"; if however because his life has de-   7
served the opposite he has no fixed abode and is doomed
to aimless wandering in a kind of exile, a bogeyman power-
less against good people but dangerous to wicked ones, the
traditional name for his class is often "larva." When how-   8
ever it is uncertain what role has been assigned to any
particular one, whether it is a "lar" or a "larva," they give
it the name of "God Manes." Clearly the word "god" is   9
also attached to them by courtesy, for one only calls those
beings "gods" who, though being of the same species,
have steered the course of their life with justice and wis-

another's knees (Latin *genua*), such prayers illustrate the close
connection between body and mind.

postea ab hominibus praediti fanis et caerimoniis vulgo
10 advertuntur, ut in Boeotia Amphiaraus, in Africa Mopsus,
in Aegypto Osiris, alius alibi gentium, Aesculapius ubique.

16. Verum haec omnis distributio eorum daemonum
2 fuit, qui quondam in corpore humano fuere. Sunt autem
non posteriore numero, praestantiore longe dignitate,
superius aliud, augustius genus daemonum, qui semper a
corporis compedibus et nexibus liberi certis potestatibus
curant, quorum e numero Somnus atque Amor diversam
inter se vim possident, Amor vigilandi, Somnus soporandi.
3 Ex hac igitur sublimiore daemonum copia Plato autumat
singulis hominibus in vita agenda testes et custodes singulos[36] additos, qui nemini conspicui semper adsint, arbitri
4 omnium non modo actorum verum etiam cogitatorum. At
ubi vita edita remeandum est, eundem illum, qui nobis
praeditus fuit, raptare ilico et trahere veluti custodiam
suam ad iudicium atque illic in causa dicenda assistere, si
qua commentiatur, redarguere, si qua vera dicat, asseve-
rare; prorsus illius testimonio ferri sententiam.

---

[36] singulos *mss. HPa,* singulis *mss. ceteri*

---

[29] In making these distinctions, Apuleius is being overly sche-
matic. The *lemures* were malevolent ghosts; the *lar familiaris* is
a different kind of being, who protected household and property
and had a special shrine in the house; *larva*, literally "mask," was
a term for ghosts as seen by the living; *Manes* is a collective term
for the spirits of the dead, and properly there was no singular "god
Manes." Cf. E. Eidinow, *OCD*[4] 616 (ghosts); C. R. Phillips, *OCD*[4]
793–94 (*lares*), 819 (*lemures*), 891 (*Manes*).

[30] Amphiaraus was a prophetic hero (divinized human) with
a celebrated shrine at Oropos in southeastern Boeotia; Mopsus,

dom, and afterward have shrines and rites granted them
by humans as divine powers, and are generally recognized;[29] such are Amphiaraus in Boeotia, Mopsus in Af- 10
rica, Osiris in Egypt, others in other lands, and Asclepius
everywhere.[30]

16. Now, all these distinctions concerned those spirits
who once occupied a human body. But there is another 2
class of spirits, higher and more venerable, not fewer in
number but far superior in rank, who have always been
free from the shackles and ties of the body, and are responsible for certain functions. Among these are Sleep and
Love, who have opposite powers, Love to keep us awake
and Sleep to make us sleep. Well, among this crowd of 3
higher spirits, so Plato affirms, particular ones are set over
particular persons to be witnesses and guardians in the
course of their life; visible to no one, they are always at
hand, observing not only their actions but their thoughts
too.[31] But when our life is done and we must return, the 4
same spirit who had been set over us immediately catches
us and drags us before the judgment seat as if we were his
prisoners, and there he stands beside us as we plead our
case, refuting any lies we tell and corroborating us in any
truths; in short, his testimony determines the verdict that
is handed down.

a similar hero, was an Argonaut who died in Libya; Osiris was an
Egyptian god who underwent death and resurrection and was
widely worshiped (cf. Apul. *Met.* 11.27–30); Asclepius, a hero who
became the Greek god of healing, was even more widely worshiped and was a principal god of Apuleius' adopted Carthage
(*Flor.* 18).

[31] Apuleius combines several passages of Plato: *Phd.* 107D,
Resp. 10.617D–E, 620D–E.

5   Deinde uos omnes, qui hanc Platonis divinam sententiam me interprete auscultatis, ita animos vestros ad quae-
6 cumque agenda vel meditanda formate, ut sciatis nihil
homini prae istis custodibus nec intra animum nec foris
esse secreti, quin omnia curiose ille participet; omnia visi-
tet, omnia intellegat, in ipsis penitissimis mentibus vice
7 conscientiae deversetur. Hic, quem dico, privus custos,
singularis praefectus, domesticus speculator, proprius
curator, intimus cognitor, assiduus obseruator, individuus
arbiter, inseparabilis testis, malorum improbator, bono-
8 rum probator; si rite animadvertatur, sedulo cognoscatur,
religiose colatur ita ut a Socrate iustitia et innocentia
cultus est, in rebus incertis prospector, dubiis praemoni-
9 tor, periculosis tutator, egenis opitulator; qui tibi queat
tum insomniis, tum signis, tum etiam fortasse coram, cum
usus postulat, mala averruncare, bona prosperare, humilia
sublimare, nutantia fulcire, obscura clarare, secunda re-
gere, adversa corrigere.

     17. Igitur mirum, si Socrates, vir adprime perfectus et
Apollinis quoque testimonio sapiens, hunc deum suum
cognovit et coluit, ac propterea eius custos—prope dicam,
Lar contubernio familiaris—cuncta et arcenda arcuit et
praecavenda[37] praecavit et praemonenda praemonuit?
2 Sicubi tamen intersaeptis[38] sapientiae officiis non consilio

---

[37] et arcenda arcuit et praecavenda *Thomas*: quae arcenda
sunt arcuit quae cavenda *mss. plerique*

[38] intersaeptis *Oudendorp*: interfectis *mss. plerique*

---

[32] Pl. *Ap.* 20E–21A.

[33] In Greek and Roman thought, the term "god" could be
applied to beings lower than gods, even to humans to whom one

Accordingly, all of you listening to this inspired doc- 5
trine of Plato, whose mouthpiece I am, must regulate your
minds in all your actions or intentions, in the knowledge 6
that a human being has no secret from those guardians,
either within his mind or without; no, they involve themselves attentively in everything, see everything, learn everything, and dwell in the very recesses of the mind as
conscience does. This being that I talk of is a personal 7
guardian, single overseer, household watchman, private
caretaker, intimate acquaintance, tireless observer, ines-
capable onlooker, inseparable witness, who reproves your
bad deeds and approves your good ones. Provided that 8
he receives proper notice, attentive recognition, scrupulous worship, as Socrates worshiped his in justice and innocence, he alerts you in uncertainty, forewarns you in
doubt, protects you in danger, supports you in need; by 9
dreams or omens, or perhaps in person if the situation
demands, he can sweep away what is evil and promote
what is good, raise up what is cast down, steady what is
tottering, illuminate what is dark, guide success and undo
failure.

17. Is it then surprising if a man of complete perfection
such as Socrates, to whose wisdom even Apollo testified,[32]
recognized and worshiped this being as his god,[33] and
therefore his guardian—I might almost say, his "household lar" because of their cohabitation—averted whatever
needed to be averted, anticipated whatever needed an-
ticipating, foretold whatever needed foretelling? Though 2
if at any time his wisdom could not serve him and he

owed gratitude for help or safety, cf. Nock, *Essays on Religion*,
145.

sed praesagio indigebat, ut ubi dubitatione clauderet, ibi
3 divinatione consisteret? Multa sunt enim, multa de quibus
etiam sapientes viri ad hariolos et oracula cursitent. An
non apud Homerum, ut ‹in›[39] quodam ingenti speculo,
clarius cernis haec duo distributa, seorsus divinationis,
4 seorsus sapientiae officia? Nam cum duo columina totius
exercitus dissident, Agamemnon regno pollens et Achilles
bello potens, desideraturque vir facundia laudatus et peritia memoratus, qui Atridae superbiam sedet, Pelidae fero-
ciam compescat atque eos auctoritate advertat, exemplis
moneat, oratione permulceat, quis igitur tali in tempore
5 medius[40] ad dicendum exortus[41] est? Nempe Pylius orator,
eloquio comis, experimentis catus, senecta venerabilis, cui
omnes sciebant corpus annis hebere, animum prudentia
vigere, verba dulcedine affluere.

18. Itidem cum rebus creperis et afflictis speculatores
deligendi sunt, qui nocte intempesta castra hostium pe-
netrent, nonne Vlixes cum Diomede deliguntur veluti
consilium et auxilium, mens et manus, animus et gladius?
2 Enimvero cum apud Aulidem[42] desidibus et obsessis ac
taedio abnuentibus difficultas belli et facultas itineris et
tranquillitas maris et clementia ventorum per fibrarum
notas et alitum vias et serpentium escas exploranda ‹est›,[43]
tacent nempe mutuo duo illa sapientiae Graiae summa

[39] in *add. ed. Rom.*
[40] medius *Thomas*: me ω
[41] exortus *ms. Pb, Wowerius*: exortatus ω
[42] ad Aulidem *Thomas*: ab Aulide ω
[43] est *add. Kiessling apud Thomas*

needed foreknowledge rather than advice, he was sustained by divination when he was hobbled by doubt. For 3 there are many, many questions which cause even men of wisdom to turn to soothsayers and oracles. Do we not clearly see in Homer, as if in a vast mirror, these two functions separated, those of divination on the one side and those of wisdom on the other? For when the two pillars of 4 the whole army are at loggerheads, Agamemnon the supreme king and Achilles the mighty warrior, and the times call for a man of renowned eloquence and acknowledged experience to lower the pride of Atrides, check the fury of Pelides, influence them both by his authority, advise them by past examples, and calm them by speech, who at such a juncture rose up between them to speak? The Pylian 5 orator, of course[34]—mild and eloquent, canny and experienced, ancient and authoritative, whom all knew to have a body weakened by age, a mind vigorous and prudent, and a style of speaking fluent and agreeable.

18. Similarly, in murky and difficult situations, when scouts must be chosen to infiltrate the enemy camp at dead of night, does not the choice fall on Ulysses and Diomedes to represent intelligence and assistance, brain and brawn, mind and sword?[35] Moreover, when the Greeks 2 were at Aulis, idled, blockaded, and ready to give up from fatigue, and needed to test whether the war would be difficult, the journey easy, the sea calm, and the winds favorable by means of omens from entrails, the paths of birds, and the scraps fed to snakes, of course those two peers of Greek wisdom, the Ithacan and the Pylian, were

[34] That is, Nestor: Hom. *Il.* 1.247–84, 2.76–83, etc.
[35] Hom. *Il.* 10.218–53.

3 cacumina, Ithacensis et Pylius: Calchas autem longe prae-
stabilis hariolari simul alites et altaria et arborem contemplatus est, actutum sua divinatione et tempestates flexit et
4 classem deduxit et decennium praedixit. Non secus et in
Troiano exercitu cum divinatione res indigent, tacet ille
sapiens senatus, nec audet aliquid pronuntiare vel Hicetaon vel Lampo vel Clytius, sed omnes silentio auscultant
aut ingrata auguria Heleni aut incredita vaticinia Cassan-
5 drae. Ad eundem modum Socrates quoque, sicubi locorum aliena sapientiae officiis consultatio ingruerat, ibi vi
daemonis praesagiari egebat.[44] Verum eius monitis sedulo
oboediebat eoque erat deo suo longe acceptior.

19. Quod autem incepta Socratis quaepiam daemon
ille ferme prohibitum ibat, numquam adhortatum, quo-
2 dam modo ratio praedicta est. Enim Socrates, utpote vir
adprime perfectus, ex sese ad omnia congruentia sibi offi-
3 cia promptus, nullo adhortatore umquam indigebat, at
vero prohibitore nonnumquam, si quibus forte conatibus
eius periculum suberat, ut monitus praecaveret, omitteret
coepta impraesentiarum, quae tutius vel postea capesseret
vel alia via adoriretur.
4 In huiuscemodi rebus [dixit][45] vocem quampiam divinitus exortam dicebat audire (ita enim apud Platonem, ne

---

[44] praesagiari egebat *Wiman*: praesagia regebat ω
[45] dixit *del. Goldbacher*

---

[36] That is, Odysseus and Nestor.
[37] Hom. *Il.* 2.278–332, where Odysseus recalls how the
Greeks at Aulis were sacrificing on altars beneath a plane tree
when a snake devoured a mother sparrow and eight of her chicks

both alike silent:[36] but Calchas, a seer of outstanding skill,   3
as soon as he had observed birds, altars, and a tree, immediately averted storms, launched the fleet, and predicted the ten years by the power of his foresight.[37] So also   4
in the Trojan army, when the situation called for divination, that wise counsel of elders was mute, neither Hicetaon, Lampo nor Clytius dared utter a word, but all lis-
tened in silence to Helenus' predictions that they did not
welcome or to Cassandra's prophecies that they did not
believe.[38] In the same way, if Socrates too anywhere stood   5
in need of advice that his wisdom was unable to supply, he
needed to be warned by his demon's power; and yet he
followed its advice scrupulously, and thus became even
more favored by his god.

19. But as to why the demon sometimes moved to
check some of Socrates' undertakings, but never to encourage them, I have in a way already given the reason. As   2
a perfect human being, ready of his own accord to perform
every duty appropriate for him, Socrates never needed
prompting, and yet did sometimes did need restraining   3
when he happened to be embarked on a path across some
concealed danger, so that after consultation he might plan
ahead, and briefly abandon his intention, either to resume
it later at less risk or to go about it some other way.

In such cases he would say he heard some kind of voice   4
of supernatural origin (for so it says in Plato, in case any-

and how Calchas predicted from this omen that the Trojan War
would last ten years.   [38] Hicetaon, Lampo, and Clytius are
mentioned among the elders of Troy at *Il.* 3.146–49; for Helenus'
prophetic powers, *Il.* 6.76. The tradition of Cassandra as a proph-
etess fated not to be believed is post-Homeric.

quisquam arbitretur omina eum vulgo loquentium capti-
5 tasse). Quippe etiam semotis arbitris uno cum Phaedro
extra pomerium sub quodam arboris opaco umbraculo
signum illud adnuntium sensit, ne prius transcenderet
Ilissi amnis modicum fluentum, quam increpitu indigna-
6 tum Amorem recinendo placasset; cum praeterea, si
omina observitaret, aliquando eorum nonnulla etiam hor-
tamenta haberet, ut videmus plerisque usu evenire, qui
nimia ominum superstitione non suopte corde sed alterius
verbo reguntur, ac per angiporta reptantes consilia ex alienis uocibus colligunt et, ut ita dixerim, non animo sed
auribus cogitant.

20. Verum enimvero, ut ista sunt, certe quidem[46] ominum harioli vocem audiunt saepenumero auribus suis
usurpatam, de qua nihil cunctentur [de qua sciunt][47] ex
2 ore humano profectam. At enim Socrates non "vocem" sibi
sed "vocem quampiam" dixit oblatam, quo additamento
profecto intellegas non usitatam vocem nec humanam sig-
nificari. Quae si foret, frustra "quaepiam," quin potius aut
"vox" aut certe "cuiuspiam vox" diceretur, ut ait illa Teren-
tiana meretrix:

audire vocem visa sum modo militis.

3   Qui vero "vocem ⟨quampiam⟩"[48] dicat audisse, aut

___

46 quidem*Wilamowitz*: quid ω   47 de qua sciunt *del.*
Thomas   48 quampiam *add. ed. Rom.*

___

39 Pl. *Ap.* 31C–D and elsewhere. In his dialogue *On the Sign
of Socrates,* Plutarch discusses speculation that the "spirit" was in
fact Socrates' inference from "sneezes and chance remarks" (*Mor.*
581F).

one supposes that he went hunting for omens in ordinary talk).[39] For even with no bystanders present, when he was 5
alone with Phaedrus outside the city limits in the deep shade of a certain tree, he sensed that same sign warning him not to cross the small stream of the river Ilissus until he had made a recantation to appease Love, whom he had irritated by a tirade.[40] Moreover, if he had been an ob- 6
server of omens, he would have treated some of them as promptings, as we see many people do. Because of their excessive reverence for omens, they let the words of others guide them rather than their own intuition, and they creep down alleyways picking up advice from other people's re- marks, thinking with their ears, so to speak, not with their brains.

20. But however that may be, those who prophesy from omens certainly do hear a voice perceived through the ears, and have no doubt that it issues from a human mouth. Socrates, though, did not say that it was "a voice" that had 2
come to him but "a certain voice,"[41] from which qualifica- tion one can readily see that he did not mean an ordinary or human voice. Had that had been so, it would have been pointless to say "a certain," but rather "a voice" or at any rate "someone's voice," as the prostitute says in Terence,

I thought I just heard the soldier's voice.[42]

But someone who says he heard "a certain voice" either 3

40 Pl. *Phdr.* 242B; for the "tirade," 237C–41D.
41 Pl. *Phdr.* 242C.
42 Ter. *Eun.* 454.

nescit unde ea exorta sit, aut in ipsa aliquid addubitat, aut
eam quiddam insolitum et arcanum demonstrat habuisse,
ita ut Socrates eam, quam sibi [ac][49] divinitus editam tem-
4 pestive accidere dicebat.[50] Quod equidem arbitror non
modo auribus eum verum etiam oculis signa daemonis sui
usurpasse, nam frequentius non vocem sed signum divinum sibi oblatum prae se ferebat. Id signum potest et
ipsius daemonis species fuisse, quam solus Socrates cer-
5 neret, ita ut Homericus Achilles Minervam. Credo plerosque vestrum hoc, quod commodum dixi, cunctantius
credere et impendio mirari formam daemonis Socrati visi-
tatam. At enim [secundum][51] Pythagoricos contra mirari
oppido solitos, si quis se negaret umquam vidisse dae-
6 monem, satis, ut reor, idoneus auctor est Aristoteles. Quod
si cuivis potest evenire facultas contemplandi divinam
effigiem, cur non adprime potuerit Socrati obtingere,
quem cuivis amplissimo numini sapientiae dignitas coae-
7 quarat? Nihil est enim deo similius et gratius quam vir
animo perfecte bonus, qui hominibus ceteris antecellit,
quam ipse a diis immortalibus distat.

21. Quin potius nos quoque Socratis exemplo et commemoratione erigimur ac nos secundo studio philosophiae pari similitudini[52] numinum aventes[53] permittimus?
2 De quo quidem nescio qua ratione detrahimur.[54] Et nihil
aeque miror quam, cum omnes et cupiant optime vivere

49 ac *del. Wowerius*
50 accidere dicebat *Thomas*: accedebat *vel* accidebat ω
51 secundum *del. ed. Rom.*
52 similitudini *Beaujeu*: similium ω
53 aventes *Vulcanius*: caventes ω
54 detrahimur *Thomas*: dei rapimur ω

does not know its origin, or is rather unsure about it, or indicates that it had something unusual and mysterious about it, as Socrates did with that voice when he maintained that it came to him at the right moment from heaven. As to that, my own belief is that he perceived his 4 demon's signs not just through the ears but through the eyes too, for he often stated openly that it was not a voice but a heavenly sign that he had received. That sign may even have been an appearance of the demon itself, perceptible only to Socrates as Minerva was to Achilles in Homer.[43] Most of you, I believe, are reluctant to believe 5 what I have just said, and are greatly surprised to hear that Socrates saw the demon's shape; and yet the Pythagoreans are usually very surprised if anyone *denies* ever having seen a demon, according to Aristotle, whose authority I believe to be good.[44] But if any person might be granted 6 the ability to observe a supernatural form, why should it not be vouchsafed to Socrates more than anyone, considering that his degree of wisdom had made him equal to any divinity, however august? For there is nothing more 7 similar or more welcome to godhead than a man of perfectly virtuous mind, who is as far above all other men as he is distant from the immortal gods.

21. Let us then be moved to action by the example and memory of Socrates, and, guided by the study of philosophy, let us eagerly devote ourselves to achieving a similar resemblance to the gods. But for some reason we become distracted, and nothing surprises me so much as that ev- 2 eryone wants to live the best kind of life, and furthermore

[43] Hom. *Il.* 1.194–98.
[44] Aristotle, fr. 175 Gigon.

et sciant non alia re quam animo vivi nec fieri posse quin,
ut optime vivas, animus colendus sit, tamen animum suum
3 non colant. At si quis velit acriter cernere, oculi curandi
sunt, quibus cernitur; si velis perniciter currere, pedes
curandi sunt, quibus curritur; itidem si pugillare valde
velis, brachia vegetanda sunt, quibus pugillatur; similiter
in omnibus ceteris membris sua cuique cura pro studio
4 est. Quod cum omnes facile perspiciant, nequeo satis
mecum reputare et proinde, ut res est, admirari cur non
5 etiam animum suum ratione excolant. Quae quidem ratio
vivendi omnibus aeque necessaria est, non ratio pingendi
nec ratio psallendi, quas quivis bonus vir sine ulla animi
vituperatione, sine turpitudine, sine labe[55] contempserit.
6 Nescio ut Ismenias tibiis canere, sed non pudet me tibicinem non esse; nescio ut Apelles coloribus pingere, sed non
pudet me non esse significem; itidem in ceteris artibus, ne
omnis persequar, licet tibi nescire, nec pudet.

22. Enimvero dic, sodes: "nescio bene vivere, ut Socrates, ut Plato, ut Pythagoras vixerunt, nec pudet me
nescire bene vivere"; numquam hoc dicere audebis. Sed
cumprimis mirandum est, quod ea, quae minime videri
volunt nescire, discere tamen neglegunt et eiusdem artis
2 disciplinam simul et ignorantiam detrectant. Igitur coti-
diana eorum aera dispungas, invenias in rationibus multa
prodige profusa et in semet nihil, in sui dico daemonis
cultum, qui cultus non aliud quam philosophiae sacra-

---

[55] labe *ed. Rom.*: labore ω

---

[45] Ismenias of Thebes was a famous player on the double
pipe (*diaulos*), and Apelles an equally famous painter, both of the
fourth century.

390

knows that he can have such a life only through the mind, and that there is no other way of living the best life than by improving the mind, and yet he does not improve his own. And yet if one is to see keenly, he must look after the 3 eyes he uses to see; if he wants to run fast, he must look after the feet he uses to run; so also if you want to be a great boxer, you must exercise the arms you use to box; and similarly with all the other parts of the body—the attention one gives to each accords with his profession. Since this is something plainly visible to all, I cannot pon- 4 der the fact enough, and marvel at it as it deserves, that people do not also improve their minds by use of their reason. Such a way to live is essential for everyone equally, 5 unlike a way to paint or a way to play the harp, skills that any person of virtue may disregard without any rebuke from his own mind, without disgrace, and without a blush. I cannot play the pipe like Ismenias, but I am not ashamed 6 not to be a piper; I cannot paint in colors like Apelles, but I am not ashamed not to be a painter.[45] So also with the other arts, not to list them all—you can be ignorant of them and not feel ashamed of being so.

22. On the other hand, just try to say, "I do not know how to live the virtuous life as Socrates, Plato, or Pythago-ras lived it, but I am not ashamed not to know how to live it": *that* you will never dare to say. But what is extremely remarkable, the very things that they least want to seem ignorant of are the ones they refuse to learn, and they belittle both learning the art of life and ignorance of it. Hence, if you tot up their daily expenses, their account 2 books will tell you that they spend very lavishly on many things, yet nothing on themselves, by which I mean on care for their own demon, care which simply means devot-

3 mentum est. Plane quidem villas opipare exstruunt et
domos ditissime exornant et familias numerosissime com-
parant. Sed in istis omnibus tanta affluentia rerum nihil
est praeterquam ipse dominus pudendum, nec iniuria:
cumulata enim habent, quae sedulo percolunt, ipsi autem
4 horridi, indocti incultique circumeunt. Igitur illa spectes,
in quae patrimonia sua profuderunt: amoenissima et ex-
structissima et ornatissima deprehendas, villas aemulas
urbium conditas, domus vice templorum exornatas, familias numerosissimas et calamistratas, opiparam supellectilem, omnia affluentia, omnia opulentia, omnia ornata
5 praeter ipsum dominum, qui solus Tantali vice in suis divitiis inops, egens, pauper non quidem fructum[56] illum fugi-
tivum captat et fallacis undae sitit, sed verae beatitudinis,
id est secundae vitae et prudentiae fortunatissimae, esurit
et sitit, quippe non intellegit aeque divites spectari debere
ut equos mercamur.

23. Neque enim in emendis equis phaleras considera-
mus et baltei polimina inspicimus et ornatissimae cervicis
divitias contemplamur, si ex auro et argento et gemmis
monilia variegata dependent, si plena artis ornamenta
capiti et collo circumiacent, si frena caelata, si ephippia
2 fucata, si cingula aurata sunt, sed istis omnibus exuviis
amolitis equum ipsum nudum et solum corpus eius et animum contemplamur, ut sit et ad speciem honestus et ad
3 cursuram vegetus et ad vecturam validus: iam primum in
corpore si sit

---

[56] fructum *van Lennep apud Thomas*: fluentem ω

ing themselves to philosophy. Of course, they build lavish 3
country houses, richly decorate their houses in town, and
buy vast numbers of slaves, and yet amid all this, amid so
great a mass of possessions, there is nothing to raise a
blush except the owner, and for good reason. For they
have heaps of things that they cherish dearly, while they
themselves go around shabby, ignorant and uncultivated.
Just look, then, at the things they have lavished their in- 4
heritances on: you will find everything comfortable, lofty,
ornate to the last degree, country houses built to look like
cities, houses in town fitted out like temples, countless
coiffured slaves, luxurious furniture, every sign of abundance, opulence and embellishment except the owner
himself. He alone is like Tantalus—destitute, needy, poor 5
in the midst of his riches; he does not strain at that elusive
fruit and thirst for that deceptive water, but hungers and
thirsts for true blessedness, that is, for a contented life and
a full measure of wisdom. He does not understand, you
see, that we should examine the rich in the same way as
we purchase horses.

23. For when buying horses too, we do not look at their
cheek pieces, examine their polished harnesses, or survey
the rich ornaments around their necks, if they are hung
with chains set off with gold, silver and jewels, if highly
wrought decorations surround their heads and necks, if
their reins are embossed, if their saddlecloths are purple
dyed, if their saddle girths gilded. No, we remove those 2
trappings and survey the bare horse himself, just his body
and his temper, making sure that he is handsome to look
at, with a good pace and a strong back: in the first place, 3
whether physically he has

Argutum caput, brevis alvus obesaque terga
luxuriatque toris animosum pectus honesti;

praeterea si

Duplex agitur per lumbos spina:

volo enim non modo perniciter verum etiam molliter per-
vehat.

4   Similiter igitur et in hominibus contemplandis noli illa
aliena aestimare, sed ipsum hominem penitus considera,
ipsum ut meum Socratem pauperem specta. Aliena autem
voco, quae parentes pepererunt et quae fortuna largita est.
5   Quorum nihil laudibus Socratis mei admisceo, nullam
generositatem, nullam prosapiam, nullos longos natales,
nullas invidiosas divitias, haec enim cuncta, ut dico, aliena
6   sunt. Sat Porthaonio[57] gloriae est, qui talis fuit, ut eius
nepotem non puderet. Igitur omnia similiter aliena nu-
meres licebit. "Generosus est": parentes laudas. "Dives
est": non credo fortunae. Nec magis ista adnumero. "Validus est": aegritudine fatigabitur. "Pernix est": stabit in
senectute.[58] "Formosus est": exspecta paulisper et non
7   erit. "At enim bonis artibus doctus et adprime est eruditus
8   et, quantum licet homini, sapiens et boni consultus." Tandem aliquando ipsum virum laudas: hoc enim nec a patre
hereditarium est nec ‹a›[59] casu pendulum nec a suffragio
anniculum nec a corpore caducum nec ab aetate mutabile.

[57] sat Porthaonio *Beaujeu*: sateprothaonio *ω*
[58] est: stabit in senectute *Thomas*: estabit in senectutem *mss.
plerique*
[59] a *add. Koziol*

Fine head, tight belly, brawny back,
A thoroughbred's bold, thickly muscled chest,[46]

and in addition

Double spine,[47]

For I want him to carry me softly and not merely quickly.

Similarly, then, when considering human beings do not   4
measure them by the usual externals, but examine the
human person closely, observe himself in his poverty like
my master Socrates; by "externals" I mean what has been
transmitted from his parents and granted him by fortune.
None of these things do I include in my praises of Socra-   5
tes, not high birth, not pedigree, not distant forbears, not
invidious wealth, for as I say all these things are externals.
Porthaon's son has glory enough in having been such a   6
man as not to disgrace his grandson.[48] Well then, we may
evaluate everything external in the same way. "He is well
born": you are praising his parents. "He is rich": I do not
trust chance. No more do I count the following. "He's
strong": illness will tire him. "He's fast": old age will halt
him. "He's handsome": wait a while and he won't be. "But   7
he has had a liberal education, he is exceptionally learned
and, as far as a man may be, he is wise and a true judge of
goodness." At last you are praising the real man: for all this   8
is not inherited from a father, dependent on chance, voted
for a single year, nor doomed to fail with the body or

[46] Verg. *G.* 3.80–81 (where *honesti* belongs to the next sentence).   [47] Verg. *G.* 3.87, where Mynors explains that the
"double spine" is a ridge of muscles on either side of the horse's
spine, enabling the rider to ride comfortably.
[48] Porthaon's son Oeneus was the father of Diomedes.

Haec omnia meus Socrates habuit et ideo cetera habere contempsit.

24. Quin igitur et tu ad studium sapientiae accingeris[60] vel properas saltem, ut nihil alienum in laudibus tuis audias, sed ut, qui te volet nobilitare, aeque laudet ut Accius Ulixen laudavit in Philocteta suo, in eius tragoediae principio?

> Inclite, parva prodite patria,
> nomine celebri claroque potens
> pectore, Achivis classibus auctor,
> gravis Dardaniis gentibus ultor,
> Laertiade.

2 Novissime patrem memorat. Ceterum omnes laudes eius viri audisti: nihil inde nec Laertes sibi nec Anticlia nec Arcisius vindicat: [nec][61] tota, ut vides, laudis huius pro-
3 pria Vlixi possessio est. Nec aliud te in eodem Ulixe Homerus docet, qui semper ei comitem voluit esse prudentiam, quam poetico ritu Minervam nuncupavit. Igitur hac eadem comite omnia horrenda subiit, omnia adversa supe-
4 ravit. Quippe ea adiutrice Cyclopis specus introiit, sed egressus est; Solis boves vidit, sed abstinuit; ad inferos demeavit et ascendit; eadem sapientia comite Scyllam praeternavigavit nec ereptus est; Charybdi consaeptus est nec retentus est; Circae poculum bibit nec mutatus est; ad Lotophagos accessit nec remansit; Sirenas audiit nec accessit.[62]

---

[60] accingeris *Lütjohann*: ingeris ω
[61] nec *del. Lütjohann*   [62] *Subscriptionem* APVLEI PLATONICI PHILOSOPHI MADAVRENSIS DE DEO SOCRATIS LIBER EXPLICIT *praebent* BMV (*om.* LIBER MV).

change with age. All these attributes my master Socrates had, and so did not care to have those other attributes.

24. Well then, you too should arm yourself to study philosophy, or at least do so soon, so that the praise you hear includes no externals, and someone wishing to extol your fame lauds you as highly as Accius lauded Ulysses in the opening of his tragedy *Philoctetes:*[49]

> O man of fame, son of a small land,
> Mighty in famous name and splendid heart,
> Moving spirit of the Achaean fleet,
> Fearful scourge of the Dardanian clans,
> Son of Laertes.

He mentions his father last: and yet you have already 2 heard all that hero's praises. None of them is claimed by Laertes, Anticleia or Acrisius: as you can see, the praise is the property of Ulysses alone. And that is just what Homer 3 teaches us in the figure of this same Ulysses when he chose to make Wisdom his constant companion, by poetic license calling her Minerva. Hence with her as his companion he faced every terror and overcame every difficulty; for with her as his helper he entered the Cyclops' cave and 4 yet emerged; he saw the cattle of the Sun and did not eat; he descended to the underworld and yet emerged; again with Wisdom by his side, he sailed past Scylla and was not devoured; he was encircled by Charybdis and not caught; he drank Circe's cup and was not transformed; he landed among the Lotus-Eaters and did not stay; he heard the Sirens and did not land.

[49] *ROL* 2.504; *Accius* (ed. Dangel [Budé]), 149, lines 195–99.

APPENDIXES

A: APULEIUS' DATE OF BIRTH

Apuleius' birthdate is commonly placed about 125, with some favoring a range of 120 to 125, others a range of 125 to 130. The earlier range seems more probable.[1]

The question can be approached by two lines of argument. One is that in a speech preserved among the *Florida,* Apuleius calls the Roman senator Strabo Aemilianus his "fellow student" (*condiscipulus, Flor.* 16.37) and also describes him as an ex-consul, who will soon be proconsul if the universal prayers are answered (*vir consularis, brevi votis omnium futurus proconsul,* 16.40). Since thirty-two was the minimum age for the consulate, and Strabo was consul in 156, he cannot have been born later than about 124. But as Ronald Syme observed,[2] "Indiscriminate application of that norm [age thirty-two for the consulate] can be harmful and misleading. . . . It would be preferable to posit the standard age of forty-two." There is no reason to suppose that Strabo would have had accelerated access to the consulate, and his consulate in 156 would *prima facie* allow a date for his birth at least as early as 115.

[1] Rohde "Zu Apuleius," 73 = *Kleine Schriften,* 50, suggested a date "um 124."

[2] R. Syme, *Tacitus* (Oxford, 1958), 653–54.

The hints that Apuleius drops about his age in the *Apologia,* ostensibly delivered in 158/9, are ambiguous. His wife, Pudentilla, was older than he was; her first son, Sicinius Pontianus, dead by the time of the trial, had been his close companion, apparently younger than Apuleius, in Athens (*Apol.* 72.3); her second son, Sicinius Pudens, had taken the *toga virilis* at the time of his brother's marriage and was still not yet of an age to represent himself in court (2.3, 87.10). Apuleius claims to be able to prove from documents that his wife was little more than forty (89.5), whereas his opponents maintained that she was sixty (89.1). They described Apuleius as a "handsome philosopher" (4.1), whereas he claims that long study had reduced him to an ugly wreck (4.10–12); elsewhere, however, he says that he was a "a grown man of no slight attractiveness" (*iuvenem neque corpore . . . paenitendum*), at least at the time of his marriage (92.5). His age at the time of the speech might have been about thirty-five, and his date of birth about 122 or 123; if Pudentilla had been married at about twenty and had a first (surviving) son soon thereafter, she might now have been in her early forties.

B: *APOL.* 23.6, 24.10
THE LOCATION OF ZARATH

At tamen parce postea, Aemiliane, paupertatem cuipiam obiectare, qui nuper usque agellum Zarathensem, quem tibi unicum pater tuus reliquerat, solus uno asello ad tempestivum imbrem triduo exarabas.

Ut mihi tu, Aemiliane, minus posthac suscenseas, potiusque ut veniam impertias, si per neglegentiam forte non elegi illud tuum Atticum Zarat [Fφ: *Zarath* edd.] *ut in eo nascerer.*

Commentators observe that Zarat, or Zarath, should be near Oea (modern Tripoli). Thus Butler and Owen (*Apulei Apologia,* 63), "The site is unknown. From the contempt with which Apuleius speaks of it, it is presumably a small village near Oea." So also Hunink (*Apuleius of Madauros* 80), "He knows even the name of Zarath, the small village near Oea where Aemilianus lived." Cf. M. Leglay, *RE* 9 A (1997): 2319, "Apul. Apol. 23 erwähnt ein Zarath . . . von wo Sicinius Aemilianus, einer seiner Ankläger, stamme. Doch diese Stadt [!] scheint in Tripolitanien zu liegen." (Apuleius, *Apologia* 23 mentions a certain Zarath . . . as the birthplace of Sicinius Aemilianus, one of his prosecutors. But this city [!] seems to lie in Tripolitania.)

The *Barrington Atlas* (35 F 2) indicates an ancient site at "Ain Zara," some ten miles south-southeast of Oea. '*Ain* is Arabic for "spring," and suggests an agricultural region, so that it is natural to wonder whether Ain Zara is a survival of the ancient Zarat or Zarath. G. W. Bowersock informs me that the precise transliteration is '*Ain Zārah,* since the Arabic name ends with a *ta' marbūta,* that is, with a soft *t* that sounds as an *h,* hence very close to *Zarath.* The site was an important agricultural center in antiquity. A mosaic discovered in 1911 shows that it contained at least one wealthy villa already in the Antonine or Severan period.[3] It seems certain that Aemilianus' Zarath (with a long first *a*) was a village on the territory of Oea and that Aemilianus was actually a citizen of Oea, who owned an estate near the city; what Apuleius says about his plowing

[3] R. Paribeni, "Il Mosaico di Áin Zára," *Bollettino d'Arte* 6 (1911): 75–77; for Christian remains from the site, S. Aurigemma, *L'Area cemeteriale cristiana di Áin Zára presso Tripoli di Barberia* (Rome, 1932).

the hard soil with only a single donkey is likely to be a malicious exaggeration.

C: *APOL.* 24.8–9
THE STATUS OF APULEIUS' FATHER

Patrem habui loco principis duoviralem cunctis honoribus perfunctum, cuius ego locum in illa re publica, exinde ut participare curiam coepi, nequaquam degener pari, spero, honore et existimatione tueor.

Commentators and translators understand *princeps* here to mean "leading citizen": thus Butler in his translation, "My father attained to the post of duumvir and became the foremost citizen of the place, after filling all the municipal offices of honour. I myself, immediately after my first entry into the municipal senate, succeeded to my father's position in the community." Similarly, Butler and Owen (*Apulei Apologia,* 66), "The *duumviri* were the chief magistrates of the *colonia* . . . Apuleius uses the adjective *duumviralis* because his father did not hold the office at the time of his death. He had held the office and ranked as the foremost citizen of the place." So also Hunink on the passage (*Apuleius of Madauros,* 84), "His father had been a *duumvir,* the highest office in a colony. *Principis* simply means 'of a leading citizen.'"

This interpretation is open to question on two grounds. One is that the singular *princeps* in Apuleius normally means "the emperor": thus *Met.* 3.29.1, *venerabili principis nomine;* 7.6.1, *procuratorem principis;* 7.7.4, *nutus magni principis;* 9.41.6, *adiurantes genium principis;* 10.13.2, *litteras ad magnum scriptas principem;* 11.17.3, *fausta vota praefatus principi magno.* One exception might be cited as a parallel to the present instance, *Flor.* 15.14, *Gillo Crotoniensium principe,* though here the genitive specifies the community of which Gillus was the "principal" (*De mundo* 35, 5 [p. 171 Thomas], *alicuius officii principem fieri,* where *princeps* means "primary actor," is different).

There is a further difficulty, in that *loco* with a genitive corresponds to English "as," German "als," in the sense of "instead of," "in the place of," not in the sense of "as being." The only other instance in Apuleius is *Met.* 6.4.5, *Veneris, nurus meae, quam filiae semper dilexi loco.* There are several instructive instances in Tacitus' *Histories:* 1.11.1, *Aegyptum copiasque . . . equites Romani obtinent loco regum;* 1.16.1, *loco libertatis erit quod eligi coepimus* (here *loco libertatis* is a predicate phrase with *esse,* but the sense is still "instead of" or "as good as"); 1.57.2, *gregarius miles viatica sua et balteos phalerasque . . . loco pecuniae tradebant.*

There is no difficulty in Apuleius' statement, "I had a father of duoviral status in place of the emperor, after he had held all (previous) offices," or, less literally, "had mayoral status in the emperor's stead and had risen through all the magistracies." It was enshrined in the charters of Roman colonies that they could ask the emperor or another member of the ruling house, or occasionally a highly placed *privatus,* to be honorary *duovir; municipia* could do the same for the position of *quattuorvir.* When this happened, a substitute (*praefectus*) had to be found among the highly regarded members of the community. Given the prestige of the nominal magistrate, usually an emperor, there could be only one such substitute in place of the normal two (or four), so that the *praefectus* had all the powers normally divided between two or four colleagues.

The rule is spelled out in the charter of Irni in Spain, granted by Domitian. As translated by Michael Crawford, this states (*JRS* 76 [1986]: 183):

> Concerning the praefectus of the Emperor Caesar Domitian Augustus. If the decuriones or conscripti or municipes of that municipium, in the common name of the municipes of that municipium, confer the duumvirate on the Emperor Caesar Domitian Augustus, father of his country, and the Emperor Caesar Domitian Augustus, father of his country, accepts that duumvirate and orders anyone to be praefectus in his place, that praefectus is to have the same rights as he would have if it had been appropriate for him to be appointed sole duumvir under this statute and he had been appointed under this statute sole duumvir for the administration of justice.

D: THE TRIALS IN *APOL.* 66.4

Neque autem gloriae causa me accusat, ut M. Antonius Cn. Carbonem, C. Mucius A. Albucium, P. Sulpicius Cn. Norbanum, C. Furius M'. Aquilium, C. Curio Q. Metellum.

The identification of the various persons mentioned in this sentence has caused problems to Apuleius no less than to his commentators. He gives five cases, as follows:

1. M. Antonius, consul in 99 and a famous orator, accused Cn. Papirius Carbo for his defeat by the Cimbri, probably in 113 (*MRR* 1.535).

2. T. (not A.) Albucius prosecuted Q. (not C.) Mucius

Scaevola (Augur) for extortion in 119; Apuleius erroneously makes Albucius the defendant (*MRR* 1.523–24).

3. P. Sulpicius Rufus prosecuted C. (not "Cn.") Norba-
nus in 94 on the charge of *maiestas* for his activities as
tribune in 103 (*MRR* 1.564).

4. "C. Furius" is a mistake for L. Fufius, who prosecuted M. Aquilius for peculation as governor of Sicily,
perhaps in 98 (Cic. *Brut.* 222; *MRR* 2.2–3).

5. The last pair, C. Curio and Q. Metellus, has caused
the most problems, but the key is given by a passage of
Asconius (ed. Clark [OCT] 63); cf. B. A. Marshall, *A Historical Commentary on Asconius* (Columbia, MO, 1985),
230–31. Probably in the early 90s, C. Scribonius Curio
(consul in 76, *MRR* 2.92) prosecuted Q. Metellus Nepos
(consul in 98, *MRR* 2.4). The dying Nepos enjoined his son
Q. Caecilius Metellus Nepos (Cicero's nemesis as tribune
in 62, consul in 57, *MRR* 2.199) to prosecute Curio in
retaliation, and Metellus began the suit but dropped it: the
date may have been circa 70.

E: *CONSULATUS* OR *PROCONSULATUS*
IN *APOL.* 94.5?

*Itaque acceptis litteris Carthaginem pergit, ubi iam prope
exacto proconsulatus* [*scripsi:* consulatus *mss. et edd.
omnes*] *sui munere Lollianus Avitus te, Maxime, opperiebatur.*

Since Lollianus Avitus was proconsul, not consul, *consulatus* might have been suspected. Apuleius thrice uses *proconsul* or *proconsularis* of the current governor, Claudius
Maximus (*Apol.* 65.8, 85.2, 103.5), and in such compounds

405

pro is usually contracted to a single *P,* and easily omitted. *OLD* sv *consul* 2b cites Cic. *Phil.* 13.16 and Nepos, *Cato* 1.3 for *consul,* "used loosely of a consul elect or proconsul," but it gives no instance of *consulatus* used instead of *proconsulatus;* the *Thesaurus Linguae Latinae* gives only this passage (4.575, 56). I have therefore put *proconsulatus* in the text.

INDEX

Parentheses preceding or following certain names either indicate that a person or thing is mentioned in two different ways in the text, e.g., "(Junius) Crassus," or aid identification, e.g., "Calvus (orator)."

INDEX

M. Antonius (consul 99 BC), *A.* 17.7, 66.4

Apelles, *F.* 7.6; *D.* 21.5

Apollo, *A.* 42.8; *F.* 3.6, 3.8–9, 3.13–14, 4*.5, 4*.7; *D.* 2.7, 17.1

Apollobex, *A.* 90.6

Appii, *A.* 72.2, 72.6

Apuleius, *A.* 9.4, 17.4, 27.10–11, 48.7, 53.4, 82.2, 82.6, 83.1, 102.7; *F.* 20.6

(M'.) Aquilius, *A.* 66.4

Arabia, *A.* 6.3, 6.5; *F.* 6.1

Archimedes of Syracuse, *A.* 16.6

Archytas, *A.* 15.14

Arcisius, *D.* 24.2

Arcturus, *D.* 2.4

Arion, *F.* 17.15

Aristides ("the Just"), *A.* 18.7

Aristippus, *F.* 2*.1–2

Aristotle, *A.* 36.3, 36.5, 40.5, 40.11, 41.4, 41.7, 50.4, 103.2; *D.* 8.2, 20.5

Arsacids, *F.* 6.1

Ascanius, *D.* 5.5

Asclepiades, *F.* 19.1, 19.8

Asclepius, *A.* 55.10–11; *F.* 18.37, 18.42; *D.* 15.10

(Atilius) Regulus, *A.* 18.11

(Atilius) Serranus, *A.* 10.6, 88.7

Athens, *A.* 24.6, 72.3, 86.1; *F.* 18.7, 18.15, 18.42, 20.4, 22.1

Atrides. *See* Agamemnon

Attica, *A.* 24.10; *F.* 18.15

Attius Navius, *D.* 7.1, 7.3

Aulis, *D.* 18.2

Avitus (Lollianus A.), *A.* 24.1, 94.3, 94.5, 94.7, 95.4–5, 95.6, 95.7, 96.2, 96.3–4

Babylon, *A.* 38.7; *F.* 9.19

Bathyllus, *F.* 15.6

Boeotia, *D.* 15.10

Brahmins, *F.* 15.16, 15.18

Brindisi, *A.* 39.3

Caecilius Statius, *A.* 5.3

Caesar, *A.* 95.5

Caesar (C. Iulius C., cos. 59 BC), *A.* 95.5

Caesars, *F.* 9.40

Calpurnianus, *A.* 6.1, 6.3, 6.5, 60.2

Calvus (orator), *A.* 95.5

Cambyses, *F.* 15.14

Camena/Camenae, *F.* 9.14, 9.30, 20.10

Capitolina, *A.* 61.7, 62.1

Cn. (Papirius) Carbo (consul 120 BC), *A.* 66.4

(Cn. Papirius) Carbo (consul 85 BC), *A.* 17.7

Carmendas, *A.* 90.6

Carthage, *A.* 94.5, 96.5–6; *F.* 9.37, 9.40, 16.25, 16.35, 16.38–41, 16.46, 17.19, 18.1, 18.8, 18.36–37, 18.41, 20.9–10

Cassandra, *D.* 18.4

Cassius Longinus, *A.* 101.6–7

(M.) Cato (M. Porcius C., consul 195 BC), *A.* 17.9, 42.8, 95.5

408

INDEX

INDEX

411

INDEX